FINANCIAL SECURITIES

Translated from French by Logotechnics CPC Ltd

THE CURRENT ISSUES IN FINANCE SERIES

Books in the Current Issues in Finance Series provide a rigorous yet readable treatment of important finance topics. This book, **FINANCIAL SECURITIES: MARKET EQUILIBRIUM AND PRICING METHODS**, by Bernard Dumas and Blaise Allaz exemplifies the objective of the series. Dumas and Allaz present a thorough and complete exposition of three important areas of modern finance: portfolio theory and asset pricing, option pricing, and fixed income valuation. Growing out of the authors' MBA courses at the HEC School of Management, this book clearly and completely explains the key concepts underlying many of the financial innovations of the last 15 years.

The publication of this book is an international effort, as it is co-published by South-Western College Publishing and Chapman & Hall, American and British subsidiaries of International Thomson Publishing. I salute them for their support of the series and thank Chris Will, in particular, for his efforts on behalf of the series. Other books in the series are **FUTURES AND OPTIONS** by Hans Stoll and Robert Whaley and **INTERNATIONAL FINANCIAL MARKETS AND THE FIRM** by Piet Sercu and Raman Uppal. Students of finance can look forward to additional volumes in the Current Issues in Finance Series that will keep them abreast of important advances in the field of finance.

Hans R. Stoll
Consulting Editor, Current Issues in Finance Series

FINANCIAL SECURITIES
MARKET EQUILIBRIUM
AND PRICING METHODS

Bernard Dumas and Blaise Allaz
School of Management
Groupe HEC
France

SOUTH-WESTERN College Publishing

CHAPMAN & HALL

London · Glasgow · Weinheim · New York · Tokyo · Melbourne · Madras

Published in the UK and rest of the world by Chapman & Hall, 2—6 Boundary Row, London SE1 8HN and in North America by South-Western College Publishing, 5101 Madison Avenue, Cincinnati, Ohio 45227, USA

Chapman & Hall, 2—6 Boundary Row, London SE1 8HN, UK

Blackie Academic & Professional, Wester Cleddens Road, Bishopbriggs, Glasgow G64 2NZ, UK

Chapman & Hall GmbH, Pappelallee 3, 69469 Weinheim, Germany

Chapman & Hall USA, 115 Fifth Avenue, New York, NY 10003, USA

Chapman & Hall Japan, ITP-Japan, Kyowa Building, 3F, 2-2-1 Hirakawacho, Chiyoda-ku, Tokyo 102, Japan

Chapman & Hall Australia, 102 Dodds Street, South Melbourne, Victoria 3205, Australia

Chapman & Hall India, R. Seshadri, 32 Second Main Road, CIT East, Madras 600 035, India

French edition 1995 *Les Titres Financiers Financiers:Equilibre du marché et méthodes d'évaluation*

© 1995 Presses Universitaires de France, 108 boulevard Saint-Germain, 75006 Paris

First English edition 1996

© 1996 Chapman & Hall and South-Western College Publishing

Typeset in the UK by Logotechnics CPC Ltd, Sheffield
Printed in Great Britain by St. Edmundsbury Press, Bury St. Edmunds, Suffolk

ISBN   1 412 53880 6 (UK and the rest of the world)
        0 538 84777 8 (North America only)

A catalogue record for this book is available from the British Library
A Library of Congress data record is available for this title

∞ Printed on permanent acid-free text paper, manufactured in accordance with ANSI/NISO Z39.48-1992 and ANSI/NISO Z39.48-1984 (Permanence of Paper)

Contents

Preface

Every day, financial theory finds new applications in the world of business, money markets and financial institutions. The range of applications is expanding with the increased power of computers and numerical analysis, making it feasible to solve equations too complex to have an explicit solution.

As a result, the student and practitioner of finance need to be kept up to date with recent economic research if they are not to become out of touch. Beyond the technical aspects, a number of principles emerge from this work, which need to be known if the practical mechanisms are to be fully understood. It is no exaggeration to say that finance is one area of business practice that has been profoundly influenced by theoretical developments. The model of a rational decision-maker, which was conceived by theoreticians in an attempt to represent in a rudimentary way the behaviour of actual decision-makers, has tended to play a normative role and has influenced the way in which financial decisions are made today. The design[1] and regulation of today's money markets are largely the product of theoretical and empirical thinking concerning optimality and the efficiency of market equilibrium. It has come to a point where it may legitimately be questioned whether modern theories can be tested on the basis of historical data.

Markets evolve at the rate at which practitioners adopt more sophisticated forms of reasoning.

This course in financial theory has been taught at the HEC School of Management since 1983, in the second year of a three-year curriculum. It is offered as an option for the benefit of students intending to specialize in the field of finance. The level of mathematics required is that of a good science-based *baccalauréat* with one additional year of college level mathematics. This book is not aimed at trained mathematicians (although mathematicians will, we hope, find nothing objectionable in it); it uses only ordinary notions of analysis and algebra. Some supplements in mathematics will be provided here, but these are not intended as substitutes for tuition in mathematics, since we also attempt to remain simple, intuitive and 'concrete' in style.

Our book covers three basic subjects fundamental to the understanding of other aspects of finance. In addition to their elementary character, these three subjects were selected because they have given rise to so many practical applications during the last twenty years. Each of the three topics is covered in one part of the book:

- **Part I:**
  behaviour of investors towards risk (Chapter 2), portfolio choices (Chapter 3) and (partial) equilibrium on the stock market (Chapters 4 and 5);

- **Part II:**
  option valuation (Chapters 6, 7 and 8);

- **Part III:**
  bond valuation and the study of interest rates (Chapters 9, 10 and 11).

The first topic has profoundly influenced the manner in which investment funds are managed, even though the equilibrium model which is the by-product of this approach (the Capital Asset Pricing Model, CAPM) does not always survive unscathed the numerous empirical tests to which it has been subjected (*see* Chapter 5). The second and third topics have provided the backbone for the extraordinary growth of option markets and interest rate hedging mechanisms. Furthermore, options theory provides a veritable 'legal algebra'[2] when drawing up financial contracts which define the rights of issuers and holders of securities, and in the valuation of the liabilities of limited companies as well as some of their assets (Chapter 8). This book should, therefore, be of great practical interest, even though it does not go into the detailed functioning of financial markets and institutions, the description of financial contracts and existing markets, or the analysis of business practices.

This book is not intended as an encyclopedia of finance; in fact, it covers only a small sector of the field. It does not study dynamic optimization, portfolio management or market equilibrium over several periods of time, although this last area is touched on in places. It does not address issues of corporate finance or the microstructure of markets, or the economic theory of financial institutions, recent developments based on game theory and information asymmetry among agents. Nor does it discuss areas of application: business management (cash management, choice of capital structure, mergers and acquisitions, dividend policy and so on), bank management, portfolio management, international finance, the economics of insurance and so on. Finally, this book devotes little space to empirical studies, although the whole of Chapter 5 is given over to modern econometric techniques which serve to test the CAPM.

Within some of the topics which we do cover, some methods are ignored. With regard to the stock market, we only discuss the CAPM, leaving aside Ross's Arbitrage Pricing Theory (APT). In our treatment of option pricing theory and bond pricing theory, we make very limited use of a modern mathematical approach, known as the 'martingale' approach, which is touched upon in Chapters 7 and 10.[3] The valuation of options and bonds ultimately requires the solution of a differential or partial differential equation. From a pedagogic point of view, we felt it would be more simple to obtain these equations directly and hence to limit ourselves to standard methods of differential and integral calculus. Even though the martingale approach is undeniably more elegant, a parallel exposition of this would have required additional coverage of mathematical topics and also a significant amount of duplication and back-tracking. We felt that a systematic survey of this method should constitute a separate pedagogic project.

We end with a word on style. Although this is a technical book, we have done our best to make room for discussion and interpretation. We have attempted to take a step back from published academic literature and to create a well-integrated book which would be more than the sum of the individual contributions of the various researchers. Frequently we have stated personal views and we have passed judgement on some approaches. The reader may decide whether or not he or she agrees.

Our thanks go to Mathieu Lepeltier and Isabelle Salaün of Crédit Commercial de France, who have taught this course at HEC, Pierre Collin-Dufresne and Bertrand Jacquillat, who have given us their comments and encouraged us to finish this work. We are grateful to them all, and to the numerous HEC students who have been generous with their remarks over the years.

Notes to Preface

1   The creation of futures contracts on stock indices is a case in point.
2   We are grateful to our colleague Romain Laufer for coining this expression for us.
3   *See* [Duffie 1992].

Reference

[Duffie 1992]   D. Duffie, *Dynamic Asset Pricing Theory*.
                                       Princeton University Press, 1992.

1

Introduction, basic concepts and reminders

1.1 What is a financial security?

A financial security may be defined by the sequence of future cash flows its holder will receive. Describing a security requires the possession of a certain amount of information: what is the payment schedule, that is, on what date will the payment of each flow take place? What will the amounts of successive payments be? What will happen in the case of non-payment? and so on.

The most simple case of a financial security is a risk-free security for which all future cash flows are known for certain at all times. Government bonds are more or less risk-free, since we can be practically certain that the government will always be in a position to pay its debts in ECU.[1]

Generally, the future flows of a security are not known for certain. The investor must assess the security from cash flow *forecasts* and thus from *random data*. For some securities, such as bonds or receivables, these forecasts are based on contractual data. For others, such as shares, they are

1

merely the results of economic analysis made by the investor: the issuing company has made no promise as to the amount of future dividends or the payment schedule.

Whatever the basis of the random flow forecasts, they are represented in the form of a *probability distribution* for each flow. But the random variables representing the successive cash flows are not generally independent of one another. In many cases, the realization of the flow at instant 1 supplies information about the amount of flow at instant 2: a commercial operation which proves a success during its first few years very often keeps going up under its own momentum; similarly, an operation which rapidly becomes a failure rarely sees its later results improve. This is called the *serial dependence* of cash flows. It is taken into account by the *joint probability distribution* of all flows relating to the financial security in question.

1.2 The financial market

The question of what a security is worth has no meaning in itself. It is out of the question to attempt to value a financial security without specifying the market on which the value is to be assessed. The first step is therefore to describe the financial market in question. The most detailed description specifies the nature and number of investors present in the market; from this we may deduce their demand for financial securities. Reconciling the forces of demand and supply, we arrive at a price for each security. This is to say that an *evaluation function* exists which links each cash flow sequence with its value on the market.

It must be stressed that this evaluation function applies uniformly to all securities. To illustrate the universality of this function and at the same time give a more concrete description, let us consider as an example the most simple case: that of the *certain future*. Suppose we have a financial security which is to produce three successive payments at instants 1, 2 and 3, equal for example to 500 ECU, 500 ECU and 10,500 ECU (this would correspond to a security with a face value of 10,000 ECU and a coupon rate of 5%). Let us also give a simplified description of the financial market by specifying that during the period 0–1 the prevailing interest rate is 6% and that it is 7% during the period 1–2 and 8% during the period 2–3.[2]

It is thus possible to calculate the exact behaviour, over time, of the price of this security on this market. In order to do this, we work from the principle that at the terminal instant $t = 3$, the security must have a price equal to its redemption price, which is 10,500 ECU. Then, tracing back in time to instant $t = 2 + \varepsilon$, we can see by discounting that the security is worth 10,500 ECU divided by 1.08. We next move from instant $2 + \varepsilon$ to instant $2 - \varepsilon$, adding 500 ECU to the price of the security.[3]

Continuing back in time, we obtain the progression of the price of the security as it appears in Figure 1.1: during the first period, the bond which pays only 500 ECU sees its value go from 9484.41 ECU to 9533.48 ECU. Its *rate of return* during this period is indeed 6%, taking into account both payments and appreciation:

$$\frac{9553.48 - 9484.41 + 500}{9484.41} = 0.06 \qquad [2.1]$$

What allows the appreciation to be produced is the fact that the initial price – which, it may be recalled, was calculated backwards – was sufficiently low to start with. If the first payment had been even smaller (400 ECU for example) the initial price would have been less than 9484.41 ECU, whereas the end-of-period price would remain that which results from later payments, namely 9553.48 ECU. Thus, the appreciation would have been larger.

By this technique, all the securities return 6% on the market during the first period, proof that the evaluation function used applies to all of them. The security considered here as an example has a coupon rate of 5%, which is less than the rate of return demanded by the market during the three successive periods. The payments being insufficient, the required rate of return is produced by an increase in value which goes to complete the payments (so that throughout its life, the value of this security is quoted above the 'par' 10,000 ECU).

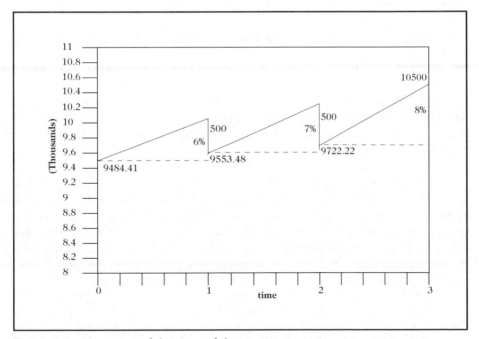

Figure 1.1   Movement of the price of the security over time

Generally speaking, *all* financial securities must, under certainty, have a price which increases in step with the period rate of interest of the market; however, when a payment is made, this causes an immediate drop in price.

We may thus state the following principle:

> The value of securities is calculated backwards and under certainty is such that there appears, over each period, a total return (taking into account payments and any appreciation) equal to the interest rate of the period.

Two types of data were needed to calculate the preceding price:

*   those characterising the security, namely the three successive payments (corresponding to a coupon rate of 5%) and
*   data depending on the description of the financial market, namely the three successive market interest rates: 6, 7 and 8%.

Price adjustment ensures coherence between these two types of data: there is nothing to prevent a security yielding only 5% from existing on a market where rates of return are higher; to do so, it need only be quoted below par, so that an increase in value may occur later.

1.3   Choices made by investors

The information supplied in the above example, according to which the interest rates in the three periods were 6, 7 and 8% respectively, is not in fact a base figure. It results from the consumption behaviour of individuals, especially *the way in which they spread their consumption between the various periods*. When they wish to consume heavily in comparison to the resources immediately available, interest rates are high; when they wish to consume little, interest rates are low. Individuals therefore make intertemporal choices which affect interest rates.

It will be recalled in this regard that in economic theory, items of choice are divided into two categories. The first consists of the *flows* obtained for the purpose of consumption. The demanded flow of consumable goods and services is a function of their purchase price (and the agents' wealth): no other economic determinant enters into in the agents' decision. The second category of items of choice consists of *stocks*. A stock is an item which may be accumulated for it to be resold or consumed later; the economic determinant which influences the quantity demanded is, therefore, not the price at the time of purchase, but the purchase price compared with the possible resale price or with the price of a purchase made at a later date. This price difference is the economic determinant of the demand for stocks. It is clear that financial securities belong to the category of stocks.

The intertemporal choices we have just mentioned are most often model-led using the *utility-of-consumption function* specific to each individual. Utility is a function of present and future consumption. Individuals spread their resources between present and future consumption in such a way that their utility function reaches the highest possible level. The marginal rate of substitution between these two consumptions is a very important factor in determining the rate of interest.[4]

However, the utility function is not only intended to represent the choices of consumption made at two different moments. It also represents the choice between a *quasi-certain* consumption (that of today) and a consumption which is random (that of tomorrow). The *behaviour of individuals towards risk*, which will be represented by their utility function, is at the very heart of this study: we will see that it creates a particular attitude towards the composition of portfolios of securities. In Chapter 3, for example, we will make the assumption that investors are concerned with the expected return and with the variance of return on their portfolio, and we will demonstrate the benefit generated by diversification. Individuals having an aversion to extremely high risks and focusing only on the overall risk of their portfolio will make a point of selecting securities whose risks compensate for one another: if one of the securities included in the port-folio yields more than expected in circumstances where others yield less than expected (and vice versa) the overall risk they assume is reduced. Diversification between securities is a standard behavioural characteristic of risk aversion.[5]

To sum up: dividing consumption between periods and diversifying between securities[6] are the essential motivating factors which influence investors' choices.

1.4 Equilibrium

The state of the market results from the conflict between the choices made by all those acting in it. Equilibrium is reached when the supply of each security is equal to the demand for each security. This is how the evaluation function will be determined. Remember that this function is applicable to all securities simultaneously in a given market.[7]

Although equilibrium may only be calculated in detail by imposing the condition of equality of supply and demand for each security, it is possible to state a minimum condition (a necessary but not sufficient condition) which must prevail at equilibrium and which may, on its own in certain cases[8], provide valuation results. This condition is the *absence of arbitrage opportunities*.

Arbitrage is defined as *an operation which generates a positive profit with no outlay of capital and no risk-taking*. For example, if there existed on the same market two identical securities at different prices, it is obvious that each investor would choose to buy the less expensive security and sell the one whose price is higher. The difference would provide an immediate profit with no risk and no capital outlay, since the sale of one would have permitted the purchase of the other.[9]

If arbitrage opportunities existed, the market could not be in equilibrium, since all operators would carry out the arbitrage operation, demanding some securities in infinite quantity and selling others in equally infinite quantity. In such conditions, the demand for each security could not be equal to its supply.[10]

The basic idea according to which a market in equilibrium cannot offer arbitrage opportunities results in an important principle which characterizes the evaluation function of all markets. This is the *value additivity principle*:

> If, in the same market, there exists a security A defined by its sequence of future cash flows, a security B also defined by its sequence of future cash flows, and a security $A + B$ whose cash flows are at all times equal to the sum of the flows of the two preceding securities, then

$$V(A + B) = V(A) + V(B)$$

The evaluation function is a linear application.

The value of the third security must be equal to the sum of the values of the first two. If this were not the case, arbitrage opportunities would exist. Let us imagine, for example, that the value of $A + B$ was greater than the value of A plus the value of B. An individual would then be able to buy A and B separately and sell $A + B$, possibly selling it short. This would involve no risk for the individual, since all the flows would cancel each other out exactly: they would receive the proceeds from A and the proceeds from B, which would allow them to pay exactly the cash flows of $A + B$ which they had sold short. Any inequality between the market values would result in an immediate profit, even though no risk had been assumed. Inequality in this direction is thus impossible; it will also be shown that it is impossible in the other direction ($V(A + B) < V(A) + V(B)$), so that only equality, and thus value additivity, is possible.

Note that the rule of additivity assumes the simultaneous existence of the three securities A, B and $A + B$. The rule does not say that in a market where only security A and security B existed, we could eliminate these securities and replace them with security $A + B$, whose value would be the sum of the values of the two preceding securities. This could not be true, since the removal of some securities and the creation of others may fundamentally change the equilibrium of the market. Where the three securities exist simultaneously on the same market, however, the principle generally applies.

We must point out that in corporate financial theory, the principle of additivity underlies the *Modigliani-Miller theorem*, according to which:

> In the absence of taxes, the total value of a firm is independent of the composition of its liabilities.

Whether the firm is financed by equity capital or by debt, the total value of these two categories of securities is not modified when their relative value is changed.[11] This result is the direct product of the value additivity principle: the value of the shares plus the value of the debt is equal to the value of the total flow resulting from the operations of the firm – its economic flow – and this value is an objective amount, independent of the financing method.

1.5 Basic reminders on probability and statistics

After this brief reminder of basic financial principles, in the next two sections we shall consider a few technical concepts arising from the theory of probability and statistics and the theory of optimization. These concepts will be useful to us in later chapters. In fact, the concept of a random variable, which is the object of probability theory, is the most frequent representation of financial risk, and optimization is the basis for the economic theory of the choices made by economic agents.

A random variable X is most often specified using its *distribution function*, defined by:

$$F(x) \equiv \Pr\,(X \leq x) \tag{5.1}$$

This function corresponds to the probability that the random variable X will take a value less than or equal to the real number x.

We may also specify the random variable X by its *probability density* $f(x)$, which is such that:

$$F(x) \equiv \int_{-\infty}^{x} f(u)\,du \tag{5.2}$$

By definition, the probability that $X < x$ is equal to the area beneath the curve $f(x)$ to the left of the value x.

Very often we make do with a more concise description of the random variable X: such a description does not allow us to know the total probability distribution, only certain descriptive parameters. The first of these parameters is *expected value*, which is a measurement of the central value of the distribution of probabilities. The expected value of the random variable X is a real number; it is defined by:

$$E(X) \equiv \int_{-\infty}^{+\infty} x f(x)\, dx \qquad\qquad [5.3]$$

This is the mean of the possible values of the random variable, weighted by their respective probabilities. In fact, the quantity $f(x)dx$ is nothing more than the probability that the variable X will take a value between x and $x + dx$. Expected value is also called the 'first moment' of probability distribution.

Since the probability distribution is in practice rarely known in its entirety, we are led to *estimate* the expected value of a random variable using a finite sample of observations. We must take care to distinguish two concepts:

- the expected value itself, which is a fixed real number, and which could be calculated from the complete probability distribution,

- an estimate, or an estimator, of this expected value which could be calculated not from the whole distribution, but from a sample of this distribution taken at random.

The most commonly used estimator of expected value is the *mean of the values* in the sample:

$$\overline{x} \equiv \frac{\sum_{i=1}^{n} x_i}{n} \qquad\qquad [5.4]$$

where the various x_i are the observations belonging to the sample.

It is crucial to understand that, since the sample was taken at random, a different sample could equally have been taken. The numeric values which make up a sample, and as a result their mean, are random variables. We may thus define their expected value: we would show that the expected value of the mean $\overline{x}$ is equal to the expected value of X. We say that $\overline{x}$ as an estimator of $E(X)$ is *unbiased*; this means that the errors contained in the estimator are of zero expected value.

A second parameter frequently used to describe the behaviour of random variables is intended to measure not the central value but the *dispersion* of the associated probability distribution or the mean size of the fluctuations of the variable. This is the *variance* of the random variable X:

$$\mathrm{Var}(X) \equiv \int_{-\infty}^{+\infty} [x - E(X)]^2 f(x) \, dx \qquad\qquad [5.5]$$

Variance is the expectation of the squares of the deviations from the expected value. Variance has the purely formal inconvenience of being measured in a unit which is the square of the unit of measurement of the random variable itself, which sometimes hinders interpretation. For this reason another measure of dispersion has been defined: *standard deviation*, to which we give the symbol σ, and which is the square root of the variance:

$$\sigma(X) = \sqrt{\mathrm{var}(X)}$$

Standard deviation has the advantage of being measured in the same units as the variable, but this is only an advantage of presentation: the two concepts are in fact equivalent. Variance is also called the 'second moment' of distribution. It would be easy to define the nth moment in similar fashion.

The most commonly used estimator of variance where we have a sample of observations, x_i, $i = \ldots n$, is defined by the formula:

$$\text{est var } (X) \equiv \frac{\sum_{i=1}^{n} \left(x_i - \overline{x} \right)^2}{n - 1} \qquad\qquad [5.6]$$

The calculation is done by obtaining the deviations of each observation from the mean, before squaring them and calculating the mean of these squares.[12]

We will sometimes need to use not one random variable but several. Their behaviour will therefore need to be described by a joint distribution function, defined by:

$$F(x, y) \equiv \mathrm{Pr} \ (X \leq x \text{ and } Y \leq y) \qquad\qquad [5.7]$$

where we have two random variables X and Y. In the same way as for a single variable (Equation 5.2), we may define a joint probability density of these two variables, written $f(x, y)$.

When dealing with several random variables, the problem arises of knowing the distribution of their sum, and more specifically, the value of the variance of their sum. The variance of the sum of the two random variables X and Y is calculated as follows:

$$\text{Var}\,(X + Y) = \text{var}(X) + \text{var}(Y) + 2\,\text{cov}(X,Y) \tag{5.8}$$

It is not equal to the sum of the variances of X and Y, except in the special case of linear independence between the two variables. Generally, there is added to the two variances a term equal to twice the covariance between X and Y; this term reflects the cancelling out of any possible randomness between X and Y. The covariance between X and Y is defined by:

$$\text{cov}(X,Y) = \int_{-\infty}^{+\infty}\int_{-\infty}^{+\infty} [x - E(X)][y - E(y)]\, f(x,y)\, dx\, dy \tag{5.9}$$

that is, by the expected product of the deviations of X and Y from their respective expected values.

Correlation is another measure of the interdependence between two variables which disregards the size of their respective fluctuations. It is defined by:

$$\text{corr}(X,Y) = \frac{\text{cov}(X,Y)}{\sigma(X)\sigma(Y)} \tag{5.10}$$

This amount necessarily lies between -1 and 1: when it equals 0, the two variables are linearly independent; when it equals 1 or -1 the two variables are perfectly linked by a linear relationship; when the correlation is positive the two variables tend to fluctuate in unison, when it is negative they fluctuate in opposition to one another. Correlation thus has a clearer intuitive meaning than covariance, to the extent that the meaning of covariance might be better understood by reading the definition of correlation in reverse: covariance is the product of the correlation and the standard deviations of the two variables. Covariance is therefore a joint measure of the degree of inter-dependence and the size of the randomness affecting the two variables. It goes without saying that it enters into the calculation of the variance of a sum: for the randomness of two variables to compensate one another, they must not only vary inversely to one another but also be of appropriate sizes.

As in the case of expected value or variance, we may obtain estimators of covariance; but for this we must have a sample of *pairs* of observations of X and Y. From a sample x_i, y_i, $i = 1...n$, we may calculate an estimator of covariance using the formula:

$$\text{est cov}(X,Y) = \frac{\sum_{i=1}^{n}(x_i - \bar{x})(y_i - \bar{y})}{n-1} \qquad [5.11]$$

that is, taking the mean of the products of the deviations of the observations of X and Y from their respective means. It is necessary to have simultaneous observations of X and Y to be able to calculate their covariance.

When considering two random variables X and Y which are not independent, it is often useful to determine to what extent the knowledge of a realization x of X supplies information about the probability distribution of Y. This relationship between a value x of X and the probability distribution of Y is expressed by the *conditional* distribution function defined by:[13]

$$F(Y|x) \equiv \frac{\Pr\ [Y \leq y \text{ and } X = x]}{\Pr\ [X = x]} \qquad [5.12]$$

applying what is known as the Bayes theorem.

The concept of conditional distribution is extremely important in finance, due to the role played by the treatment of information on the financial markets.[14] Suppose Y is the future return on a security, which we are attempting to forecast, whereas X is a relevant piece of information, likely to help with the forecast. When the information X is known and we know that it takes the value x, the forecast for Y is generally improved by it. The conditional probability distribution is 'more precise', or more informative, than the *a priori* probability distribution.[15]

We associate with conditional probability distribution, by the same method as before, the concept of *conditional* expected value, written $E(Y|x)$, as well as that of conditional variance, written var$(Y|x)$, and also the general one of conditional moment. The conditional expected value of Y, given the value x, is *a function of x*. It is no longer, as in the case of unconditional expected value, a simple number: it gives the forecast central value of Y, given the realized value of x.

Conditional expectations are linked to unconditional expectations by the rule:

$$E[E(Y|X)] = E(Y) \qquad [5.13]$$

This rule holds that the unconditional expected value of Y is obtained from the expected value conditional on x by integrating over all the possible values of x, weighted by their probabilities. In fact, mathematicians use the more general rule:

$$E[g(X).E(Y|X)] = E[g(X).Y] \text{ for all } g \text{ functions} \qquad [5.14]$$

as the definition of conditional expectation.[16]

It is sometimes possible to state that $E(Y|x)$ is a linear function of x, which is the same as saying that Y is equal to a linear function of X plus a random variable with a zero expected value, given x:

$$Y = \alpha + \beta X + \varepsilon \qquad E(\varepsilon|x) = 0. \qquad [5.15]$$

This relationship is called a 'regression of Y on x' and the β coefficient is called the 'regression coefficient'. It may be verified that:[17][18]

$$\frac{\text{cov}(X,Y)}{\text{var}(X)} = \beta \qquad [5.16]$$

It is often legitimate to estimate the β coefficient by what is known as the 'method of least squares', which produces an estimator of β equal to the ratio of the estimates of $\text{cov}(X, Y)$ and $\text{var}(X)$ already given.

1.6 Reminders on optimization

In the following pages, we always assume that economic agents make decisions which are the best possible ones in view of a well-defined criterion which they set themselves. The optimization of this criterion – also called 'objective function' – by a choice appropriate to the value of the decision, allows us to represent the behaviour of the agent.[19] The simplest case of optimization is *unconstrained optimization*.

Suppose an agent wishes to take a decision x which is the best possible in view of a criterion, or an objective function, $f(x)$, to be maximized. The optimum decision is calculated quite simply by noting that the apex of the curve representing the function $f(x)$ is reached at a point where the slope of the curve is reduced to zero. We know that the slope of a function is obtained by calculating its first derivative; the optimum value x^* of x is thus such that:

$$\frac{df}{dx}(x^*) = 0 \qquad [6.1]$$

This equation, known as a *first-order condition*[20], is only one necessary condition of optimality; it would remain to be established that the point obtained is a maximum and not a minimum or a plane. On the other hand, this method of calculating the optimum decision supposes that the criterion f is differentiable with respect to the decision x.

In the more general case, where not one but *several* decisions have to be taken simultaneously – to maximize a criterion which depends on all of them – the optimum value of each decision may be obtained by equating each of the *partial* derivatives of the objective function f to zero.[21] We thus have a system containing as many equations as there are decisions to be taken, and which will then have to be solved.

In economics, however, it is rarely possible to optimize without constraint. Limited resources, and the necessary balancing of receipts and expenses, are amongst the constraints which economic agents are obliged to take into account.

Let us imagine that two decisions x and y have to be taken in order to maximize a criterion $f(x,y)$, whilst respecting a constraint $g(x,y) = 0$:

$$\text{Max } f(x,y)$$
$$\text{subject to } g(x,y) = 0 \qquad\qquad [6.2]$$

The solution to this problem may be obtained in two different ways. The first is more natural but less often viable than the second, known as the 'Lagrange method', which is much more easily put into practice.

The first method involves substituting the constraint into the objective function. We know that the two decisions to be taken x and y are linked by the relationship $g(x,y) = 0$ which we are strictly obliged to verify. Suppose we may express the same constraint in the form:

$$y = \Phi(x) \qquad\qquad [6.3]$$

To take this into account in an optimization problem, we may substitute $y = \Phi(x)$ into the objective function to obtain a new criterion to be maximized:

$$\text{Max } f(x, \Phi(x)) \qquad\qquad [6.4]$$

We then have an unconstrained optimization problem with a single decision x. However, the method is generally of little use as it is difficult to calculate the value of y satisfying $g(x,y)$ for each value of x, that is, to obtain $y = \Phi(x)$.

The Lagrange method, on the other hand, leads easily to a system of optimal conditions. It involves modifying the criterion $f(x,y)$ by introducing into it a 'penalty' which takes effect in the case of violation of the constraint, then adjusting the rate of this penalty so that the decisions satisfy the constraint exactly. In other words, we construct what is known as a '*Lagrangian*':

$$L(x,y) = f(x,y) - \lambda.g(x,y) \qquad\qquad [6.5]$$

The 'penalty' is equal to the deviation from the constraint, $g(x,y)$, multiplied by the 'Lagrange multiplier', λ. Once the Lagrangian is constructed, we have to deal with an optimization problem which is formally without constraint and which involves maximizing L by an appropriate choice of three decision variables x, y and λ. The first-order optimality conditions are accordingly obtained by partial derivation with respect to these three variables:

$$\frac{\partial f}{\partial x}(x,y) - \lambda \frac{\partial g}{\partial x}(x,y) = 0$$
$$\frac{\partial f}{\partial y}(x,y) - \lambda \frac{\partial g}{\partial y}(x,y) = 0 \qquad\qquad [6.6]$$
$$g(x,y) = 0$$

The system thus obtained is a system of three equations with three unknowns, allowing x, y and λ to be determined.

Its solution may be arrived at by all the usual methods, but the economic significance of the calculation is particularly clear when we proceed as follows: we first solve the first two equations, from which we obtain x and y in terms of λ, that is, the decisions in terms of the penalty. We then substitute the functions $x(\lambda)$ and $y(\lambda)$ thus obtained in the third equation, which gives:

$$g(x(\lambda), y(\lambda)) = 0 \qquad\qquad [6.7]$$

When obtainable, the solution of this equation supplies the value of λ, so that the constraint is satisfied exactly (at this stage the penalty is adjusted). It only remains to substitute the value of λ thus obtained into the functions $x(\lambda)$ and $y(\lambda)$ to obtain the optimum decisions.

The value of the Lagrange multiplier λ has an interesting economic significance: it is equal to the increment of the criterion f, per unit of increase or displacement of the constraint.[22] When the constraint is relaxed, it is generally possible to attain a higher value of the criterion f; the multiplier λ

indicates the rate at which this increment takes place. The multiplier thus provides an indication as to the more or less 'restrictive' nature of g.

If, for example, the constraint g reflects a limitation on resources, the multiplier is a measure of the more or less precious nature of these resources in relation to the optimization problem to be solved. If we envisage acquiring an extended quantity of resources, we may take this decision by comparing the value of the multiplier with the acquisition cost of a unit. The Lagrange multiplier is an index of rarity of resources, similar in many ways to a price.

1.7 Conclusion

Any good account of financial theory assumes the reader is familiar with the basic principles of microeconomics, optimization and probability theory. We have at the very most listed the tools which we shall use in the remainder of this book. Readers wishing to acquire some degree of mastery of these concepts should consult the three textbooks referred to in the bibliography.

It now remains for us to develop the theory of (partial) equilibrium on the financial market. In order to do this, we must first of all equip financial investors with an objective function capable of representing the choices which they make between more or less random securities (Chapter 2). We then deal with the effective calculation of these choices, that is, determine the individuals' optimum portfolios (Chapter 3), then deduce from them the equilibrium prices on a financial market where a given collection of such individuals transact (Chapter 4).

Notes to Chapter 1

1   It must be said, however, that the real purchasing power of the ECU in ten years' time is not, strictly speaking, certain. The flows of government bonds are thus risk-free in face value only. They are probably risky in terms of real value.

2   As we have said, a complete description of the market involves indicating exactly what the population of investors is. Interest rates constitute a summary description of this population: these are the rates at which investors, taking account of their preferences and their assets, are prepared to exchange future ECU against present ECU.

3   If, on the other hand, we move forward in time, the price of a security falls at the moment of the payments. This is logical, since at that moment the security 'loses some of its substance'.

4   See a standard microeconomics textbook (such as [Varian 1978] or [Zisswiller 1975]).

5   Note also that the intertemporal dimension of the choices and the attitude to risk act jointly to induce a behavioural trait of *'intertemporal' diversification*. Since the periods of investment and reinvestment follow one another, investors must concern themselves with the way in which the rate of return on a security over one period may be linked to opportunities for reinvestment which may present themselves during subsequent periods. In the case where such a probabilistic link exists, investors may be led to choose their portfolio in such a way that an abnormally small return during the first period is followed by exceptionally favourable opportunities for reinvestment, whereas an abnormally high rate of return during the first period would be followed by extremely weak opportunities for reinvestment. There appears therefore a mechanism for the *compensation of risks over the periods*. This is what we have called intertemporal diversification.

6   And intertemporal diversification.

7   *See* Chapter 4.

8   *See* Chapters 6 *and* 7, for example.

9   We know that thanks to the various mechanisms for short selling, it is possible to sell a security even though one does not own it. The monthly settlement market of the Paris Stock Exchange, for example, authorizes vendors only to deliver at the end of the month a security which they sold during the month. It is thus perfectly possible for them to sell a security which they do not hold. In the United States, where there exists only one spot market, intermediaries are prepared to lend securities to operators who may thus sell them without possessing them, thus avoiding having to deliver the sold security. Whatever the institutional details, the general idea is the same: unjustifiable price differences cannot exist for very long in a correctly organized market.

10   Supply is the number of securities put into circulation by firms, a finite quantity.

11   By issuing equity capital to pay off a debt, for example.

12   As shown by the formula, it is preferable to calculate this last mean by dividing by $n-1$ rather than by n. This manipulation is aimed at obtaining an unbiased estimator of variance; dividing by the number n of observations would produce an estimated variance whose expected value would differ from the true variance of X. *See* a textbook on statistics.

13   The definition given here is meaningful only if X is a 'discrete' random variable, that is, for example, a variable which may take only integer values. In fact, if X were a non-discrete variable (taking its values, for example, from the set of real numbers) the event $X = x$ would have a probability of zero. It is possible, however, to extend this definition to non-discrete variables. *See* [Métivier 1979] page 130.

14   *See* Chapter 4.

15   *Cf* [Blackwell 1951].

16   *See* [Métivier 1979].

17   $E(\varepsilon|x) = 0$ for all x implies by virtue of [5.14] that $\text{cov}(\varepsilon,X)$, which is equal to $E(\varepsilon X)$, is zero.

18   Be careful to distinguish regression coefficient and correlation coefficient.

19   Chapter 3 will give a sample application of this principle. See also a microeconomics textbook, such as [Varian 1978].

20   Since it involves the first derivatives of the function f.

21   Consider a function of two variables $f(x,y)$. The partial derivative of f with respect to $x, \partial f/\partial x$, is obtained by a derivative calculation in which the other variable, y, is treated as a constant.

22    $g(x,y) = \varepsilon\ (\varepsilon > 0)$ rather than $g(x,y) = 0$.

References

[Blackwell 1951]   D. Blackwell, The Comparison of Experiments, *Proceedings of the Second Berkeley Symposium on Mathematical Statistics and Probability*, University of California Press, 1951, 93–102.

[Varian 1978]   H. R. Varian, *Microeconomic Analysis*. Norton, 1978.

[Métivier 1979]   M. Métivier, *Notions fondamentales de la théorie des probabilités*. Paris, Dunod, 1979.

[Zisswiller 1975]   R. Zisswiller, *Microéconomie et analyse financière*. Dalloz, 1975.

Part I

Equilibrium in the stock market

2

The attitude of a rational individual towards risk

The prices of financial securities on the stock market are dictated by the forces of supply and demand. Since most securities yield random revenues, it follows that demand cannot be explained without *a model of investors' behaviour towards risk*. It is in effect this behaviour which determines investors' preference for more or less risky securities and for the higher or lower returns they expect from them.

Games of chance provide us with a convenient experimental base to use in assessing the attitude of an individual in a situation of risk.[1] These attracted very early on the attention of philosophers such as Blaise Pascal and Pierre de Fermat, who commonly accepted the idea that the attraction of a lottery X opening up the prospect of gains $(x_1, \ldots x_n)$ with the probabilities $(p_1, \ldots p_n)$ was completely measured by the expected value $E(X) = \sum_i x_i p_i$.

The St. Petersburg paradox[2] formulated by the Swiss mathematician Nicholas Bernoulli in 1728 was to call this idea into question. Gabriel Cramer and Daniel Bernoulli [Cramer and Bernoulli 1738] suggested generalizing the hypothesis of Pascal and Fermat: there is no reason to think that a gain of 200 ECU would necessarily have, in the eyes of a gambler, twice the value of a gain of 100 ECU (one or the other resulting from the same lottery). They put forward the idea that an (increasing) concave[3] function had to be applied to the gains before taking their expected value. The effect of such a transformation was to reduce the attraction to the gambler of very high values of gain such as could result from the St. Petersburg game. It was thus admitted that individuals possess what today is called a *utility function*, and that they evaluate lotteries not on the basis of their expected value of gain $E(X) = \sum_i x_i p_i$, but on that of their expected utility $E(X) = \sum_i u(x_i) p_i$.[4]

This idea is at the historical origin of the *expected utility theorem*, which was to find its axiomatic justification only with the *von Neumann and Morgenstern theorem* [von Neumann and Morgenstern 1947].

This theorem is the subject of the first section of this chapter. Then, in Section 2.2, we introduce the *risk aversion theory* of [Arrow 1965] and [Pratt 1964]. We show that the attitude of an investor towards risk is related to the concavity of his or her utility function. Finally, in Section 2.3, we present a collection of the utility functions most commonly used in financial economics.

2.1   The theory of von Neumann, Morgenstern and Savage[5]

All economic theory is based on behaviour hypotheses. These constitute the axiomatic basis of the theory. Any hypothesis may be criticized: once formulated, it may exclude from the scope of the theory unsuspected modes of behaviour which may explain certain real phenomena. In spite of everything, we cannot allow investors to behave in an arbitrary fashion, as the theory would then be devoid of consequences and incapable of producing any statements. It would then be unusable.

John von Neumann and Oskar Morgenstern sought to formulate hypotheses on investors on the stock exchange which led to an easy-to-handle, and thus productive, economic theory[6]. These assembled hypotheses constitute a possible definition of the 'rational individual'. By this we understand a person who systematically pursues a simple objective. In the present case, the simple objective is the expected value of utility.

There are three basic concepts to the von Neumann and Morgenstern theory:

- *the set S of possibilities* or of the various states of nature (indexed s): these offer a description of the world of such precision that the information according to which a particular state of the world should prevail removes all uncertainty in the mind of the decision-maker.

Conversely, this description of the world makes it possible to identify objectively the state of nature which arises.[7] States of nature are mutually exclusive: only one occurs at a time, never two simultaneously. The drawing of the states of nature is assumed to be entirely outside the control of the decision-maker.[8] We may also define an *event* or a *circumstance* as being a subset of S;

- *the set C of consequences* (indexed c): a consequence is any sort of phenomenon which directly motivates the decision-maker. Financial gains are the only consequences we consider here;

- *the set A of actions* (indexed a): an action a is any mapping $c(a,s)$ of the set of states of nature on the set of consequences.

The expected utility theorem summarizes the choices of the rational individual by means of only two indices:

- an index which applies to the *consequences* which his or her actions will have in the various future circumstances; we call this the '*utility*' of these consequences;

- an index which applies to the various future circumstances, and which, out of convenience, we call the '(subjective) *probability*' of these circumstances, as it is perceived by the investor.[9]

It is often useful to describe the elements of a decision problem by means of a table whose columns correspond to the various states of nature, whose rows correspond to the actions, and whose body indicates for each action, a, and each state of nature, s, the consequence, $c(a,s)$, to which the decision-maker is subjected. The example illustrating this section is presented in this form in Table 2.1 Panel A. The example refers to three states of nature α, β and γ, and three possible consequences 1, 2 and 3, giving a total of $3 \times 3 \times 3 = 27$ different actions.[10]

Let us suppose a questionnaire has been completed by the decision-maker, or, better still, that a sufficient number of choices made by him have been observed. In this way, a complete list of these actions in decreasing order of preference has been established. This appears in Table 2.1, which has been drawn up *in a comprehensive form and without any contradictions appearing* between the individual's choices, due to the absence of transitivity. This means that, for the rational individual:

Axiom 1:
   A complete ordering exists in the set A of all the envisageable actions.[11]

The question is whether, for greater convenience, this ordering may be reproduced using only two indices. This would obviously be impossible if the ranking were arbitrary.

	State		
	alpha	beta	gamma
Action			
1	1	1	1
2	2	1	1
3	1	2	1
4	1	1	2
5	3	1	1
6	2	2	1
7	2	1	2
8	1	2	2
9	3	2	1
10	1	3	1
11	3	1	2
12	2	2	2
13	2	3	1
14	1	1	3
15	3	2	2
16	2	1	3
17	1	3	2
18	3	3	1
19	1	2	3
20	2	3	2
21	3	1	3
22	2	2	3
23	3	3	2
24	3	2	3
25	1	3	3
26	2	3	3
27	3	3	3

Table 2.1   Panel A

But the ranking of actions in Table 2.1 is not arbitrary. By carefully deciphering this table, we can uncover the logic which guides the steps of the decision-maker. For example, he prefers action 1 to action 2. This allows us to think that, all other things being equal, he prefers consequence 1 to consequence 2.

This deduction is confirmed by examining actions 8 and 12, 6 and 12 and so on. In fact, the decision-maker applies this preference to the consequences in a coherent fashion. Similarly, we can observe his preference

Index of preference on the consequences	alpha 0.2	beta 0.35	gamma 0.45	Reconstruction of the preferences by means of subjective probability and the index of preferences between consequences
(1)	(2)	(3)	(4)	(5)
100	20	35	45	100
	11.68	35	45	91.68
	20	20.44	45	85.44
	20	35	26.28	81.28
	0	35	45	80
	11.68	20.44	45	77.12
	11.68	35	26.28	72.96
	20	20.44	26.28	66.72
	0	20.44	45	65.44
	20	0	45	65
	0	35	26.28	61.28
58.4	11.68	20.44	26.28	58.4
	11.68	0	45	56.68
	20	35	0	55
	0	20.44	26.28	46.72
	11.68	35	0	46.68
	20	0	26.28	46.28
	0	0	45	45
	20	20.44	0	40.44
	11.68	0	26.28	37.96
	0	35	0	35
	11.68	20.44	0	32.12
	0	0	26.28	26.28
	0	20.44	0	20.44
	20	0	0	20
	11.68	0	0	11.68
0	0	0	0	0

Table 2.1   Panel B

for action 2 compared to action 3, which allows us to conjecture, taking into account what has just been said, that he considers event {β} to be more probable than event {α}. Also on this point, our conjecture can be systematically verified (*see* actions 14 and 19 and so on).

In short, we can verify that the arrangement of Table 2.1 corresponds to the behaviour of an individual whose choices in a situation of risk obey, in addition to Axiom 1, three other axioms which we state below.

Some definitions are given where necessary during the course of this statement. They introduce some new concepts of preference which are all deduced from the ordering affecting the actions. The aim is to reduce a relatively complex field of preferences covering 27 different actions to two more simple fields, one covering the three consequences and the other the three basic events. We then show that the scalar product of these two reduced fields does indeed reproduce the relative preference for the various actions given at the beginning.

Definition of conditional ordering:

Actions a and b on the one hand, a' and b' on the other hand being linked as follows:[12]

$$c(a, s) = c(b, s)$$
$$c(a', s) = c(b', s) \quad \text{for all } s \text{ belonging to } E \text{ and}$$
$$c(b, s) = c(b', s) \quad \text{for all } s \text{ belonging to } \tilde{E}$$

we say that action a' is not preferred to action a, given event E, if and only if $b \geq b'$.[13]

Axiom 2:

For all events E, the ordering conditioned by E, which we have just defined on set A, exists and is complete.

Event E being given, Axiom 2 postulates that the relative ranking of actions a and a' is well defined: it is the same whatever the actions b and b' to which a and a' are compared, or whatever the values taken by these actions b and b' on $\tilde{E}$.[14] Actions b and b' compared unconditionally lead to a conditional ranking of a and a'. According to this axiom, if we know that event E must occur (thus that $\tilde{E}$ will not occur) we may make a coherent choice between all the actions without having to be concerned with the consequences which would result from these choices in the – now impossible – event of $\tilde{E}$ occurring.[15]

Let us check that the ranking in Table 2.1 obeys Axiom 2. Let us examine for example the ranking conditioned by event $E = \{\alpha \text{ or } \beta\}$ and actions 2, 3, 7, 8, 16 and 19. According to the conditional ordering,

$$
\begin{aligned}
2 \geq 3 \quad &\Rightarrow 7 \geq 8 \text{ given } E; \\
&\Rightarrow 16 \geq 19 \text{ given } E; \\
7 \geq 8 \quad &\Rightarrow 2 \geq 3 \text{ given } E; \\
&\Rightarrow 16 \geq 19 \text{ given } E; \\
16 \geq 19 \quad &\Rightarrow 2 \geq 3 \text{ given } E; \\
&\Rightarrow 7 \geq 8 \text{ given } E; \\
&\Rightarrow 7 \geq 3 \text{ given } E.[16]
\end{aligned}
$$

Note that no contradiction appears in the ordering conditioned by E.

Axiom 2, which plays a crucial role in the expected utility theorem, is given different names by different authors. Some call it the *'independence axiom'* ([Samuelson 1957]), since it means in substance that various mutually exclusive future events do not intervene conjointly in the determination of preferences between the various actions[17]. Others call it the *'sure thing principle'* ([Savage 1954]), referring to the idea that a rational decision should not take into account events which the decision-maker has learned are impossible.

Definition of subjective impossibility:
   An event E is null (that is, subjectively impossible) if, whatever the actions a and a', a' is not preferred to a given E.

   Or, event E is null if:
   a' is not preferred to a given $\tilde{E}$, if and only if a' is not preferred to a.

Definition of preference between consequences:
   E being any event other than a null event, and a and a' being two constant actions on E, taking on E the values c and c', consequence c is not preferred to consequence c' ($c' \geq c$) if and only if $a' \geq a$ given E.[18]

Axiom 3:
   The ordering, which we have just defined on the set of consequences C, exists and is complete.

Axiom 3 postulates that the classification of consequences c and c' is well defined: it is the same whatever the event E considered in the definition. In other words, knowledge of the state of nature or of the event which must prevail in no way modifies the preference between the various consequences. We say that the decision-maker has no preference for states of nature.[19]

We can easily verify that the classification in Table 2.1 obeys Axiom 3: whatever the event envisaged, the decision-maker does not prefer consequence 3 to consequence 2, nor consequence 2 to consequence 1. This is true if the event in question is the full set of possibilities (action 27 is not preferred to action 12, nor action 12 to action 1). But it is also true whatever the event; let us for example examine event $\{a \text{ or } \beta\}$: the classification of actions 1, 6 and 18 (or that, identical under the terms of Axiom 2, of actions 4, 12 and 23)[20] produces the same result. The same is also true for events $\{a\}$, $\{\beta\}$, $\{\gamma\}$, $\{\beta \text{ or } \gamma\}$ and $\{a \text{ or } \gamma\}$.

Definition of preference between events (subjective probabilities):
   Let us consider two consequences c and c' such that $c \geq c'$. Consequences c and c', events E and E' and actions a and a' being linked as follows:[21]

$c(a, s) = c$ for all s belonging to E
$c(a, s) = c'$ for all s belonging to $\tilde{E}$
$c(a', s) = c$ for all s belonging to E'
$c(a', s) = c'$ for all s belonging to $\tilde{E}'$,

we say that event E' is not preferred to event $E (E \geq E')$[22] if and only if $a \geq a'$.

In other words, if decision-makers prefer to 'bet on' event E rather than on event E', it is because they consider the first to be more probable. Since decision-makers naturally opt for the action $(a \geq a')$ which produces the preferred consequence $(c \geq c')$ with the greatest probability, the subjective probability of the events is revealed by observing their acts.

Axiom 4:
The ordering which we have just defined on the set of events exists and is complete.

Axiom 4 postulates that the ordering on the events is well defined: it is independent of the two consequences c and c' envisaged in the definition.[23] The choice of an event on which a person decides to bet does not depend on the nature of the prospective gains. If I prefer a pink elephant to a white elephant, I choose the action which will give me a pink elephant in the case of the most probable event occurring; likewise, if I prefer a pink butterfly to a white butterfly, I choose the action which will give me a pink butterfly in the case of the most probable event occurring, the meaning of 'the most probable' being the same in both cases. Thus no ambiguity appears in the concept of 'most probable'.

Let us check that the classification in Table 2.1 obeys Axiom 4: event $\{\alpha\}$, for example, is at least as probable (subjectively) as event $\{\beta\}$, whatever the pair of consequences used to verify it. That is clear if we consider the bets on the consequences 1 and 2 (action 7 is not preferred to action 6); but also if we examine the bets on consequences 2 and 3 (action 24 is not preferred to action 23)[24]. In the same way, we may establish that event $\{\beta\}$ is at least as probable as event $\{\alpha\}$, that event $\{\alpha$ or $\beta\}$ is at least as probable as event $\{\gamma\}$[25], and so on.

On the basis of these four axioms characterizing the behaviour of the so-called rational individual, we may state the *expected utility theorem*:

Theorem:
There exists a measure of probability[26] Pr (E) on the set of events and a real function $u(c)$ on the set of consequences, such that:

$a \geq a'$ if and only if:

$$\sum_i \mathrm{Pr}\,(E_i).u(c_i) \geq \sum_{j'} \mathrm{Pr}\,(E_{j'}).u(c_{j'})$$

where we have stipulated that:

$c(a, s) = c_i$ for all s belonging to E_i

$c(a', s) = c_j$, for all s belonging to E_j

This theorem means that the orderings on the consequences and on the events may be represented by a utility function and a measure of probability. These allow us to code the ordering on the actions by means of a simple comparison of the expected utilities of these actions. This is, therefore, a considerable simplification of the representation of the attitude of individuals towards risk; it will be used throughout this book.[27]

The complete proof of this theorem is not given here.[28] In the appendix to this chapter, we illustrate only the principal stages of the proof by means of the numerical example in Table 2.1. Each one allows us to appreciate the restrictions successively imposed on the structure of the preferences of the decision-maker.

To illustrate the theorem, let us observe only that the behaviour of the decision-maker in Table 2.1 may be entirely coded using five numbers:[29]

- three values of the utility-of-consequences index:

$u(1) = 100 \quad u(2) = 58.4 \quad u(3) = 0$

- the subjective probabilities of two of the three basic events:

$\mathrm{Pr}\,(\{\alpha\}) = 0.2 \quad \mathrm{Pr}\,(\{\beta\}) = 0.35$

The first column of Table 2.1 Panel B contains the three values of the utility of the consequences, while the subjective probabilities appear on the last line of the same panel. Columns 2, 3 and 4 of Panel B contain the quantities $Pr\,(E).u(c)$ and column 5 (the sum of columns 2, 3 and 4) indicates for each action the value resulting from the expected utility. These values reproduce faithfully the ranking of actions given at the start.

The theorem of von Neumann and Morgenstern may be generalized to an infinite number of consequences. A few additional technical axioms are then necessary; the statement of these may be found in [Arrow 1970].[30] In the remainder of this book, the set of consequences will be that of the positive real numbers representing the quantities consumable by the decision-maker. We shall assume simply that the choices may here again be modelled by maximization of the expected value of the utility of these consumable quantities, and that the index (or the function) of utility is continuous and differentiable as required.

2.2 Risk aversion in the sense of Arrow and Pratt (1964–1965)

We wish to restrict further the behaviour of financial investors. We not only require them to be rational in the sense of von Neumann and Morgenstern, but we also demand that they do not take risks lightly. Finance being a theory of the remuneration of risks, it is undesirable that individuals should appear on the market who will take risks for nothing, or worse still, who are prepared to pay to take them (as is the case in games of chance). We therefore wish to know which property of the utility function will be likely to represent risk averse behaviour.

Definition:
Individuals are risk averse if they always prefer to receive a fixed payment to a random payment of equal expected value.

Let us consider an individual who, at a future instant, will have access to a risk-free consumption c from which he will derive a utility $u(c)$. He is offered the opportunity of modifying this prospect by means of a financial contract. This will yield him the consumable quantities $+h$ (gain) or $-h$ (loss) with equal probabilities with no other compensation. This individual's risk aversion must lead him to refuse this offer. By virtue of the expected utility theorem, we write:

$$u(c) \geq (1/2)u(c - h) + (1/2)u(c + h);$$

from which it results that:

$$u(c) - u(c - h) \geq u(c + h) - u(c).$$

We may thus establish that the slope of such an individual's utility function is decreasing, and that his utility function is concave (*see* Figure 2.1). Risk averse individuals are thus characterized by a *concave utility function*. Conversely, a *risk neutral* individual possesses a linear utility function whose intercept and slope are irrelevant: such individuals take their decisions on the basis of the expected value of the gains, as Pascal and Fermat supposed. For the remainder of this book we use concave utility functions only.

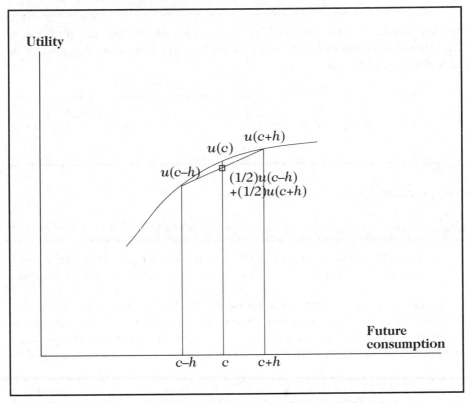

Figure 2.1   The curvature of the utility function reflects the risk aversion

The qualitative relationship between concavity and risk aversion leads to a quantitative relationship. This will prove useful in the following chapters, concerning the determination of the the risk premiums demanded by investors on securities of different risk levels.

Let us offer the individual a compensation (or premium) p of a size just sufficient to induce him not to refuse the random contract:[31]

$$u(c) = (1/2)u(c + p-h) + (1/2)u(c + p + h) \qquad [2.1]$$

This being a non-linear equation, we cannot generally obtain the value of p in an explicit form. But suppose that h is a small risk compared to the pre-existing consumption c, in which case the same will be true of the premium p. We may thus apply to the right-hand side of [2.1] a Taylor expansion in the vicinity of c, to obtain an approximation of the value of p, an approximation which is an exact limit when h approaches zero:[32]

$$u(c) = (1/2)[u(c) + u'(c)(p - h)] + (1/2)[u(c) + u'(c)(p + h)] + (1/2)u''(c)h^2$$

[2.2]

In this expansion, the term in h^2 has been added due to the cancelling out of the preceding terms in h. All eliminations having been made, the root value of p of this equation is:

$$p = \frac{1}{2}\left[-\frac{u''(c)}{u'(c)} \right]h^2$$

[2.3]

The premium demanded, p, is linked to:

- the size of the risk incurred, measured by h^2, which is interpreted as the variance of the probability distribution of consumption, and
- a characteristic of the utility function $-u''(c)/u'(c)$, called local[33] risk aversion[34], which is in fact positive when the function $u(c)$ is concave.

In general, the absolute risk aversion which we have just defined is a function of c, the level of consumption. A moment of reflection should be enough to convince the reader that absolute risk aversion should be a decreasing function: as individuals become richer and consume more, they will generally tend to take risks of a given ECU size more easily.

The premium p having increased the expected value of future consumption, and h^2 being the variance of consumption resulting from the contract, Equation 2.3 above shows that, in the case of 'small risks', the individual simply balances expected value against variance, by weighing the latter by a coefficient equal to half the risk aversion.[35] We shall use this decision-making criterion frequently in the next chapter.

Note, to close this section, that Equation 2.3 may be written as a relative value:

$$\frac{p}{c} = \frac{1}{2}\left[-c\frac{u''(c)}{u'(c)} \right]\left[\frac{h}{c} \right]^2$$

[2.4]

The relative premium demanded, p/c, is linked to the relative size of the risk, $(h/c)^2$, by an amount - $cu''(c)/u'(c)$, which is naturally called the 'relative risk aversion'.

2.3   A toolkit of utility functions

Readers will find it useful to have at their disposal a collection of functions commonly used to model the behaviour of financial investors, and to know their main properties.

Quadratic function:[36]

$$u(c) = c - ac^2; \quad a > 0. \tag{3.1}$$

The principal significance of this function is that the expected value $E[u(c)]$ is expressed simply as a function of the first two moments (expected value and variance) of the random variable c:[37]

$$E[u(c)] = E[c] - a\, E[c]^2 - a\, \mathrm{var}[c]. \tag{3.2}$$

We shall see in Chapter 3 that this property considerably simplifies portfolio choices.

On the other hand, the other characteristics of the quadratic function make it somewhat less commendable:

- it assumes a maximum at the point $c = 1/(2a)$, which means that beyond this point every additional unit of consumption will lead to a reduction in utility. Since saturation of needs is not a credible hypothesis in economics, the function may only be used if we can reduce to zero the probability of exceeding $c = 1/(2a)$;

- the absolute risk aversion which it induces:

$$-\frac{u''(c)}{u'(c)} = \frac{2a}{1-2ac} \tag{3.3}$$

is an increasing function of the level of consumption, which is not consistent with the likely behaviour of individuals;

- contrary to the suggestion made by [Levy and Markowitz 1979], it is not generally possible to introduce the quadratic function as an approximation, obtained by a Taylor expansion[38], of any utility function. In fact the behaviour of the decision-maker in the various states of nature (and over time) is not such that c remains in the vicinity of a fixed point; the coefficient 'a' of the Taylor expansion taken to the second order cannot therefore be a constant. Quadratic approximation may still be used in the case of 'small risks', as the analysis of the Pratt-Arrow theory in the previous section showed. Even in this case, the Taylor expansion would remain problematic in a multi-period model of choice because the reference level of consumption, c, would move over time.

Logarithm function:

$$u(c) = \log(c); \quad c > 0. \tag{3.4}$$

This is a very special function, as no parameter allows the behaviour of the decision-maker to be adjusted.[39] Relative risk aversion is equal to a fixed number: 1, and absolute aversion to $1/c$. The latter has the advantage of decreasing in relation to consumption.

The logarithm function shares with the power function shown below the property that:

$$u'(0) = + \infty. \tag{3.5}$$

In other words, marginal utility becomes extremely large when consumption falls. For this reason, decision-makers endowed with such a utility function must ensure that their consumption does not become zero (or negative) under any circumstances (if this is feasible). This property makes economists' work much easier, since it saves them having to impose constraints of non-negativity on c, or having to incorporate a default clause into contractual mechanisms.

The logarithm function is unbounded:

$$\lim_{c \to 0} u(c) = -\infty \text{ and } \lim_{c \to \infty} u(c) = + \infty.$$

This is sometimes considered to be an inconvenience: it could be shown that to any unbounded utility function we may oppose a paradox of the St. Petersburg type (see supra).

Power function:[40]

$$u(c) = \frac{1}{\gamma} c^\gamma \qquad \gamma < 1 \tag{3.6}$$

This function possesses the same properties as the logarithm function, but the exponent γ allows the relative risk aversion to be adjusted. It is constant and equal to $1-\gamma$. We can demonstrate that the decisions obtained by letting γ go to 0 reproduce the decisions of a 'logarithmic' decision-maker.

Exponential function:[41, 42]

$$u(c) = -\exp[-ac]; \quad a \geq 0. \tag{3.7}$$

The essential characteristic of this function is that it generates an absolute risk aversion which is constant and equal to the parameter a.[43] In addition, it has an upper limit but does not have the property of default avoidance exhibited by the two preceding functions, since $u'(0) = a$.

When the probability distribution of consumption is normal, an extremely useful formula allows the expected utility of consumption to be obtained:

$$E[-\exp(-ac)] = -\exp\{-a\ [E(c) - a\ \mathrm{var}(c)/2]\}, \tag{3.8}$$

an objective function which, from a decision-making point of view, is equivalent to:

$$E(c) - a\ \mathrm{var}(c)/2. \tag{3.9}$$

We thus arrive at an objective function which depends only on the expected value and the variance of consumption.

'HARA' functions:

All the functions which we have examined until now have the property that the tolerance to risk which is associated with them is linear in relation to consumption:[44]

$$-\frac{u'(c)}{u''(c)} = A + Bc \tag{3.10}$$

In the case of the logarithm function and the power function, this linear relationship was reduced to a relationship of proportionality ($A = 0$; $B = 1/(1-\gamma)$). In the case of the exponential function, it was reduced to a constant value of tolerance ($A = 1/a$; $B = 0$). Lastly, the quadratic function corresponded to the values $A = 1/(2a)$, $B = -1$.

However, these are not the only functions having this property of linearity. The complete family is obtained by integration of the above definition equation:

$$u(c) = -A\exp[-c/A] \qquad \text{when } B = 0 \qquad [3.11a]$$

$$u(c) = \log[c + A] \qquad \text{when } B = 1 \qquad [3.11b]$$

$$u(c) = \frac{1/B}{1 - 1/B}(A + Bc)^{1-1/B} \qquad \text{in other cases} \qquad [3.11c]$$

This family of utility functions contains all the commonly used functions, which are distinguished from one another by the values of two parameters A and B only. What is more, these functions lend themselves to analytical treatment: the calculation of equilibrium is greatly simplified when all the investors operating in a financial market have utility functions of this type and the value of parameter B is the same for everyone.[45]

Mean-variance functions:[46]

Under somewhat restrictive conditions, the expected utility of consumption may be expressed as an (increasing) function of the expected value and a (decreasing) function of the variance of consumption, without any other moment of the probability distribution coming into the picture.

$$E[u(c)] = G(E[c], \text{var}[c]). \qquad [3.12]$$

These conditions may be of two types:

- they may have to do with the utility function $u(c)$: we have already seen that property [3.12] is satisfied when $u()$ is a quadratic function (on condition that an upper limit is placed on consumption so that the saturation of needs does not occur), or when the quadratic function may serve as a close approximation to the true utility function (this is the case, it will be recalled, when the risks incurred are 'small' in size);

- they may have to do with the probability distribution of c:[47] $E[u(c)]$ can in general only be a function of the distribution parameters of c. It will be remembered that the parameters of the normal law are rightly interpreted as the expected value and the variance of the random variable. Hence, if the probability distribution of c is normal, $E[u(c)]$ is a function of the expected value and the variance of c.[48] But the normal law is not the only probability distribution which permits this conclusion: the binary law (the variable taking two possible values as with Arrow-Pratt), the binomial law (the variable in this case being a sum of a finite number of binary variables identically distributed) and the log-normal law (the logarithm of the variable in this case being normally distributed) are other examples of this. Generally, any distribution having two parameters which are linked one-to-one to expected value and variance will involve this property. This is in fact the family of distributions which may be obtained from the binary law.

Chapters 4 and 5 of this book are based on the assumption of 'mean-variance' behaviour on the part of the investor.

2.4 Recent developments

Are individuals – particularly investors on the stock exchange – rational in the restricted sense of von Neumann and Morgenstern? Some experimental evidence leads us to doubt that they are. The earliest evidence of that kind has become known as the 'Allais paradox'.[49]

To understand the scope of the Allais paradox, it is probably useful to have in mind a relatively recent geometrical interpretation of the axioms of von Neumann and Morgenstern.[50] Let us consider, for the purposes of two-dimensional graphical representation, the set of lotteries containing only three possible fixed gains $x_1 < x_2 < x_3$ occurring with the variable probabilities (p_1, p_2, p_3) $(p_1 + p_2 + p_3 = 1)$. Remember the significance of the expected utility theorem: the preference between these lotteries is given by the expression $p_1u(x_1) + p_2u(x_2) + p_3u(x_3)$ which is *linear in relation to the probabilities*. We may represent the lotteries in question, which are entirely defined by the triplets (p_1, p_2, p_3), by the points of an right-angled triangle in the (p_1, p_3) plane (Figure 2.2). Movements towards the top of the triangle increase p_3 to the detriment of p_2 (shifting the probabilities of gain x_2 towards the higher gain x_3); similarly movements to the left reduce p_1 to the benefit of p_2 (shifting the probabilities of gain x_1 to the higher gain x_2). These movements, and more generally any movement to the north-west, consequently lead to preferred lotteries, whatever the (increasing) utility function of the decision-maker.

The indifference curves in this diagram are *parallel lines* of equation:

$$E(u) \equiv \Sigma_{i=1}^{3} u(x_i)p_i \equiv u(x_1)p_1 + u(x_2)(1 - p_1 - p_3) + u(x_3)p_3 = \text{constant}   [4.1]$$

the indifference curves corresponding to higher levels of expected utility being situated to the north-west of those representing lower levels. It turns out, moreover,[51] that in the case of a risk averse individual, the indifference curves are more steeply sloped than would be those representing constant levels of expected value of gains, the latter having as an equation:

$$E(x) \equiv \Sigma_{i=1}^{3} x_i p_i \equiv x_1 p_1 + x_2 (1 - p_1 - p_3) + x_3 p_3 = \text{constant} \qquad [4.2]$$

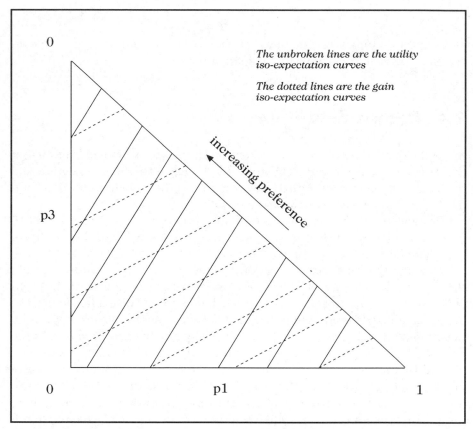

Figure 2.2   Another representation of the preferences

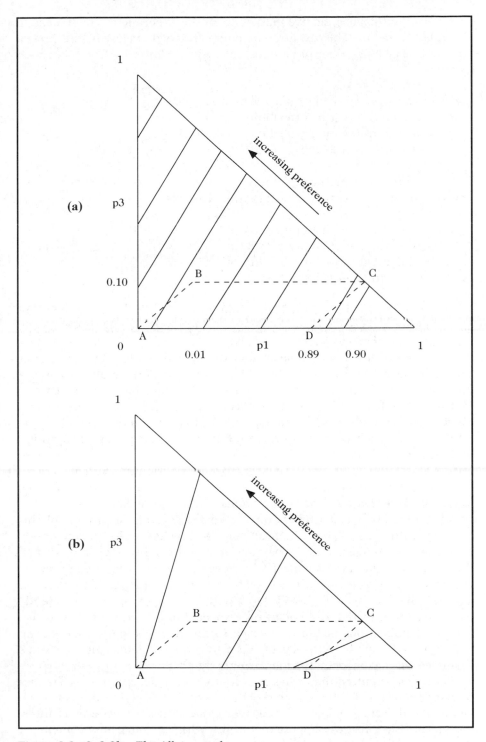

Figure 2.3a & 2.3b   The Allais paradox

Guided by this diagram, we may perform the experiment which leads to the Allais paradox. This experiment comprises two stages. In the first, a subject is asked his or her preference between two lotteries A and B defined as follows:[54]

A: certainty of receiving 1 million ECU
B: 5 million ECU with a probability of 0.10
    1 million ECU with a probability of 0.89   [4.3]
    0 ECU with a probability of 0.01.

In the second stage, the same subject is asked to indicate his or her preference for lottery C or lottery D, these being defined as:

C: 5 million ECU with a probability of 0.10
    0 ECU with a probability of 0.90   [4.4]
D: 1 million ECU with a probability of 0.11
    0 ECU with a probability of 0.89

If we define $(x_1, x_2, x_3) \equiv (0\ \text{ECU}, 1\ \text{million}, 5\ \text{million})$, it will be seen that these four lotteries form a parallelogram in the triangle (p_1, p_3), as shown in Figure 2.3. According to the theory of expected utility, a preference for lottery A in the first choice would indicate that the individual's indifference curves are fairly steep (as in Figure 2.3a); this should therefore result in a preference for lottery D in the second choice. On the other hand, in the case of less steep indifference curves, the subject might prefer lottery B in the first choice, but he or she must in that case prefer lottery C in the second.

It turns out, however, that in several experiments carried out by Allais and other researchers, the subjects preferring lottery A to lottery B, but also lottery C to lottery D formed the largest group. So their indifference curves are not parallel to one another, but rather tend to fan out – and in fact no longer have any reason to be straight lines – as in Figure 2.3b.

Numerous other experiments have revealed several 'deviations' of this type or of different types, which all tend to invalidate the theory of von Neumann and Morgenstern. A complete and particularly clear inventory of these may be found in [Machina 1987]. Several theories have been proposed in order to take account of these real-world behaviour patterns; they are also described in [Machina 1987]. None of them has yet become sufficiently established to threaten to supplant the expected utility theorem. Because of this, few applications of these theories to financial economics have been demonstrated. For the purposes of this book, we shall continue to assume that decision-makers obey the four axioms stated above.

Let us also mention that it has proved difficult to specify the preferences of decision-makers in an intertemporal context. By this is meant a situation where the decision-maker is faced over time with a succession of interdependent risks. Must we suppose that utilities arising from gains occurring at different times are simply added together (a present value factor taking into account where necessary the fact that an early gain is preferable to a late gain)? If this is the case, and if the utility of each period is of the von Neumann-Morgenstern type, the form of the global objective function is very restrictive, as it comprises a double addition of time and states of nature,[53] which implies that the gains of a given future period, occurring in a given state of nature, point the decision-maker to his or her choices independently of the gains which must occur at other times or in other states of nature. Various more general approaches have been proposed by [Drèze and Modigliani 1972] and [Kreps and Porteus 1978].[54] Research is under way in this area.

2.5 Conclusion

Chapters 3 and 4 of this book suppose that investors are endowed with an objective function of the 'mean-variance' type. Such behaviour rests, as we have seen, both on the axioms of von Neumann and Morgenstern and on additional hypotheses depending on either the utility function or the probability distribution of consumption.

'Mean-variance' behaviour is justified mainly when investors are confronted with 'small' risks. This is the case especially when investors have an option, if they wish, to hold securities for only an infinitely short time, and financial prices follow continuous processes.[55] Gains and losses are then necessarily small over a short holding period.

Appendix 2.1

Outline proof of the expected utility theorem

In this appendix, we explain how the successive axioms progressively restrict the form of the index of preference of decision-makers and simplify the coding of their behaviour.

Axiom 1 by itself simply allows us to state that the relative preference for the various actions may be represented by a real function: if actions a and a' are defined by their consequences c_s and c'_s in the various states s (that is, by the rows of Table 2.1), the ordering between the actions is indicated by the values of index U:

$$a \geq a' \text{ if and only if } U(c_s; s = 1,2,...) \geq U(c'_s; s = 1,2,...)$$

In the context of the example in Table 2.1, Axiom 1 means that there are 27 numbers $u(c_\alpha, c_\beta, c_\gamma)$ indicating the relative level of preference for an action producing consequence c_α (c_α = 1, 2 or 3) in state α, consequence c_β in state β and consequence c_γ in state γ.

Note: knowing such a set of 27 numbers, another set, representing the same ordering on the set of actions, may be obtained by subjecting the first numbers to any monotonically increasing transformation.

Axiom 2 allows the individual's preferences to be summed up more simply. It implies the existence of functions $u_E(c_s;$ s belonging to E) such that two actions a and a' (defined by their consequences c_s and c'_s) may be compared as follows:

$$U(c_s;s = 1,2..) \geq U(c'_s;s = 1,2...) \text{ if and only if}:$$
$$u_E(c_s;s \in E) + u_{\tilde{E}}(c_s;s \in \tilde{E}) \geq$$
$$u_E(c'_s;s \in E) + u_{\tilde{E}}(c'_s;s \in \tilde{E}), \text{ whatever } E. \quad [A2.1]$$

In particular:
$$u(c_\alpha,c_\beta,c_\gamma) \geq u(c'_\alpha,c'_\beta,c'_\gamma) \text{ if and only if}:$$
$$u_\alpha(c_\alpha) + u_\beta(c_\beta) + u_\gamma(c_\gamma) \geq u_\alpha(c'_\alpha) + u_\beta(c'_\beta) + u_\gamma(c'_\gamma).$$

By virtue of Axiom 2, the index of preference takes a less general form than before: it is now additive, each term reflecting separately the distinct contribution of each event or of each state of nature.[56] Nevertheless, the index of preference $u_s()$ which applies to each state s remains specific to this state: this is the behaviour called 'preference for states of nature' which the next axiom has the effect of eliminating.

In the context of the example in Table 2.1, this means that there are nine numbers $u_s(c)$ reflecting the preference for consequence c in state s and allowing all the decisions to be represented.

Note: knowing such a set of 9 numbers, another set, representing the same ordering on the set of actions, may be obtained by subjecting the first numbers to any increasing linear transformation.

Axiom 3 allows us to state the existence of a single function $u(c)$ (that is, in the context of Table 2.1, three numbers $u(c)$ for c = 1, 2 and 3), such that:

$$u(c) \geq u(c') \text{ if and only if:}$$
$$u_E(c) \geq u_E(c'), \text{ whatever } E \qquad \text{[A2.2]}$$

Note: knowing such a set of 3 numbers $u(c)$, another equivalent set may be obtained by subjecting the first to any increasing linear transformation.

Finally, Axiom 4 allows us to state the existence of numbers $P(E)$ such that:

$$Pr(E) \geq Pr(E') \text{ if and only if:}$$
$$u_E(c) \geq u_{E'}(c) \text{ whatever } c \qquad \text{[A2.3]}$$

these numbers satisfying the property of additivity:

$$Pr(E \text{ or } E') = Pr(E) + Pr(E') \text{ for all mutually exclusive events E and E'}$$

In the case of Table 2.1, only two numbers (for example, $P(\{\alpha\})$ and $P(\{\beta\})$ are sufficient to represent the ordering on the events.

Statements A2.2 and A2.3 taken together lead to the conclusion that:

$$u_E(c) \text{ on the one hand, and } Pr(E).u(c) \text{ on the other}$$

establish the same conditional ordering whatever the event E and the consequence c in question. This result, coupled with statement A2.1, leads to the theorem.

Notes to Chapter 2

1   Nevertheless, the analogy between games of chance and investment on the stock exchange does not entirely hold and may even distort the argument. In principle, investors in the stock market have only one aim: to make money, whereas the gamblers who inhabit the casinos are also, perhaps above all, seeking the pleasure of playing. For the analogy to be viable, we must assume that the pleasure of playing is identical to the satisfaction of winning.

2   This was a game played with a coin. The gambler having chosen 'heads' received 2^n ECU if heads came up for the first time on the nth throw. This event having a probability of $1/2^n$ of occurring, the expected value of this game is infinity ($\sum_{n=1}^{\infty} 2^n 1/2^n = \infty$). However, it is obvious that no rational human being would prefer this wager to a large fixed sum. It thus proved necessary to generalize the thesis of Pascal and Fermat to take account of individuals' real behaviour.

3   A function $y = f(x)$ is said to be concave if its curvature turns downwards. If f is increasing and concave, y grows at a decreasing rate for higher and higher values of x.

4   As a result of this transformation, the certain gain which would bring the gambler the same utility as the St. Petersburg game is of the order of 9 ECU if the function U is, for example, a logarithm function (see Section 2.3), even though the expected value of the gain is, as we have seen, infinity. This figure seems reasonable and conforms to what we know intuitively of human behaviour.

5   The following account is inspired largely by [Savage 1954] Chapters 2–5, [Arrow 1970] and [Drèze 1974].

6   The progression of von Neumann and Morgenstern is the inverse of that of Gabriel Cramer and Daniel Bernoulli. Cramer and Bernoulli stated that a pre-existing theory (that of Pascal and Fermat) was too restrictive since it led to a conclusion incompatible with the real behaviour of individuals, namely an excessive evaluation of the St. Petersburg wager. von Neumann and Morgenstern, on the other hand, start from the arbitrary behaviour of an individual and seek, by means of plausible axioms, to restrict it gradually until they also arrive at the expected utility theorem.

7   This condition is of no immediate interest; it will only be important when the present theory is applied to financial contracts concluded between several parties. See subsequent chapters.

8   This is to say that there is no 'behaviour risk' or 'moral hazard'.

9   In the original theory expounded in [von Neumann and Morgenstern 1947], the probabilities of the various circumstances were presumed given and the authors had 'merely' demonstrated the existence of the utility index. In fact we are setting out here a later theory attributable to [Savage 1954], which deduces the existence of the two indices simultaneously from the supposedly rational behaviour of the individual (see also [Ramsey 1926] and [de Finetti 1937]). This new theory thus avoids having to begin by justifying the concept of probability: the probabilities are 'revealed' by the decisions which the individual makes (and may later serve to reproduce them). We thus demonstrate that any decision-maker implicitly has subjective probabilities in mind which apply to the events with which he or she is confronted. The necessary existence of such probabilities is interesting, as it constitutes a response to the objections of those who claim that individuals do not use this concept in their decisions. However, from an empirical point of view, only experimentation would allow us to measure subjective probabilities. Economic science being more often a science of observation than an experimental science, we are forced to suppose that subjective probabilities are identified with the effectively observed realisation frequencies (objective probabilities).

10 We do not assume that the decision-maker can make use of all these actions (some may not be feasible, as is the case when a budgetary constraint limits the choices of an economic agent). We assume only (see Axiom 1) that the decision-maker is in a position to express his relative preference for all these actions. It must be made clear that a limitation is imposed here on the empirical content of the theory, as some of these actions will in practice never be observed.

11   This means that for any $a, a' a''$ belonging to A:

   –   Either a' is not preferred to a (written: $a \geq a'$), or a is not preferred to a' ($a' \geq a$), or else the two propositions are true simultaneously, in which case we say that there is indifference between a and a' (completeness);

   –   If $a'' \geq a'$ and $a' \geq a$, so $a'' \geq a$ (transitivity);

   – $a \geq a$ (reflexivity).

12   In other words, actions a and b on the one hand, and a' and b' on the other, have identical consequences on E, and actions b and b' have identical consequences on the complement $\tilde{E}$ of E, actions a and a' having unspecified consequences on $\tilde{E}$.

13   For this definition to mean anything, actions b and b' satisfying the above conditions must appear in the decision-maker's ranking. This is why we have posited (Axiom 1) that all the envisageable mappings $c(a, s)$ are ranked by him.

14   It will however be recalled that the definition imposes the condition that b and b' have the same consequences on $\tilde{E}$. We shall explain below (note 16) the reasons for this hypothesis.

15   Another statement of Axiom 2, avoiding the concept of conditional preference, would be as follows:
Axiom 2': Whatever the event E,
$a \geq a' \Leftrightarrow b \geq b'$

if $c(a, s) = c(b, s)$ for all s belonging to E
     $c(a', s) = c(b', s)$

     $c(a, s) = c(a', s)$ for all s belonging to $\tilde{E}$
     $c(b, s) = c(b', s)$

16   We now see the cogency of the restriction $c(b,s)=c(b's)$ on $\tilde{E}$ introduced in the definition of conditional preference: $8 \geq 16 \nleftrightarrow 3 \geq 7$ given E.

17   The same idea would perhaps be better expressed by calling it the 'axiom of separability'. If regret involves appreciating the gains received in one state of nature by comparison with the gains which would have been received in another state of nature, an individual whose choices *ex ante* aim to avoid regret *ex post* has a behaviour incompatible with Axiom 2.

18   Recall once again that we assumed that all the envisageable actions, and in particular the constant actions on E, were ranked by the decision-maker. In Table 2.1 constant actions on the full set of possibilities S are actions 1, 12 and 27; they are the actions which lead to the same consequence whatever the prevailing state of nature. Similarly, action 4 is a constant action on subset $E=\{\alpha,\beta\}$ and so on.

19   The reader will no doubt object that rain or bad weather constitute states of nature which noticeably affect people's preference for umbrellas. It is entirely fair to call Axiom 3 into question. We then obtain a system of preference which is not that of von Neumann-Morgenstern, but which is nonetheless easily manipulated (on preference for states of nature, *see* [Hirshleifer 1971]).

20   Or that of actions 14, 22 and 27.

21   Again, remember that all the envisageable actions, including actions a and a' below, have been ranked.

22   Or, more vividly, that event E is at least as probable as event E'.

23   The definition did not only refer to two consequences c and c'. It also referred to two actions a and a', but these two actions were not picked independently: this was a pair of actions linked, as stipulated, to the two consequences c and c' and to the two events E and E'.

24   Or the bets on consequences 1 and 3 (action 21 is not preferred to action 18).

25   For this, compare actions 6 and 4.

26 Satisfying the property of additivity.

27 The interested reader will find a summary of the critiques levelled against this theory in [Drèze 1974]. *See also* Section 2.4.

28 *See* [Savage 1972], [Drèze 1974].

29 This is not the only combination of numbers allowing the behaviour of the decision-maker to be coded. It will be seen quite easily that the *u* numbers are determined up to a linear transformation. Here utility is 'cardinal'.

30 Where the set of consequences is not only infinite but also unbounded, it is preferable for the utility index to be bounded, in order to rule out any paradox of the St. Petersburg type. [Arrow 1970], in fact, uses such an assumption in his proof of the existence of the utility index.

31 It is by a calculation of this type that we may find the fixed payment equivalent to the St. Petersburg lottery. It will be remembered that this lottery offers a possibility of 1/2 of winning 1 ECU, 1/4 of winning 2 ECU, and so on. Let us give the individual a choice between a fixed payment x and the random payment which would result from this lottery. The individual would be indifferent if:

$$u(W + x) = (1/2).u(W + 1) + (1/4).u(W + 2) + (1/8).u(W + 4) + ...$$

where W is the previous wealth of the individual. If u is the logarithm function the solution to this equation is approximately 9 ECU, as indicated earlier.

32 $u'(c)$ designates the value of the first derivative of u at point c and $u''(c)$ the value of the second derivative.

33 Since we have dealt only with small values of h.

34 This is what is known as absolute risk aversion, as opposed to relative risk aversion, which we shall define in a moment.

35 *See* [Samuelson 1970].

36 *See* [Adler 1969].

37 In the expected value–standard deviation plane, the following equation produces indifference curves which are circles centred on the point ($E[c]=a/2$, standard deviation $[c]=0$). In the expected value–variance plane, these would be parabolas. Taking into account the shape of these curves, only their ascending sections are really indifference curves.

38 Any approximation of a utility function should really be pushed to the second order to take account of risk aversion.

39 A more general function would be: $\log(c \pm a)$. This was the subject of a study by [Rubinstein 1976].

40 An application of this function is demonstrated by [Merton 1971].

41 It does not matter that the values of this function are negative. It will be recalled that a utility function serves only to establish preferences between various actions and that its level is thus unimportant. exp[] stands for the exponential function; this is to say that exp[x] means 'number e to the power x'.

42 [Lintner 1969] and [Diamond and Verrechia 1981] are examples of the application of this function.

43 This property does not agree with the idea that risk aversion should be decreasing. However, it does have the effect that, where a non-risky security exists, the amount of random securities demanded by an individual is independent of his wealth, only his demand for non-random securities being linked to wealth.

For the same reason, the aggregation of individuals having this utility function and participating in the same market is extremely simple to perform: if it is a question of determining prices, a collection of individuals of this type may simply be replaced by a representative individual for whom the inverse of the coefficient a (the 'tolerance to risk') is the sum of each of their tolerances to risk. Thus the distribution of wealth plays no role in the determination of asset prices. These considerations are outside the scope of this book.

44 Which is to say that absolute risk aversion is a hyperbolic function of consumption. 'HARA' stands for 'Hyperbolic Absolute Risk Aversion'. [Rubinstein 1974] offers a complete description of the properties of these functions.

45 This is the subject of Rubinstein's article [Rubinstein 1974]: he shows that in this case, prices are calculated by replacing the population of investors by a representative investor also having a HARA utility function. Rubinstein calls the B coefficient the 'cautiousness parameter'.

46 Markowitz' application of mean-variance functions [Markowitz 1959] had a great impact on financial theory (*see* Chapter 3).

47 In an economic model, consumption is a decision variable and thus an endogenous variable; it is not in principle legitimate to state hypotheses about its behaviour. Hypotheses should cover only exogenous variables: endowments, production and so on.

48 If $u()$ is increasing and concave, and if the probability distribution of c is normal, $E[u(c)]$ is effectively increasing in relation to $E[c]$ and decreasing in relation to var[c].

49 [Allais 1953].

50 An exposition of the proof of von Neumann and Morgenstern which refers to this graphical approach can be found in [Hirshleifer 1971].

51 *See* [Hirshleifer 1971] *or* [Machina 1987].

52 Readers are invited to note their own choice of lottery.

53 We thus say that it is doubly separable. We have seen that Axiom 2 involves the separability of states of nature. It has the effect that the objective function takes an additive form in relation to the various future events, as confirmed by the statement of the expected utility theorem. The decision maker's resulting behaviour is such that the various, mutually exclusive, future events do not enter conjointly into the determination of preferences between the various actions.

54 See the applications demonstrated by [Caperaa and Eeckoudt 1975], [Brys *et al.*1985].

55 The process followed by a financial price is said to be continuous if the probability is equal to 1 is that the trajectory of the price is a continuous function of time. *See* Chapter 7.

56 *Cf. supra*, our interpretation of Axiom 3: 'the knowledge of the state of nature or the event which prevails in no way modifies the preference between the various consequences.'

References

[Adler 1969]   M. Adler, Geometric Properties of the Quadratic Utility Function, *Quarterly Journal of Economics*, 1969.

[Allais 1953]   M. Allais, Le comportement de l'homme rationnel devant le risque; critique des postulats et axiomes de l'Ecole américaine, *Econometrica*, 21, 503–546.

[Arrow 1965]   K. J. Arrow, Exposition of the Theory of Choice under Uncertainty, in K. J. Arrow, *Essays in the Theory of Risk Bearing*. Amsterdam: North-Holland, 44–89.

[Arrow 1970]   K. J. Arrow, The Theory of Risk Aversion, lecture 2 in K. J. Arrow, *Aspects of the Theory of Risk Bearing*. Helsinki: Yrjö Jahnsonin säätiö.

[Bernoulli 1738]   D. Bernoulli, *Specimen Theoriae Novae de Mensura Sortis*. Commentarii Academiae Scientarium Imperialis Petropolinae, 5, 175–192; English translation: *Econometrica*, 22, 23–36.

[Briys *et al.* 1985]   E. Briys, L. Eeckoudt and H. Loubergé, *Endogenous Risks and the Risk Premium*. Research Paper, Department of Economics, University of Montreal, 1985.

[Caperaa and Eeckoudt 1975]   P. Caperaa and L. Eeckoudt, Delayed Risks and Risk Premiums. *Journal of Financial Economics*, 2, 1975, 309–320.

[Diamond and Verrechia 1981] D. W. Diamond and R. E. Verrechia, Information Aggregation in a Noisy Rational Expectations Economy, *Journal of Financial Economics*, 9, 1981, 221–237.

[Drèze 1974]   J. Drèze, Axiomatic Theories of Choice, Cardinal Utility and Subjective Probability: a Review *in* J. H. Drèze, ed., *Allocation under Uncertainty: Equilibrium and Optimality*. New York: John Wiley & Sons, 1974, 3–23.

[Drèze and Modigliani 1972] J. Drèze and F. Modigliani, Consumption Decisions under Uncertainty, *Journal of Economic Theory*, 5, 1972, 308–335.

[de Finetti 1937] B. de Finetti, La prévision: ses lois logiques, ses sources subjectives, *Annales de l'Institut Henri Poincaré*, 1937, 7, 1–68.

[Hirshleifer 1971] J. Hirshleifer, *Investment, Interest and Prices*, Prentice-Hall, 1971.

[Kreps and Porteus 1978] D. Kreps and E. Porteus, Temporal Resolution of Uncertainty and Dynamic Choice Theory, *Econometrica*, XLVI, 1978, 185–200.

[Levy and Markowitz 1979] H. Levy and H. Markowitz, Approximating Expected Utility by a Function of Mean and Variance, *American Economic Review*, 69, 1979, 308–317.

[Lintner 1969] J. Lintner, The Aggregation of Investors' Diverse Judgments and Preferences in Purely Competitive Security Markets, *Journal of Financial and Quantitative Analysis*, 1969, 347–400.

[Machina 1987] M. J. Machina, Choice under Uncertainty: Problems Solved and Unsolved, *Journal of Economic Perspectives*, 1, 1987, 121–154.

[Markowitz 1959] H. Markowitz, *Portfolio Selection*. New York: John Wiley and Sons, Inc., 1959.

[Merton 1971] R. C. Merton, Optimum Consumption and Portfolio Rules in a Continuous-time Model, *Journal of Economic Theory*, 3, 1971, 373–413.

[Pratt 1964] J. W. Pratt, Risk Aversion in the Small and in the Large, *Econometrica*, 32, 1964, 122–136.

[Ramsey 1931] F. P. Ramsey, Truth and Probability, in *The Foundations of Mathematics and Other Logical Essays*. London: Routledge and Kegan, 1931, 156–198.

[Rubinstein 1974] M. Rubinstein, An Aggregation Theorem for Securities Markets, *Journal of Financial Economics*, 1974, 1, 225–244.

[Samuelson 1952]   P. A. Samuelson, Probability, Utility and the Independence Axiom, *Econometrica*, 1952, 20, 670–678.

[Samuelson 1970]   P. A. Samuelson, The Fundamental Approximation Theorem of Portfolio Analysis in Terms of Means, Variances and Higher Moments, *Review of Economic Studies*, 36, 1970, 537–542.

[Savage 1954]   L. J. Savage, *The Foundations of Statistics*. New York: John Wiley & Sons, 1954. Revised and enlarged edition, New York: Dover, 1972.

[von Neumann and Morgenstern 1944]   J. von Neumann, and O. Morgenstern, *Theory of Games and Economic Behavior*. Princeton: Princeton University Press, 1944.

3

Portfolio choices

In Chapter 2, we described the attitude of individuals towards risk in general terms. We shall now apply the ideas developed there to model the behaviour of investors towards financial securities, which we know to differ from one another mainly in their level of risk. We will then be in a position to determine the demand for securities, which will allow us, in Chapter 4, to deduce their value.

Two constituent elements are necessary to formulate the present model. The first is the *time scale*: we are dealing here with a 'static' situation characterized by two instants $t = 0$ and $t = 1$. At instant $t = 0$, individuals invest their disposable wealth in a portfolio of securities chosen optimally. At instant $t = 1$, they consume all their wealth, including the revenues from the portfolio, and disappear. It is clear that this time specification is restrictive and should be generalized to a succession of periods in order to obtain a 'dynamic' model.[1] In practice it corresponds to the behaviour of an investor interested exclusively in short-term gains.

The second constituent element is the special hypothesis regarding the attitude of individuals towards risk. The portfolio chosen at $t = 0$ generates at $t = 1$ a wealth which is random. For this reason, choosing the composition of a portfolio is the same as choosing an action or a lottery in the context of the von Neumann-Morgenstern theory. The theory of portfolio choices which we are about to explain takes into account all the axioms of von Neumann and Morgenstern. The expected utility theorem thus allows us to state that investors make up their portfolio so as to maximize the expected utility of the future wealth which will result from this portfolio. In other words, the expected utility of wealth is their 'objective function'.

We further restrict this objective function by supposing that it depends only on *the expected value of future wealth and the variance of this wealth*, which amounts, as we saw in Chapter 2 (Section 2.3), to making additional hypotheses, either about the utility function, or about the probability distribution of future wealth.[2] Original wealth being a fixed piece of information, the objective function may still be expressed as a function of the expected value and of the variance of the *rate of return* on the portfolio, since this is no more than the increase of the wealth at $t = 1$ compared to the wealth at $t = 0$. In the objective function, the relative weight of the variance relative to the expectation will represent the risk aversion of the individual concerned. The less risk aversion he has, the higher will be the level of risk – and the expected return – of the portfolio he chooses.

For the time being, let us leave aside the problem of maximizing the objective function of a particular investor (endowed with a particular risk aversion) and consider, in Sections 3.1, 3.2, 3.3.1 and 3.3.2, a wider problem. This involves identifying the complete set of portfolios which an investor of any risk aversion might consider holding, the only constraint which we shall impose on his behaviour being that he wishes to profit from as high an expected value of return as possible for a given variance. We specify later (Section 3.3.3) the choice which a given individual would be forced to make between these two dimensions. Portfolios belonging to the set which we shall seek to define are called 'efficient' portfolios. Section 3.4 establishes the structure of this set. Finally, Section 3.5 describes some of the difficulties in implementing the theory of portfolio choices.

3.1   Numerical example with two financial securities

Let us begin with an extremely simple case: an individual has access to only two securities and must choose what proportion of his original wealth to invest in each one. The rate of return on these two securities is described by a joint probability distribution shown in Table 3.1. This is a particularly basic distribution, since it only shows three possible circumstances. It will immediately be noted that the data show a negative correlation between the two securities: when security 1 has a higher than expected rate of return,[3] security 2 has a lower than expected rate of return, and vice versa.

Probability	Security 1	Security 2
0.4	3%	5%
0.3	4%	4%
0.3	6%	3%

Table 3.1

It is a straightforward matter to calculate the rate of return on a portfolio made up of these two securities, according to the composition we give to it. Table 3.2 gives this rate of return for a portfolio made up of 75% of security 1 and 25% of security 2. It is obtained by calculating, in each of the future circumstances, the average of the rates of return on these two securities, and by weighting this average in the proportions 0.75 and 0.25.

Probability	Portfolio
0.4	0.75 × 3% + 0.25 × 5% = 3.5%
0.3	0.75 × 4% + 0.25 × 4% = 4%
0.3	0.75 × 6% + 0.25 × 3% = 5.25%

Table 3.2

The probability of each possible future circumstance being given, and the rate of return on the portfolio in each of these circumstances having been calculated, it is easy to obtain the expected value of the rate of return on the portfolio and its variance. These two values are respectively:[4] 4.175% and 0.5979 10^{-4}.

Proportion of security 1	100%	75%	50%	0%
E(R)	4.2%	4.18%	4.15%	4.10%
var(R)	1.733 10^{-4}	0.5979 10^{-4}	0.0583 10^{-4}	0.767 10^{-4}

Table 3.3

The same calculation may be made for different compositions of the portfolio. We thus obtain Table 3.3, which shows the performance of the portfolio in terms of expectation and variance, according to the proportion of wealth allotted to security 1. Figure 3.1, drawn as a graph of expected rate of return against variance of rate of return, shows the same results as Table 3.3. The curve described by varying the proportion allotted to the two securities is a parabola.[5] The same graph could have been drawn by plotting expectation against standard deviation; the curve would then have been a hyperbola branch.

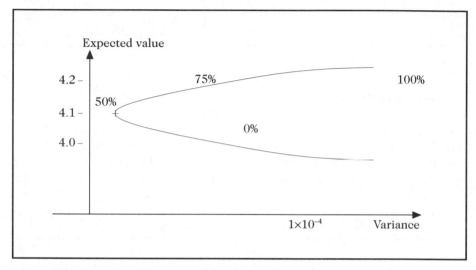

Figure 3.1   Linear combinations of two financial securities

In both graphs, the portions of the curve corresponding to a proportion allotted to security 1 greater than 100% or less than 0% have the following meaning: above 100%, security 2 is *sold short*, and this sale finances a purchase of security 1 greater than the original wealth; conversely, below 0%, security 1 is sold short.[6]

The portfolio chosen by a particular individual will necessarily be situated on the upper half of the parabola. The particular point which he chooses on the semi-parabola depends on his degree of risk aversion, that is, on the relative importance which he attaches to the expected return and to the variance of the rate of return.

3.2 Risk reduction: the effect of correlation between securities

Figure 3.1 highlights a very important result: it is possible to bring the variance of the portfolio to a distinctly lower level than that of the variances of the securities which it contains (without noticeably reducing the expected rate of return). What we have revealed is a *diversification* effect: since the correlation between the two securities is negative, a judicious weighting between them allows a very effective compensation of risks to be obtained. When a security yields more than expected, the gain is compensated by an unexpected loss on the other security, thus reducing the total risk. The diversification effect is obvious here because of the negative correlation, but we shall show that it exists in all cases.

Consider two risky securities. Let us call the security with the smaller variance 'security 1' and the other security 'security 2'. Let us now call x the portion of security 2 in a portfolio made up of these two securities. If we allow x to take positive values as well as negative values,[7] it is *almost always possible* to bring the variance of the portfolio below that of security 1. On the other hand, if only positive weightings are allowed, this objective can only be attained if the correlation and the variances of the two securities satisfy certain restrictions.

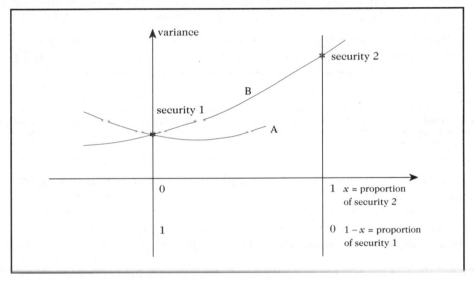

Figure 3.2   The diversification effect

For proof, consult Figure 3.2. The variance of the portfolio:

$$\text{var}(R_p) = (1-x)^2 \, \text{var}(R_1) + x^2 \, \text{var}(R_2) + 2x(1-x)\text{cov}(R_1, R_2) \qquad [2.1]$$

is a second degree function of the composition x. The corresponding curve is therefore a parabola (whose curvature is turned upwards) which has only two possible configurations, 'A' and 'B' in Figure 3.2. In both cases, coincidence excepted,[8] the minimum of the parabola is situated at a level of variance lower than that of Security 1. In configuration A, a value of x greater than 0 allows the minimum variance to be attained; in configuration B, x must take a negative value for the same result to be arrived at.

The distinction between configurations A and B is shown by the derivative of var (R_p) with respect to x at the point $x = 0$:

$$\frac{d\mathrm{var}(R_p)}{dx}\bigg|_{x=0} = 2[\mathrm{cov}(R_1,R_2) - \mathrm{var}(R_1)]$$

[2.2]

If the value of the derivative is negative, the configuration is of type A. If it is positive, the situation is of type B. In the exceptional case where the derivative is zero, it is not possible to diversify the risks of security 1 by means of security 2, as security 1 corresponds exactly to the minimum of the parabola.

If negative values of x are not permitted, only configuration A allows the risks of security 1 to be diversified by those of security 2. In this case risk reduction is only possible if derivative [2.2] is negative, which may be expressed in three equivalent ways. The first two are:

$$\mathrm{cov}(R_1, R_2) < \mathrm{var}(R_1)$$

[2.3]

or:

$$\mathrm{corr}_{1,2} < \frac{\sigma_1}{\sigma_2}$$

[2.4]

We obtain [2.4] from [2.3] using the definition of the correlation between two random variables[9]. In order for the randomnesses of Security 2 to compensate those of security 1, both being held positively, the correlation between the two types of randomness must be lower than the ratio of their mean fluctuation margins (standard deviations). If the two securities are of a roughly equal level of risk, as given by their standard deviations, a possibility exists for risk compensation even if their correlation is close to 1. On the other hand, if security 2 has a much higher standard deviation than that of security 1, the correlation between them must be small.

The third expression of the necessary condition for diversification calls for the introduction of what will prove to be an extremely useful concept: the β coefficient. The beta of Security 2 with respect to security 1, written $\beta_{2|1}$, is the coefficient of a regression of the rate of return on security 2 on that of security 1:[10]

$$\beta_{2|1} = \frac{\mathrm{cov}(R_1, R_2)}{\mathrm{var}(R_1)}$$

[2.5]

On the basis of this definition, we may rewrite condition [2.3] in the form:

$$\beta_{2|1} < 1$$

[2.6]

In order to be able to diversify the risks of security 1 using security 2 held positively, it is necessary (and sufficient) for the beta of security 2 with respect to security 1 to be less than 1.[11]

More generally, for any composition $(x, 1 - x)$, the derivative of the total risk [2.1] of the portfolio with respect to its composition is given by the following expressions:

$$\frac{d\mathrm{var}(R_p)}{dx} = 2(1-x)\,\mathrm{cov}(R_1, R_2) + 2x\,\mathrm{var}(R_2)$$

$$- 2(1-x)\,\mathrm{var}(R_1) - 2x\,\mathrm{cov}(R_1, R_2)$$

$$= 2\,\mathrm{cov}(R_2, R_p) - 2\,\mathrm{cov}(R_1, R_p) \qquad [2.7]$$

$$= 2\,\mathrm{var}(R_p)[\beta_{2|p} - \beta_{1|p}] \qquad [2.8]$$

In other words, increasing the weight of security 2 in the portfolio, by reducing that of security 1, reduces the total risk if and only if the covariance of security 2 with the existing portfolio is lower than that of security 1 (Equation 2.7). A similar statement for a comparison of the β coefficients may be obtained from Equation 2.8. These statements allow us to interpret the covariance of a security with a portfolio – or, equally, the beta of this security with respect to the portfolio – as a measure of the *marginal risk* of this security. This is because, all other things being equal, the covariance shows how much the total variance would be raised by increasing the portion of the security in the portfolio.

3.3 The first-order condition for portfolio choice in the general case of *n* securities

Let us stay with the hypothesis according to which the investor is aiming for the highest possible expected rate of return for a given variance of return. His decision affects the composition of the portfolio, that is, the relative weight allotted to each of the securities in it.

3.3.1 The rate of return on a portfolio of *n* securities

The first step involves calculating the rate of return on the portfolio from those of the securities, according to the portfolio's composition. This is done using the following formulae:

$$\tilde{R}_p = \sum_{i=1}^{n} x_i \tilde{R}_i \qquad\qquad [3.1]$$

$$E(\tilde{R}_p) = \sum_{i=1}^{n} x_i E(\tilde{R}_i) \qquad\qquad [3.2]$$

$$\text{var}(\tilde{R}_p) = \sum_{i=1}^{n} \sum_{j=1}^{n} x_i x_j \, \text{cov}(\tilde{R}_i, \tilde{R}_j) \qquad\qquad [3.3]$$

Equation 3.1 is the general formula for calculating the random rate of return $\tilde{R}_p$ on the portfolio: $\tilde{R}_i$ is the random rate of return on security i, and x_i the relative weight of security i in the portfolio.[12] As these are relative weightings, we always impose the constraint: $\Sigma_i \, x_i = 1$. Equation 3.2 allows the expected value of the rate of return on the portfolio to be calculated. Since expected value is a linear operator, the result may immediately be deduced from the previous equation.

Equation 3.3 gives the variance of the rate of return on the portfolio; it takes the form of a double sum generalizing formula [2.1] above, which dealt with a portfolio of only two securities. To make writing easier, we shall use the convention: $\text{cov}(\tilde{R}_i, \tilde{R}_j) = \text{var}(\tilde{R}_i)$ when $j = i$. Formula [3.3], for n random variables, appears in most probability textbooks and is deduced from formula [2.1] by induction over the number of securities.[13] As in the case of two securities, the presence of covariances by pairs $\text{cov}(R_i, R_j)$ $(i \neq j)$ corresponds to the mutual reduction of risks, between securities taken two at a time.

3.3.2 Portfolio optimization

Suppose an investor wishes to obtain the highest possible expected rate of return for a given level of variance equal to σ^2:

$$\max_{\{x_i\}} \sum_{i=1}^{n} x_i \, E(\tilde{R}_i) \qquad\qquad [3.4a]$$

$$\text{constraints: } \sum_{i=1}^{n} \sum_{j=1}^{n} x_i x_j \, \text{cov}(\tilde{R}_i, \tilde{R}_j) = \sigma^2 \qquad\qquad [3.4b]$$

$$\sum_{i=1}^{n} x_i = 1 \qquad\qquad [3.4c]$$

This is a problem of optimization under constraint which is solved by the Lagrange method (*cf* Section 1.1.6):

$$L = \sum_{i=1}^{n} x_i E(\tilde{R}_i) + \tfrac{1}{2}\theta[\sigma^2 - \sum_{i=1}^{n}\sum_{j=1}^{n} x_i x_j \operatorname{cov}(\tilde{R}_i,\tilde{R}_j)]$$
$$+ \mu(1 - \Sigma_{i=1}^{n} x_i)$$

[3.5]

This expression is that of the Lagrangian; $1/2\theta$ is the Lagrange multiplier corresponding to the constraint which sets the level of variance, and μ the multiplier of the constraint stipulating that the sum of the weights of the securities is equal to 1. The Lagrangian being thus written, we maximize it by treating each of the x_i, θ and μ as unconstrained decision variables. The necessary first-order conditions are obtained by equating the derivatives of the Lagrangian with respect to these three variables to zero:

$$\frac{\partial L}{\partial x_i} = E(\tilde{R}_i) - \theta \sum_{j=1}^{n} x_j \operatorname{cov}(\tilde{R}_i \tilde{R}_j) - \mu = 0$$

[3.6a]

$$i = 1, \dots n$$

$$\frac{\partial L}{\partial \theta} = \sigma^2 - \sum_{i=1}^{n}\sum_{j=1}^{n} x_i x_j \operatorname{cov}(\tilde{R}_i \tilde{R}_j) = 0$$

[3.6b]

$$\frac{\partial L}{\partial \mu} = 1 - \sum_{i=1}^{n} x_i = 0$$

[3.6c]

Equations 3.6b and 3.6c, which are the derivatives of the Lagrangian with respect to θ and μ, reproduce the constraints. As for the n equations of System 3.6a, these are obtained by partial differentiation of L with respect to each of the weightings x_i. It will be noted that the differentiation of the double sum of the second term with respect to x_i generates a coefficient 2: in fact the same variable x_i is encountered explicitly in this double sum in the form x_i, but also as x_j for $j = i$.

Equations 3.6a, b and c constitute a system of $n + 2$ equations with $n + 2$ unknowns $(x_i, i = 1 \dots n; \theta, \mu)$, which is easily solved (in Appendix 1, we shall solve a very similar problem). We thus obtain the optimum composition of the portfolio for a given risk σ^2.

We may isolate the equation system 3.6a to state the following theorem:

Theorem:

A necessary condition of the efficiency of a portfolio p defined by the weightings x_i, $i = 1...n$, is that there are two numbers μ and θ such that:[14]

$$E(R_i) = \mu + \theta \sum_j x_j \, \text{cov}(\tilde{R}_i, \tilde{R}_j) \text{ for all } i = 1, ...n \qquad [3.7]$$

Since the sum of the right-hand side of [3.7] may be successively rewritten: $\text{cov}(R_i, \sum_j x_j R_j)$ then $\text{cov}(R_i, R_p)$, the same theorem may be stated as follows:

Theorem:

A necessary condition of the efficiency of a portfolio is that a linear relationship exists between the expected rate of return on each security and the covariance of this security with the portfolio.

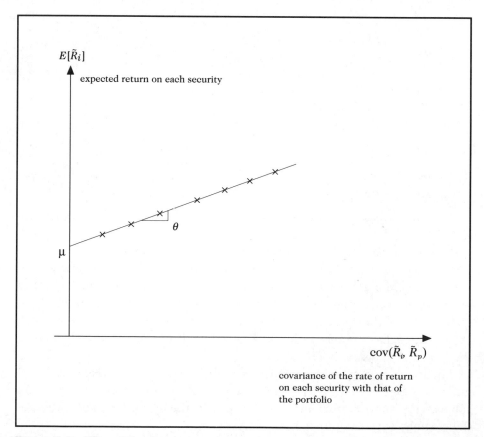

Figure 3.3   The market line

The economic significance of this relationship is as follows. As we saw in Section 3.2, the covariance of the security with the portfolio determines the marginal contribution by the security in question to the total variance; this is a measure of the *marginal risk* of the security in question. The expected rate of return required of each security must therefore be linked linearly to its marginal risk. In the graph of expected rate of return against marginal risk, all the securities lie on one line (*see* Figure 3.3). If this were not the case, it would mean that the portfolio is badly made up, and that no investor would wish to hold it.

In Equation 3.7 the number μ represents the rate of return (or the expected rate of return) on a security or a portfolio of securities which would be risk-free or perhaps have a zero covariance with the portfolio of the investor; $\theta > 0$ is the increase in expected rate of return demanded by the investor per additional unit of risk. We shall use this below as a measure of risk aversion.

A few comments are required regarding the definition of marginal risk. First, remember that it is defined not by the variance of the security itself, but by the *covariance* of the security with the portfolio: covariance is a *measure of the security's contribution to the total risk of the portfolio*. Next, in contrast to the variance of the security, the marginal risk *may* be negative: this is not uncommon, especially if financial securities are taken to include forward commodities or exchange contracts used by investors as a means of protection.[15] Lastly, the marginal risk thus defined has the important property of being linear in relation to the rate of return on the security, so that the risks of several securities may easily be combined: the marginal risk of the sum of two securities or of a mean of two securities is equal to the sum or to the mean of the individual marginal risks, calculated with respect to the same portfolio.[16]

3.3.3 The portfolio choice of an investor of given risk aversion

We have just established the first-order conditions which must be satisfied by a portfolio of given risk σ^2. As we have seen, the optimum composition of the portfolio may be calculated, like the Lagrange multipliers μ and θ, by solving globally System 3.6. In the next section, we intend to explore the set of optimal portfolios obtained, from a fixed collection of securities, by varying the assumed level of risk σ^2.

However, a different approach could have been adopted. Instead of fixing *a priori* the level of risk borne by an investor, it would perhaps have been more natural to fix his risk aversion and to deduce from this the level of risk he wishes to take. Fortunately, to solve this second problem, we have only to adopt a different interpretation of what we have already done. If we examine the expression of the Lagrangian [3.5] which was constructed from the maximization problem [3.4], we can see that a very similar Lagrangian would have resulted from the following problem:

$$Max_{\{x_i\}} \sum_{i=1}^{n} x_i E(\tilde{R}_i) - \frac{1}{2}\theta \sum_{i=1}^{n} \sum_{j=1}^{n} x_i x_j \, \text{cov}(\tilde{R}_i, \tilde{R}_j) \qquad [3.8a]$$

with only one constraint:

$$\sum_{i=1}^{n} x_i = 1 \qquad [3.8b]$$

The objective function [3.8a] of this new problem contains (first term) the expected value of the rate of return on the portfolio to be constructed, and (second term) its variance affected by a negative coefficient $-1/2\theta$. We may interpret [3.8] as a mean-variance utility function, the coefficient $\theta > 0$ representing the relative importance which the investor in question attaches to the risk relative to the expected rate of return, and the minus sign representing the fact that he wishes to avoid risk whereas, on the contrary, he is seeking a high expected rate of return. In this utility function, the coefficient θ represents the relative risk aversion of the investor. This interpretation is reinforced by the Arrow-Pratt theory which was presented in Section 2.2.2. We saw there that the premium demanded by an investor taking a risk was equal to half his risk aversion multiplied by the variance of the risk taken.[17] This is the same form which we find in objective function [3.8a].

Thus problem [3.8] is the one which an investor of given relative risk aversion θ would solve. It leads to a Lagrangian equivalent to [3.5][18] and to first-order conditions identical to [3.6a] and [3.6c], [3.6b] no longer appearing as a condition of optimality since θ, instead of being a Lagrange multiplier to be determined, is now a given parameter. By solving the restricted system [3.6a, 3.6c], we obtain the composition $\{x_i(\theta)\}$ of the portfolio chosen by an individual of aversion θ, as well as the corresponding value $\mu(\theta)$ of the multiplier μ.[19] An examination of equation system [3.6a], [3.6c] shows that the solution $x_i(\theta)$ is linear in $1/\theta$ (see Appendix 3.1). The expected rate of return on this portfolio is equal to $\sum_{i=1}^{n} x_i(\theta)E(R_i)$ and the total risk taken by this individual is:

$$\sigma^2(\theta) = \sum_{i=1}^{n} \sum_{j=1}^{n} x_i(\theta) x_j(\theta) \, \text{cov}(\tilde{R}_i, \tilde{R}_j)$$

We can show that this relationship between σ^2 and θ is monotonically decreasing;[20] the greater the individual's risk aversion, the less risks he will decide to take. It will thus be equivalent if we vary σ^2 or θ.

3.4   The efficient frontier and separation theorems

Definition:
> We call 'efficient portfolios' all optimal portfolios obtained, from a fixed collection of securities, by varying the level of risk taken σ^2 by the procedure in Section 3.3.2, or by varying the level of risk aversion θ by the equivalent procedure in Section 3.3.3.

Individuals differing from one another in their risk aversion will choose different portfolios, but they will all choose portfolios belonging to this set, as long as their utility function is of the mean-variance type. By construction, there are no portfolios which are preferable to these, either in the dimension of expected rate of return or in the dimension of risk. And choosing a portfolio which, at a given risk, would give an expected rate of return inferior to that of an efficient portfolio would be irrational.

3.4.1 The Markowitz frontier

For each level of risk – or for each value of risk aversion – the expected rate of return on the efficient portfolio is the maximum performance which can be achieved with a given collection of financial assets. This performance is described in Figure 3.4: on the x axis is the level of risk (the variance of the portfolio) and on the y axis, the maximum expected rate of return achieved. The curve obtained is a parabola 'on its side'[21] of which we are only interested in the top half: this is the efficient frontier, called the 'Markowitz frontier' after its inventor.[22] This frontier is rising: the higher the level of risk accepted, the more it becomes possible to achieve a high expected rate of return.

The slope of the frontier at the point σ^2 on the x axis is $1/2\theta$, as we saw in Section 3.3.3 and as shown by an examination of statement [3.8] of the optimization problem. Conversely, the x axis σ^2 at the point on the frontier where the slope is $1/2\theta$ gives us the level of risk which an investor of given risk aversion θ would choose to take. This is the nature of the correspondence between σ^2 and θ. The Markowitz frontier is concave: the smaller the aversion to risk, the higher the level of risk accepted.

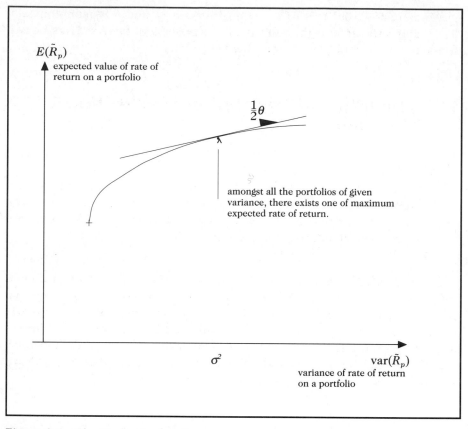

Figure 3.4   The Markowitz frontier

3.4.2 The Black separation theorem

We may now state a fundamental property of the Markowitz frontier, or more precisely, of the set of efficient portfolios. This property[23] is known as the 'Black separation theorem',[24] which may be stated in two parts:

1. **Proposition:** Any convex combination of efficient portfolios is an efficient portfolio.[25]
   From a portfolio 1 and a portfolio 2, which are both on the Markowitz frontier, we may make up a portfolio 3 by taking an average made up, for example, of 75% of portfolio 1 and 25% of portfolio 2. *This new portfolio also lies on the frontier.*

2. **Counter-proposition:** All efficient portfolios may be written in the form of linear combinations of two efficient portfolios chosen arbitrarily.[26]

The procedure involving the combination of portfolio 1 and portfolio 2 is exhaustive: it allows all the efficient portfolios to be obtained without leaving any out. When the relative weight of the two portfolios is varied, the whole parabola is described by a moving point corresponding to portfolio 3. In other words, we only need to know two efficient portfolios to know the whole frontier.

3.4.3. The Tobin separation theorem

There is a special case of the Black theorem known as the *Tobin theorem*, which concerns the case in which a risk-free asset – that is, an asset of zero variance – is effectively present in the market. It may easily be shown that by placing ourselves in the graph of expected rate of return against standard deviation of rate of return (instead of expected rate of return against variance of rate of return), a random combination of a risk-free asset and any risky asset allows us to move along a straight line.[27] The efficient frontier is thus determined in two steps:

- eliminate for the moment the risk-free asset and draw the efficient frontier of the portfolios made up solely of risky assets (this gives us a branch of a hyperbola);

- combine the risk-free asset with a combination of risky assets so as to obtain a frontier (thus a straight line) as high as possible, in order to maximize the rate of return for a given risk. A glance at Figure 3.5 shows that this line is at a tangent to the efficient frontier of the risky assets. Hence Tobin's theorem:[28]

Theorem:
All efficient portfolios are combinations of the risk-free asset and the 'tangent portfolio'. The global efficient frontier is a straight line,[29] called the 'Capital Market Line'.

Equation system 3.6a,c remains a necessary first-order condition of the portfolio of an individual of risk aversion θ. However, if we isolate from this the equation corresponding to the risk-free security with a fixed rate of return r (the rate of interest) we obtain:

$$r = \mu.$$

From this we may obtain a simple interpretation of the number μ allowing the system of first-order conditions to be written as follows:

$$E(\tilde{R}_i) = r + \theta \sum_{j=1}^{n-1} x_j \operatorname{cov}(\tilde{R}_i, \tilde{R}_j); \ i = 1, \ldots, n-1 \qquad [4.1]$$

for any security i, other than the risk-free security (to which we have assigned the number n).

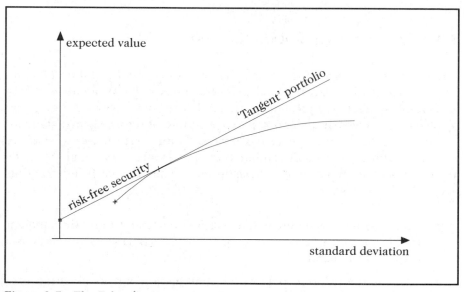

Figure 3.5   The Tobin frontier

As the 'tangent portfolio' is the only efficient portfolio which does not contain the risk-free asset, its composition may be obtained from system [4.1] by imposing

$$\sum_{i=1}^{n-1} x_i = 1$$

We must then treat θ as an unknown, which is normal since we do not know *a priori* the level of risk aversion of an investor who wishes to hold exactly the tangent portfolio.

3.5 Implementation

The implementation of the investment programme recommended by portfolio theory runs into two difficulties, one more serious than the other. The first is linked to the amount of information it is necessary to have before carrying out optimization. Imagine we wish to optimize a modest portfolio of $n = 100$ securities. We would need to know the expected rate of return on each security, which is $n = 100$ parameters, as well as the variance of each and the covariance between each pair, which is $n(n + 1)/2$ parameters. This gives a total of 5150 parameters. Some simplification is obviously required.

It has therefore been suggested[30] that the dependence between the various securities can be summed up by the following statistical formula:

$$\tilde{R}_i = a_i + b_i\tilde{M} + \tilde{\varepsilon}_i \qquad\qquad\qquad\qquad [5.1a]$$

$$\mathrm{cov}(\tilde{\varepsilon}_i, \tilde{\varepsilon}_j) = 0, \qquad i \neq j \qquad\qquad\qquad [5.1b]$$

$$\mathrm{cov}(\tilde{\varepsilon}_i, \tilde{M}) = 0 \qquad\qquad\qquad\qquad\qquad [5.1c]$$

where a_i and b_i are coefficients specific to security i, M is a random factor common to all the securities and ε_i a random factor specific to each security. The condition of independence [5.1b] between the specific risks of the various securities means that a single common factor is sufficient to sum up the interdependence between the securities. The specific nature of the risk ε_i is expressed by the condition of independence [5.1c] between the specific risks and the common factor. This model is called the 'diagonal model' or 'market model'. For n risky securities in the portfolio, all that is required is a knowledge of $3n$ parameters (which, for $n = 100$, is 300 parameters) which are sufficient to calculate all expected returns, variances and covariances. These $3n$ parameters are the coefficients a_i and b_i and the specific risk variances ε_i. The variance of the common factor M is arbitrary.

A second problem of implementation, much more serious than the first, is linked to the quality of the information used. The theory developed until now assumes that the expected rates of return, variances and covariances are known, thanks to which the investor bears only the risk of his investment, a risk minimized by an appropriate policy of diversification. In reality, the investment risk is not the only risk incurred, since we must add to this the uncertainty regarding the value of the parameters used. Expectations, variances and covariances are often estimated on the basis of a sample of rates of return observed in the past. The estimators obtained are imprecise and, more importantly, random: having obtained a particular sample, we should not lose sight of the fact that different samples would have been possible and even probable. The random character of the estimators reflects the imperfect information available to the investor – that is to say his or her incomplete knowledge of the joint probability distribution of the rates of return – and implies the existence of an additional risk called the 'estimation risk'. As the estimation risk is often significant, it would be dangerous to ignore it. Appendix 3.2 of this chapter offers a possible solution to this thorny problem, known as the *Bayesian technique*. This technique involves not basing the decision entirely on information drawn from the past, but tempering this by *a priori* conjectures.

3.6 Conclusion

In this chapter we have revealed two essential results:

- The risk of a security is relative to the portfolio held by an individual: it is measured marginally by its covariance with the portfolio. A necessary first-order condition of the portfolio is that a linear relationship exists between the expected rate of return on each security and its marginal risk.

- The Black theorem stipulates that any combination of efficient portfolios is an efficient portfolio and that the set of efficient portfolios may be obtained from only two efficient portfolios, chosen arbitrarily.

Appendix 3.1

Properties of equation system [3.6a,c] and the Black theorem

1. The solution to system 3.6a,c is linear in terms of $1/\theta$.

    For convenience, let us use matrix and vector notations. Let Ω represent the matrix of variance-covariance of the rates of return:

$\Omega = [\Omega_{ij}]; \qquad \Omega_{ij} = \text{cov}(\tilde{R}_i, \tilde{R}_j); i = 1...n; j = 1...n;$

$\underline{R} = [E(\tilde{R}_i)]; \qquad i = 1.....n;$

$\underline{x} = [x_i]; \qquad i = 1...n;$

$\underline{1} = [1]$

By solving part (a) of system [3.6] which is linear in x, we obtain:

$\underline{x} = (1/\theta)\Omega^{-1}(\underline{R} - \mu\underline{1}).$

Substituting this result into part (c) of the system gives (a prime $'$ denotes a transposed vector):

$(1/\theta)\underline{1}'\Omega^{-1}(\underline{R} - \mu\underline{1}) = 1$

---

and therefore:

$\mu = [\underline{1}'\Omega^{-1}\underline{R} - \theta]/[\underline{1}'\Omega^{-1}\underline{1}]$

Thus:

$\underline{x} = (1/\theta)\Omega^{-1}\left\{\underline{R} - [\underline{1}'\Omega^{-1}\underline{R} - \theta]/[\underline{1}'\Omega^{-1}\underline{1}]\underline{1}\right\}$

$\underline{x} = (1/\theta)\Omega^{-1}\left\{\underline{R} - [\underline{1}'\Omega^{-1}\underline{R}]/[\underline{1}'\Omega^{-1}\underline{1}]\underline{1}\right\} - \Omega^{-1}\underline{1}/[\underline{1}'\Omega^{-1}\underline{1}]$

---

which is indeed linear in $1/\theta$.

2. The variance of the resulting portfolio is quadratic in $1/\theta$.

   The variance of the portfolio is written as $\underline{x}'\Omega\,\underline{x}$; it is thus indeed linear in $(1/\theta)^2$. Given that $1/\theta$ is limited to positive real values, this establishes a bijective relation between θ and the variance σ^2. System 3.6, including 3.6b may therefore be solved by solving a simple quadratic equation, selecting the positive solution for θ. (It must be shown that one solution is positive and the other negative.)
   The expected rate of return on the portfolio is written as $\underline{x}'\underline{R}$; it is thus linear in $1/\theta$ and the expected rate of return versus variance frontier is a parabola.

3. Proof of the Black theorem

   Once the composition of an efficient portfolio is shown to be linear in $1/\theta$, it is clear that two portfolios are sufficient to describe the set of these portfolios, for example the portfolio corresponding to $1/\theta = 1$:

$$\underline{x}_1 = \Omega^{-1}\underline{R} - \Omega^{-1}\underline{1}.[\underline{1}'\Omega^{-1}\underline{R} - 1]/[\underline{1}'\Omega^{-1}\underline{1}]$$

and that corresponding to $1/\theta = 0$:

$$\underline{x}_0 = \Omega^{-1}\underline{1}/[\underline{1}'\Omega^{-1}\underline{1}]$$

Appendix 3.2

Introduction to some Bayesian considerations

We now come to consider the degree of precision with which the composition of the optimal portfolios is known. This is another way of taking account of the estimation risk, as well as the difficulties of implementing optimal portfolio diversification policies.

To illustrate this problem, we carried out a simulation of two financial assets, one risk-free, with a rate of return (interest rate) equal to 10%, and the other risky, with an expected rate of return equal to 11% with a standard deviation of 10%. One of the optimal portfolios (in this case, the one corresponding to a risk aversion equal to 1) has the following composition: 100% allotted to the risky security and 0% allotted to the risk-free security.[31]

In practice, the expected rate of return and the standard deviation of a risky security are not known *a priori* and must be estimated from a sample of observations. The simulation involved drawing at random six samples of thirty-two observations each. After each sample was drawn, the mean rate of return and the standard deviation of the risky security were estimated and the optimal portfolio calculated.

The mean composition of the portfolio, obtained over six experiments of this type, was as follows: 86% allotted to the risky security and 14% to the risk-free security, which is some way from the true optimum of 100% allotted to the risky security. Even more seriously, the optimal decision fluctuates considerably from one sample to the next, as its standard deviation over the same six experiments was 130%. This means that an investor possessing only past observations (32 in this case) from which to make his decision could just as well be led to invest:

$$86\% + 2 \times 130\% = 346\%$$
or:
$$86\% - 2 \times 130\% = -174\%$$

of his wealth in the risky security. In the first case, he borrows at the risk-free rate of 10% (if this is possible) to invest more than his original wealth in the risky security; in the second, on the other hand, he sells this short! The recommendations of the theory as to the portfolio to hold evidently lack precision if their implementation relies on sampled rates of return (observed in the past).

The Bayesian technique is intended to get round this difficulty, at least in part. To apply it, we must have an 'a priori hypothesis', namely one dictating the behaviour of an individual possessing no information concerning the future rates of return of the securities, apart from the fact that some of them (bank deposits) offer nominally risk-free rates of interest. In this situation of ignorance, it is possible that the investor will resort to one of three approaches:

(1) he may choose exclusively risk-free deposits;

(2) he may decide to invest equal parts in the various available securities;

(3) he may decide to invest, in the various securities, parts equal to those of the market portfolio, assuming these are known to him.

The first approach corresponds to an a priori hypothesis according to which all the securities have an expected return equal to the risk-free rate. The second approach corresponds to a very egocentric a priori hypothesis, according to which system 3.6a, 3.6c is verified by $x_i = 1/n$, for the degree of risk aversion of the investor himself. The third approach corresponds with the a priori hypothesis according to which the CAPM is correct and the investor's risk aversion is equal to that of the market.

In general, the investor does not operate in complete ignorance, nor with perfect information regarding the probability distribution of future rates of return. He is rather in possession of limited information; for example, he has a number, essentially finite, of observations of past rates of return and he is conscious of the pitfalls of the estimation risk. Intermediate behaviour therefore seems likely.

This intermediate behaviour is dictated by a statistical theory known as Bayes' theorem. The essence of this theorem is contained in a formula deriving the probability that an event, A, will occur given that an event, B, has occurred (called the *a posteriori* probability $Pr(A|B)$) from the *a priori* probability that A and B will occur together ($Pr(A$ and $B)$) and that B will occur ($Pr(B)$):

$$Pr(A|B) = Pr(A \text{ and } B)/Pr(B)$$

This formula is based crucially on the specification of the *a priori* probability distribution of events A and B, modified by incorporating the information according to which event B has occurred.

The investor in question is in the situation envisaged by the Bayes formula. He wishes to know the probability distribution of future rates of return given the observations of past rates of return, the *a priori* distribution of the rates of return being, in the example of *a priori* attitude no. 2, one which would lead him to invest equal parts of his wealth in each financial security.

Imagine for a moment that the investor begins his career with zero information. He would thus hold equal parts of each security. The next instant, he would observe the rates of return and prudently change his initial decision to one in line with his observations. Progressively, the events observed would acquire more weight in his decision.

The Bayesian technique thus involves using not just past information when choosing a portfolio, nor just the *a priori* hypothesis, but a weighted average of the two. Thus, in the simple case where an investor's ignorance relates solely to the expected returns and not the variances and covariances, the portfolio chosen is a weighted average of the portfolio deduced from historical observations and the *a priori* portfolio of his choice (according to one of the three approaches mentioned above).

For more details, *see* [Jorion 1985] and [Dumas and Jacquillat 1990].

Notes to Chapter 3

1   This book does not address dynamic portfolio choices explicitly. However, Parts II (Arbitrage Models) and III (Bond Valuation) contain models and results of partial equilibrium which may be incorporated into a dynamic model of general equilibrium without any contradiction appearing. For more information on the subject of dynamic portfolio choices, *see* [Merton 1971].

2   This hypothesis is important. It would be useful to compare portfolio decisions taken according to this criterion and decisions taken on the basis of another utility function (which, however, would still be of the von Neumann-Morgenstern type).

3   By which we mean, 'higher than its own expected value'.

4   $0.4 \times 3.5 + 0.3 \times 5.25 = 4.175$;
$0.4 \times (3.5 - 4.175)^2 + 0.3 \times (4 - 4.175)^2 + 0.3 \times (5.25 - 4.175)^2 = 0.5979$.
Note: it is simpler to do the latter calculation as follows:
$0.4 \times (3.5)^2 + 0.3 \times (5.25)^2 + 0.3 \times (5.25)^2 - (4.175)^2 = 0.5979$

When rates of return are measured in percent (that is, $\times 10^{-2}$), variances are expressed in 'per ten thousand' (that is, $\times 10^{-4}$). Their root, the standard deviation, would once again be in percent. A process at least as transparent would involve expressing all rates of return and variances of rates of return in crude figures (without multiplication by one hundred leading to the figure in percent).

5   The reader may be more accustomed to thinking of a parabola as a graph of the equation $y = ax^2 + bx + c$. In the present case it is a parabola 'lying on its side', as the axes are interchanged. the variance (on the x axis) gives the y dimension and the expectation (on the y axis) gives the x dimension.

6   In practice, short selling is subject to restrictions which are not taken into account in the present formulation of this model. Almost all the results which follow depend on the hypothesis of free short selling.

7   When we say that x takes a negative value, this means that the investor loses money when the negatively held security has a positive rate of return. This is what is achieved in practice by short selling (the mechanics of which were briefly described in Chapter 1). An individual who has borrowed a security in order to sell it, must buy it back in order to be able to give it back. In the event of a positive rate of return, he buys it back at a higher price. $x < 0$ may therefore be interpreted as a short sale.

8   Where the minimum of the parabola is exactly at the point $x = 0$ corresponding to security 1.

9   *See* Section 1.1.5.

10   Take care to distinguish the correlation coefficient from the regression coefficient. *See* Section 1.1.5.

11   Hedging is a technique which involves protecting oneself from a risk by means of another risk. The β coefficient may be interpreted as a 'hedge ratio'.

12   The Spanish tilde ~ is often used to signify that a symbol designates a random variable.

13   The variance of the rate of return on the portfolio is a quadratic form constructed on the matrix of variances/covariances of the rates of return.

14   It is easy to show that the number θ must be positive. Any relaxation of the constraint of variance (additional risk-taking) allows a higher expected rate of return to be produced.

15   *See* Section 3.2.

16   This property will prove essential for equilibrium prices (*see* Chapter 4) to satisfy the value additivity principle (*see* Chapter 1).

17   At least as far as small-scale risks are concerned.

18   The term $(1/2)\theta\sigma^2$ in [3.5] was a constant which only played a part in determining θ (first-order condition 3.6b).

19   μ would represent the rate of interest which this investor would be prepared to pay or to receive for a risk-free loan or investment.

20   σ^2 is a second degree function in $1/\theta$ defined only for positive values of $1/\theta$.

21 *See* Appendix 3.1 for proof.

22 *See* [Markowitz 1952].

23 Which gives the set of efficient portfolios the structure of a convex space of dimension 2 in a linear space of dimension n;

24 *Cf.* [Black 1972]. Proof of this theorem may be found in Appendix 3.1.

25 A convex combination is a linear combination with positive coefficients. The concept of an efficient portfolio could be adapted to objective functions which are not of the mean-variance type. The proposition would remain true. As far as constraints are concerned, however, extensions are generally false: only strict linear constraints taking the form of equalities (such as the budget constraint $\Sigma_i x_i = 1$) are permitted. Constraints taking the form of inequalities (such as one preventing short selling $x_i \geq 0$) would invalidate this theorem. No separation theorem has been established which applies in the case of inequality constraints.

26 Here we have written 'linear combination', not 'convex combination' as it may be necessary to use negative weights to describe the entire set of efficient portfolios. The two portfolios referred to form a basis for the set of efficient portfolios. The counter-proposition, as opposed to the proposition, is based on the hypothesis that investors have a mean-variance objective function. Other objective functions would generally require a wider basis.

27 Let us call the rate of return on the risk-free asset r and that of the risky asset R. The rate of return on a portfolio made up of these two securities is

$R_p = (1 - x)r + xR$ and we have:

$E(R_p) = (1 - x)r + xR, \sigma(R_p) = x\sigma(R)$;

Therefore: $E(R_p) = r + (R-r)\ \sigma(R_p)/\sigma(R)$.

28 [Tobin 1958].

29 That is, to a geometrician, a branch of a degenerate hyperbola.

30 [Sharpe 1963].

31 The formula giving the optimal portfolio of an investor with (relative) risk aversion equal to 1 is: $(ER - r)/\sigma^2$, where ER is the expected return on the risky security, r the risk-free rate, and σ the standard deviation of the risky security.

References

[Black 1972] F. Black, Capital Market Equilibrium with Restricted Borrowing, *Journal of Business*, 45, 1972, 444–455.

[Dumas and Jacquillat 1990] B. Dumas, and B. Jacquillat, Performance of Currency Portfolios Chosen by a Bayesian Technique: 1967–1985, *Journal of Banking and Finance*, 14, 1990, 539–558.

[Jorion 1985] P. Jorion, International Portfolio Diversification with Estimation Risk, *The Journal of Business*, 58, 1985, 259–278.

[Markowitz 1959] H. Markowitz, *Portfolio Selection*. New York: John Wiley and Sons, Inc., 1959.

[Sharpe 1963]   W. F. Sharpe, A Simplified Model for Port-
                       folio Analysis, *Management Science*, 9,
                       1963, 277–293.

[Sharpe 1970]   W. F. Sharpe, *Portfolio Theory and Capital
                       Markets*. New York: McGraw Hill, 1970.

[Tobin 1958]   J. Tobin, Liquidity Preference as Behavior
                       Towards Risk, *Review of Economic Studies*,
                       25, 1958, 65–86.

4

The Capital Asset Pricing Model: statement and use

1994 marked the 30th anniversary of the publication of William Sharpe's article ([Sharpe 1964]; *see also* [Treynor 1963], [Lintner 1965], [Mossin 1966]) which gave birth to the Capital Asset Pricing Model (CAPM). This model – which will be demonstrated and its uses presented in this chapter, before some criticisms are made in Chapter 5 – has had a considerable influence on the terms and conditions of financial investment. One of its principal uses, which we shall study in this chapter, was to measure the performance of portfolio managers. Almost all studies having concluded that managed portfolios did not produce a better performance than could have been achieved by holding the securities used to calculate the stock exchange index (Standard & Poors 500 or Dow Jones, or the CAC Index in France), the idea arose of managing invested funds mechanically, by reproducing the composition of the market. This idea gave birth to more or less specialized index funds.

The previous chapter was devoted to the concept of diversification and to individual investors' demands for financial securities. The next step logically

involves dealing with the market equilibrium which results from this behaviour. This will supply us with the CAPM: let us suppose that all investors
behave as was stated in Chapter 3 – that is, that they choose efficient
portfolios – and let us add together these individual demands and compare
their sum with the total supply of securities. The equality of supply and
demand must lead to the prices of financial securities relative to one
another. The result is the *Capital Asset Pricing Model* (Section 4.1). We
take careful note of its significance in the global context of a production or
exchange economy (Section 4.2) before examining three uses of the CAPM:
the identification of over- or under-valued securities (Section 4.3), the
measurement of managers' performance in a situation of risk (Section 4.4)
and the selection of investment projects (Section 4.5). Before summing up
(Section 4.7), we mention some recent developments (Section 4.6).

4.1   The CAPM

4.1.1 Definition of the market portfolio

The statement of the capital asset pricing model is based on the concept of a
market portfolio, which requires a definition. A market portfolio is a portfolio
which has the same composition by value as the whole of the market. If firm
A represents 3% of the total capitalization[1] of a given market, firm B 5%, and
so on, a portfolio of any size containing 3% of firm A, 5% of firm B, and so
on, is called a market portfolio. Once we know the composition of the
market portfolio, we know the values of the various securities relative to one
another.

4.1.2 Proof and statement of the CAPM

Given this definition, we can now move on to the proof of the CAPM. This is
most often done using algebra.[2] Here, we shall do it using a method of pure
logic which will perhaps appear more direct: the syllogism. By definition, a
syllogism consists of three propositions: a major, a minor and a conclusion:

- Major: any convex combination of efficient portfolios is an efficient
  portfolio, by virtue of the Black theorem.[3]

- Minor: in a state of market equilibrium, the market portfolio is a
  convex combination of efficient portfolios. In effect, supply being
  equal to demand, the securities are all held in individuals' portfolios,
  each of these portfolios being, by hypothesis, efficient and having a

positive weight in the market portfolio to the extent that the wealth of each person is positive.

- Consequently, the market portfolio is efficient. It lies on the efficient, or Markowitz, frontier.

The conclusion according to which the market portfolio is efficient is a complete statement of the CAPM. It implies, by application of the necessary first-order condition stated in Chapter 3 (Equation 3.7), that a *linear relationship must exist between the return on a security and its risk*, the risk of each security being measured by its *covariance with the market portfolio*, since this is the portfolio which is supposed to be efficient.

Theorem:
In a condition of market equilibrium, two numbers $\theta > 0$ and μ exist such that:

$$E(\tilde{R}_i) = \mu + \theta \operatorname{cov}(\tilde{R}_i, \tilde{R}_m) \quad \text{for all } i. \tag{1.1}$$

In this equation, the number θ has the same general meaning as in Equation 3.7 of Chapter 3:[4] it is a risk aversion. But we are now dealing with the risk aversion of an average investor, a weighted average[5] of the individual risk aversions.

What condition [1.1] means is that for the average investor to wish to hold the market portfolio, the riskier securities must yield more, the risk being measured by the covariance between the return on each security and that of the market portfolio.

The linear relationship [1.1] provides a basis for comparison between the various securities present on the same financial market. Figure 4.1 shows this relationship: the levels of risk of the various securities appear on the x axis, and the expected values of the rate of return appear on the y axis. All the securities, in equilibrium, are on the line.

If we wish to use the model to determine the required return of each security, Equation 1.1 for each security i supplies the answer directly. But the true meaning of [1.1], as an *asset pricing model*, is better understood by expanding the market rate of return $\tilde{R}_m$ in the form $\sum_i x_i \tilde{R}_i$ ($\sum_i x_i = 1$) and interpreting [1.1] as an equation system, where the unknowns are the relative values x_i of the various securities. We solve the equation system as we did system 3.7 in Chapter 3, which gave us the composition of an individual's portfolio. Here we obtain the composition of the entire portfolio; but as we have said, once we know the composition of the market portfolio, we know the values of the various securities relative to one another.[6]

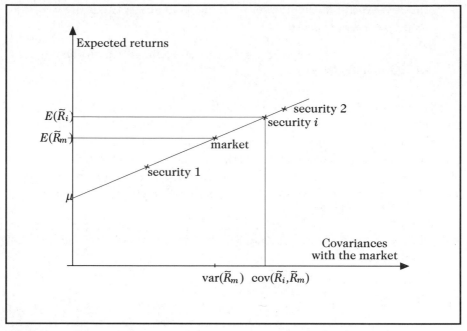

Figure 4.1   Every security must have an expected return in relation to its risk, the latter being measured by the covariance with the market.

4.1.3 Another statement of the CAPM: measurement of risk by the beta coefficient

The CAPM is very often written in a different form, which is obtained by an interpretation of the numbers μ and θ. This is simply a difference in presentation.

The number μ, the intercept term of the linear relationship, may be interpreted as the expected return on a portfolio having a zero covariance with the market (often written as portfolio z). This is written:

$$\mu = E(R_z) \tag{1.2}$$

In the special case where a risk-free security exists, the interpretation of μ is even simpler: in this case it is the fixed rate of return on this security (or the risk-free rate of interest).

Since each security lies on the line, the market portfolio, as indeed any portfolio (efficient or not), also lies on it, at the point $[E(R_m), \text{var}(R_m)]$ in Figure 4.1. By 'knowing' two points on this line, corresponding to portfolios m and z, we may easily obtain the expression of its slope θ in the form:

$$\theta = \frac{E(\tilde{R}_m) - E(\tilde{R}_z)}{\text{var}(\tilde{R}_m)} \qquad [1.3]$$

By substituting expressions [1.2] and [1.3] into Equation 1.1, we obtain the most commonly encountered form of the CAPM:

$$E(\tilde{R}_i) = E(\tilde{R}_z) + [E(\tilde{R}_m) - E(\tilde{R}_z)]\,\beta_i \qquad [1.4]$$

where:

$$\beta_i = \frac{\text{cov}(\tilde{R}_i, \tilde{R}_m)}{\text{var}(\tilde{R}_m)} \qquad [1.5]$$

In the case where a risk-free asset exists, the CAPM is also written as:

$$E(\tilde{R}_i) = r + [E(\tilde{R}_m) - r]\,\beta_i \qquad [1.6]$$

The meaning of this relationship is still the same; only the presentation is different. We have shown here a coefficient β_i specific to each security and equal to its covariance with the market, divided by the variance of the market. This is a new measurement of risk which corresponds to the risk linked to the market. This measurement is dimensionless,[7] the benchmark of risk being the market which has a beta equal to 1. Equation 1.4 supplies the expected rate of return required from security i from two components: the first is the risk-free rate of return, and the second is a *risk premium proportional to beta,* where *the risk premium benchmark* is the market premium: $E(\tilde{R}_m) - E(\tilde{R}_z)$.

4.1.4 The calculation of beta and one more interpretation of the CAPM

The β coefficient is, according to definition [1.5], the coefficient of a linear regression of the rate of return $\tilde{R}_i$ of security i on the rate of return $\tilde{R}_m$ of the market (both random). It thus measures the link between one particular security and the whole market.

This is why we often say that it represents the 'systematic risk', that is the part of the risk of security i linked to the movements of the whole financial market.

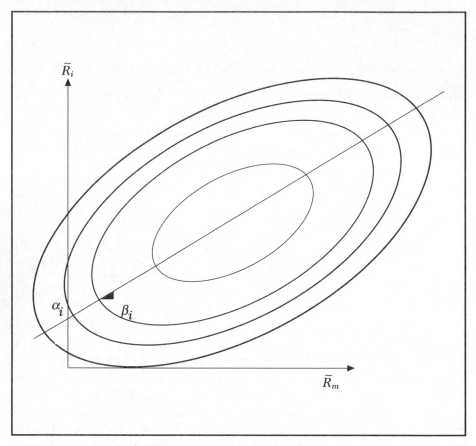

Figure 4.2   Breakdown of the random rate of return on a security into systematic part and specific part, by means of a regression. The regression is the product of a joint probability distribution of $\tilde{R}_i$ and $\tilde{R}_m$, whose isoprobability lines are elliptical.

By referring to the linear regression of $\tilde{R}_i$ on $\tilde{R}_m$ represented in Figure 4.2:[8]

$$\tilde{R}_i = \alpha_i + \beta_i \tilde{R}_m + \tilde{\varepsilon}_i \tag{1.7}$$

we may break down the total variance of the rate of return of security i as follows:

$$\operatorname{var}(\tilde{R}_i) = \beta_i^2 \operatorname{var}(\tilde{R}_m) + \operatorname{var}(\tilde{\varepsilon}_i) \tag{1.8}$$

The first component of the total variance of security i is the systematic variance, and the second is that of a variable independent from the market rate of return, which is often called the 'diversifiable risk' or the risk 'specific' to security i.

Thus the CAPM, Equation 1.4, means that the rate of return on each security must be linearly linked to its systematic risk, the 'diversifiable' risk on its own playing no role and being, as it were, neglected by investors. The corresponding line (Figure 4.3), is called the 'Securities Market Line'.

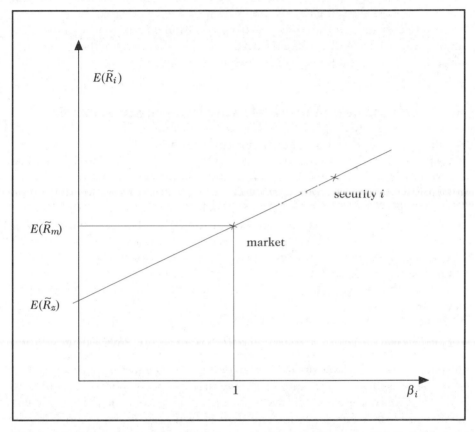

Figure 4.3   Equivalent to Figure 4.1, but using beta as a measure of risk on the x axis. The line is called the 'Securities Market Line' or 'Market Line'.

It is crucial not to confuse this line with Markowitz's efficient frontier, which is reduced to a straight line in the graph of expected return against standard deviation, where a non-risky asset exists (*see* Section 3.4.3 on Tobin separation), and which is sometimes called the 'Capital Market Line'. Also do not confuse this with Sharpe's diagonal model or 'market model' (Equation 5.1a of Chapter 3), which is merely a simplification of the variance-covariance structure of the securities and is in no way a model of economic behaviour. Finally, do not confuse this with Equation 1.7 above, which is simply a means of calculating the 'beta' coefficient.

4.2 The macro-economic context of the CAPM

Financial markets, financial decisions and financial prices are only reflections of an underlying system of production and distribution of goods and services. Our presentation of the CAPM left this more general context in the background. In the formulation used up to now, the probability distribution of the rates of return on the securities was given and was imposed on the market. In fact, adjusting the relative prices of the securities to give equality of supply and demand modified the composition of the market portfolio, apparently without the rates of return being affected by the investors' behaviour. Where did these rates of return come from?

4.2.1 The case of an infinitely elastic supply of securities

We may suppose that the rates of return, until now simply taken as given, are, in fact, imposed by the random production processes, with constant returns to scale,[9] of firms. In this interpretation, firms adjust their capital passively, in response to investors' demands for securities, issuing (or buying back) all the securities demanded and investing (or disinvesting) the product of these issues in the physical production process; physical investment is made at the discretion of the financial investors.[10] The case considered until now is therefore one of an *infinitely elastic supply* of securities:[11] in equilibrium, the composition of the market portfolio dictates the relative size of the firms, that is, the proportion of available physical capital assigned to each one.

Imagine, for example, a stock-market economy in which there were only two firms producing at constant returns to scale according to the joint probability distribution given in Table 4.1. Knowing, furthermore, that the investors present on the stock market lend to and borrow from one another at the supposedly risk-free rate of 8%, we may deduce from this the proportion of the economy's capital invested in each firm. Let x be the proportion invested in firm 1 and $1 - x$ that invested in firm 2. From Equation 1.1, this is written as:

$$0.10 = 0.08 + \theta[(0.08)^2 x + (0.08 \cdot 0.11 \cdot 0.6)(1 - x)]$$
$$0.12 = 0.08 + \theta[(0.11 \cdot 0.08 \cdot 0.6) x + (0.11)^2 (1 - x)]$$

[2.1]

The solution is:

$$x = 0.17 \qquad (1 - x = 0.83)$$
$$\theta = 3.66$$

[2.2]

Therefore:

$$V_1 = \frac{0.17}{0.83} V_2 \qquad\qquad [2.3]$$

where V_1 and V_2 are the capitalizations of the two securities. These are proportional to one another.

The Capital Asset Pricing Model is worthy of its name; thanks to it, we have just determined the relative prices of the two securities.[12]

	Expected rate of return	Standard deviation of rate of return	Correlation
Firm 1	10%	8%	
			0.6
Firm 2	12%	11%	

Table 4.1   Market expectations (probability distribution corresponding to the case of infinitely elastic supply)

4.2.2 The case of an infinitely inelastic supply of securities

We can also consider the case of an *infinitely inelastic supply*, which is diametrically opposed to the preceding case.[13] Let us suppose that firms have taken 'immutable' investment and production decisions. The quantities of securities offered are thus fixed and the securities are defined, not by the probability distribution of their rates of return, but by that of their future payments X_i (a random sum of ECU of a given probability distribution). The rate of return R_i on each security is then calculated as follows:

$$1 + \tilde{R}_i = \frac{\tilde{X}_i}{V_i} \qquad\qquad [2.4]$$

where V_i is the market capitalization of security i. Note that, in this new context, a modification of prices leads to a modification of rates of return. By substituting definition 2.4 into the CAPM 1.1, we obtain several relationships between the prices of the securities (generally $n - 2$ linear relationships where n is the number of securities).

Let us take a different look at the preceding example and imagine a stock-market economy comprising only two firms, which produce immutable but random quantities according to the joint probability distribution of Table 4.2. Let us further specify that loans between operators are made at the rate of 8%. Equation 1.1 supplies the system:

$$
\begin{cases}
\dfrac{10}{V_1} = 1.08 + \theta\left[\dfrac{8^2}{V_1{}^2}\dfrac{V_1}{V_1+V_2} + \dfrac{8 \cdot 11 \cdot 0.6}{V_1 \cdot V_2}\dfrac{V_2}{V_1+V_2}\right] \\[4mm]
\dfrac{12}{V_2} = 1.08 + \theta\left[\dfrac{11 \cdot 8 \cdot 0.6}{V_1 \cdot V_2} + \dfrac{V_1}{V_1+V_2}\dfrac{11^2}{V_2{}^2}\dfrac{V_2}{V_1+V_2}\right]
\end{cases}
\tag{2.5}
$$

which we may also write as:

$$
V_1 = \frac{10 - \dfrac{\theta}{V_1+V_2}(8^2 + 8 \cdot 11 \cdot 0.6)}{1.08}
\tag{2.6a}
$$

$$
V_1 = \frac{12 - \dfrac{\theta}{V_1+V_2}(8 \cdot 11 \cdot 0.6 + 11^2)}{1.08}
\tag{2.6b}
$$

which, after cancelling out $\theta/(V_1 + V_2)$, gives:

$$
\frac{\dfrac{10}{1.08} - V_1}{8^2 + 8 \cdot 11 \cdot 0.6} = \frac{\dfrac{12}{1.08} - V_2}{11^2 + 11 \cdot 8 \cdot 0.6}
\tag{2.7}
$$

	Expected cash flows	Standard deviation of flows	Correlation
Firm 1	10 ECU	8 ECU	
			0.6
Firm 2	12 ECU	11 ECU	

Table 4.2　Market expectations (probability distribution corresponding to the case of infinitely inelastic supply)

Equations 2.6, expressing the prices of the securities, contain a numerator, which is discounted at the risk-free rate. The numerator is called the certainty equivalent of the future random flow X, since it is to be discounted at the risk-free rate of 8%. The certainty equivalent consists of the expected value of the flow, adjusted by a *penalty*, determined here by the variance of the flow (the first term of the expression in brackets) plus its covariance with the flow of the other firm (second term), which is to say that the penalty is determined by the covariance of the flow of the firm with the total flow of the economy.

Relationship 2.7, which links the prices V_1 and V_2, is linear, but is not a pure relationship of proportionality, in contrast to what happened in the preceding economy (Equation 2.3).

Whatever the economy in question, the CAPM allows us to obtain the prices of securities relative to one another, but the relationship linking them differs according to the macroeconomic context.

We can now turn to the applications of the CAPM which have been demonstrated.

4.3   Identifying over- or under-valued securities

Some securities may appear over- or under-valued to an investor whose anticipations differ from those of the market taken as a whole. A speculative operation then becomes possible. If the investor's anticipations are correct, he will be able to reap the rewards of his operation in the form of capital gains as soon as the market comes round to his point of view. Otherwise, he will have to wait until the security he has bet on brings him payoffs (dividends, coupons, repayments) conforming to his expectations.

	Expected rate of return	Standard deviation of rate of return	Correlation
Firm 1	11.5%	8%	
			0.5
Firm 2	12%	11%	
	Risk-free rate = 8%		

Table 4.3   Probability distribution reflecting the expectations of an isolated investor (and which is also the *ex post* empirical distribution)

By way of an example, let us look again at the economy with constant returns to scale described in Table 4.1, the rate of interest being 8%. As this table represents the anticipations of the market, the capitalizations of the two securities are, as we have seen, in the ratio 0.17/0.83 (result 2.3 above). The composition of the market portfolio resulting from this is: 17% of security 1, 83% of security 2 and 0% risk-free security, as the latter is only an instrument of borrowing and lending between investors. The three securities plotted on a diagram of expected return against beta (or expected return against covariance with the market) are therefore correctly aligned.

Imagine for the moment an investor who has the same risk aversion as the market as a whole ($\theta = 3.66$),[14] but whose anticipations are different, namely those of Table 4.3. To check whether the prices quoted on the stock exchange – which, remember, are in the ratio 0.17/0.83 – conform to his anticipations, he plots the three securities on a diagram of expectation against covariance with the market (Figure 4.4) or, which amounts to the same thing, a diagram of expected return against beta (Figure 4.5), and notes that the rate of return on security 1 is excessive relative to that of security 2. This means that *in his eyes*, security 1 is undervalued by comparison with security 2.

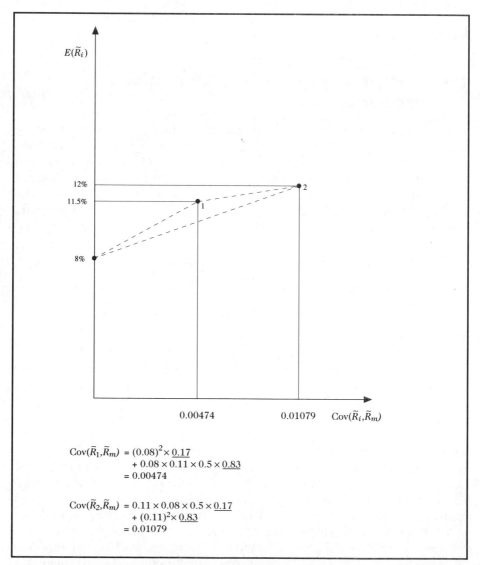

$$\text{Cov}(\tilde{R}_1, \tilde{R}_m) = (0.08)^2 \times \underline{0.17}$$
$$+ 0.08 \times 0.11 \times 0.5 \times \underline{0.83}$$
$$= 0.00474$$

$$\text{Cov}(\tilde{R}_2, \tilde{R}_m) = 0.11 \times 0.08 \times 0.5 \times \underline{0.17}$$
$$+ (0.11)^2 \times \underline{0.83}$$
$$= 0.01079$$

Figure 4.4 (data: Table 4.3) By comparing expected return with risk (measured by the covariance with the market) the investor observes a lack of alignment and therefore an under-valuation of security 1 relative to security 2.

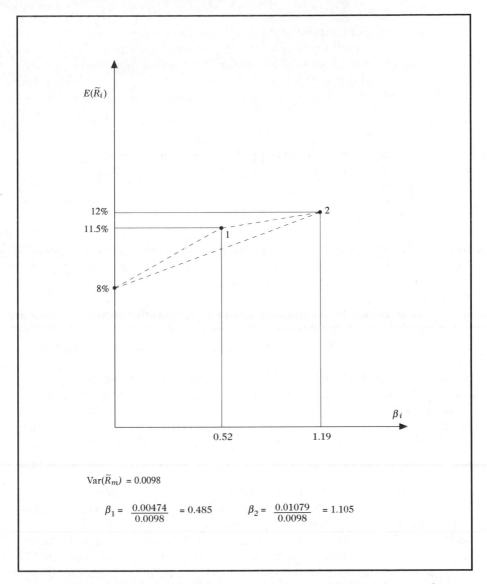

Figure 4.5   (data: Table 4.3) This figure is equivalent to Figure 4.4, but uses beta as a measure of risk.

As confirmation, let us calculate this investor's optimal portfolio, by solving the equation system:

$$0.115 = 0.08 + 3.66[(0.08)^2 x + 0.08 \cdot 0.11 \cdot 0.5y]$$
$$0.12 = 0.08 + 3.66[0.11 \cdot 0.08 \cdot 0.5x + (0.11)^2 y]$$

[3.1]

where:

---

x = proportion of his wealth invested in security 1
y = proportion of his wealth invested in security 2
$1 - x - y$ = proportion of his wealth invested (or borrowed if < 0) at
         the risk-free rate.

We obtain:

$$x = 1.17$$
$$y = 0.48$$
$$1 - x - y = -0.65$$

[3.2]

---

from which the investor concludes that, if the market shared his point of view, it would have to be an overall borrower, which is impossible, and above all, that it would have to give security 1 a value more than double that of security 2.[15]

As this is evidently not the case here, the investor decides to speculate against the market. The mode of operation in this speculation differs according to case. We shall consider here two extreme cases, leaving it up to the reader to deal with those in between.

In the first case, the investor is almost certain that the market will come round to his way of thinking almost immediately. In the second, by contrast, he believes that the market will persist in its 'error' until the final maturity of the securities. This vital distinction illustrates an important point: in order to implement a speculative operation, it is not enough to know the 'true' probability distribution of the rates of return on the securities; it is also necessary to forecast the mechanism by which the appearance of one piece of information or another will (more or less suddenly) rock the market.

If the investor considers that the market will agree with him almost immediately, he is tempted to adopt a reckless attitude. When security 1 is under-valued, he will tie up all his wealth in this security, plus any amount he is able to borrow at the rate of 8%, and sell, even short sell, security 2 in order to invest the amount earned in security 1. If, as he predicted, every-one very quickly adopts the anticipations of Table 4.3, a new equilibrium appears. Since the relative risk aversion of the market is supposedly fixed and equal to 3.66, the new equilibrium cannot be established at the former prices or at the former 8% rate of interest. It is established at the new relative prices x and $1 - x$ (for securities 1 and 2 respectively)[16] and at the new rate of interest z, such that:

$$0.115 = z + 3.66[(0.08)^2 \cdot x + 0.08 \cdot 0.11 \cdot 0.5 \cdot (1 - x)]$$
$$0.12 = z + 3.66[0.11 \cdot 0.08 \cdot 0.5x + (0.11)^2 \cdot (1 - x)]$$

[3.3]

---

which gives:

$$x = 0.65$$
$$1 - x = 0.35 \qquad\qquad\qquad [3.4]$$
$$z = 0.0941 = 9.41\%$$

Thus security 1, which was under-valued, undergoes an increase in value relative to security 2, and the rate of interest increases. The price modifications obviously go in the direction envisaged by the investor, and the increase in the rate of interest is consistent with the fact that at the previous rate, the market, like the speculator, would have been a borrower.[17]

The investor's profit is equal to the amount of his purchase of security 1 multiplied by the rate of appreciation on this security plus, possibly, the amount of his short-sale of security 2 multiplied by the rate of depreciation on this security.[18] If the operations we are considering remain modest in size relative to the total capitalization, they have no influence on the original price, and the rates of appreciation and depreciation are dictated by the prices which we have already calculated:[19]

$$\frac{0.65 - 0.17}{0.17} = 2.84 = 284\% \text{ on security 1 bought}$$
$$\qquad\qquad\qquad\qquad\qquad\qquad\qquad\qquad [3.5]$$
$$\frac{0.35 - 0.83}{0.83} = -0.582 = -58\% \text{ on security 2 sold}$$

which represents substantial rates of return in a very short time! On the other hand, if the orders to buy security 1 and the orders to sell security 2 placed by the speculator are large enough to affect the original prices, not only may the potential rates of appreciation be reduced, but also the other operators may come to suspect that an individual, better informed than they are, is attempting an operation. The investor will thus no longer find another party in the market and his manoeuvre will become impossible.[20]

In the second of the extreme cases mentioned above, *the speculator considers that the market will persist in its error* and that his expectations will only be rewarded by payoffs of securities (distribution of dividends, and so on). His attitude is therefore much more prudent. He adopts on his own account the diversified portfolio [3.2] which corresponds to his anticipations: he borrows and invests the sums earned, plus his initial wealth, in the two securities, favouring security 1, which he considers to be under-valued.

The rate of return on this portfolio is obviously random and it could well happen, by chance, that at the end of the period, the investor records a considerable loss, even though his anticipations (which are those of Table 4.3) and his actions reflect the true probability distribution of the rates of return. Nevertheless, his behaviour will have been optimal with regard to the 'expectation-variance' criterion. As Table 4.4 demonstrates,[21] his behaviour brings him, by construction, a higher price of the *ex ante* criterion:

expected rate of return on the portfolio
$-\frac{1}{2}\,\theta\cdot$ variance of the portfolio,

than if he had simply adopted the market portfolio [2.2].

	Portfolio of composition [3.2] 1.17; 0.48; −0.65	Market portfolio of composition [2.2] 0.17; 0.83; 0
Expected rate of return	1.17×0.115 0.48×0.12 -0.65×0.08 $= 0.14001$ $= 14\%$	$0.17 \times 0.115 + 0.83 \times 0.12$ $= 0.11915$ $= 11.92\%$
Variance of rate of return (standard deviation)	0.0164 $= 164 \cdot 10^{-4}$ (12.81%)	0.0098 $= 98 \cdot 10^{-4}$ (9.88%)
Expectation criterion $-1/2\ \theta \times$ variance ($\theta = 3.66$)	0.1100	0.1013

Table 4.4   Comparison of the levels of utility on the basis of the *ex post* distribution (data: Table 4.3)

In this way, the CAPM allows an individual, knowing a probability distribution of future rates of return, to identify over- or under-valued securities and to implement a speculative strategy. Such over- or under-valuations may occur in two types of situation, equally exploitable.

1. The investor and the market have *the same anticipations*, but the market portfolio, contrary to the statement of the CAPM, is not correctly diversified.[22] This means that the investors present on the market do not apply the expectation-variance criterion and do not diversify their portfolios as we envisage. In this case, the CAPM will be empirically false. But the isolated investor – himself having an objective of the expectation-variance type – and wishing to profit from what in his eyes is a 'bad' diversification, could still use the CAPM diagram to draw a diagnosis from it. The strategy presented above is thus directly applicable.

2. The investor and the market choose efficient portfolios, but on the basis of different anticipations. This is the situation which we have described in this section.

When a situation of this type is encountered, we must investigate the origin and the possible justification of a difference in anticipations between the individual investor and the market. Both derive their anticipations from the information available to them. It is thus essential for speculators to have at their disposal private information which allows them to justify, in their eyes or in the eyes of their principals, the divergence of their anticipations from those of the market. What is this information? is it verified? does the market know it already? and so on.

All investors, and therefore the market, have in common at least one extremely well-worn element of information; namely, the history of market rates of return. An extremely large number of past observations allows an empirical distribution of the rates of return to be established which is – averaging out sampling errors – the 'true' distribution as it prevailed in the past. If, *on the sole basis of this distribution*, – called empirical, or observed, or *ex post* – we detect a non-alignment of the points corresponding to the various securities in the diagram of expected rate of return against beta, we must be extremely careful. In fact, the most likely explanation is that the market has the empirical distribution at its disposal, but has decided not to take it completely into account, expecting that the future will be different from the past. Before implementing a speculative combination, it would therefore be useful to discover the market's reasons, which are certainly based on additional information (other than past rates of return). As a rule, the empirical distribution *on its own* does not constitute usable information.

4.4 Measuring the performance of portfolio managers

Whenever the expected results of management depend on external random factors – which is obviously the general case – performance measurement is a delicate operation. Clearly, it cannot be done from a single observed result, since this is partly the product of chance. For performance measurement to have any meaning, we must have a sufficient number of observations, gathered independently of one another, to allow statistical conclusions to be drawn.

Besides the need to differentiate between the result of chance and the product of good management, there is also the problem of *checking the level of risk*. On a financial market, it is generally very easy to achieve a higher average result by taking more risks. So a manager who shows, on average, better results than another is not necessarily a 'better' manager; it may be that the level of risk in the portfolio he or she has selected is higher. Any measurement of performance must incorporate a measurement of the level of risk taken.

The procedure suggested by [Jensen 1968] to solve both aspects of the problem simultaneously is as follows: let $R_{m,t}$ and $R_{p,t}$ respectively be the market rate of return over a period of time t and that, simultaneously, of a portfolio p whose performance we wish to measure. Now let r_t be the rate of interest quoted at the start of the same period. From a time series of observations, $t = 1, ...T$, we may calculate the linear regression:

$$R_{p,t} - r_t = \hat{\alpha}_p + \hat{\beta}_p (R_{m,t} - r_t) + \varepsilon_{p,t}; t = 1 ... T \qquad [4.1]$$

where the $\varepsilon_{p,t}$ are the deviations from the regression, of zero mean, statistically independent from $R_{m,t} - r_t$, and $\hat{\alpha}_p$ and $\hat{\beta}_p$ are the estimates of the intercept and its slope respectively. If the CAPM (Equation 1.6) is correct, that is, if the market portfolio is efficient with regard to the true probability distribution, we have:

$$E(\tilde{R}_p) - r = \beta_p (E(\tilde{R}_m) - r)$$

therefore:

$$E(\hat{\alpha}_p) = 0 \qquad [4.2]$$

On the other hand, if portfolio p is efficient, and the market portfolio is not, we have:[23]

$$E(\hat{\alpha}_p) > 0 \qquad [4.3]$$

This is true whatever the reasons dictating the choice of the two portfolios: calculations of the diversification of portfolios p and m on the basis of the same probability distribution, one being a correct calculation and the other not, or knowledge by the manager of the true probability distribution, where this is not known by the market. Whatever the cause of the performance, the $\hat{\alpha}_p$ estimated by regression [4.1] may be used to measure it. It will however be noted that this measurement is meaningless unless the β_p, that is, the *level of risk taken*, is *constant* throughout the observation period.[24]

To illustrate this process, let us imagine that the investor whose operations we described in Section 4.3 is working for a financial institution, and that, as outside observers, we wish to evaluate his management. To do this, we assemble a large number of observed rates of return for the managed portfolio; if the manager's anticipations are correct, the empirical distribution (*ex post* distribution) will converge towards the probability distribution of Table 4.3. It is on this basis that we must calculate the regression [4.1]. A large part of the necessary calculation work is already contained in Table 4.4 above, as well as in the key to Figures 4.4 and 4.5. We find:[25]

$$\beta_p = 1.17 \times 0.485 + 0.48 \times 1.105 = 1.1$$
$$\alpha_p = 0.14 - 0.08 - 1.1 \times (0.1192 - 0.08) \qquad [4.4]$$
$$= 0.017 = 1.7\%$$

Since $\alpha_p > 0$, we cannot question the performance of the manager.

The *sign* of Jensen's measure, α, has the merit of being independent from the level of risk of the portfolio. On the other hand, its value does not have the same property. Let us imagine that the manager's relative risk aversion was $\theta = 2$ instead of $\theta = 3.66$. By redoing the calculations in the previous section, we can determine his new portfolio choice:

Security 1:	2.13
Security 2:	0.88
Risk-free security:	−2.01

with the result that:

$$\beta_n = 2.005$$
$$E(\tilde{R}_p) = 0.1897$$
$$\alpha_p = 0.031 = 3.1\% > 0$$

The α_p is still positive, but it takes a different value, showing that it would be incorrect to establish a ranking of managers on the basis of the α they achieve: for an unchanged level of expertise on the part of the manager,[26] the α obtained is, in fact, proportional to the level of risk (β) incurred.

What is more, the fact that $\alpha_p > 0$ does not, strictly speaking, allow us to treat the manager's performance as exceptional: if p is efficient when m is not, we do have $\alpha_p > 0$; but $\alpha_p > 0$ may well result from a situation where neither m nor p is efficient.[27]

To demonstrate superiority of management, we would have to draw a comparison such as we made in Table 4.4: this was a direct comparison of the levels attained by the mean-variance criterion, the basis on which portfolio p or portfolio m is held. However, a comparison of this type is meaningful only if we know *a priori* that the manager and the market have the same risk aversion. In practice, that of the market is not observable if the market's anticipations are not known.

We must therefore make an adjustment. Since the manager's relative risk aversion is equal to θ, we compare:

$$E(R_p) - 1/2\,\theta\,\mathrm{var}(R_p) = 0.1100 \tag{4.5}$$

not to:

$$E(R_m) - 1/2\,\theta\,\mathrm{var}(R_m) = 0.1013$$

but to:

$$\underset{x}{Max}\quad [xE(\tilde{R}_m) + (1-x)r - 1/2\,\theta x^2\,\mathrm{var}(\tilde{R}_m)] \tag{4.6}$$

or:

$$r + \frac{1}{2}\frac{1}{\theta}\frac{(E(\tilde{R}_m)-r)^2}{\mathrm{var}(\tilde{R}_m)} = 0.1015$$

In other words, we compare the quality of management p to that which the manager would have achieved by combining optimally the market portfolio m and the risk-free security, taking into account the *ex post* distribution and his risk aversion.

This adjusted comparison is, in fact, equivalent to the more simple comparison[28] of the *ex post* excess rate of return ratios per unit of standard deviation, *whose use was suggested by* [Sharpe 1966]:[29]

$$\frac{E(\tilde{R}_p)-r}{\sqrt{\mathrm{var}(\tilde{R}_p)}} = 0.468 \quad \text{as regards portfolio p} \tag{4.7}$$

$$\frac{E(\tilde{R}_m)-r}{\sqrt{\mathrm{var}(\tilde{R}_m)}} = 0.396 \quad \text{for the market portfolio} \tag{4.8}$$

The relationship between comparison [4.5–4.6] and comparison [4.7–4.8] is illustrated by Figure 4.6, drawn as a graph of expected rate of return against standard deviation: the Sharpe ratio of a portfolio is simply equal to the slope of the line joining the portfolio to the risk-free security. In our example, this slope is greater for portfolio p than for portfolio m, which establishes that portfolio p is superior to portfolio m.

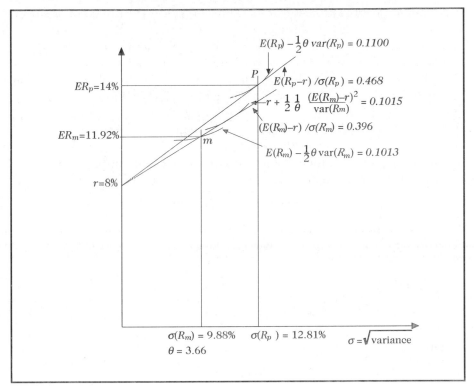

$E(R_p) - \frac{1}{2}\theta \, var(R_p) = 0.1100$

P

$E(R_p - r) \, /\sigma(R_p) = 0.468$

$r + \frac{1}{2}\frac{1}{\theta}\frac{(E(R_m)-r)^2}{var(R_m)} = 0.1015$

$(E(R_m)-r) \, /\sigma(R_m) = 0.396$

$E(R_m) - \frac{1}{2}\theta \, var(R_m) = 0.1013$

$ER_p = 14\%$

$ER_m = 11.92\%$

m

$r = 8\%$

$\sigma(R_m) = 9.88\%$ $\sigma(R_p) = 12.81\%$ $\sigma = \sqrt{variance}$

$\theta = 3.66$

Figure 4.6 (based on the probability distribution of Table 4.3). The measurement of portfolio performance by means of Sharpe's ratio amounts to a comparison of utility levels.

The reasoning we have just followed in the comparison of the managed portfolio, p, with the market portfolio applies equally to the comparison of any pair of portfolios. In contrast to Jensen's α, Sharpe's ratio therefore allows investment funds to be ranked relative to one another. It is perhaps for this reason that it is more widely used in practice.

4.5 Choice of investment projects

The choice of investment projects using the CAPM is based on the same logic as the identification of over- and under-valued securities, apart from the fact that the 'security' in question is not yet on the market. Since investors have not yet had the opportunity to introduce the project into their portfolio, there is no reason for it to be on the line of securities quoted in the diagram of the expected rate of return against beta. It is thus structurally over- or under-valued,[30] which means that its acquisition cost allows a negative or positive net present value to be produced. The decision to adopt or reject the project follows from this: reject the project if it is over-valued, that is, if it is below the line.

However, implementing this procedure is problematic to the extent that it requires the beta of a project to be determined by pure economic analysis. No macroeconomic model is sufficiently precise to allow calculation of the link between the rate of return of a project and that of the global economic system.[31]

Let us assume that this difficulty is resolved and that, in one of the economies envisaged here – that of Table 4.1 (where investment was carried out at the discretion of financial investors) – an investment project is drawn up. This may be of fixed or variable size.

Cost of the investment	100 ECU
Expected end-of-period flow	120 ECU
Standard deviation of the end-of-period flow	17.5 ECU
Correlation of the end-of-period flow with the rate of return on security 1	0.2
Correlation of the end-of-period flow with the rate of return on security 2	0.5

Table 4.5   Investment project of fixed size

- **First case:**
  If the investment is of fixed size, it is defined by its start- and end-of-period cash flows – for example, those of Table 4.5.[32] The acquisition cost of the project being 100 ECU, the rate of return for whichever firm takes it on is: $E(R) = 20\%$, $\sigma(R) = 17.5\%$. As the market comprises 17% of firm 1 and 83% of firm 2, the beta of the project is:

$$\beta(R) = \frac{0.17 \cdot 0.175 \cdot 0.08 \cdot 0.2 + 0.83 \cdot 0.175 \cdot 0.11 \cdot 0.5}{(0.17)^2 \cdot (0.08)^2 + (0.83)^2 \cdot (0.11)^2 + 2 \cdot 0.17 \cdot 0.83 \cdot 0.08 \cdot 0.11 \cdot 0.6} \quad [5.1]$$

$$= \frac{0.00848}{0.0100} = 0.848$$

The relative merits of the project, in comparison to securities 1 and 2, are shown in Figure 4.7. The project is evidently acceptable since:[33]

$$20\% > 8\% + [11.66\% - 8\%] \cdot 0.848 = 11.11\% \qquad\qquad [5.2]$$

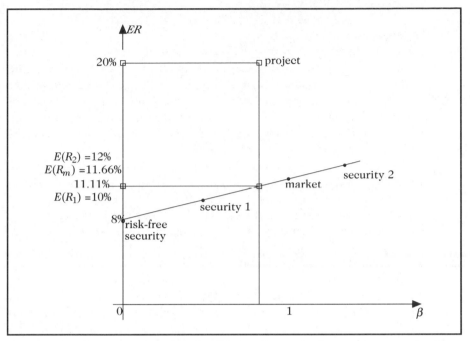

Figure 4.7   The project is undervalued; its net present value is positive; it should be undertaken.

The project has an expected return, *relative to its acquisition cost*, greater than that of the required return, which is 11.11%, taking into account its risk. At this cost, it is 'under-valued' and produces a positive net present value:

$$\text{present value} = \frac{120}{1.1111} = 108 \text{ ECU}$$

$$\text{net present value} = 108 \text{ ECU} - 100 \text{ ECU} = 8 \text{ ECU} \qquad\qquad [5.3]$$

This net present value has a simple interpretation: if the financial market takes account of the new project immediately, the market capitalization of the firm which implements it must undergo an immediate appreciation of 8 ECU.

Even in the case where the market does not immediately recognize the presence of the new project and does not signal its satisfaction by this appreciation, a manager who decides to undertake it anyway will see its merits justly recognized *a posteriori*: his management will produce a positive Jensen's α.[34] No matter how quick or slow the market's reaction, he is well advised to undertake a project with a positive net present value.

- **Second case**
  If the size of the project may be varied at will, and if the net present value is positive, it is theoretically desirable to increase the size of the project infinitely. But we must also consider that it would partly supplant the other economic activities and significantly change the composition of the market portfolio. It is therefore important to determine the optimum size of the project, that is, the size which maximizes the value of the firm.

  Let us consider a project similar to that described in Table 4.5, which was of fixed size, with the difference that its size, measured in acquisition cost, may now be 200, 300, 400... ECU. The rate of return is constant and equal to 20 ECU per 100 ECU invested (20%), with a standard deviation of 17.5%. Imagine that we have already multiplied the unit project to the point where it represents a fraction $1 - x - y$ of the economy's capital (whereas the former activities 1 and 2 absorb fractions x and y of the capital). Should we continue on this path? We have seen (Equations 5.2 and 5.3) that when the return on a project exceeds its expected return it produces an increase in value for the firm undertaking it. At equilibrium, there must therefore be equality between the return and the required return:

$$
\begin{aligned}
0.2 = r + 3.66 \cdot [& x \cdot 0.175 \cdot 0.08 \cdot 0.2 \\
& + y \cdot 0.175 \cdot 0.11 \cdot 0.5 \\
& + (1 - x - y) \cdot (0.175)^2]
\end{aligned}
\qquad [5.7a]
$$

Furthermore, with investors diversifying their portfolios, we have, as in Chapter 3:

$$
\begin{aligned}
0.10 = r + 3.66 \cdot [& x \cdot (0.08)^2 \\
& + y \cdot 0.08 \cdot 0.11 \cdot 0.6 \\
& + (1 - x - y) \cdot 0.08 \cdot 0.175 \cdot 0.2]
\end{aligned}
\qquad [5.7b]
$$

$$
\begin{aligned}
0.12 = r + 3.66 \cdot [& x \cdot 0.11 \cdot 0.08 \cdot 0.6 \\
& + y \cdot (0.11)^2 \\
& + (1 - x - y) \cdot 0.11 \cdot 0.175 \cdot 0.5]
\end{aligned}
\qquad [5.7c]
$$

where r is the new equilibrium rate of interest, after the introduction of the project. The solution to system 5.7 is:

$$x = 0.1722$$
$$y = -0.2058$$
$$1 - x - y = 1.0336$$

As it is impossible to make activity 2 operate negatively, we must close it down ($y = 0$) and produce a fresh solution for the system comprising only [5.7a] and [5.7b] (setting $y = 0$). This solution is:

$$x = 0.018$$
$$1 - x = 0.987$$
$$\text{and } r = 8.95\%$$

The new activity has eliminated the old activity 2, reduced the proportion of activity 1 and now occupies 99% of the economy's capital. The risk-free rate of interest is increased.

4.6   Recent developments

In the next chapter, we examine the criticisms which have been levelled against portfolio theory and the CAPM. A number of recent developments have set out to reduce the shortcomings of this model. This is not the place to discuss them; however, it is appropriate to summarize here the recent developments in the most important application of the CAPM: performance measurement (Section 4.4 above). In this respect, Jensen's measurement has been the subject of some important methodological debates.[35]

We may expect a measurement of performance to take a positive value when a manager possesses and makes correct use of information which is better than that held by the market. As mentioned by [Jensen 1972] himself, as well as [Admati and Ross 1985] and [Dybvig and Ross 1985], this requirement is not satisfied by Jensen's α if the β of the managed portfolio is not constant. Consider the case of a manager who directs the composition of the portfolio he manages towards securities with a high β when he anticipates (correctly) a rise in the market and who, conversely, reduces his β when the market is about to fall (a strategy known as 'market timing'). It may be shown that, in this case, the β of the portfolio, measured *ex post*, is biased upwards compared to the average β. The risk is therefore over-estimated and, as a result, the α measured may be negative, even though the manager has shown himself capable of anticipating the market.[36]

Let us illustrate this tendency using Figure 4.8, which represents the excess return (over and above the risk-free rate) on the managed portfolio against that of a reference portfolio (for example the market portfolio), in the manner of Equation 4.1 above. For the purposes of the illustration, let us imagine simply that the manager must make a choice between a high beta portfolio, corresponding to the more steeply sloping line, and a low beta portfolio corresponding to the less steeply sloping line. If the reference portfolio is efficient, both lines pass through the origin, as the above result [4.2] showed.

The manager is assumed to be capable of forecasting the return on the reference portfolio. This means that he receives a *signal* which tells him sometimes that the excess return on the reference portfolio will take the value R_1, and sometimes that it will take the value R_2 $(R_1 > R_2)$.[37] If he is in a position to make use of this knowledge, he will choose the high beta portfolio and position him at point A when he receives a signal of type 1, and position him at point B in the event of a signal of type 2.

Let us now consider the view of an outside observer to whom the manager's return results were announced, but who did not know the details of purchases and sales of securities at each moment, and therefore did not know of the market timing strategy pursued. This observer would consider that the risk of the portfolio managed in this way was equal to the slope of the dotted line AB. This slope is greater than either of the two betas between which the portfolio oscillates. The risk is therefore overestimated. The *intercept* (point C) of the dotted line is negative. That is to say that the Jensen's α measured using this method wrongly indicates a poor performance. Moreover, this example for Figure 4.8 shows that a systematically erroneous strategy, involving choosing a low beta portfolio in the event of an upward signal and a high beta portfolio in the event of a downward signal, would produce a positive α (line $A'B'$)!

[Grinblatt and Titman 1989] recently developed a new performance measure which does not lead to error. They call it the 'Positive Period Weighting Measure' (PPWM). The PPWM is a weighted average of the *ex post* returns obtained by the managed portfolio, as was Jensen's α. They show, however, that the α is an average in which the weight attributed to each observation is sometimes positive and sometimes negative, and that this is where the origin of the error lies. In the calculation of the PPWM, the weightings are always positive, which eliminates the problem. In addition, the weightings are designed to be higher when R_m is weak and lower when R_m is strong, in order to represent the idea of timing: management is better if the results obtained are high at the very moment that the market is falling, and relatively low when the market is rising.

Besides the ability to anticipate the market (timing) the manager may possess an ability to *select financial securities* (selectivity). In Section 4.4, we kept the beta of the portfolio constant; we therefore based the manager's performance entirely on this ability. Our examination was based on the idea that the market held an inefficient portfolio (with regard to the true probability distribution revealed *ex post*), whereas the manager himself chose an efficient portfolio. In this case he produced a positive α. This presentation assumes that the market has anticipations corresponding to a probability distribution constantly different from what will be the *ex post* distribution, which is known to the manager. A different information structure, envisaged by [Mayers and Rice 1979], seems more realistic and is also capable of producing a non-zero Jensen's α.

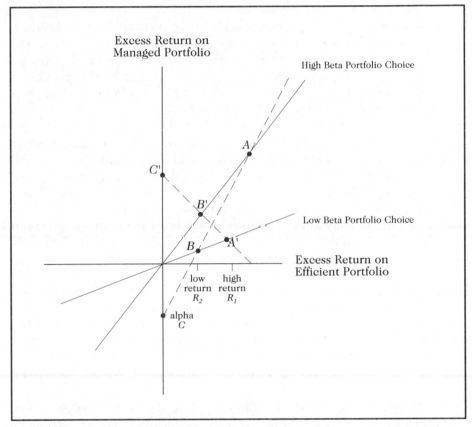

Figure 4.8   The erroneous results of the Jensen measure when the portfolio beta is not constant. *Source*: [Grinblatt and Titman 1989].

In the scenario presented by Mayers and Rice, the market and the manager have, *on average*, the same probability distribution. The manager's information advantage, his 'expertise', which we are attempting to demonstrate, stems from the fact that, at the start of each period, he receives *signals* pointing to the return on one security or another over the coming period. He then infers a joint probability distribution, *conditioned by the value of the signals received*, which is used as the basis of his portfolio choice for that period. His portfolio changes constantly in order to profit from the signals; this is *active management*. The market itself receives no signals; the probability distribution it uses is merely the unconditional probability distribution.[38] Due to a lack of information, the market is not in a position to adjust its portfolio over time; it practices *passive management*, which is only correct on average. Thus, period by period, the manager may accumulate higher gains than those of the market, since he chooses securities by benefiting from a certain foresight. Active management, based on genuine expertise, beats passive management. The α measures the manager's degree of foresight which allows him to select securities better than the market.

In connection with the persistent error of the market which it assumed, the presentation of Section 4.4 was also somewhat contradictory to the spirit of the CAPM, since the manager could only produce a non-zero α if the reference portfolio was inefficient *ex post* with respect to the expectation-variance criterion. If we were to find it difficult identifying the market portfolio (*see* Roll's critique [Roll 1977, 1978] in Chapter 5), there would be no question of using any efficient portfolio in its place, since that would automatically have produced an α equal to zero, whatever the managed portfolio comprised. On the other hand, in the information structure of Mayers and Rice, it is logical to use as a reference portfolio[39] the market portfolio, or *any other portfolio which is efficient* on the basis of the distribution observed (*ex post*). In practice, it would seem normal to include in the reference portfolio only those securities to which the manager has access or which reflect the speciality of the fund in question (for example, a fund specializing in the choice of oil securities would be compared with an *ex post* efficient portfolio made up entirely of oil securities).

We could even claim that it is preferable to choose as a reference a portfolio calculated as being efficient, rather than the market portfolio, which is only efficient *if* the CAPM is true. We examine the validity of the CAPM in Chapter 5, where we see that it is called into question by a number of anomalies in the rate of return: for example, in the USA between 1975 and 1984, the smaller firms quoted on the American Stock Exchange and the New York Stock Exchange had a rate of return, adjusted for risk, distinctly higher than the larger firms. Taking this into account, a manager whose portfolio accorded the small firms a greater weight than they were given by the market portfolio would have produced an exceptional performance. What significance could we grant to this performance?

Conversely, we may claim that any efficient portfolio lacks the unquestionable benchmark character of the market portfolio. This is all the more true since the calculation of efficient portfolios raises several difficulties (*see* Chapter 5).

As we can see, performance measurement, otherwise quite well understood in its method, runs up against one fundamental problem: the choice of the reference portfolio to which the management of a fund may be compared. As a result of this problem, a whole new industry has come into being to calculate reference indices. Nowadays, under the influence of portfolio theory, the management objective of an investment fund is commonly set by giving it the mission of beating a certain index. And in order to reduce management costs, some funds, called 'index funds', even have as their mission only to *equal*, that is, to reproduce or imitate the behaviour of a given index.

We shall leave a few additional remarks on performance measurement until Chapter 5 (Section 5.2.3).

4.7 Conclusion

The CAPM is a relatively simple equilibrium model which bases capital allocation, between the various industrial activities of an economy, on the expected return and the variance of these activities, but also on the covariances between them. At equilibrium, it indicates the market values of the various activities, whether these are in elastic or inelastic supply, or – which amounts to the same thing – it indicates the required return on each according to its risk.

Amongst the possible applications of the CAPM, the most developed is the measurement of portfolio managers' performance, which is done today on the basis of a reference portfolio or a reference index. A recent trend (Section 4.6) leads us to use as a reference portfolio an efficient portfolio calculated *ex post*. This has the advantage that the measurement no longer depends on the validity or non-validity of the CAPM.

Two other possible applications of the CAPM have been studied. The first is the *ex ante* identification of over- or under-valued securities; this runs up against some problems of logical consistency. The second is the choice of investment projects in an uncertain world; although this may be by far the most important potential application for the real world, methods of implementation in industry remain to be specified.

The following chapter is devoted to a critique and evaluation of this model which remains, despite everything, a conceptual basis for modern finance.

Appendix

Justification of Jensen's α

We shall show below that, if a managed portfolio p is efficient, whereas the market portfolio is not, we have: $\alpha_p > 0$, which means, for a sufficiently large sample: $E[\alpha_p] > 0$, if the estimator of α is unbiased.

In the presence of a risk-free asset, the managed portfolio being efficient, $\theta > 0$ such that:

$$E[R_i] - r = \theta \operatorname{cov}[R_i, R_p] \text{ for all } i$$

and therefore, by combination:

$$E[R_p] - r = \theta \operatorname{var}[R_p]$$

and:

$$E[R_m] - r = \theta \operatorname{cov}[R_m, R_p]$$

By definition:

$$\alpha_p = E[R_p] - r - \{E[R_m] - r\} \cdot \operatorname{cov}[R_p, R_m] / \operatorname{var}[R_m]$$

Therefore:

$$\alpha_p = \theta \operatorname{var}[R_p] - \theta \{\operatorname{cov}[R_p, R_m]\}^2 / \operatorname{var}[R_m]$$
$$= \theta \operatorname{var}[R_p]\{1 - [\operatorname{corr}[R_p, R_m]]^2\}$$

where $\operatorname{corr}[R_p, R_m]$ is the correlation between the managed portfolio and the market portfolio. If the latter does not equal 1, we do indeed have $\alpha_p > 0$.

Notes to Chapter 4

1   The capitalization of a market is the total value of this market, namely, the total number of securities in circulation multiplied by the price of each security. By the same token, we call capitalization of a particular security the number of shares of this security multiplied by the price quoted.

2   *See*, for example, [Sharpe 1964, 1970].

3   *See* Section 3.4.2.

4   *See* the interpretation given of θ in Section 3.3.

5   A demonstration of the theorem using algebra would have allowed us to check that the $1/\theta$ of the market is the average of the $1/\theta$ of the individual investors, weighted by the wealth of each one. The most well-off investors have the greatest weight in the determination of the risk premium required by the securities. The algebraic proof would start from Appendix 3.1, where we calculated the composition of the portfolio of each investor (this is linear in $1/\theta$). We simply write that the average of the compositions of all these portfolios, weighted by the wealth of each person, is identical to the composition of the market portfolio.

6   *See* two example solutions in Section 4.2.

7   In definition 1.5, the dimension of the covariance is $(\%)^2$ or 10^{-4}. It is the same for the variance. Their ratio is thus dimensionless.

8   Where the variables R_i and R_m have a bivariate normal distribution, the isoprobability curves are elliptical and the conditional expectation, $E[R_i|R_m]$, is a linear function of R_m. This is shown in Figure 2.

9   We say that a production process exhibits constant returns to scale if doubling input, all other things being equal, has the effect of doubling output in all states of nature.

10   [Ingersoll 1987] speaks of 'discretionary investment'. Exchange which takes place between investors and firms can be expressed more precisely: investment is made over a period of time [0, 1]. At date 0, the investors, knowing the firms' production possibilities, make up their portfolios and put their physical resources into the various firms. At date 1, the firms' output is produced; it is distributed, in the form of cash dividends, to the investors who consume it.

11   Or infinitely elastic demand for funds (or capital).

12   Another way of formulating the problem would have been to adopt the average risk aversion, θ, of the investors and deduce from this the relative values of V_1/V_2 as well as the risk-free rate of interest.

13   The intermediate case in which investment incurs adjustment costs was considered by [Huffman 1985].

14   The optimum behaviour of a speculator having a different risk aversion could be explored as an exercise.

15   The investor is only in a position to draw such a precise conclusion if he knows that the risk aversion of the market is equal to 3.66. This is rarely the case in practice. On the other hand, the diagnosis of over-or under-valuation by non-alignment of the points, which we carried out above, requires no such knowledge.

16   Remember that risk-free rates are used only for lending and borrowing between investors. Overall, they invest nothing in the risk-free security, and the available capital is thus divided exclusively between the two firms.

17   If the new equilibrium, consistent with the anticipations of Table 4.3, produced a negative value of x or one greater than 1, the firm which became unprofitable would have to close down.

18   ...less, where applicable, the financial fees for borrowing at the rate of 8%.

Note: The new interest rate of 9.41% does not affect the speculator in question.

19   This is a matter of relative appreciation and depreciation (that is, of one security relative to the other), leaving aside any possible variation in market capitalization, as this aspect is outside the scope of the present theory as we have presented it here.

20   *Cf* [Tirole 1982].

21   Calculated from the data in Table 4.3

22   That is, according to the expectation-variance norm.

23   *See* the proof in the appendix. It is also assumed that portfolios p and m are not perfectly correlated.

24   *See* the critique of Jensen's α in Section 5.4.6.

25   For the purposes of this numerical illustration, we assume a rate of interest remaining equal to 8%, and put ourselves in the case where the speculator holds the diversified portfolio [3.2].

26   That is, for two unchanged probability distributions, one corresponding to the (correct) anticipations of the manager, the other to those of the market.

27   Conversely, if m is efficient with regard to the empirical distribution, $\alpha_p = 0$, whatever the composition of p.

28   As it does not require the data for the manager's relative risk aversion.

29   Sharpe's ratio (as opposed to Jensen's measure α) is only applicable when there is a risk-free asset.

30   Or, purely by coincidence, correctly valued.

31   It was with the idea of solving this problem that [Breeden 1989] attempted to apply the 'consumption CAPM' developed by himself ([Breeden 1979]) to the choice of investment.

32   Of the data in this table, it is determining the correlations of the project with the existing securities which presents the most difficulties in practice.

33   **Reminder:** 11.66% is the expected return on the market portfolio.

34   Imagine, for example, that the project is taken on by firm 1. Let us specify that the expected future flow of this firm, apart from the project, is 1000 ECU, and bear in mind that the expected rate of return of this firm is 10%. At the end of the period, it will produce an average rate of return of:

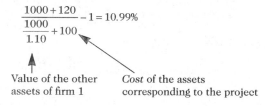

$$\frac{1000+120}{\dfrac{1000}{1.10}+100}-1=10.99\%$$

Value of the other   *Cost* of the assets
assets of firm 1   corresponding to the project

whereas the rate of return required from it is a weighted average of the rate of return required of the project (11.11%) and that required of the other assets (10%), which gives:

$$\frac{1000+120}{\dfrac{1000}{1.10}+108}-1=10.12\%$$

Market value of the assets corresponding to the project

The Jensen's α resulting from the adoption of the project will be equal to:
$\alpha = 10.99\% - 10.12\% = 0.87\% > 0$.

35   *See* [Grinblatt and Titman 1989]

36   As early as 1966, Treynor and Mazuy suggested a method of measuring this aspect of a manager's expertise. They pointed out that a manager applying such a strategy generates a *non-linear* random relationship (of positive curvature) between the rate of return on his portfolio and the market rate of return. The validity of this point will be more apparent after examining Figure 4.8.

37   $E(R_m) = p_1 \cdot R_1 + p_2 \cdot R_2$, where p_1 and p_2 are the probabilities of receiving one signal or the other. More generally, $E(R_m)$ would be the unconditional expectation of the reference portfolio and R_1 and R_2 the expectations conditioned by the two signals.

38   That is to say, the average of the probability distributions conditioned by the different possible values of the signals, weighted by the probabilities that the signals will take these different values (see Section 1.1.5).

39   This is the portfolio whose rate of return appears on the right-hand side of Equation 4.1, defining α.

References

[Admati and Ross 1985]   A. Admati and S. Ross, Measuring Investment Performance in a Rational Expecta-
tions Equilibrium Model, *Journal of Business*,
58, 1985, 1–26.

[Breeden 1979]   D. T. Breeden, An Intertemporal Asset
Pricing Model with Stochastic Consumption
and Investment Opportunities, *Journal of
Financial Economics*,7 1979, 265–296.

[Breeden 1989]   D. T. Breeden, Capital Budgeting with Con-
sumption, Working Paper, Duke University,
June 25, 1989, article présenté aux Journées
Internationales de l'AFFI, Université Paris-
Dauphine, June 1989.

[Dybvig and Ross 1985]   P. Dybvig and S. Ross, Differential Information and Performance Measurement Using a
Security Market Line, *Journal of Finance*,
40, 1985, 383–399.

[Grinblatt and Titman 1987]   M. Grinblatt and S. Titman, The Relation
Between Mean-Variance Efficiency and
Arbitrage Pricing, *Journal of Business*, 60,
1987, 97–112.

[Grinblatt and Titman 1989]   M. Grinblatt and S. Titman, Portfolio Performance Evaluation: Old Issues and New
Insights, *The Review of Financial Studies*,
2, 1989, 393–421.

[Huffman 1985]   G. W. Huffman, Adjustment Costs and Capital Asset Pricing, *Journal of Finance*, 40, 3,
1985, 691–705.

[Ingersoll 1987]   J. Ingersoll, *Theory of Financial Decision
Making*. Rowman & Littlefield, 1987.

[Jensen 1968]   M. Jensen, The Performance of Mutual Funds
in the Period 1945-1964, *Journal of Finance*,
23, 1968, 389–416.

[Jensen 1972]   M. Jensen, Optimal Utilisation of Market
                                 Forecasts and the Evaluation of Investment
                                 Portfolio Performance, in Szego and Shell,
                                 eds., *Mathematical Methods in Investment
                                 and Finance*. Amsterdam: North-Holland,
                                 1972.

[Lintner 1965]   J. Lintner, The Valuation of Risk Assets and
                                 the Selection of Risky Investments in Stock
                                 Portfolios and Capital Budgets, *Review of
                                 Economics and Statistics*, 47, 1965, 13–37.

[Mayers and Rice 1973]   D. Mayers and E. Rice, Measuring Portfolio
                                 Performance and the Empirical Content of
                                 Asset Pricing Models, *Journal of Financial
                                 Economics*, 7, 1979, 3–29.

[Mossin 1966]   J. Mossin, Equilibrium in a Capital Asset
                                 Market, *Econometrica*, 34, 1966, 768–783.

[Roll 1977]   R. Roll, A Critique of the Asset Pricing
                                 Theory's Tests; Part I: On Past and Potential
                                 Testability of the Theory, *Journal of Finan-
                                 cial Economics*, 4, 1977, 129–176.

[Roll 1978]   R. Roll, Ambiguity When Performance is
                                 Measured by the Securities Market Line,
                                 Journal of Finance, 33, 1978, 1051–1069.

[Roll 1979]   R. Roll, A Reply to Mayers and Rice,
                                 Journal of Financial Economics, 7, 1979,
                                 391–400.

[Rubinstein 1973]   M. Rubinstein, A Comparative Statics Ana-
                                 lysis of Risk Premiums, *Journal of Business*,
                                 46, 1973, 605–615.

[Sharpe 1964]   W. F. Sharpe, Capital Asset Prices: A Theory
                                 of Market Equilibrium under Conditions of
                                 Risk, *Journal of Finance*, 19, 1964, 425–442.

[Sharpe 1966]   W. F. Sharpe, Mutual Fund Performance,
                                 Journal of Business, 39, 1966, 119–138.

[Sharpe 1970]   W. F. Sharpe, *Portfolio Theory and Capital
                                 Markets*. New York: McGraw Hill, 1970.

[Tirole 1982]   J. Tirole, On the Possibility of Speculation under Rational Expectations, *Econometrica*, 50, 1982, 1163–1182.

[Treynor 1963]   J. Treynor, 1963, Memorandum

[Treynor 1965]   J. Treynor, How to Rate the Management of Investment Funds, *Harvard Business Review*, 43, 1965, 63–75.

[Treynor and Mazuy 1966] J. Treynor and F. Mazuy, Can Mutual Funds Outguess the Market?, *Harvard Business Review*, 44, 1966, 131–136.

5

Critique and evaluation of the CAPM

Assuming the financial market to be efficient, (that is, not systematically mistaken about the information it receives),[1] the joint probability distribution of the returns on all the securities is equal to the distribution observed empirically. In particular, the expected return required from each security may be estimated using the average realized return. This is true for each security as well as for the market portfolio.

According to the CAPM, the average market rate of return (over and above the risk-free rate) multiplied by the beta of a security gives a second estimator of the expected return required from this security.

If the data originating from the stock market were arbitrary, these two methods of calculating the expected return on a security would produce results which bore no relation to one another. But, if the theory of portfolio choices is correct, the data are not arbitrary. The CAPM forces them to conform to a *restriction*; the two values of the expected return must be equal. Thus the two estimators of this expectation which correspond to them must not be significantly different from each other.

Verifying the CAPM empirically means determining whether the restriction imposed by the CAPM is or is not rejected by a statistical test.

There have been so many tests of the CAPM that it is impossible to give a comprehensive summary of them here. In this chapter, we set out merely to raise a certain number of questions of method which will place a limit on the operational content of this model. In Section 5.1, we touch on the 'static' nature of the CAPM, which conflicts with the fluctuating nature of the financial market. In Section 5.2, we address a 'philosophical' question: does the econometrician possess the data and the means necessary to test the CAPM? The fluctuations of the market parameters must be modelled in order to implement the test; this is the subject of Section 5.3. In Section 5.4, we describe two ways of testing and briefly show what results they have given. Section 5.5 gives a few examples of deviations from the model.

5.1 The static nature of the CAPM

5.1.1 Single-period versus multi-period models

The investor we considered in Chapters 3 and 4 was concerned with the expected value and the variance of the rate of return which his portfolio would produce during a single investment period. His investment horizon was therefore very short: we could say that this investor was 'short-sighted'.

An individual's investment horizon is dictated by a parameter which we have not yet mentioned. This parameter, which could be called the degree of psychological impatience, measures investors' intertemporal preferences. The more impatient individuals are to consume, the shorter their investment horizon; the more patient they are, the longer their horizon.

Investors, taking into account the fact that throughout their life they will need to produce an investment revenue allowing them to consume, will normally have a long investment horizon. We do not mean by this that they will deprive themselves of freedom to manoeuvre by keeping their securities for longer. Just like investors with short horizons, they will keep the option of adjusting their portfolio at any time but, in contrast to them, they will plan their investments over several periods. They will not be content, therefore, with examining the rate of return and risk relating to the immediate period. They will also be concerned with the *reinvestment risk*. By taking their investment decision today, they will view the consequences of this investment at the end of a period, not only in terms of return, or of increasing wealth, but also with regard to the later use which could be made of the wealth accumulated (consumption and reinvestment).

To illustrate the concept of reinvestment risk, let us compare two debenture securities: one with close maturity, only one period away (a short-term asset) the other with a distant maturity (a long-term asset). The immediate risk of the long security is greater than that of the short security, as its price will fluctuate in accordance with fluctuations in market rates, whereas the immediate return on the short security is assured.[2] But the short security exposes its holder to more reinvestment risk. Once the certain return from the first period has been pocketed, holders of the short security must reinvest their money; they will do this at a market rate which will have shifted. On the second investment period, the new short rate will be riskless; but, at the initial moment, this rate will be unknown and will therefore constitute a risk: the reinvestment risk of the short security.

In summary, the CAPM is based on an extremely short investment horizon (an arbitrarily short holding period), which cannot be justified. We say that the CAPM is a single-period model, or a *static model*.

5.1.2 IID versus non-IID rates of return: information or instrumental variables

There is a case in which the unjustifiable short-sightedness of the CAPM investor would not make any difference: the case where his decisions would be identical whatever his horizon. This is a situation in which the joint probability distribution of market rates of return repeats itself identically, period after period. The rates of return therefore have a constant distribution and the rates of return of one period of time are independent from the rates of return of all other periods (IID = *Independently, Identically Distributed*).

In this case, time passes by without any noticeable change occurring in the economic world. The stock exchange is a lottery where the draw may give different results from one period to the next, but the lottery is renewed identically period after period with no variation of the probabilities of gain and loss.[3]

[Rosenberg and Ohlson 1976] pointed out that the IID hypothesis is untenable, since it leads to a conclusion which is obviously in conflict with reality. Let us imagine for a moment that we are in an IID world: at the start of every period, investors face the same choices and therefore make the same decisions. They always assign the same proportions of their wealth to the various financial securities,[4] so that at market level, the market capitalizations of all the securities all fluctuate proportionally to one another, the only source of fluctuation – common to all securities – being the overall wealth of the investors, which may find itself diminished by a poor year or suddenly increased by a good year. Thus, between two successive instants, the appreciations or depreciations of the various securities will all be perfectly correlated, which is obviously far from what we see on a daily basis.

At any rate, direct observation of market rates of return suggests that these are probably not IID.[5] It will therefore be necessary to model variations over time in the joint probability distribution of the returns on securities. This may develop in relation to previous actual returns or in relation to certain variables which are not themselves returns, but which it may be useful to know in forecasting future rates of return.

In the case where past returns have an influence on the probabilities of future returns, we speak of the serial dependence of rates of return. It may be, for example, that high actual returns increase the probability of low returns later on: the serial correlation is therefore negative. In the long term, there is a tendency to revert to an average level of return.

When variables, past realizations of returns, or variables other than rates of return may help to forecast rates of return, we call them information variables, or 'instrumental variables' in the parlance of econometricians. They do not enter directly into the statement of the CAPM, but influence the values, variable over time, of the terms of the CAPM equation. All the variables currently used by financial analysts in their attempts to guess the future fall into this category: money supply, political deadlines, term structure of interest rates, and so on. In Section 5.3.3, we list the instrumental variables which have been used by researchers.

The concepts of conditional probability and conditional moment, which were introduced in Chapter 1, give us the means to express mathematically the relationship which exists between rates of return and instrumental variables. For example, at instant $t - 1$, the investor will be interested in the expected return, R_t, of a security over the period of time $[t - 1, t]$ given the value at instant $t - 1$ of an information variable z: $E(R_t \mid z_{t-1})$, which is often abridged to $E_{t-1}(R_t)$. This quantity, remember, is a function of z_{t-1}.

The form of this function (linear, quadratic, exponential?) depends on the joint probability distribution of R and z. In the case where R and z obey a normal bivariate law, we can show that the relationship is linear:

$$E(R_t \mid z_{t-1}) = a + bz_{t-1} \qquad [1.1]$$

Researchers will often postulate a linear relationship of this form *ab initio* for the first moments of rates of return.

Even if the time series of observed market returns violate the IID hypothesis, making the investor's short-sighted behaviour less plausible, it is not impossible to view the one-period CAPM as an approximation of reality. It is entirely possible that the investors' more or less distant horizon has an effect on the equilibrium of the stock market which is quantitatively negligible. We may well attempt to determine whether a model is verified or invalidated by the data, even though we know by analysis that it contains some theoretical flaws. A model must not be judged on its hypotheses but on its capacity to account for certain observations. But we must at least take proper account of the non-IID nature of the data.

5.1.3 Conditional and unconditional CAPM

If the IID hypothesis is violated, we must understand the CAPM as a relationship between conditional moments.[6] If the probability distribution of market returns develops over time in more or less close harmony with certain economic variables or with their past realizations (serial dependence), it is inconceivable that investors, when making their portfolio decisions, will not use the information they possess about these variables or about past rates of return. These information variables or 'instrumental variables' must therefore play a role in the formulation of the model.

To understand the role which they must play, let us re-examine the investor's portfolio choice, which was described in Chapter 3. This choice was made from the moments (expected values, variances and covariances) of the rates of return on the various securities; we arrived at a first-order condition Equation 3.3.7. Aggregating the various investors' first-order conditions in Chapter 4, we obtained the CAPM.

Now, if the rates of return are not IID, the expectations, variances and covariances vary over time in harmony with the instrumental variables. What the investor takes into account are the expected values, variances and conditional covariances, given the values of the instrumental variables. The CAPM must therefore be understood as follows:

At market equilibrium, two processes θ_t and μ_t exist such that:[7]

$$E_{t-1}(R_{i,t}) = \mu_{t-1} + \theta_{t-1}\,\mathrm{cov}_{t-1}(R_{i,t}, R_{m,t})\ \text{for all } i \qquad [1.2]$$

We have just stated the CAPM *in its conditional form*. There are as many possible conditional forms as there are conceivable sets of information variables. We therefore need to know what information the investors actually use. What is more, the functional form of the relationship established between the moments of rates of return and the information variables depends, as we have seen, on the probability laws which govern them. These laws are very difficult to clarify. In contrast, the *unconditional CAPM* would be obtained by postulating that investors do not use any information and assume that the rates of return are IID (consequently of fixed moments) over time.

Let us state again that, in theory, it makes no sense to think of a static, conditional CAPM in the presence of non-IID rates of return. A static CAPM may, nonetheless, be a correct approximation of reality, even if reality is dynamic. This is the point we consider in Sections 5.4 and 5.5 below.

5.2   Conceptual shortcomings of the CAPM

Before examining empirical tests of the CAPM, we should pause to consider whether such tests are feasible in the first place. Do econometricians actually possess the elements of information which will enable them to reach a conclusion? Two arguments have been put forward which suggest that the CAPM is not testable. By this we mean that a rejection of a statistical hypothesis on the basis of the available data cannot be interpreted as a conclusive rejection of the model itself. These two arguments were presented by [Roll 1977], and by [Hansen and Richard 1987] respectively.

5.2.1 Roll's critique

The reader will recall the benchmark role played by the market portfolio in the statement of the CAPM: from one security to the next, a linear relationship exists between return and risk, risk being measured by the covariance of each security (or its beta) with the market. A second statement, equivalent to the first, is that the market portfolio belongs to the set of efficient portfolios: it lies somewhere on the Markowitz frontier.[8]

When the CAPM is implemented, it is not a simple matter to observe the composition of the market portfolio. If we are considering a worldwide financial market, we must take into account all the world's assets – a vast project indeed! Some day, we may well be able to draw up a complete list of quoted securities.[9] But some assets, such as gold, are held in secret. The majority of assets held by investors worldwide are not listed in an exchange: real estate, and, above all, human capital.[10] Future taxes which investors will have to pay (this is a liability which must be given a negative weighting in the composition of the market portfolio) will need to be taken into account, but they are in fact in return for the public services which citizens receive free of charge. Even amongst traded securities, many raise unresolved conceptual problems: bonds issued by firms must obviously be included in the market portfolio, but government bonds will be reimbursed by the government from fiscal revenues; if we cannot include investors' fiscal debts in the liabilities of the market portfolio, perhaps it is better to avoid including amongst the assets their claims on the government. Last but not least, how do we value and take account of the liquid assets which investors hold in order to carry out transactions? The monetary base is a claim on the government, of which we have just spoken. Money provides liquidity services; must we include in the portfolio held by the set of investors the value of future liquidity services which will be supplied by the monetary base?

In practice, users of the CAPM have used as the rate of return on the market portfolio the return on a stock index. They have turned equally to the NYSE, the Dow Jones index, or one of the Standard & Poors indices, where the USA is concerned, and the CAC or INSEE index in France. For any given country, the choice of reference portfolio need not be important, since they are all very highly correlated. Does this mean that an imperfect measure of the market portfolio gives us at least an approximately correct CAPM?

[Roll 1977] gives a negative reply to this question. Unfortunately, the high correlation between the indices does not imply that it is immaterial which one is used.[11] Quoting one of the first empirical tests of the CAPM by [Black *et al.* 1972], which led them to reject the CAPM, he observes that with the same data we could have formulated *de novo* (and *a posteriori*[12]) a market index other than the one used, which would have led to an exact verification of the CAPM and would have given a rate of correlation with the index used of 0.895. So a test of the CAPM only has a well-defined meaning if we know exactly the composition of the market portfolio. It is not sufficient to find an approximate portfolio which is highly correlated with the true market portfolio.

As we have seen, we do not know the true market portfolio exactly: far from it. The measurement benchmark on which the very significance of the CAPM rests is itself unmeasurable.

5.2.2 Hansen and Richard's critique

Given that market rates of return are not IID, investors most certainly use the information at their disposal to forecast future rates of return. This means that only a conditional CAPM is justified. Obviously, the set of data at each investor's disposal is vast and unobserved; the econometrician therefore measures, and uses as instrumental variables, a reduced set of information variables. Having rejected the tested statistical hypothesis, is he entitled to conclude that the model must be rejected?[13]

[Hansen and Richard 1987] answer this question in the negative. They point out that a portfolio – a market portfolio or another portfolio of variable composition – which, amongst all the conceivable investment strategies, is conditionally efficient with respect to a wide set of information, is not necessarily conditionally efficient with respect to a restricted set of information.

To justify this finding by Hansen and Richard, let us consider a set of financial securities. Let us enrich this set of securities by adding to it all the 'active' strategies, or managed portfolios whose composition is variable over time although not based on any foresight, but simply on the information available to the investor at each instant.[14] Amongst these portfolios, some will be conditionally efficient; they will always lie on the time-varying Markowitz frontier constructed from the conditional moments. Next, let us obtain the unconditional moments of the rates of return of all the portfolios and construct the unconditional Markowitz frontier. The conditionally efficient portfolios have no reason to lie exactly on the unconditional frontier; many of them are unconditionally inefficient.[15]

It would take too long here to give explicit examples of conditionally efficient strategies which are not unconditionally efficient, but it would not be at all difficult to find some. We understand intuitively that active strategies generate an increased risk from the vantage point of an individual who does not have the information on which they are based, and cannot therefore take them into account when investigating their efficiency. A ship's captain who manoeuvres to avoid obstacles, static or mobile, may give a distant observer the impression that the ship is following a nonsensical random course.

Thus, the market portfolio may very well belong to the set of conditionally efficient portfolios in relation to the wide set of information without being conditionally efficient in relation to the restricted set. The theory in no way states that the market portfolio is efficient in relation to the restricted set of information to which the econometrician has access. Therefore, if the restricted hypothesis is rejected, this does not permit the 'true' conditional CAPM to be rejected.

5.2.3   A digression on performance measurement

The distinction between conditionally and unconditionally efficient portfolios gives us an opportunity to make a brief digression, extending the discussion in Chapter 4 about the measurement of portfolio managers' performance and Jensen's α (Sections 4.4 and 4.6). There, the discussion was expressed entirely in terms of unconditional efficiency and we implicitly assumed that the rates of return were IID. We may now refine that discussion.

We considered the case of a portfolio manager who knew the true probability distribution of the returns, whilst the market followed a different distribution. We showed that, if this manager held a portfolio which was efficient with regard to the true distribution, he had to produce a posteriori a positive Jensen's α.

If the rates of return are not IID, the conclusion is less clear. Indeed it is likely that the individual carrying out the performance measurement (who may be the bearer of shares in a unit trust or a mutual fund) does not possess the information which the manager possesses. He or she therefore calculates an unconditional α. The managed portfolio, which is efficient with respect to the information used by the manager, is not generally unconditionally efficient. Therefore the α calculated has no reason to be positive, even though the manager has managed the portfolio correctly (perhaps even very well).[16] To save themselves from the trouble which can occur during performance evaluation, portfolio managers would be well advised to choose, from all the portfolios they regard as conditionally efficient, those which are also unconditionally efficient.

We also observed in Chapter 4 that an $\alpha > 0$ may very well result from a situation where neither the market nor the managed portfolio is efficient. This observation applies especially where the rates of return are not IID. Since, in general, neither the managed portfolio nor the market portfolio is unconditionally efficient, we may well obtain a positive unconditional α even though the portfolio is badly managed (conditionally inefficient).

5.3   Stability of the components of the CAPM

In this section, we attempt to find out whether the moments of the returns on securities are stable over time. We wish to know, in particular, whether the moments which appear in the actual expression of the CAPM, namely the betas (or the covariances) and the expected returns, vary. More precisely, what is the nature of their variations? These may be purely the result of chance, or they may be systematic, as when one month's returns are linked to past realizations (Sections 5.3.1 and 5.3.2) or to other economic variables (Section 5.3.3). This information will condition the form of the statistical model which we shall implement in testing the CAPM (Section 5.4).

5.3.1   Stability of the betas

In an early study, [Sharpe and Cooper 1972] attempted to show that the betas were stable, but it seems that their own results may be turned against them. Using the monthly returns from the period 1937–1967, divided into six subperiods of five years, they sorted the securities of the NYSE into ten classes of risk (class no. 1 containing low beta securities, and class no. 10 high beta securities). The beta of each security having been calculated over five years of monthly observations, the security was assigned to a class and its moves from one class to another between the five-year periods were observed.[17] Table 5.1 shows the average proportion of securities in each class which remain in the same class (Column 1), and the proportion of securities which remain in the same class or in an adjacent class (Column 3). Columns 2 and 4 serve as a reference and give those proportions, as they would have been if the betas of two successive subperiods had been totally independent of one another. The comparison of Columns 1 and 2 on the one hand and 3 and 4 on the other appears to prove Sharpe and Cooper right: the successive betas of a security are not totally independent of one another. But, if we also compare the percentages measured with what they would have been in the event of perfect stability, namely 100%, it will be noted that the reality is 'closer' to the hypothesis of total independence than to the hypothesis of total stability. [18]

Class	Proportion of securities which are in the same class five years later (%)		Proportion of securities which are in the same class or move into an adjacent class (%)	
	Observed proportion	Hypothetical proportion*	Observed proportion	Hypothetical proportion
10	32.2	10.	69.3	20.
9	18.4	10.	57.3	30.
8	16.4	10.	45.3	30.
7	13.3	10.	40.9	30.
6	13.9	10.	39.4	30.
5	13.6	10.	41.7	30.
4	13.2	10.	40.2	30.
3	15.9	10.	44.6	30.
2	21.5	10.	60.9	30.
1	40.5	10.	62.3	20.

*This is the proportion as it would be if the successive betas of a security were completely independent of one another. On the other hand, in the case of perfect stability, the proportion of securities remaining in the same class is 100%.

Table 5.1   The degree of stability of the beta coefficients. *Source:* [Sharpe and Cooper 1972]

To give the reader an idea of the severity of the statistical problem facing researchers, it is useful to quote some figures. Let us examine, for example, the work of Fama and MacBeth,[19] which for a long time has been the authority on this subject and to which we return in Section 5.4.5 below. These authors estimated the beta coefficients of twenty portfolios made up from several hundred shares quoted on the NYSE (from 400 to 800 depending on the periods),[20] between 1930 and 1966. The betas of the portfolios are spread out between approximately 0.3 and 1.6, and are estimated over five years of monthly rates of return (sixty observations for each portfolio). The standard deviation (measuring the uncertainty over the estimate) of these betas is in the order of 0.03. If, following tradition, we consider a confidence interval equal to plus or minus two standard deviations, we arrive at a margin of imprecision on a *portfolio* beta equal to ±0.06. Taking into account the size of the portfolios and the degree of interdependence between the securities within a portfolio, Fama and MacBeth also show that the uncertainty of estimation on the beta of a share taken individually would be three to seven times as large, which implies a margin of imprecision on a beta *of an individual security* of approximately ±0.18 or ±0.42. So monitoring a security every month for five years in no way enables its beta to be calculated precisely.

The studies which we have just quoted aimed only to quantify the degree of variation of the betas. A more recent study by [Collins *et al.* 1987] examines the particular question which interests us:[21] are these variations the result of chance (sampling variations due to the randomness of the returns or randomness in the betas) or are they systematic? Of course, we cannot ask whether they are systematic in general; we must, for the purposes of this analysis, specify the systematic behaviour of which we are speaking. Collins *et al.*, like Sharpe and Cooper, chose to research autoregressive systematic behaviour: to what extent do the betas of a period depend on the betas of recent previous periods? Collins *et al.*[22] estimate the following statistical model for the betas of the securities:

$$\beta_t = \bar{\beta} + \varepsilon_t + \delta_t \qquad [3.1]$$

where

$$\delta_t = \Phi\delta_{t-1} + d_t \qquad [3.2]$$

$\{\varepsilon_t\}$ and $\{\delta_t\}$ being two series of IID random variables with zero mean and variances equal to σ_ε^2 and σ_d^2. $\bar{\beta}$ represents the long-term mean of beta; the first random term of [3.1] represents the IID (transitory) random fluctuations of beta and the second the autocorrelated variations (that is, those which depend on past realizations) which persist some time after a shock. This model breaks down the total variance of beta, VARTOT = $V(\beta_t)$ into two components:

$$
\begin{aligned}
\text{VARTOT} &= \text{VARRAN} + \text{VARSEQ} \\
V(\beta_t) &= V(\varepsilon_t) + V(\delta_t) \\
&= \sigma_\varepsilon^2 + \sigma_d^2 / (1 - \Phi^2)
\end{aligned}
\qquad [3.3]
$$

The first term, VARRAN = σ_ε^2, measures the purely random variability (not serially correlated and therefore transitory); the second, VARSEQ = $\sigma_d^2/(1-\Phi^2)$, measures the 'sequential' or serial (correlated) component of the variability of beta.

In the study by Collins *et al.*, the model [3.1, 3.2] was adjusted to data from weekly returns, covering individual securities as well as portfolios. The sample contained 500 securities chosen at random and 500 portfolios containing 10, 50 or 100 securities made up at random, from securities quoted on the New York Stock Exchange and the American Stock Exchange. For each security or portfolio, the parameters were estimated over 250 and 500 weeks selected at random during the period from July, 1962 to December, 1981. The return on the market portfolio calculated by the Center for Research in Securities Prices (CRSP) at the University of Chicago was used as an approximation of R_m in calculating the betas, with weightings corresponding with the market capitalizations.

We can summarize the results obtained by Collins *et al.* as follows. The ratio of the random variation to the sequential variation, VARRAN/VARSEQ, is approximately equal to 4:1 in the case of securities taken individually, and 3:1 in the case of portfolios containing 100 securities. Therefore, almost a quarter of the variability of the betas is of an autocorrelated, systematic nature. Since this autocorrelated variation affects portfolios almost as much as individual securities, we may conclude that it results from influences of a macroeconomic nature (for example, unexpected changes in the rate of inflation or a change in the rate of interest) which affect the majority of securities simultaneously. The tests of the hypothesis, covering 10 years (500 weeks) of observations make it reasonable to conclude that there is a statistically significant[23] autocorrelated variation for 10% of the individual securities, and 15%, 30% and 45% of the portfolios, depending on their size (10, 50 or 100 securities respectively).

5.3.2 Stability of expected returns for securities and the market; stability of the slope of the market line

Let us now examine the variations of two other constituent parameters of the CAPM: the intercept, μ in the notation of Chapter 4, which is the risk-free rate of return, and the slope of the postulated linear relationship, which, in the formulation of Equation 1.6 of Chapter 4, is the expected excess rate of return of the market.

Fama and MacBeth calculated these two figures every month, from 1935 to 1968, from the rates of return on twenty portfolios of securities on the NYSE. The intercept fluctuates considerably from one month to the next: it has a mean of 0.0061 (0.6% per month, which is significantly more than the rate of interest) with a standard deviation of 0.038. So over 402 months of observations, the average intercept of the CAPM has the following confidence interval:[24]

$$0.0061 \pm 0.0038$$

or:[25]

$$7.32 \pm 4.55\% \text{ per annum}$$

A similar calculation regarding the slope of the relationship produces:

$$10.20 \pm 7.90\% \text{ per annum}$$

To sum up, imagine we are dealing with a security whose true beta (which, of course is unknown) is equal to 1, and that we wish to know whether this security is above or below the line, perhaps with the aim of determining whether it is under- or over-valued.

The beta of this security, measured over sixty observations, will have a non-negligible probability of being 1.42 at one extreme or 0.58 at the other (*see* page 122), whereas a degree of uncertainty, which we have just quantified, affects the position of the line itself. So the annualized monthly average rate of return on the security may lie between:

$$7.32 - 4.55 + (10.20 - 7.90) \times 0.58 = 4.10\% \text{ per annum}$$

at the minimum, and:

$$7.32 + 4.55 + (10.20 + 7.90) \times 1.42 = 37.57\% \text{ per annum}$$

at the maximum without enabling us to conclude anything at all about the position of the security relative to the line.

In their well-known finance textbook, [Brealey and Myers 1982] put the results of Fama and MacBeth into the form of graphs which are reproduced in Figure 5.1. These show the average returns (on the y axis) and the estimated betas (on the x axis) of a set of portfolios.[26] Observe how much this estimated slope varies from one five-year period to the next.[27]

Recent research has shown that the variations in expected return which we have just mentioned are not random variations. [Fama and French 1988a] showed that these variations have a systematic character, especially where rates of return over long periods are concerned. The authors calculated the serial correlation of the weekly returns, then that of the monthly, quarterly, annual and pluriannual returns of a portfolio of stocks on the NYSE. We may sum up this work using Figure 5.2, taken from [Kandel and Stambaugh 1988]. This shows on the x axis the number of months the portfolio is held and on the y axis the autocorrelation of the corresponding rate of return, which measures the degree of serial dependence.[28]

It will be noted that the autocorrelation is positive over short periods (a few weeks), becoming negative in the longer term. The rates of return calculated over four or five years have an autocorrelation in the order of –0.5. Since $(0.5)^2 = 0.25$, knowing these past rates of return allows the uncertainty (variance) of the rates of return over four or five years to be reduced by 25%.[29]

In other words, market rates of return, especially long-term rates of return, can be forecast from their past realizations. High realized rates of return tend to be followed by low realized rates of return and vice versa.

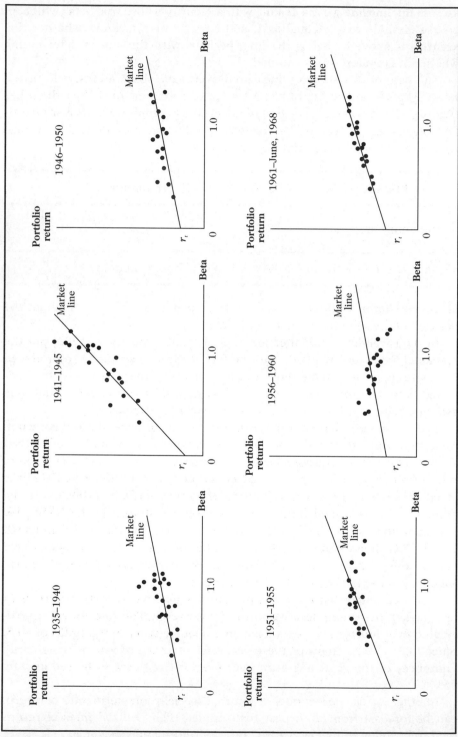

Figure 5.1 The fluctuations of the securities market line. *Source:* [Brealey and Myers 1982]

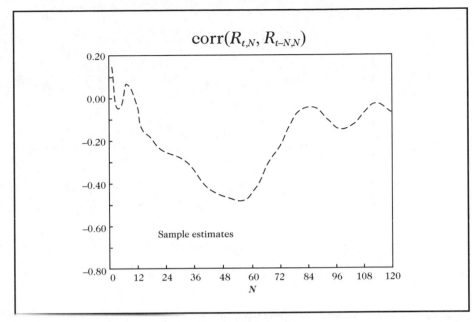

Figure 5.2   Estimated autocorrelation of market rates of return for holding periods of N months. The estimates are obtained by regressing the rate of return of N months of investment on its value lagged by N months. *Source:* [Kandel and Stambaugh 1988]

5.3.3 Instrumental variables used to specify the conditional CAPM

Some variables other than past realizations of returns can help in forecasting future rates of return. [Fama and French 1988b] showed, for example, that the dividend yield (dividend payment divided by price) had this property. This is obviously the dividend yield of a security or a portfolio, calculated at instant t, which is linked to the rate of return on the same security or portfolio over a later period $[t, t + N]$. A similar forecasting power has been attributed in various studies to the default risk premium on corporate bonds, compared to government bonds, and to the term premium (yield to maturity[30] of long-term bonds minus the yield of short-term securities on the money market).

Figure 5.3, also taken from [Kandel and Stambaugh 1988], sums up well the results of research undertaken in this field. The x axis, as in Figure 5.2, shows the duration in months of the holding period over which the rate of return is calculated, and the y axis shows the R^2 of a regression of the rate of return on the instrumental variables which were mentioned in the previous paragraph. The longer the period, the better these variables allow the later rate of return to be forecast. Over a period of four years, knowledge of past returns therefore allows the variance of the rates of return over four or five years to be reduced by 40%.[31]

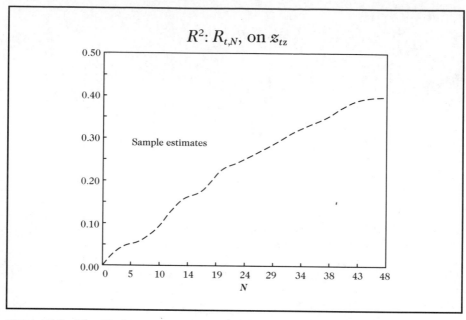

Figure 5.3   The R^2 obtained by regressing the actual returns produced during N months of holding the NYSE portfolio weighted uniformly on three forecasting variables, *viz.* the yield of the Baa bonds minus that of the Aaa bonds, the Aaa yield minus the rate of the Treasury Bills and the dividend yield of the shares. The successive observed rates of return correspond to overlapping periods.

Why do the variables shown have this power? It is impossible to respond seriously to this question without having available a model of the economy in general. Only a general equilibrium model could tell us the variables which may be thought, on a theoretical basis, to anticipate market rates of return.

The CAPM on its own may only be used as a fishing net. We may use it to try out various possible variables. This trial takes place in two steps. First, we check that a set of variables has forecasting power. Second, we test the CAPM conditioned by these variables. A rejection of the model may mean two things. Either the CAPM is false, or the set of variables used, although having forecasting power, is not the complete set used by investors.

5.4   Empirical tests of the CAPM

This is not the place to present the reader with the elements of econometric theory. Besides, the first empirical checks of the CAPM rely quite simply on multiple regression techniques; these are presented in Section 5.4.1. Modern empirical studies resort to two, more elaborate, statistical methods, and the reader will wish to know the basics of them: Gibbons' 'multivariate method' [Gibbons 1982] which relies on a hypothesis of normality of rates of return, and Hansen's 'Generalized Method of Moments', GMM [Hansen 1982], which is non-parametric, meaning that it does not require the probability distribution of the rates of return to be stipulated exactly.[32]

As we saw in Chapter 4, writing the linear relationship of the CAPM is equivalent to assuming that the market portfolio is efficient (or on the Markowitz frontier). We may therefore test either the linear relationship or the efficiency of the market portfolio. We explain below the method for testing the efficiency of the market portfolio by the multivariate method (Section 5.4.2) and the method for testing the linear relationship by the GMM method (Section 5.4.3). However, both the GMM and the multivariate method, may be used to test the hypothesis in either way: there are thus $2 \times 2 = 4$ possible procedures.

Section 5.4.4 provides a briefer description of some other methods aimed at solving particular problems.

There is no doubt that the results of the tests of the CAPM differ according to the methods and samples used. However, it is probably fair to say that most modern tests reject the CAPM. That is why empirical research has established an inventory of deviations from the model (Section 5.5) and theoretical research has adopted the aim of understanding the causes of the deviations and formulating more flexible models.

5.4.1 Early studies: the work of [Fama and MacBeth 1973]

As a general rule, the empirical studies carried out during the 1970s proceeded in two stages. The first stage involved calculating the betas of the individual securities or portfolios which were the subject of the study. This was done using a regression of the return on each security or portfolio on the market rate of return, a regression in which various observations were taken from successive periods (time series). In the second stage, the returns on the various securities over one period (cross-section) were regressed on their betas. A major problem appeared at this stage: since the measure of the betas was marred by measurement errors, the estimated slope of the regression in the second stage was biased downwards.[33] To reduce the size of this effect, the tests covered the CAPM applied not to individual securities but to portfolios of securities. We know that portfolio betas are more precisely estimated than those of individual securities. In order for the second-stage regression still to produce an accurate estimate of the relationship, the betas of the portfolios in question had to differ from each other as much as possible. Securities were therefore grouped into portfolios on the basis of the betas of the individual securities, the first portfolio containing the securities with the lowest betas, and so on up to the portfolio with a very high beta. The security betas, which were used for grouping, were calculated over periods preceding those used for measuring portfolio betas.

By way of an example, let us describe in more detail the already quoted work of [Fama and MacBeth 1973], which covered several hundred securities quoted on the NYSE (435 to 845 securities depending on the period) and monthly observations running from 1926 to 1968. This global list was divided into nine study cycles, each containing three subperiods of five years.

The eighth cycle, for example, ran from 1951 to 1966. The betas of individual securities were calculated for this cycle over the period 1951–1957 (some 84 months of observations for each security), and these were taken as the basis for obtaining the composition of the portfolio.[34] The betas of the portfolios thus formed were calculated *de novo* using the observations from the period 1958–1962 (some 60 months of observations). Finally, the cross-section regression allowing the portfolios to be compared with one another was done for each month in the period 1963–1966.

By this process, Fama and Macbeth obtained a cross-section regression for each month from January 1935 to June 1968, which represents a respectable number of observations of the intercept and slope of the linear relationship of the CAPM, allowing the hypotheses to be tested.

Since the study we have just described was carried out on the returns on shares, we may attempt to discover whether the intercept of the CAPM is significantly different from the risk-free rate, at the 5% threshold. To do this, we examine the sample of monthly observations and count the months when the estimated intercept is larger or smaller than the risk-free rate. Fama and MacBeth concluded that the intercept of the CAPM is significantly greater than the risk-free rate, which invalidates the model. The slope itself is significantly greater than zero, which is reassuring.

More recent studies by [Ferson and Harvey 1989] use a similar process to test a generalized CAPM, including several risk premiums.

The Fama–MacBeth method presents a serious weakness. Remeasuring the betas periodically is not a very reliable statistical method: if they move a great deal, they must be remeasured frequently. Fama and MacBeth update the betas once every five years. How can we tell whether this is often enough? A better method would involve modelling or taking account of the way in which a beta varies. We shall study this in Sections 5.4.3 and 5.4.4.2.

5.4.2 The multivariate method illustrated by the work of [Gibbons 1982] and [Gibbons *et al.* 1989]

Applying the statistical theory of maximum likelihood (Maximum Likelihood Estimation, MLE) [Gibbons *et al.* 1989], showed that Sharpe's ratio (*see* Section 4.4) could be used to design a test of the efficiency of the market portfolio. This method is easiest to describe in the simple case where rates of return are IID and where a risk-free asset exists. But its application is not limited to this case; in fact, in Section 5.4.2.2 we study the MLE estimate of a model in which the variance of the rates of return varies over time. One hypothesis is, however, indispensable: the rates of return on the various securities and on the various periods (as well as the instrumental variables, where applicable) must obey a multivariate normal law.

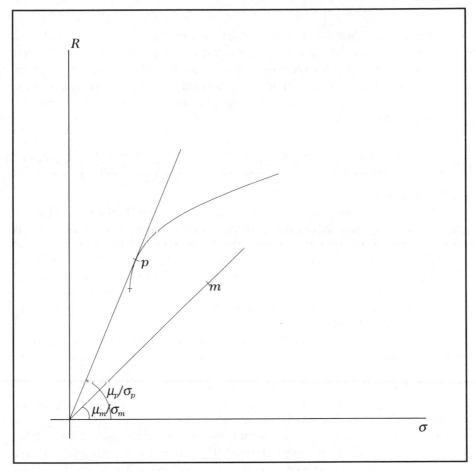

Figure 5.4   Comparing the performance of two portfolios

We proceed as follows to determine whether the market portfolio does or does not lie on the Markowitz frontier. The procedure is illustrated by Figure 5.4. On the basis of the observed returns on N securities, we construct the Markowitz frontier of the risky assets. Since a risk-free asset exists, the frontier is a tangent, at the point p, to the frontier of the risky assets (*see* Tobin's theorem in Chapter 3). The average return R_p and the standard deviation σ_p are both estimates from a sample of past rates of return. The slope of this tangent R_p/σ_p is Sharpe's ratio, or the return/risk ratio, of the *ex post* efficient portfolios. It is also easy to calculate Sharpe's ratio R_m/σ_m for the market portfolio.[35]

On the basis of a Maximum Likelihood line of reasoning, [Gibbons 1982] arrived at the following statistic:

$$T.ln\{[1 + (\bar{R}_p / \sigma_p)^2] / [1 + (\bar{R}_m / \sigma_m)^2]\} \tag{4.1}$$

where T is the number of observations in the time dimension. Gibbons showed that the statistic thus formulated has a probability distribution approaching the chi-squared distribution with $N - 1$ degrees of freedom, where the number of observations tends towards infinity. Under the hypothesis of normality [Gibbons *et al.* 1989] showed that, on a sample of finite size, a slightly different statistic, namely:

$$[1 + (\bar{R}_p/\sigma_p)^2] / [1 + (\bar{R}_m/\sigma_m)^2] - 1 \tag{4.2}$$

had an F distribution.

From its expression, it is clear that Statistic 4.1, or Statistic 4.2, has the aim of determining whether the return/risk ratio of the market portfolio is significantly smaller than that of the efficient portfolios. If the market portfolio is *ex ante* efficient, as claimed by portfolio theory, its ratio must be close to the ratio of the *ex post* efficient portfolios, and Statistic 4.1 or 4.2 must be close to zero, which leads us not to reject the null hypothesis.

What results did Gibbons, Ross and Shanken obtain by this method? In their study, the Markowitz frontier is not drawn directly from individual securities, but from portfolios made up earlier. In order to construct a frontier, it is necessary to have a number of observations in the time dimension at least equal to (and preferably much greater than) the number of securities plus two. The length of a given time series of returns therefore limits the number of investment lines in the calculation of the efficient portfolios.

Everything therefore depends on how the portfolios are composed. Gibbons, Ross and Shanken use the monthly returns of the period 1931–1965 and carry out three tests. In the first test, the portfolios, numbering ten, are made up of securities arranged in order of their beta. These do not reject the null hypothesis of market portfolio efficiency. In a second test, twelve portfolios group together the securities of twelve industrial sectors; these reject the null hypothesis. A third test leads them to group together the securities in order of their total market capitalization (the size of the issuing firm therefore dictates the groupings). These do not reject the null hypothesis.

5.4.3 The GMM illustrated by the work of [Harvey 1989]

The GMM (Generalized Method of Moments) is less powerful than the MLE method.[36] But, as we have said, it has the advantage over the MLE method of being 'non-parametric'.

To understand the GMM, we need to master two concepts: that of 'moment condition' and that of 'overidentifying restriction'.

The first of these can be illustrated using the traditional multiple regression applied to market rates of return. Consider a vector, z, of instrumental variables made up of the variables z_1, z_2, and so on. Let us start by formulating an equation for forecasting the rate of return on a security, of the type envisaged by Fama and French:

$$R_t = \delta_0 + \delta_1 z_{1,t-1} + \delta_2 z_{2,t-1} + .. u_t \qquad [4.3]$$

The aim here is to model the conditional expected return, R, of any security.[37] The $\delta.z$ terms in the right-hand side serve to forecast the rate of return R. We therefore desire that $E[R_t|z_{t-1}] = z_{t-1}.\delta$, and therefore that $E[u_t|z_{t-1}] = 0$.

In the context of the GMM, we do not generally use the whole force of this condition, but only an induced restriction which produces an unconditional expectation:[38]

$$E[u_t|z_{t-1}] = 0 \Rightarrow E[u_t \cdot z_{t-1} \mid z_{t-1}] = 0$$
$$\Rightarrow E[u_t \cdot z_{t-1}] = 0 \qquad [4.4]$$

Equation 4.4 is an example of a 'moment condition' which we shall impose, in the context of the GMM, to estimate the values of the parameters. Its meaning is as follows: if Equation 4.3 represents a forecast of rates of return, the unconditional expected value of the product of the forecasting error, u, and the instrumental variables, z, used for forecasting, must equal zero.[39]

Restriction 4.4 allows the δ coefficients of Equation 4.3 to be identified. From a sample of n observations $\{R_t, z_{t-1};\ t = 1, 2,...n\}$, the coefficients to be estimated may be obtained, for example, by solving the following system, which is the transcription of [4.4] and which contains as many equations as unknowns, δ:

$$\sum_{t=2}^{n} (R_t - \delta_0 - \delta_1 z_{1,t-1} - \delta_2 z_{2,t-1} ...)z_{j,t-1} = 0 \text{ for all j} \qquad [4.5]$$

Form 4.5 of Moment Condition 4.4 is identical to the moment conditions (called 'normal equations') of ordinary-least-squares multiple regression. System 4.4 is exactly identified: all equations of [4.4] may be satisfied on any sample of data.

It is in this sense that we may say that Regression 4.3 is purely descriptive and has no economic content at all. If it did, 'overidentifying restrictions' would exist which could be tested. Rejection of these conditions would mean rejecting the economic theory which they represented.

The CAPM is an example of an economic theory capable of creating over-identifying restrictions. As we shall see in the sections which follow, there are various ways of writing these restrictions, depending on the additional assumptions which are made. By way of an illustration, let us develop in detail one particular way of writing them. This illustration follows the work of [Harvey 1989].

Let us write the conditional CAPM, conditioned by the information variables z, taking account of [4.3]. The model states that the rate of return, $R_{i,t}$ on each security is such that:[40]

$$z_{t-1} \cdot \delta_i = \mu_{t-1} + \theta_{t-1} \cdot E[u_{i,t} \cdot u_{m,t} | z_{t-1}] \qquad [4.6]$$

for the μ and θ common to all the securities. Let us define the 'pricing' error affecting security i:

$$h_{i,t} = z_{t-1} \cdot \delta_i - \mu_{t-1} - \theta_{t-1} \cdot u_{i,t} \cdot u_{m,t} \qquad [4.7]$$

We may now rewrite [4.6] as

$$E[h_{i,t} | z_{t-1}] = 0 \qquad [4.8]$$

which leads to the unconditional restriction:

$$E[h_{i,t} z_{j,t-1}] = 0 \text{ for all } i \text{ and } j \qquad [4.9]$$

Restrictions [4.9] and [4.4] constitute the system of equations, or 'moment conditions', which, once applied to a sample of data (as was done in [4.5]), must be solved in order to obtain estimates of the set of parameters.

The behaviour of μ and θ over time remains to be modelled. When we consider, not the rates of return on the securities, but the excess returns (over and above the risk-free rate), it is often legitimate to write: $\mu \equiv 0$. The various implementations of the tests differ, amongst other things, as regards the modelling of θ – the market price of the covariance risk. For his part, Harvey assumed that $h_{m,t}$, defined as:

$$h_{m,t} = z_{t-1} \cdot \delta_m - \mu_{t-1} - \theta_{t-1} \cdot u_{m,t} \cdot u_{m,t} \qquad [4.10]$$

was exactly equal to zero, which allows us to substitute θ_{t-1} into each of the equations for the individual securities [4.7, 4.8, 4.9].

To the extent that the economic theory of the CAPM has a restrictive content, system [4.4, 4.9] is overidentified: it contains more conditions to satisfy than unknowns.[41] A compromise must therefore be established between the various equations which will in no case have a right-hand side reducing exactly to zero. The deviations must be incorporated into an objective function, and the values of the parameters are chosen so as to minimize this objective function. We minimize, for example, the sum of the squares of the deviations from the various equations. Thus, each has its deviation reduced as far as possible.

The GMM is slightly more elaborate than this (it is in this sense that it is a 'generalized' moment method): it weights the deviations of the various equations in order to give less weight to the deviations which have a greater variance.[42]

Econometricians ([Hansen 1982]) have demonstrated that the objective function thus formulated has a probability distribution approaching the chi-squared distribution[43] when the number of observations tends towards infinity. When the sample is sufficiently large, this result allows us to test hypotheses. In particular, the level of chi-squared indicates whether we must reject the overidentifying restrictions of the CAPM.

The GMM severely limits the number of securities which may be taken into account. We must therefore consider carrying out preliminary groupings of securities into portfolios. [Harvey 1989] studies ten portfolios, the preliminary grouping of the securities having been decided according to their capitalizations (size of the company). The observation period is September 1941 to December 1987, using securities on the NYSE. The instrumental variables (measured, it will be recalled, in $t - 1$ when forecasting the rates of return of the period $[t - 1, t]$) are as follows: a constant, the excess return on the market portfolio, a seasonal variable for the month of January,[44] a term structure premium (monthly return on a 90-day bill minus the rate of a 30-day bill), a default risk premium (yield to maturity of a BAA bond minus that of an AAA bond) and the dividend yield of the Standard & Poor's over and above the risk-free rate. In this test, Harvey rejects the overidentifying restrictions of the CAPM.

5.4.4 Other statistical models

5.4.4.1   Constant beta and latent variable: the solution to Roll's problem?

A statistical model known as the 'latent variable' model was first used by [Hansen and Hodrick 1983], on foreign exchange data, and [Gibbons and Ferson 1985], on stock market data. To explain this model, let us take as a starting point the CAPM equation in its conditional form:

$$E_{t-1}(R_i) = r_{t-1} + \theta_{t-1} \, \text{cov}_{t-1} \, (R_i, R_m) \qquad [4.11]$$

The aim of the method is to test this relationship by allowing the conditional expectations to move with time where the market portfolio, m, is not observable. Let us use a portfolio, p, to interpret θ:

$$E_{t-1}(R_i) - r_{t-1} = [E_{t-1}(R_p) - r_{t-1}] \cdot \beta_i \qquad [4.12]$$

where: $\beta_i = \text{cov}(R_i, R_m)/\text{cov}(R_p, R_m)$. In this method, the β_i are assumed constant over time. Under these conditions, Equation 4.12 means that the variations with time of the expected excess returns on all the securities have one factor in common, namely $E_{t-1}(R_p) - r_{t-1}$. The problem is therefore to determine empirically whether one common factor accounts for all the excess expected returns.

To this end, let us postulate that the excess return on portfolio p is linked linearly to a certain number of instrumental variables, z:

$$R_{p,t} - r_{t-1} = \Sigma_j \delta_j \cdot z_{j,t-1} + u_t \qquad [4.13]$$

with the restriction:

$$E(u|z) = 0 \qquad [4.14]$$

which implies:

$$E(u \cdot z) = 0 \qquad [4.15]$$

By substituting [4.13] into [4.12], we obtain:

$$E(h|z) = 0 \qquad\qquad\qquad\qquad [4.16]$$

where the vector h is defined by:

$$R_{i,t} - r_{t-1} = \beta_i \cdot [\Sigma_j \delta_j \cdot z_{j,t-1}] + (u_t \cdot \beta_i + h_{i,t}) \qquad\qquad [4.17]$$

Equation 4.16 implies that:

$$E(h_i \cdot z) = 0 \qquad\qquad\qquad\qquad [4.18]$$

Equations 4.15 and 4.18 put together have the obvious consequence that:

$$E[(u \cdot \beta_i + h_i) \cdot z] = 0 \qquad\qquad\qquad [4.19]$$

which means that the residuals of [4.17] have a zero covariance with the instruments.

The procedure is therefore as follows. First we use the GMM to estimate Equation 4.17 as an unconstrained regression:

$$R_{i,t} - r_{t-1} = \Sigma_j \gamma_{ij} \cdot z_{j,t-1} + \varepsilon_{i,t} \qquad\qquad [4.20]$$

Next, we again estimate [4.17] by GMM by forcing the coefficients into the form. $\gamma_{ij} = \beta_i . \delta_j$. Finally, we compare the levels of chi squared of the two regressions. If there is a significant difference between them, the restrictions of the pricing model are rejected.

We will not be reviewing the results of the application of this method here. The reader may wish to consult: [Hansen and Hodrick 1983], [Gibbons and Ferson 1985], [Hodrick and Srivastava 1984], [Giovannini and Jorion 1987], [Giovannini and Jorion 1989], [Campbell and Hamao 1992], [Bekaert and Hodrick 1991] and [Cumby 1990].

To the extent that it avoids having to observe the market portfolio, the latent variable method appears to answer Roll's critique (Section 5.2.1) However, it merits serious reservations.

First, the latent variable method ignores one problem. Suppose we accept the model and thus that some behaviour over time of θ_{t-1} or $E_{t-1}(R_p) - r_{t-1}$ may account for expected excess rates of return in the form of risk premiums. The question which is not addressed is whether or not the amplitude (variance) of the fluctuations of this variable is excessive compared to that which would result from a portfolio choice model based on risk aversion.[45]

In his critique of the latent variable model, [Wheatley 1989] supplies a fine illustration of the pitfall which may result from imposing auxiliary arbitrary assumptions when models are applied empirically. He first points out that the constant beta assumption could not be verified separately from the data since, by hypothesis, the market portfolio m is not observed. Consequently, the test which is carried out is the test of a joint hypothesis: if the assumption concerning the betas is false, the test may reject the hypothesis concerning the factor common to all the expected excess returns, even though it is true. This goes without saying.

More surprising and more important is Wheatley's inverse argument. This shows that the latent variable method may well conclude that the common factor hypothesis is acceptable even though it is actually false. The argument is as follows. There is an infinite number of portfolios, p, which exactly verify Equation 4.12 with $\beta_i = \text{cov}(R_i, R_p)/\text{var}(R_p)$.[46] If one of the portfolios has by chance the property that the betas of all the securities measured relative to it are constant, the econometrician will conclude wrongly from the validity of [4.12] that a common factor exists.

It is likely that arguments of this type may be found against any test of a model which economic theory does not specify completely, as is the case with the CAPM. Properly speaking, it is impossible to verify the workings of part of the economic system without investigating it is its entirety. As a rule, we need a completely specified general equilibrium model; such a model would be falsifiable without any methodological difficulty appearing. Unfortunately, existing stochastic general equilibrium models are based on exceedingly restrictive hypotheses, more restrictive, in fact, than all the auxiliary hypotheses which have been put forward to complete the CAPM.

5.4.4.2   AutoRegressive Conditional Heteroskedasticity (ARCH)

ARCH is a statistical model which allows us to estimate a process for the second moments of random variables. It is a quite natural generalization of autoregressive models with constant variance. According to this model the variations in variance are persistent, in the sense that a change over one period leads to changes in variance over several later periods. The most simple ARCH model concerning a univariate time series $\{R_t\}$ is written:

$$R_t = \Phi R_{t-1} + \varepsilon_t \tag{4.21}$$

$$\varepsilon_t \sim N(0, h_t)$$

$$h_t = \Omega + \alpha \varepsilon_{t-1}^2 \tag{4.22}$$

where $|\Phi| < 1$, $\Omega > 0$ and $\alpha \geq 0$. A more elaborate version (called the Generalized ARCH in Mean) is written:[47]

$$R_t = \Phi R_{t-1} + \theta h_t + \varepsilon_t \qquad\qquad [4.23]$$

$$\varepsilon_t \sim N(0,h_t)$$

$$h_t = \Omega + \alpha \varepsilon_{t-1}^2 + \beta h_{t-1} \qquad\qquad [4.24]$$

ARCH models are most commonly estimated by the method of maximum likelihood.

If $\{R_t\}$ is a time series of rates of return, for example that of the market, it will be seen that Equation 4.23 constitutes a rudimentary single-asset CAPM which states that conditional expected return is proportional to the conditional variance, h_t. ARCH and GARCH models may be extended to several assets. They then allow a test of the CAPM in cross section.

The market price of risk, θ, is assumed to be constant. This hypothesis is extremely restrictive.

ARCH models allow limited movement of the second moments. In particular, it will be noted that the equation of the variance [4.24] contains no random error. A functional relationship exists between the path of the variable, R, and the path of its variance.

Finally, the structure of the model is not invariant in relation to temporal aggregation. If a variable follows an ARCH process in a daily cycle, it does not follow an ARCH process in a weekly cycle. This is why it is important to view ARCH processes in continuous time. But since data are obviously observed at discrete time intervals, estimation by maximum likelihood becomes extremely complex.

5.5 Anomalies

By 'anomalies', we mean all forms of deviation from the CAPM, and more generally from the doctrine of efficient markets, which have been noted in various empirical studies. Thomas Kuhn underlined the important role played by anomalies in the development of knowledge. 'Discovery commences with the awareness of anomaly, i.e., with the recognition that nature has somehow violated the paradigm-induced expectations that govern normal science'. The list of anomalies concerning the CAPM is a long one. In every case, we are dealing with a form of behaviour of market rates of return which gives cause to doubt that the beta of a security is the only relevant measure of its risk, to the exclusion of all other attributes of the security.

The first research into anomalies went along with the first tests of the CAPM. The total risk of a security (its variance or its standard deviation) as opposed to its diversifiable risk (its beta) was used as a basis for an alternative cross-sectional relationship linking rate of return and risk. [Miller and Scholes 1972], repeating an earlier study by Douglas and Lintner and using as data the rates of return of the period 1954–1963, regressed the annual rate of return of 631 companies on their beta (systematic risk) and their specific risk (variance of the error in the regression of the rate of return on the security on that of the market). In this cross-section regression, they found a Student's t statistic of the beta coefficient equal to 7.4 and a Student's t statistic of the coefficient of specific risk equal to 11.7. The specific risk appeared to explain the compared rates of return of the securities at least as well as the systematic risk! Miller and Scholes managed, however, to show that this type of test is not conclusive, due to errors in the measurement of beta which, in their study, was calculated over the same period as that used for the cross-section regression. This is what led the authors of later research, such as Fama and MacBeth, to group securities into portfolios and measure the betas over earlier periods, in order to reduce errors in the measurement of the betas and to make them independent of the rates of return of the test period.

In addition to the betas of the various portfolios, [Fama and MacBeth 1973] tested the influence of specific risk as an additional explanation of the rates of return, using the method described in Section 5.4.1. Over all the periods of their study, they found coefficients of this additional term whose Student's t statistics were not significant. It must be noted, however, that in this study the individual securities were grouped into portfolios on the basis of their earlier betas. This procedure was aimed at maximizing the significance of the beta coefficient in the cross-section, not at maximizing that of the specific risk coefficient. The study would have to be redone building up the portfolios from specific risks.

The linearity of the return-risk relationship of the CAPM has also been the subject of anomaly research, quite similar to that concerned with the specific risk. Researchers added to the cross-section CAPM relation an additional term in beta squared. The coefficient of this term has a significant Student's t statistic in two of the nine time-cycles of Fama and MacBeth's study.

Research into sundry and various anomalies may be pursued indefinitely whenever a new attribute of the various securities is considered and introduced into the cross-section. Studying the same database of the same American firms over the same period, researchers were bound to find, sooner or later, an attribute of these firms which played as important a role as beta in the explanation of the compared rate of return of the securities. This unconstrained exploration of a database bears the rather pejorative name of 'data mining'. Out of a hundred attributes chosen at random independently of one another, five of them will very probably produce statistically significant results at the 5% threshold, without this having any sort of significance.

All the same, let us mention several attributes of securities whose price appears to be at least as good an explanation of the compared rates of return as beta. [Banz 1981] showed empirically that small firms (size being measured by market capitalization) have higher average rates of return than large firms. [Basu 1977, 1983] established that securities having a low (multiple) PER have above-average performances of rates of return later. [Rosenberg *et al.* 1985] showed that market rates of return are positively correlated with the ratio, measured earlier, of the book value of a firm to its market value. [Keim 1985] discovered that, amongst firms which pay a dividend, market rates of return increase with the dividend yield. However, the highest rates of return are those of firms who do not pay a dividend.[48] Dividend yield is not particularly correlated with beta. [de Bondt and Thaler 1985, 1987] showed that firms with low rates of return subsequently have high rates of return although their betas are not higher, and vice versa.[49]

All these relationships[50] are the subject of systematic verification on the French market in a recent book by [Hamon and Jacquillat 1992]. [Hawawini and Keim 1994] produced an excellent review and critique of the research done on the various world markets.

Recently, [Fama and French 1992] reexamined these various effects separately and simultaneously on a unified American database. They conclude that two attributes of securities, namely the size of the firm and the book value/market value ratio, offer a simple and effective description of the difference in rates of return on securities, more effective in fact than the betas measured according to the Fama and MacBeth method. They find it unlikely that these attributes are disguised measures of beta, which may be less marred by mistakes than the estimated beta itself. Nevertheless, this is exactly what [Jagannathan and Wang 1993] attempted to demonstrate in a recent article.

5.6 Conclusion

At the time of writing, there is nothing that allows us to state that the CAPM is false. In many recent empirical studies the tests lead to a rejection of the hypothesis tested. How the conclusion is rated, however, will depend very much on a subjective evaluation of the method used. This is why, in this chapter, we wished to give at least a little space to questions of method.

No statistical study will ever allow us to conclude that a theory is correct. We will therefore never be able to say that the CAPM is correct, but, at best, that one type of test or another does not allow us to reject it, due to the test's lack of power or to an insufficient amount of data. However, the data concerned here are market data covering thousands of securities, which have been continuously observed, at least weekly, since the 1920s in the United States and since the 1960s in most European countries. When such a mass of data is used, it is probably permissible to conclude that the non-rejection of a statistical test equates to a confirmation of the hypothesis.

Several of the testing procedures of the CAPM which were considered here lead to a non-rejection. This is particularly true of the tests relating to the conditional CAPM. But even in this case, it is almost always true that the measure of risk proposed by the CAPM does not explain a large part of the variation in cross-section of market rates of return.

In the absence of a convincing alternative, the CAPM remains an extremely common paradigm in modern financial thought. As we saw in Chapter 4, this model has had a powerful influence on business practice, mainly on that of investment fund management.

Notes to Chapter 5

1   This hypothesis must be used in any case when the CAPM is implemented, since anticipated returns are replaced by actual returns.

2   *See* Chapter 9.

3   Let us state again why the IID hypothesis is essential to the traditional CAPM: without it, it would not be enough for investors to take into account the probabilities of loss and gain over a single period (that of the immediate future); they would have to plan their purchases and sales up to a very distant horizon. The result would be a much more complex CAPM than the model traditionally taught.

4   We are greatly simplifying Rosenberg and Ohlson's argument; in fact, an individual's risk aversion, and thus the portfolio chosen, may vary from one period to the next. *See* their article for more details.

5   We return to this problem in Section 5.3.

6   *See* Chapter 1 for the definition of conditional expectation and (by way of consequence) conditional variance.

7   A process is a sequence of random variables. *See* Chapter 7.

8   The statement, which is equivalent to the conditional CAPM, refers to the conditional Markowitz frontier, which is formulated at each date (that is, for each value of the information variables) on the conditional moments of the rates of return. *See* Section 5.2.2.

9   Even this raises some questions to which the model itself provides no answer: many securities are barely liquid (rarely traded) and some are not accessible to all categories of investor (foreigners, for example). How can they be included in the benchmark portfolio?

10   'Human capital' refers to the discounted value (at what rate?) of the increase in earned income received by individuals due to qualifications they have obtained.

11   Roll also showed that the value of the beta of a financial security could vary considerably according to whether it is calculated with respect to one market index or another, even if these two indices are highly correlated.

12   To construct his counter-example, Roll used actual returns to calculate the efficient portfolio with the maximum correlation with the market index which was used in the study by Black, Jensen and Scholes.

13   Bear in mind that a statistical test supplies information only if a tested hypothesis is rejected. Non-rejection may be due to a lack of data or to a lack of power in the test used: it therefore has no positive significance.

14   One element must be carefully noted in these various comparisons: when we say that a strategy is efficient, conditionally or unconditionally, we are speaking in both cases of the same set of possible investment strategies amongst which the strategy in question is optimal.

15   Conversely, Hansen and Richard show that a portfolio which is conditionally efficient in relation to a restricted information set is also conditionally efficient in relation to a wider set. In particular, all strategies which are unconditionally efficient (*UE*) are conditionally efficient (*CE*) whatever the information set. Indeed, suppose otherwise, that is, that there exists a UE strategy which is not CE. Since this strategy is not CE, another strategy exists with the same conditional expected return and a smaller conditional variance. By applying to this conditional expectation and variance the operator of unconditional expected value (*see* Chapter 1), we may conclude that this second strategy has the same unconditional expectation and a smaller unconditional variance than the first, which contradicts the hypothesis that the first is UE.

16   This is a generalization, encompassing all aspects of the probability distribution, of the critique of [Admati and Ross 1985], which was touched on in Section 4.6 and dealt with the case where the betas of the securities were variable over time.

17   Similar data covering the French market were measured by [Altman *et al.* 1974]. *See also* [Jacquillat and Solnik 1989], page 104.

18   In any case, as a test of independence, Sharpe and Cooper's experiment was not ideal. Their hypothetical probabilities, as they appear in the table, are clearly based on a joint hypothesis linking independence *and* uniform probability distribution of the beta of a security between the various classes of risk. Nobody could seriously accept this second part of the hypothesis, which would involve stating that the securities have intrinsically the same risk, only the realized risk varying from one period to another. If we seriously wished to test the independence of the betas of the securities over time, we would have to allow the beta of each security to have its own probability distribution, each security beta having, amongst other things, a different expected value.

19   [Fama and MacBeth 1973].

20   As we shall see, the betas of portfolios of securities can be more accurately estimated than those of securities taken on their own.

21   *See also* [Ohlson and Rosenberg 1982].

22   As did Ohlson and Rosenberg, *op. cit.* before them.

23   At the 5% threshold.

24 $2 \times 0.038/\sqrt{402} = 0.0038$.

25 $0.0038 \times 12 = 0.0455$. We multiply the standard deviation of the monthly rate of return by twelve to obtain the standard deviation of the annualized monthly rate of return. This cannot be compared with the standard deviation of the annual rate of return, which we could construct from the monthly rates of return by assuming the independence of the successive monthly rates of return. To obtain this amount, we would have to multiply the monthly standard deviation by $\sqrt{12}$ instead of 12.

26   In Section 5.4.3, we return in greater detail to the method followed by Fama and MacBeth.

27   [Merton 1980] stressed the difficulty of estimating the market rate of return.

28   We must be aware that successive points of the curve are not independent of one another, since they are based on the same observed trajectory of the price of the portfolio.

29   More accurately, the conditional variance, given the past rates of return, is 25% less than the unconditional variance.

30   Yield to maturity is defined in Chapter 9.

31   Conditional variance, given the values of these variables, is 40% less than the unconditional variance.

32   We need only postulate that the random process followed by the rates of return over time reaches a stationary rate after a sufficient interval.

33   It is biased downwards when the theoretical slope is positive, consistent with the CAPM. *See*, for example, [Maddala 1992], Chapter 11.

34   Fama and MacBeth chose the composition of the portfolios so as to minimize the variance of the portfolios, with a given beta. This procedure allowed them to maximize the accuracy of measurement of the portfolio betas.

35   The market portfolio is itself made up of the N securities.

36   That is, it is less apt to reject the CAPM, as a hypothesis to test, if the data are not consistent with this model.

37   The instrumental variables, z, are common to all the securities. The coefficients, ∂, are specific to each.

38   The last implication below is based on the rule: $E\{E[X|Y]\} = E[X]$. *See* Chapter 1.

39   The procedure leading to [4.4] implies a loss of information relative to the starting condition: $E[u|z] = 0$. But this cannot be used directly, since we cannot really use a data sample except in order to impose an unconditional restriction.

40   Since the instrumental variables are common to all the securities, an equation similar to [4.1] applies to the rate of return, $R_{m,t}$, of the market portfolio. The residual in this equation is written $u_{m,t}$.

41   Here, for example, is the breakdown corresponding to the implementation of the test by Harvey. If the test covers N securities plus the market portfolio (observed independently), and involves L instrumental variables, there are $L \times (N + 1)$ conditions (4.4) and $L \times (N + 1)$

forecasting coefficients, δ. Conditions [4.9], for their part, number $L \times N$. There are therefore $L \times N$ overidentifying conditions.

42 The objective is a quadratic expression formulated on the inverse matrix of the variance-covariance matrix estimated from the $u.s.$.

43 The reader is reminded that the distribution called chi-squared is the distribution of a random variable which would be the sum of a certain number of squares of normal variables. The number of squares included in the definition is called the 'number of degrees of freedom'; the distribution differs according to the number of degrees of freedom (consult a statistical table for proof). In the GMM method, the test of the overidentifying restrictions must be applied with a number of degrees of freedom equal to the number of overidentifying restrictions (which is the total number of moment conditions minus the number of parameters to be estimated).

44 *See* Section 5.5.

45 Remember that θ_{t-1} is, as a rule, the relative risk aversion of the market. This number must fall within a reasonable range (say between 1 and 10).

46 These are all the *ex post* efficient portfolios, p.

47 'Generalized' is a reference to the presence of the term h_{t-1} in the equation of h_t and 'in Mean' refers to the presence of the term in h_t of the 'equation of the mean', the first equation of the system.

48 In addition, excessive rates of return for groups who pay no dividend or who pay the highest dividend seem to appear especially in January.

49 The effect is not quantitatively symmetrical.

50 Other anomalies, such as the January effect and the weekend effect, relate to compared market rates of return from one instant to the next. These effects may be taken into account in tests of the CAPM using instrumental variables but do not directly constitute a divergence from it. Note, however, that [Tinic and West 1984] concluded that the influence of beta on the rate of return in cross-section only manifests itself clearly in January!

References

[Altman *et al.* 1974]   R. Altman, B. Jacquillat and M. Levasseur, La stabilité des coefficients bêta, *Analyse Financière*, 16, 1974, 43–59.

[Banz 1981]   R. W. Banz, The Relationship Between Return and Market Value of Common Stock, *Journal of Financial Economics*, 9, 1981, 3–18.

[Basu 1977]   S. Basu, Investment Performance of Common Stocks in Relation to Their Price-Earnings Ratios: A Test of the Efficient Market Hypothesis, *Journal of Finance*, 33, 1977, 663–682.

[Basu 1983]   S. Basu, The Relationship Between Return and Market Value of Common Stocks, *Journal of Financial Economics*, 9, 1983, 3–18.

[Bekaert and Hodrick 1992]   G. Bekaert and R. J. Hodrick, Characterizing Predictable Components in Excess Returns on Equity and Foreign Exchange Markets, *Journal of Finance*, 47, 1992, 467–511.

[Black *et al.* 1972]   F. Black, M. C. Jensen and Myron Scholes, The Capital Asset Pricing Model: Some Empirical Tests, in M. C. Jensen, ed., *Studies in the Theory of Capital Markets* (Praeger Publishers).

[Brealey and Myers 1982]   R. Brealey and S. Myers, *Principles of Corporate Finance*. Second edition, 1982.

[Campbell and Hamao 1992]   J. Y. Campbell and Y. Hamao, Predictable Stock Returns in the United States and Japan: A Study of Long-term Capital Market Integration, *Journal of Finance*, 47, 1992, 43–70.

[Collins *et al.* 1987]   D. W. Collins, J. Ledolter and J. Rayburn, Some Further Evidence on the Stochastic Properties of Systematic Risk, *Journal of Business*, 60, 1987, 425–448.

[Cumby 1987]   R. E. Cumby, Consumption Risk and International Equity Returns: Some Empirical Evidence, *Journal of International Money and Finance*, 9, 1987, 182–192.

[de Bondt and Thaler 1985]   W. F. de Bondt and R. H. Thaler, Does the Stock Market Overreact?, *Journal of Finance*, 40, 1985, 793–805.

[de Bondt and Thaler 1987]   W. F. de Bondt and R. H. Thaler, Further Evidence on Investor Overreaction and Stock Market Seasonality, *Journal of Finance*, 42, 1987, 557–581.

[Fama and French 1992]   E. F. Fama and K. R. French, The Cross-section of Expected Stock Returns, *Journal of Finance*, 47, 1992, 427–466.

[Fama and MacBeth 1973]   E. F. Fama and J. MacBeth, Risk, Return and Equilibrium: Empirical Tests, *Journal of Political Economy*, 71, 1973, 607–636.

[Gibbons 1982]   M. R. Gibbons, Multivariate Tests of Financial Models: A New Approach, *Journal of Financial Economics*, 10, 1982, 3–28.

[Gibbons and Ferson 1985]   M. R. Gibbons and W. Ferson, Tests of Asset Pricing Models with Changing Expectations and an Unobservable Market Portfolio, *Journal of Financial Economics*, 14, 1985, 217–236.

[Gibbons *et al.* 1989]   M. R. Gibbons, S. A. Ross and J. Shanken, A Test of the Efficiency of a Given Portfolio, *Econometrica*, 57, 1989, 1121–1152.

[Giovannini and Jorion 1987]   A. Giovannini and P. Jorion, Interest Rates and Risk Premia in the Foreign Exchange and the Stock Market, *Journal of International Money and Finance*, 1987, 107–123.

[Giovannini and Jorion 1989]   A. Giovannini and P. Jorion, The Time-Variation of Risk and Return in the Foreign Exchange and Stock Markets, *Journal of Finance*, 1989, 307-325.

[Hansen 1982]   L. P. Hansen, Large Sample Properties of Generalized Methods of Moments Estimators, *Econometrica*, 50, 1982, 1029–1054.

[Hansen and Hodrick 1983]   L. P. Hansen and R. J. Hodrick, Risk Averse Speculation in the Forward Exchange Market: and Econometrical Analysis of Linear Models, in *Exchange Rates and International Macroeconomic*, J. A. Frenkel, ed. University of Chicago Press, Chicago, 1983.

[Hansen and Richard 1987]   L. P. Hansen and S. F. Richard, The Role of Conditioning Information in Deducing Testable Restrictions Implied by Dynamic Asset Pricing Models, *Econometrica*, 55, 1987, 587–613.

[Harvey 1989]   C. R. Harvey, Time-Varying Conditional Covariances in Tests of Asset Pricing Models, *Journal of Financial Economics*, 24, 1989, 289–317.

{Hawawini and Keim 1994]   G. Hawawini and D. B. Keim, On the predictability of Common Stock Returns: Worldwide Evidence, in R. A. Jarrow; V. Maksimovic; and W. T. Ziemba, eds., *Handbooks in Operations Research and Management Science*. North Holland, Amsterdam, 1994.

[Hodrick and Srivastava 1984]   R. J. Hodrick and S. Srivastava, An Investigation of Risk and Return in Forward Foreign Exchange, *Journal of International Money and Finance*, 3, 1984, 5–29.

[Jacquillat and Solnik 1989]   B. Jacquillat and B. Solnik, *Marchés financiers; gestion de portefeuille et des risques*. Dunod, 1989.

[Jagannathan and Wang 1993]   R. Jagannathan and Z. Wang, The CAPM is Alive and Well, Working Paper 517, Federal Reserve Bank of Minneapolis, 1993.

[Kandel and Stambaugh 1988]   S. Kandel and R. F. Stambaugh, Modeling Expected Stock Returns for Long and Short Horizons, Working Paper, Wharton School of the University of Pennsylvania, 1988.

[Keim 1985]   D. B. Keim, Dividend Yields and Stock Returns: Implications of Abnormal January Returns, *Journal of Financial Economics*, 14, 1985, 473–489.

[Maddala 1992]   G. S. Maddala, *Introduction to Econometrics*. Second edition, MacMillan, 1992.

[Merton 1980]   R. C. Merton, On Estimating the Expected Return on the Market: An Exploratory Investigation, *Journal of Financial Economics*, 8, 1980, 323-362.

[Miller and Scholes 1972]   M. H. Miller and M. Scholes, Rates of Return
                                 in Relation to Risk: A Re-examination of
                                 Some Recent Findings, in: *Studies in the
                                 Theory of Capital Markets,* M. C. Jensen,
                                 ed., Praeger Publishers, 1972.

[Ohlson and Rosenberg 1982]   J. Ohlson and B. Rosenberg, Systematic
                                 Risk of the CRSP Equal-weighted Common
                                 Stock Index: A History Estimated by
                                 Stochastic Parameter Regression, *Journal of
                                 Business*, 55, 1982, 121–145.

[Roll 1977]   R. Roll, A Critique of Asset Pricing Theory's
                                 Tests: on Past and Potential Testability of
                                 the Theory, *Journal of Financial
                                 Economics*, 4, 1977, 129–176.

[Rosenberg and Ohlson 1976]   B. Rosenberg and J. A. Ohlson, The Station-
                                 ary Distribution of Returns and Portfolio
                                 Separation in Capital Markets: a Fundamen-
                                 tal Contradiction, *Journal of Financial and
                                 Quantitative Analysis*, 1976, 393–401.

[Rosenberg *et al.* 1985]   B. Rosenberg, K. Reid and R. Lanstein,
                                 Persuasive Evidence of Market Inefficiency,
                                 Journal of Portfolio Management, 11,
                                 Spring 1985, 9–16.

[Sharpe and Cooper 1972]   W. M. Sharpe and G. M. Cooper, Risk-
                                 Return Classes of NYSE Common Stocks,
                                 1937-167, *Financial Analysts Journal*, 28,
                                 1972, 46–54.

[Tinic and West 1984]   S. Tinic and R. R. West, Risk and Return:
                                 January and the Rest of the Year, *Journal of
                                 Financial Economics*, 13, 1984, 561–574.

[Wheatley 1989]   S. M. Wheatley, A Critique of Latent
                                 Variable Tests of Asset Pricing Models,
                                 Journal of Financial Economics, 23, 1989,
                                 325–338.

Part II
Options and arbitrage

The Capital Asset Pricing Model, which we studied in Part I of this book, was an equilibrium model based on the demand and supply behaviour of economic agents. It was, in principle, capable of pricing *all* securities in relation to one another.[1] This extremely wide field of application lead, on the other hand, to limited success in empirical tests.

In Part II of this book, we consider a very narrow category of securities, namely secondary securities, and set ourselves a much more limited target, namely that of pricing secondary securities *in relation to primary assets*. A secondary (or derivative)[2] security is a security whose cash flows depend, by construction, on the flows or prices of one or more other securities (which we shall call primary securities or underlying securities).

The principle used for pricing will be that of *arbitrage*: where two securities or two combinations of securities bring equal revenues, they must have the same price, if the market is functioning correctly. The justification of this principle is simple: if these two securities did not have the same price, an arbitrageur could buy one and sell the other, thus making an immediate profit with no risk and no capital outlay. A market in equilibrium, where each investor is seeking to profit from payoff opportunities, does not allow arbitrage opportunities to remain.[3]

For an investor to be able to profit from any arbitrage opportunity completely, exactly and perfectly, one would have to assume that:

- any individual may borrow or lend at the same risk-free rate of interest;

- individuals who sell securities short receive all the proceeds of this sale and all the revenues which may result from the reinvestment of these proceeds;

- transactions costs are zero on all securities;

- transactions carried out by individuals have no impact on the taxes the individuals pay.

As any model of reality, the arbitrage pricing theory is only an approximation which must be judged on its empirical validity and not on its hypotheses, which may be unrealistic.

The arbitrage pricing theory raises a mathematical difficulty when we allow operators to use arbitrage combinations containing an infinite sequence of transactions. This difficulty is well illustrated by the 'doubling strategy'.[4] A strategy exists for producing a certain revenue of 1 ECU for a zero capital outlay, thus violating the principle of the absence of arbitrage. Let us illustrate this strategy by means of a game of tossing a coin in which a player receives 1 ECU in the case of a winning bet and pays 1 ECU in the case of a losing bet:

(a) Bet 1 ECU on heads on the first throw. If you win, stop. If not, bet 2 ECU on heads on the second throw.

(b) On the nth throw, if you have lost on all preceding throws, bet $(2)^{n-1}$ ECU on heads. If you win, stop: the gains will cover the preceding losses plus 1 ECU. If you lose, bet 2^n ECU the next time, and so on.

Obviously the probability of winning 1 ECU is equal to 1 minus the probability of losing on all the throws. This last probability tends towards zero when the number of throws increases indefinitely!

By this process, it appears that from any game of chance, and by extension any financial market, a certain amount may be extracted with no capital outlay, on the condition of being allowed to play indefinitely.[5] *To avoid such pathologies, it is sufficient to prevent the gambler from borrowing indefinitely, by making margin calls, for instance.*[6]

Since revenues earned by secondary securities are systematically linked to those earned by primary securities, an arbitrage established between these two categories will give us the price of one in terms of the price of the other. This procedure is compatible with general equilibrium but avoids a particular model of general equilibrium. It does however require us to postulate (arbitrarily, therefore) the behaviour of primary securities. That behaviour may not be compatible with general equilibrium, that is, it may not result from the portfolio optimization of economic agents.

Part II contains three chapters. Chapters 6 and 7 consider mainly secondary securities created on the market by the investors themselves – such as options – whilst Chapter 8 examines the secondary securities issued by firms.

Notes to the introduction to Part II

1   The CAPM nevertheless remained a partial equilibrium model since it did not allow securities to be priced in relation to commodities.

2   We avoid the term 'conditional securities' which is used by some authors, but which should be reserved for a wider set of securities than that of secondary securities. For example, a bond indexed on the cost of living index is a conditional security – since the payments to which it gives rise are conditioned by a future random event, namely the level of the index – but it is not a secondary security.

3   The principle of the absence of arbitrage has already been mentioned in Chapter I, where we pointed out that it underlies an important property which must be satisfied by the value of financial securities, namely *the property of additivity*, a corollary to which is the Modigliani and Miller theorem. The absence of arbitrage is a minimum condition (necessary but not sufficient) of equilibrium.

4   Our presentation of the paradox is borrowed from [van Hulle 1988]. The following articles contain a more detailed treatment: [Harrison and Kreps 1979], [Harrison and Pliska 1981], [Heath and Jarrow 1987].

5   This strategy has an expected value of gain which is not defined ($\Sigma^{\infty}_{n=1}(-1)^n 1/2$).

6   [Heath and Jarrow 1987] show that the option pricing formula which we establish in the next chapter, namely the Black-Scholes formula, is not invalidated by margin calls.

References

[Harrison and Kreps 1979]   J. Harrison and D. Kreps, 'Martingales and Arbitrage in Multiperiod Securities Markets', *Journal of Economic Theory*, 20 (1979), 381–408.

[Harrison and Pliska 1981]   J. Harrison and S. Pliska, 'Martingales and Stochastic Integrals in the Theory of Continuous Trading', *Stochastic Processes and Their Applications*, 11 (1981), 215–260.

[Heath and Jarrow 1987]   D. Heath and R. Jarrow, 'Arbitrage, Continuous Trading and Margin Requirements', *Journal of Finance*, Dec 1987, 1129–1142.

[van Hulle 1988]   C. van Hulle, 'Option Pricing Methods: an Overview', *Insurance: Mathematics and Economics*, 7 (1988), 139–152.

6

Option pricing by the arbitrage method

The method of pricing securities by absence of arbitrage is applicable to all secondary securities. As options are the oldest and most commonly encountered example of a secondary security, we shall use this example to illustrate the method, and our account therefore begins by describing these financial instruments. This is the subject of Section 6.1. The pricing method, which is the subject of this chapter,[1] is applied to options in Sections 6.2 and 6.3. These two sections differ in the hypothesis used concerning the passage of time, Section 6.2 introducing the hypothesis, intended here as no more than a teaching tool, that time is divided into discrete periods, whereas, in Section 6.3, we make the interval separating two instants tend towards zero in order to arrive at continuous time. Section 6.4 addresses the problems which arise when implementing the pricing method. Section 6.5 is an assessment of the empirical validity of pricing formulae. Section 6.6 extends the discussion beyond options to consider other examples of secondary securities, or securities derived from other securities, to reveal how wide the field of application of the method studied here can be.

157

The following chapter (Chapter 7) examines arbitrage again but using a mathematical procedure which allows continuous time to be addressed directly.

6.1   Options: definitions and payoffs

There are two categories of option: call options and put options. A call option is an acquired *right* to buy a particular security, called an underlying security (for example, a share of stock), at a price set in advance, called the '*exercise price*', at a fixed date – or, according to case, before a fixed date – called the '*maturity date*'. The price of this right (often referred to as the value of the option) is called the *premium*. The definition of the put option is symmetrical to the preceding one: a put option is a right which is acquired to sell a particular security at a fixed price, on or before a fixed date.

As we saw in Chapter 1, a security is defined by the cash flows to which it gives rise. Figure 6.1 represents the cash flows produced by a call option at maturity. Two cases may arise. Either the security which is the object of the option (the underlying security) is quoted on the market at a price, S_0, above that of the exercise price; in this case, the holder of the call option has every interest in exercising his option and buying the security at the exercise price (K in Figure 6.1) in order to resell it on the market at the price S_0 thus producing a profit $S_0 - K$. Or the price S_0 on the market is less than the exercise price K, and the bearer of the option has no use for his right; the latter has a zero value. Thus the value C_0 of the call option at maturity is calculated by the formula:

$$C_0 = \text{Max}\ [0, S_0 - K] \tag{1.1}$$

where Max means 'the greater of the next two numbers'.

This equation, represented in Figure 6.1, reflects the point of view of the bearer of the option. An individual can only buy an option if he or she can find another person to buy it from. The seller would naturally have a graph of the final result which would be the opposite of the one we have just drawn (Figure 6.2). The right-hand part, reflecting a loss of cash which occurs where the price on the market is greater than the exercise price, corresponds to the circumstance where the option is exercised to the detriment of the seller.

At any time prior to maturity, an option is said to be 'in the money' if the price of the underlying asset is such that the bearer would choose to exercise it if the instant in question were the exercise date. It is 'out of the money' in the opposite case. For example, a call is in the money on the date preceding maturity by t units of time if $S_t > K$.

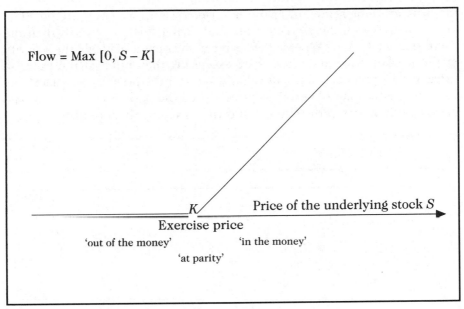

Figure 6.1   Call option: profile of the cash flow on maturity

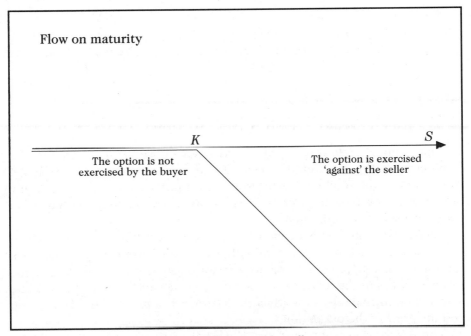

Figure 6.2   Position of an individual having sold a call option

The characteristics of a put option are similar to those of a call option, except that it is a right to sell. The gains of the bearer of a put option at maturity are represented in Figure 6.3. Here again, two cases are possible: either the price on the market of the underlying stock, S_0, is less than the exercise price K, in which case the bearer of the option may buy the security at the market price and resell it by exercising the option at the exercise price K, thus producing a positive flow $K - S_0$. Or the price of the underlying stock is greater than the exercise price K, and the option has no value. The price P_0 at maturity of the put option is thus given by the formula:

$$P_0 = \text{Max} \, [0, K - S_0] \tag{1.2}$$

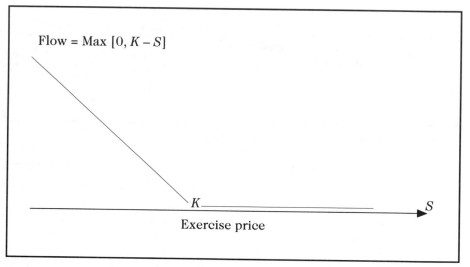

Figure 6.3   Put option: profile of the cash flow on maturity

The point of view of the seller of the put option would obviously be symmetrical. By comparing Figures 6.2 and 6.3, we can see that selling a call option is not at all equivalent to buying a put option: the buyer of any option can only receive positive flows on maturity, whereas the potential losses of a seller are unlimited.

Figures 6.2 and 6.3 also demonstrate that buying a put option attached to the sale of a call option, where both are of the European type and have the same exercise price, equates to a forward sale of the underlying stock. From this results a *relationship known as put–call parity* (called the 'conversion formula' by practitioners) between the price of the call option and the price of the put option.[2]

The description of options which we have just given is only valid for 'European' options; there are also 'American' ones. Simplifying somewhat, we can say that an 'American' option may be exercised at any time between its date of purchase and its maturity date, whereas a 'European' option may only be exercised at certain precise dates (including the maturity date).

6.2   Principles of option pricing: discrete-time

As we have just seen, the very nature of the option contract implies a profile of gain at maturity which is not a straight line, but a broken line. This is an essential difference from, for example, a forward contract, which obliges the contractor to buy or sell at the price fixed in advance whatever the cash price prevailing at the moment of conclusion. A forward contract would result in the contractors gaining or losing the difference between the original forward price and the cash price realized. This would be a profile of linear gain and it would be quite simple to determine by arbitrage what the forward price must be, depending on the simultaneous cash price: it is sufficient to compare a forward purchase to a cash purchase accompanied by a combination of financing of an appropriate, fixed amount (*see* Section 6.6.1 below).

In the case of options, we must resort to a process of pricing by 'dynamic' arbitrage.

6.2.1   Options with one period to maturity

Let us start with the most simple case and examine an option with only one period of time to maturity; we shall generalize to several periods in Section 6.2.3.

At today's date, the underlying stock has a value S. Let us suppose – still for simplification's sake – that during the final period of the life of the option, this price can only change in two ways: either it rises by a certain percentage, or it falls by a certain percentage. The movement of the price of the underlying stock is therefore purely binary. We have represented such a case in Figure 6.4: the price of the underlying stock today is 105 ECU; this price may rise by 5% to 110.25 ECU, or fall by 5% (equality of the percentages of rise and fall being a purely arbitrary stipulation) to 99.75 ECU.

The option in question has an exercise price of 100 ECU and the rate of interest covering the period of time separating today's date from the date of maturity is 0.5%.[3]

An examination of this situation is relatively simple: if the underlying stock rises to 110.25 ECU, the holder of the option at maturity will receive 10.25 ECU; if the security falls to 99.75 ECU, he will have 0 ECU.

It is possible to check that the same random pair of flows [10.25; 0] would result from another investment combination. We can verify that, instead of buying an option, individuals could, with the same terminal payoff, borrow at the risk-free rate of 0.5% a sum whose final repayment value is equal to 97.375 ECU and simultaneously buy a fraction equal to 0.97619 of the underlying security. If they do this, they will receive at the end of the period the value of their asset minus the repayment of their debt:

- if the underlying asset is at 110.25:

$$0.97619 \cdot 110.25 - 97.375 \text{ ECU} = 10.25 \qquad [2.1a]$$

- if the underlying asset is at 99.75:

$$0.97619 \cdot 99.75 - 97.375 = 0 \qquad [2.1b]$$

which are exactly the same amounts in the two possible cases as if they had held the option.

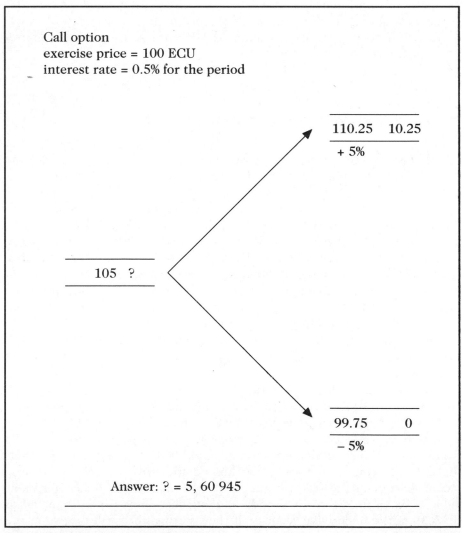

Call option
exercise price = 100 ECU
interest rate = 0.5% for the period

110.25   10.25
+ 5%

105   ?

99.75   0
− 5%

Answer: ? = 5, 60 945

Figure 6.4   Evaluation principle (1)

It is easy to see how we obtained the two numbers 97.375 ECU and 0.97619. These numbers were chosen precisely so as to obtain a match between the option and the other mode of investment. We obtained them by solving an equation system similar to equalities [2.1] where the amount of ECU to be borrowed is an unknown, D, and the fraction of the underlying asset to be bought is another unknown, h:

$$h \cdot 110.25 - D = 10.25 \qquad\qquad [2.2a]$$

$$h \cdot 99.75 - D = 0 \qquad\qquad [2.2b]$$

The number h obtained by solving this equation is equal to: $(10.25 - 0)/(110.25 - 99.75) = 0.97619$, which is the ratio of the increase in price of the option to the increase in the price of the underlying asset. This is often called the *hedge ratio*.

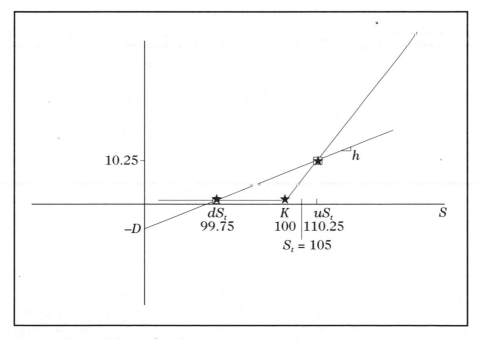

Figure 6.5   Breakdown of a call option into a loan plus an investment in the underlying asset

In graphical terms, this algebraic manipulation is the same as drawing a line through the only two pertinent points in the payoff profile of the option, namely those corresponding to the two possible realizations of the price of the underlying asset (*see* Figure 6.5). The hedge ratio, h, is the slope of the line and the final value of the amount borrowed, D, is the intercept. We may state:

Proposition 1:
>   A call option can be analysed as a combination of a riskless loan and an investment in the underlying security.

In a correctly functioning market, the option must have the same initial value as this other investment combination. The investment value at the start of the period of the other investment combination is quite clear. The investment in the underlying asset is worth 0.97619 times the value of a portion of the underlying asset, which is: 0.97619 · 105 ECU and the amount borrowed to make 97.375 ECU at maturity is equal to 97.375/1.005 ECU. Net, we obtain:

$$0.97619 \cdot 105 - 97.375/1.005 = 5.609 \text{ ECU.} \qquad [2.3]$$

This price is necessarily the price of the call option today if the price of the underlying stock is 105 ECU. If it were anything else, arbitrage would be possible.

It will be noted that the result of 5.609 ECU owes nothing to knowing the true probability of a rise or a fall in the underlying security. However, basic economic reasoning indicates that the price of the option must depend on these probabilities: the higher an option's probability of being exercised, the more value it has. The solution to this paradox is as follows: these probabilities are implicitly contained in the price of the underlying stock, which is 105 ECU today. If, for example, the probability of a rise had been higher, the price at the start of the period would have been higher than 105 ECU. The information that the price today is 105 ECU is sufficient to represent what we need to know about the future of the security in order to price the option.

6.2.2 'Risk-neutral' probabilities

These ideas may be presented differently by using a concept which we have already encountered (see Chapter 1, for example): there exists a linear mapping, called the *evaluation function*, which on a given market always links together the cash flows of any security and its market value. As this mapping is linear, we may postulate the existence of two coefficients Φ_1 and Φ_2, which we shall call present value factors,[4] corresponding to the two circumstances which may exist at the end of the period. The price of each security is obtained by applying these two coefficients to the two possible values of the cash flow accruing to the security and adding them together.

For the underlying stock itself, this formula is written:

$$105 = \Phi_1 \cdot 110.25 + \Phi_2 \cdot 99.75 \qquad [2.4a]$$

In the context of risk-free investment or borrowing, it will be noted that the investment of 1/1.005 ECU at the start of the period leads to 1 ECU being received at the end of the period in both of the two future circumstances:

$$1/1.005 = \Phi_1 \cdot 1 + \Phi_2 \cdot 1 \qquad [2.4b]$$

Equation system 2.4 has only one solution:

$$\Phi_1 = 0.5472, \ \Phi_2 = 0.4478 \qquad [2.5]$$

which we may then use to price the option:

$$\Phi_1 \cdot 10.25 + \Phi_2 \cdot 0 = 0.5472 \cdot 10.25 + 0.4478 \cdot 0 = 5.609 \qquad [2.6]$$

By rewriting, we may make this procedure even clearer. Let $\pi = \Phi_1/(\Phi_1 + \Phi_2)$. Recall also that the rate of interest is 0.005. We may now rewrite [2.4a, b] as follows:

$$105 = [\pi \cdot 10.25 + (1 - \pi) \cdot 99.75]/(1 + 0.005). \qquad [2.7]$$

Given the price of 105 ECU for the underlying stock and an interest rate of 0.005, Equation 2.7 allows us to deduce $\pi = 0.55$. The value of the option is therefore equal to:

$$[\pi \cdot 10.25 + (1 - \pi) \cdot 0]/1.005 = 5.609. \qquad [2.8]$$

We have pointed out that the true probability of a rise or a fall in the underlying stock is not involved in determining the price of the option. It will be seen that in its place there appears a quantity π, which we may interpret as an adjusted probability. Reading Equations 2.7 and 2.8 shows that π gives the value of any security – that of the underlying stock as well as that of the option – simply by taking the expected value of its future payoffs, then discounting this expected value at the risk-free rate of interest. In other words, the value of any security is such that the expected value of its rate of return, calculated on the basis of adjusted probability, is equal to the risk-free rate of interest. This method of calculation is exactly that which would be applicable in an economy where all the investors were indifferent to risk and where the probability of a rise in the price of the underlying stock was exactly π. We can now state:

Proposition 2:
- Options are valued *as if* the investors were indifferent to risk and the underlying asset had an expected return equal to the risk-free rate of interest.

In the light of what has gone before, this result is not particularly surprising. If there exists a method of reproducing the payoffs of an option by a combination of risk-free security and underlying asset, the relationship which results between the price of the option and that of the underlying asset, which is a pure arbitrage relationship, is certainly independent of the degree of risk aversion of the economic agents. If this is the case, we must be able to obtain this relationship by dealing with the most simple case, that of zero risk aversion. In an economy where individuals are indifferent to risk, *every security* has an expected rate of return equal to the risk-free rate of interest.

6.2.3 Options with any number of periods to maturity: the binomial technique

The reasoning based on reproducing the flows produced by the option by means of a different investment combination may be generalized to any number of periods. Let us imagine, for example, that we go back to an instant which precedes the date of maturity by two periods. We may now repeat the procedure which we have just followed by moving backward; this gives what is known as the *binomial* evaluation technique.

Since the price of the security may at any stage rise or fall by 5%, the result is a tree structure which is shown in Figure 6.6. Three states of affairs are possible at the end of the second period (the maturity date, which we call $t = 2$): at the highest terminal node, the security is worth 110.25 ECU and the option whose exercise price is 100 ECU is worth 10.25 ECU; at the central node, the security is worth 99.75 ECU and the option 0 ECU, and at the lower node the security is worth 90.25 ECU and the option 0 ECU.

At the intermediate instant $t = 1$, which precedes maturity by one period, arbitrage reasoning, based on the same numbers as before, has already shown that at the upper node, the share being worth 105 ECU, the option is worth 5.609 ECU. At the lower node of $t = 1$, the share is worth 95 ECU and the option is worth 0 ECU since, whatever happens, it can only pay 0 ECU at maturity.

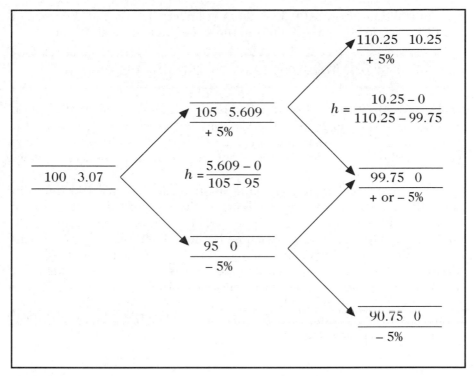

Figure 6.6   Evaluation principle (2)

It only remains to redo an arbitrage reasoning covering the two conditions for the intermediate instant: 105 ECU and 95 ECU, then go back one step further and return to the initial instant $t = 0$ where the share is worth 100 ECU. The calculation of the hedge ratio and of the amount to borrow at the risk-free rate is done as before; it leads to 3.07 ECU as the value of the option at the initial instant. The hedge ratio by which to multiply the price at step $t = 0$ to $t = 1$ is $h = (5.609 - 0)/(105 - 95) = 0.5609$ and the amount to borrow is $B = -53.2898$ (in units of ECU from instant $t = 1$). These numbers are different from those which we found when dealing with the last period ($h = 0.97619$ and $B = -97.375$ ECU). We therefore state:

Proposition 3:
The combination of risk-free borrowing and investment in the underlying asset which reproduces an option is a combination which varies over time.

However, it is very important to note that this combination is self-financing in the course of execution. Let us take account of the flows entering and leaving at instant $t = 1$ (measured in ECU of this instant) at the upper node: we repay 53.2898 ECU, but we receive 97.375/1.005 ECU by way of a new loan; in addition, we resell 0.5609 units of underlying asset at the price of 105 ECU, but we buy 0.67619 units at the same price. In total:

$$-53.2898 + 97.375/10.005 + (0.5609-0.97619) \cdot 105 = 0$$

In net, the continually adjusted combination which reproduces the option does not at any time require the slightest outlay of capital, nor does it generate any. This is what authorizes us to say that at the origin it must have the same value as the European option, which also produces no flows until the end.

The binomial technique has shown us the general concept of the arbitrage pricing method, which is as follows: we have reproduced the profile of the flows yielded by the option by a combination of other securities, a combination which may vary over time but for which we may easily calculate the initial value. Beyond its theoretical interest, the binomial technique is also a method commonly used by practitioners to obtain the value of an option in the numerous cases where no exact formula (such as that in the next section) is available.[5] When applying it, it is necessary to check the accuracy of the answer supplied; for this we use a 'control problem' to which we know the exact solution.[6]

6.3 Continuous time: the Black-Scholes formula

Multiplication of the time steps has allowed us to enrich the world of possible terminal circumstances: instead of two possible values of the underlying security at the end of one step, we have three at the end of two steps.

A multiplication of steps, which we obtained by increasing the number of periods, may also be obtained within the same period, by subdivision. We may even continue this subdivision indefinitely to the point of having infinitely small subperiods in an infinitely large number. We can thus enrich the world of terminal states to obtain a *continuum* of possible values. (The passage to the limit is explained in detail in the appendix.)

The result of the pricing method which we have just described converges towards a limit which is known as the *Black-Scholes Formula*[7] [Black and Scholes 1973]. This formula – valid for European options on non-dividend-paying securities – is given in Table 6.1.[8]

The formula contains two terms representing the payments which will be made on maturity: in the case of exercise, the bearer will receive one unit of the underlying stock worth S_0 and will pay out the exercise price K. The values at today's date (t units of time before maturity) of these two payments correspond exactly to the two terms of the formula: the first is the discounted value of the security which is received, and the second corresponds to the discounted value of the exercise price which is paid.

Price of a call option:

$$C_t = S_t N(d_1) - K e^{-rt} N(d_2)$$

$$d_1 = \frac{ln(S_t / K e^{-rt})}{\sigma \sqrt{t}} + \frac{1}{2} \sigma \sqrt{t}$$

$$d_2 = \frac{ln(S_t / K e^{-rt})}{\sigma \sqrt{t}} - \frac{1}{2} \sigma \sqrt{t}$$

Variables:
   t is the number of units of time left to run until maturity of the option;
   C_t is the cash price of a call option t units of time before maturity;
   S_t is the cash price of the underlying stock at the same moment.
Parameters:
   σ is the volatility (the standard deviation of the rate of return) of the underlying asset;
   K is the exercise price;
   ($K e^{-rt}$ is the discounted value of the exercise price).[9]
The function N is the area under the normal law.

Note: $\dfrac{\partial c}{\partial s} = N(d_1)$ $\dfrac{\partial c}{\partial k} = c^{-rt} N(d_2)$

Table 6.1   [Black and Scholes 1973]

The coefficient $N(d_2)$, by which $K e^{-rt}$ is multiplied, corresponds to the probability of exercise calculated by supposing fictitiously that the underlying stock has a price which grows on average at the rate of interest r. The interpretation of the coefficient $N(d_1)$, by which S is multiplied, is more complex. Writing S_0 and S_t for the price of the underlying stock on the day of maturity and t units of time before maturity respectively, and $\Pr(S_0 \geq K S_t)$ for the probability of exercise calculated as we have just stated, we have:

$$N(d_2) = \Pr(S_0 \geq K S_t)$$

We may now interpret $N(d_1)$ as follows:

$$N(d_1) = E[S_0/S \mid S_t, S_0 \geq K] \cdot \Pr(S_0 \geq KS_t) \cdot e^{-rt}$$

where $E[]$ is the conditional expected value, given that the exercise takes place,[10] of the value of the underlying stock on maturity relative to its value S today, the calculation being made here again, by assuming fictitiously that the price of the underlying stock changes on average at the rate r.

The graph of the Black-Scholes function, which links the price of the option to the price of the underlying stock, may be found in Figure 6.7. Naturally, the price of the option is an increasing function of the price of the share, but it is lower. For high values of the price of the underlying stock the curve approaches an asymptote. This asymptote gives a lower bound; the price of the option is always greater than the price of the underlying stock reduced by the discounted value of the exercise price.

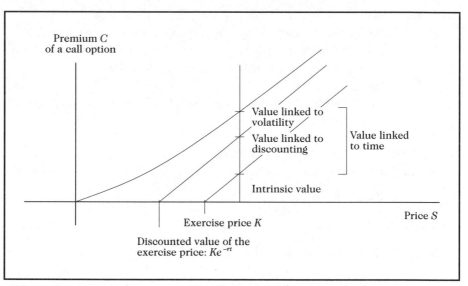

Figure 6.7

It is customary to break down the total value of the option into two elements: the 'intrinsic' value and the value 'linked to time'. The intrinsic value is that which would be received by the bearer of the option if he exercised it today, which is: $\text{Max}[0, S - K]$. If the price is less than the exercise price, the intrinsic value is zero: if it is greater, the intrinsic value of the option is the difference between the value of the underlying stock and the exercise price. The value linked to time, which justifies its name by the fact that it tends towards zero when approaching maturity, may itself be broken down into two parts: the value linked to discounting, which is equal to the exercise price minus its own discounted value, and the value linked mainly to volatility, which contains the residual value attributable neither to the intrinsic value nor to the value linked to discounting.

The price of an option as given by the Black-Scholes formula depends on three parameters: the volatility of the rate of return on the underlying stock σ, the rate of interest r and the time left to maturity t. The value of an option (call or put) is greater as the volatility of the underlying stock is higher, since this increases the payoff prospects. The value of a call option is also an increasing function of the interest rate, since buying an option allows the date of purchase of the share and the corresponding payout to be delayed: the inverse would be true for a put option. Finally, the value of a call option increases with the length of time remaining to maturity, for two reasons: the first is the delay to the payment of the exercise price, and the second is linked to the greater payoff prospects offered by possible fluctuations in the price of the underlying stock, which become greater as the period of time envisaged gets longer. In the case of a put option these two effects would operate in opposite directions, so the net effect would remain ambiguous.

The expected value of the rate of return on the underlying stock is not one of the parameters in the formula.[11] If we think that the underlying security has a good chance of appreciation, we may be led to buy this security or an option written on this security, but this in no way affects the price of the option, once the price of the underlying stock is given. In our study of the binomial technique, we pointed out that the price of the option did not depend on the true probability of a rise or a fall in the underlying asset. The two properties are identical. The explanation we have given for one applies equally to the other.

The various derivatives of the Black-Scholes formula are at least as important as the formula itself, since they are used as a management tool. For example, the derivative $\partial C/\partial S = N(d_1)$ – called the 'delta' of the option – and the elasticity $(S/C)(\partial C/\partial S)$ serve as a method of checking the risk incurred by the buyer and the seller of the option.[12] In fact, in the context of Black and Scholes' hypotheses, fluctuations in the price of the underlying stock are the only source of risk affecting the option. As a result, the volatility σ_C *of the option* is obtained from the volatility σ of the underlying asset by the formula:

$$\sigma_C = \frac{S}{C}\frac{\partial C}{\partial S}\sigma$$

Since what we call 'volatility of the underlying asset and volatility of the option' are in fact the standard deviation of the *rate of return* on the underlying asset and on the option respectively, it is naturally the elasticity, and not simply the derivative, of the function C which links one to the other. The level of risk of the option corresponds to a level of expected rate of return α_C of the option, which may be obtained – the option and the underlying asset being perfectly correlated – by using as a benchmark the expected rate of return, written α, of the underlying asset:[13]

$$\alpha_C - r = \frac{S}{C}\frac{\partial C}{\partial S}[\alpha - r] \qquad\qquad [3.4]$$

We shall look at this relation again in Chapter 8.

The Black and Scholes formula seems daunting, but it may easily be programmed into a pocket calculator.[14] Its empirical validity is attested by numerous statistical studies, of which we study a sample in Section 6.5 below.

6.4. Implementation

As pointed out by Fischer Black himself,[15] the Black-Scholes formula is based on at least ten somewhat unrealistic assumptions. These may however be relaxed. We must return to the above arguments to clarify the assumptions and examine their validity and possibilities for extension. The formula also raises a difficult problem of estimation. We shall examine successively:[16]

- the assumed behavioural characteristics of the underlying stock;
- in particular its volatility, which is assumed constant;
- the assumption of a constant rate of interest;
- the effect of dividends and the possibilities of exercise before maturity of American options;
- the problem of estimating volatility.

6.4.1 The stochastic process of the underlying asset

Although the Black-Scholes formula gives the price of the option as a function of the price of the underlying asset, the formula itself is based on a knowledge of the underlying stock which goes far beyond the price quoted today. A general hypothesis which has guided the development of the formula is that *we know several aspects of the stochastic process governing the movements of the security*. We know first of all that it is a process which in discrete time takes a *binomial* form.[17] Starting from the price quoted at any instant, the price at the next instant can only take *two* possible values: the tree structure which describes the possible movements of the security (*see* Figure 6.6) produces only two branches at each point. This hypothesis cannot be relaxed and is common to all option pricing formulae. A more general hypothesis (for example a trinomial process) would have prevented us from reproducing the cash flow profile of the option by means of the underlying stock and the risk-free security.[18]

To arrive at the special case of the Black-Scholes formula we must also assume that the price of the underlying security follows a continuous sample path and has a volatility (written σ in the formula) which is constant. These two hypotheses were not made explicit: their role becomes clear in the mathematical reasoning which leads to the limit in continuous time (*see* the appendix to this chapter or Chapter 7).

The hypothesis of continuity of the sample path is violated if the price of the underlying security is subject (occasionally) to *sudden jumps*, as is sometimes the case when important news is announced concerning the issuing firm.[19] If the market estimates that this event, if it occurs, will be of a favourable nature, call options out of the money have a higher market value (and put options in the money a lower value) than the theoretical value given by the formula.[20] If it estimates that the event will be unfavourable, call options in the money have a lower market value (and put options out of the money a higher market value) than indicated by the formula.[21] A jump which may be either favourable or unfavourable will have a total effect on option prices which may be deduced by composition of these various effects.

Several formulae exist which allow jumps in the underlying asset to be incorporated. They are unfortunately of limited interest. One of them, attributable to [Cox and Ross 1976], is based on the hypothesis that (i) jumps may only occur in one direction and that (ii) they constitute the only random element in the movement of the underlying stock. So the security follows a path which for most of the time is deterministic, but which is broken by some jumps occurring infrequently at random instants.[22] Another formula, attributable to [Merton 1976], allows a risk affecting the continuous path and the risk of a jump to coexist. But it assumes the jump risk to be 'diversifiable' in the sense of portfolio theory (*see* Chapter 4); jumps which may affect the whole of the market are not admissible.[23]

6.4.2 The constant volatility hypothesis

The volatility (the σ of the formula) of the underlying stock[24] is never truly constant. Changes in volatility have a considerable percentage impact on the price of options, especially options which are out of the money. Consider for example a six-month call option with an exercise price of 40 ECU covering a share whose volatility is 20% per annum and which is currently worth 28 ECU, whilst the interest rate is zero: by applying the Black-Scholes formula we obtain a premium equal to 0.00884 ECU. If, all other things being equal, we increase the volatility to 40% per annum, we obtain a premium of 0.465 ECU. This doubling of the volatility has led to a multiplication by 53 of the price of the option.[25] Options are a means of betting on the volatility of the underlying asset. We can state:

Proposition 4:
To buy an option is to buy volatility.

This is so true that often, on the market, the quotation of options is done not in terms of ECU, but in terms of units of underlying volatility, the correspondence between the two forms of quotation being conventionally established by mechanical application of the Black-Scholes formula.

But if the volatility can change, it is necessary in all logic for the pricing formula to take account of the manner in which it will change. The price of the option must depend on the future anticipated progression of the volatility and also on the uncertainty regarding the volatility (the volatility of the volatility). If the volatility follows an autonomous progression, it is no longer possible to price the option purely and simply by arbitrage reasoning.[26]

If, on the other hand, the volatility only changes with time and with the price of the underlying asset, the task becomes simple once again. For proof, refer to the binomial technique explained above. When constructing the tree structure in Figure 6.6, nothing obliged us to subject the underlying asset to increases and decreases of 5% at every stage. They could, for example, have been ±5% during the first period and ±7% during the second: we would therefore have been concerned with a case where the volatility varied purely according to time. The variations could also have been different during the second period according to whether we started from the upper intermediate node or from the lower node: we would then have been dealing with a case where the volatility of the underlying asset varied according to the price level reached. By redoing the calculations, the reader will be able to check that these variations in volatility in no way prevent the application of the binomial technique.

These generalizations are invaluable as it has been proved empirically that the volatility of shares over time is systematically linked to their price level. A fall in the price of a share is most often accompanied by an increase in its volatility and vice versa. If Fischer Black is to be believed,[27] it is not unusual for a share worth 20 ECU and having a typical daily price movement of 0.50 ECU to change to an average daily price movement of 0.375 ECU if its price doubles to 40 ECU. The reasons for this empirical phenomenon are yet to be completely elucidated. It is thought to be a leverage effect. When a firm's share price falls, while its debt remains constant, its financial leverage increases, which increases the risk of rate of return borne by the shareholders.[28] This also affects the risk of bankruptcy, which is itself borne by the debtors.

Two formulae for evaluation in continuous time have been proposed which take into account this phenomenon affecting the underlying asset:[29] both may be obtained as limits of the binomial technique with variable volatility which we have just outlined. The first is attributable to Cox and Ross, who merely postulate the relation between volatility and price, in the form of a power function:

$$\sigma = aS^{\gamma-1}, \gamma \le 1. \tag{4.1}$$

The elasticity of the volatility relative to the price being equal to (S/σ) $(\partial\sigma/\partial S) = \gamma - 1$, we therefore say that the underlying asset follows a process of *Constant Elasticity of Variance (CEV)*.[30] When $\gamma < 1$, the Black-Scholes formula, which corresponds to the limit case $\gamma = 1$, undervalues the call options which are out of the money and the put options which are in the money. The exact pricing formulae corresponding to the special cases $\gamma = 1/2$ and $\gamma = 0$ may be found in [Cox and Ross 1976], and the general formula in [Cox and Rubinstein 1985].[31]

The second formula – called the compound option formula and attributable to [Geske 1979] – is based on the idea that the leverage effect is at the origin of the fluctuations in the volatility of shares. Geske assumes that the volatility of the *assets* of a firm, and not that of its shares, is constant.[32] As we shall *see* in Chapter 8, shares issued by a firm, due to the limited liability clause, may be analysed as call options on the assets of the firm. So an option on a share is really *an option on a call option* on the assets, or a *compound option*. We know that, even when the volatility of the underlying asset is constant, that of the option is not. Since the share is an option, its volatility varies, as indicated by the Black-Scholes formula: this takes account of the leverage effect. In short, if the volatility of the first level underlying asset is constant, the value and the volatility of the intermediate-level underlying asset are given by the Black-Scholes formula, whilst the value (and the volatility) of the option, a third-level security, are given by Geske's formula [Geske 1979].[33]

6.4.3 The constant interest rate assumption

The risk-free rate of interest r which appears in the Black-Scholes formula is assumed constant during the entire lifetime of the option. This hypothesis is somewhat unrealistic for long maturity options. Moreover, for this category of options, and only for them, fluctuations in the rate may have a not inconsiderable effect on the price of the option.

The term structure of interest rates (*see* Chapter 9) indicates what fluctuations are anticipated by the market. [Merton 1973] showed that, where the short-term interest rate is not constant – and even where it varies in a random, autonomous way – it is sufficient, in order to re-establish the validity of the Black-Scholes formula, to replace the term e^{-rt} by the present value B_t of a *zero-coupon bond, with the same maturity as the option, and having a redemption price of 1 ECU*, and to use as volatility σ not that of the underlying asset S_t but that of S_t/B_t which is the price of the underlying asset *measured in the ECU of the maturity date*.

Of course, no such bond may exist on the market, in which case the arbitrage reasoning, strictly speaking, would no longer apply. However, the value of such a bond may be deduced from those of the existing bonds by statistical interpolation processes which we shall study in Chapter 9. This interpolated value thus allows us to obtain an excellent approximation of what the option is worth.

This transformation envisaged by Merton, based on a bond having the same maturity date as the option, is quite simply *a change of measurement unit*.[34] Generally speaking, it would have been simpler to price the European options (with a fixed maturity date) and to develop the arbitrage reasoning, using as a unit of measurement in the price calculations not the ECU of the current date, but the ECU of the maturity date (the ratio of transformation between these two units being given exactly by B_t, the price today of a bond worth one ECU on the maturity date). Thus, the price which would have been used as the reference price of the underlying security would have been, not its cash price S, but its forward price (for the maturity date of the option); and the price obtained for the value of the option would have been its *undiscounted* price, that is the value taken by the premium if it had to be paid at the end of the contract. In the absence of a dividend, the forward price of a share t units of time before maturity is equal to S_t/B_t and the value of the *undiscounted* premium is C_t/B_t. As for the exercise price K, this is already an amount expressed in ECU of the maturity date.

The Black-Scholes formula now takes the following form:

$$C_t / B_t = (S_t / B_t) \cdot N(d_1) - KN(d_2)$$

$$d_1 \text{ and } d_2 = \frac{\ln[(S_t / B_t) / K]}{\sigma\sqrt{t}} \pm \frac{1}{2}\sigma\sqrt{t}$$

or:

$$C_t = S_t N(d_1) - KB_t N(d_2),$$

that is, the formula amended by Merton. Remember: in this formula, σ is the volatility of S/B and not that of S.

6.4.4 Exercise before maturity and dividends paid on the underlying asset

The Black-Scholes formula applies to options which (i) are European – only able to be exercised at maturity – and (ii) pay no dividend on the underlying asset. Its generalization to options on dividend-paying securities or to American options is not self-evident. Possible exercise before maturity often brings an increase in value to American options.

In the case of a *call option whose underlying asset pays no dividend*, [Merton 1973] shows that the bearer has no interest in exercising the option before maturity, as this would only make him pay the exercise price earlier with no compensating advantage. In this case, American options are equivalent to European options and the Black-Scholes formula applies equally to both.[35]

However, we may be interested in exercising, prior to maturity, put options generally and calls on securities for which a dividend will be paid during the life of the option, two categories of option which raise similar problems.

When exercising his option, the bearer of a *put receives* an amount of cash equal to the exercise price. If the option is *American* and if he exercises before maturity, he may reinvest this cash, at the risk-free rate for example, and will then receive a *continuous income* during the remaining lifetime of the option, an income which he would not have received if he had not exercised the option. It is the appeal of this income that may prompt him to exercise at any time, while the drawback of exercising is that the bearer loses a potential gain which may result from a drop in the price of the underlying asset. We shall show in a moment exactly how to take the best possible exercise decision.

Consider for a moment the case of a *European* call option on a security which pays a *continuous dividend*, the dividend yield D/S being a constant δ.[36] In this case, we may adjust the Black-Scholes formula to take account of the dividend which will be received by the bearer of the underlying security, but not by the bearer of the option. This adjustment involves replacing every S, the current value of the underlying asset, by $Se^{-\delta.t}$. This is simply a second example (*see* Section 5.4.3) of the use of the ECU of the maturity date as a unit of measurement, the forward price of the underlying asset, given a flow of dividends at the certain rate of yield δ, being none other than $Se^{-\delta.t}/B_t$ (*see* Section 5.6.1).

We may even take the case of a random dividend – paid continuously or discretely – together with a random rate of interest to make the case more general. Here, to value the European option we need only have a direct quotation of the *forward price* of the underlying asset for the same maturity as that of the option. The forward price bypasses, as it were, the dividend which will be paid during the life of the option. A formula of the Black-Scholes type results from this.[37]

If we now consider an *American* call option on a dividend paying security, we once again face the problem of exercise before maturity which we have already encountered with regard to the put option, and for the same reasons (or symmetrical reasons): if the bearer exercises his option, he receives the security which will bring him a dividend, whereas the option would not have brought him one. If the dividend is paid continuously,[38] the question of exercise before maturity may arise at any time. If the dividend is paid at a discrete instant in time, it is obvious that the question only arises at the final second preceding the dividend payment.[39]

How should the problem of the optimum exercise decision be approached? Two methods are available. The first is the generalization of the binomial technique: we shall examine this here. The second – which offers two variations depending on whether the dividend is paid continuously or discretely – assumes that we know the valuation of options by differential methods: we shall look at this in Chapter 7.

To take into account the possibilities of exercise before maturity using the binomial technique, we need only compare the price of the option not exercised to its exercised price at each node of the tree structure. We thus obtain the price of the option, on the condition, however, that the dividend does not fluctuate autonomously: in other words, it must be either non-random, or a simple function of the price of the underlying asset and time.

We can now modify the tree structure in Figure 6.6 and modify the lattice to take into account a dividend of 2 ECU paid at the intermediate instant, without altering any other aspect of the problem. We thus obtain Figure 6.8. Consider the upper intermediate node, for which the price of the underlying asset with coupon is 105 ECU and the ex-coupon price is 103 ECU; the displayed value of the option is 5 ECU. How was this value obtained? Operating backwards, as always, we determine the combination of underlying asset and risk-free security which would reproduce the pair of end values of the option [8.15; 0]. The result is as follows:

- the fraction to be invested in the underlying asset at the intermediate instant: 0.7913;

- the amount to borrow in the risk-free security: an end value of 77.425 ECU at maturity.

In this way, we obtain the value of the option not exercised at the intermediate instant at the upper node:

$$-77.425/1.005 + 0.7913 \cdot 103 = 4.4602 \text{ ECU}$$

But, as this price of the option not exercised is less than the exercise price of 105 − 100 = 5 ECU, every bearer would choose to exercise, which brings the option to a price of 5 ECU. An additional stage of calculation gives the price of the option at the initial instant: 2.7363 ECU.

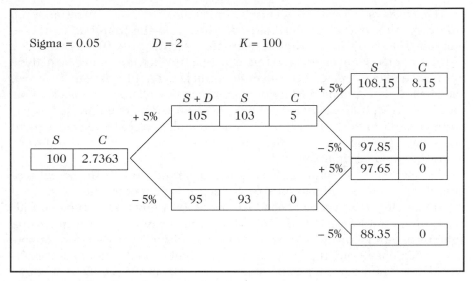

Figure 6.8   The effect of a dividend

6.4.5 Estimation of the volatility parameter σ

Now that we have dealt with most of the problems which are linked to the assumptions of the Black-Scholes formula,[40] there only remains the problem of implementation which would arise even if all the hypotheses were satisfied, namely estimating the volatility parameter σ. We have seen that the price of an option is heavily dependent on the volatility of the underlying security; we cannot hope to obtain a reliable value for the price of the option if the estimator σ introduced into the equation is not itself reliable.

This estimate may be carried out in two ways (a combination of the two is also possible). The first method involves measuring the variance from a sample of past returns on the security by using, quite simply, the unbiased variance estimation formula, mentioned in Chapter 1: this is what is known as the 'historical' approach. A variation of this approach is applicable when the available list of past prices is reduced to the single item of information giving the highest and lowest prices of the underlying asset: this is Parkinson's formula [Parkinson 1980]:

$$\sigma = \frac{0.627}{n} \Sigma_{i=1}^{n} \log (H_i / L_i).$$

in which H_i and L_i represent respectively the highest and lowest prices for one day.

The prices of the options themselves may also be used to determine the volatility: this is the second method, known as the 'implicit variance' method. *This is by far the more preferable.* Starting from the quoted price of the options, it involves inverting the Black-Scholes formula to deduce from it the implied value of σ: since the formula cannot be directly inverted, we do this using a numerical method of successive approximations such as the Newton-Raphson method.[41] It obviously brings the price provided by the formula closer to the actual price;[42] it is not tautological, however, since there are always several options, with different exercise prices and different maturities, quoted simultaneously.

The method of selecting and using these various options in the calculation of σ plays a very important role. In fact, it appears that the volatility of the underlying asset varies depending on the future period of time considered: for example, periods during which the results of a firm are to be announced are characterized by a higher volatility.[43] It is therefore important, when comparing the prices of various options and estimating volatilities, that we limit ourselves to the same time horizon: we cannot expect two options with vastly different maturities to have the same implicit volatility at the same instant.

This said, we still have to use the prices of various options with the same maturity but with different exercise prices, to obtain from them an average estimate of σ which minimizes errors of measurement due, for example, to the non-simultaneity of quotations. A weighted average of the implicit volatilities of the various options seems natural, but we must still choose the system of weighting. Some options have a price which is more especially affected by volatility; it is useful to give these a larger weighting.[44] [Latané and Rendleman 1976] suggest optimizing the weighting of the various available options by minimizing the sum of the squares of the deviations between the theoretical and observed prices. [Whaley 1982] considers that errors of measurement stem mainly from the fact that the prices of some less frequently dealt options are, to some extent, out of date. He therefore suggests weighting the various options according to their transaction volume.

Lastly, [Black 1976b] envisages using the historical approach and the implicit approach simultaneously, since they may be regarded as complementing each other, one measuring long trends and the other being more period specific. His method is purely empirical: it uses what he believes to be certain regularities, for example the negative correlation already noted between volatility and price level or the fact that the volatilities of different shares have a tendency to evolve in unison.[45]

6.5 Empirical tests

Although our aim is to offer readers an account with the emphasis on the theoretical aspects of finance, it is probably useful to discuss, at least briefly, to what extent the Black-Scholes formula corresponds to the reality of the prices quoted. Most improperly, we shall sum up the state of knowledge in this field by citing the results of only two studies: that of [MacBeth and Merville 1979] and that of [Rubinstein 1985]. These two studies covered options on shares of stock.

MacBeth and Merville compared the daily prices of call options covering the securities of six American firms with a high transaction volume during 1976. Figure 6.9 illustrates the results obtained for IBM options, other securities having produced similar results. It will be noted that the prices quoted may exceed the theoretical prices of 16%, whereas the deviation in the other direction may reach 24%. In addition, options out of the money have a market value which appears systematically too low and the opposite is true for options in the money.

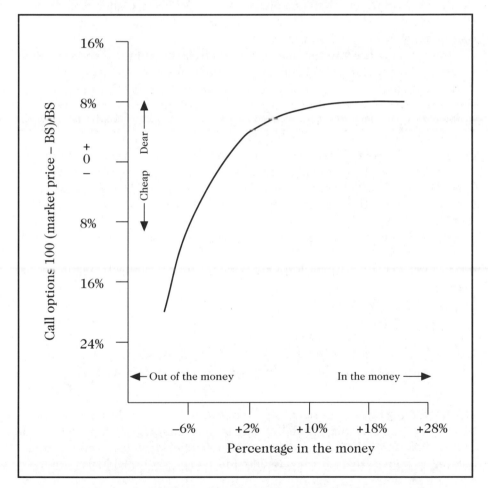

Figure 6.9   The results of [MacBeth and Merville 1979]. This figure gives the percentage of overquote ((observed price − theoretical price)/theoretical price) according to the position of the underlying asset in relation to the exercise price. % in the money = (stock price/discounted strike price less 1) 100. The chart gives the distribution of percentage for over 1000 IBM call options with more than 90 days to run; the thick line gives the mean.

During two successive periods, from 21 August, 1976 to 21 October, 1977, then from 24 October, 1977 to 31 August, 1978, [Rubinstein 1985] recorded the prices quoted on the Chicago Board Option Exchange (CBOE) at the very second that each transaction occurred, as well as, at the same time, the prices offered, the size of the transactions and the price of the underlying asset quoted on the Stock Exchange. He then grouped the prices in pairs, the two options for a pair covering the same share, with similar exercise prices, their prices being observed over a period where the price of the underlying asset did not move. Since the options for a pair thus differed only in their maturity, the hypothesis tested by Rubinstein was that the implicit volatility per unit of time of the longer option (calculated using the Black-Scholes formula) had one chance in two of being higher than that of the option closer to maturity. In reality, for 94.1% of the pairs the shorter option had a higher implicit variance!

Rubinstein carried out an analogous comparison on homogeneous pairs, whose options this time had similar maturities but different percentages of deviation from parity. For the first period of time (1976–1977), he arrived at the same conclusions as MacBeth and Merville: options in the money are undervalued by the Black-Scholes model. A surprising result was found during the second period (1976–1977), for which, for reasons unknown, the deviation for options of relatively distant maturity was systematically in the reverse direction! In addition, a comparison of the various models mentioned in Section 6.4 led Rubinstein to believe that none of them is systematically superior to the others over the various periods of time, although some dominate occasionally.

On the whole, only one conclusion appears to emerge from the empirical tests for all the periods and all the securities: the market overvalues, relative to the Black-Scholes formula, options close to maturity which are in the money.

6.6   Other secondary securities and other applications of the arbitrage principle

In Chapter 8 we study in detail the applications of the arbitrage principle which are linked to the pricing of assets and liabilities of industrial and commercial firms. We limit ourselves now to a few examples of applications relating to derivative securities, issued and bought by individuals, although covering an underlying security issued by a firm. For investors taken as a whole, investment in derivative securities of this type, such as options, futures contracts and so on, constitutes, a zero-sum game: what one wins, the other loses. It is in this that they are distinct from the basic securities issued by companies producing new resources and distributing dividends.

6.6.1 Futures contracts on financial securities

Futures contracts are in many respects, similar to simple forward contracts, except for the fact that the losses and gains of a bearer of a futures contract are registered at the end of every day and debited or credited to his or her account. This procedure is called 'marking to market'.

The forward price of any financial instrument is established, by arbitrage reasoning, at its 'parity value'. Consider, for example, a share whose cash price was today – t units of time before the maturity date – equal to S_t, whereas the dividend yield it is to distribute between today and the maturity date of the forward contract is equal to a non-random amount d_t. If the price today of a zero coupon bond of the same maturity as the contract and paying one ECU is written B_t, or, which amounts to the same thing, the yield on this bond (which is the rate of interest to run until the maturity date) is written r_t ($B_t \equiv 1/(1 + r_t)$), the forward price (quoted for example on the Paris monthly settlement market) is:

$$F_t = S_t/[B_t(1 + d_t)] = S_t(1 + r_t)/(1 + d_t) \qquad [6.1]$$

If we use a different formulation in which r and d are the rates from day to day – or rather the instantaneous rates – assumed constant during the lifetime of the contract, and compounded continuously, we have:

$$F = S\, e^{(r - d)t} \qquad [6.2]$$

or even:

$$F\, e^{-r.t} = S\, e^{-d.t} \qquad [6.3]$$

t being here the length of time to maturity of the contract.

Formula 6.3 will be understood if it is realized that holding the primary security allows dividends to be received, whilst holding the forward contract allows the interest on the money to be saved (by only paying the forward price on maturity).

The evaluation of futures contracts is less simple and may not in principle be done purely and simply on the basis of arbitrage reasoning, unless future rates of interest are considered to be non-random.[46] In all cases, the price of futures is very close to the forward price. The small deviations stem from the marking to market procedure, which produces daily cash flows, whereas a forward contract produces no cash flow until maturity.

To illustrate the impact of this procedure, consider the evaluation of a forward contract and that of a futures contract on the same underlying security with a one month maturity. If an investor makes a forward purchase of the underlying asset today, at the end of one month he will have made a profit equal to the difference between the cash price quoted on maturity and the forward price quoted today. But if he buys a futures contract on the same underlying asset, his total loss or gain will depend on what happens day after day during the month of holding. Every day, one of the following two events will occur:

- either the futures price of the underlying asset will have increased relative to what it was the previous evening; the bearer of the futures contract pockets a payoff the same day, which he may reinvest at the market rate of interest until the end of the month, thus producing an additional payoff, compared with the total deviation between the futures price at the start and the cash price on the day of maturity;

- or the futures price will have fallen during this day; the bearer must therefore finance this loss by a loan whose financial cost will constitute an additional loss at the end of the month, compared with the total deviation between the futures price at the start and the cash price on the day of maturity.

If the interest rates available during this time are fixed, the reinvestment or financing of the interim cash flows will be done in both cases at the same rate of interest (apart from the borrowing–lending rate difference) and, from the point of view of the starting date, the prospect of additional gains will cancel out in value the prospect of additional losses.

However, if the payoffs received on the futures contract during this time have a tendency to be reinvested at higher rates of interest than those at which the losses during this time are financed, then it is clear that the futures contract offers an additional advantage which must translate into a higher price. Therefore, depending on whether the correlation between futures price and interest rate is positive or negative, the original futures price must be greater or less than the original forward price.

Amongst futures contracts, those covering a stock market index are particularly useful since they allow us to cover the risks of upwards and downwards fluctuation in the securities market taken as a whole. Unfortunately, significant and inexplicable price differences have appeared between the value (quoted, for example, in Chicago) of futures contracts on indices and the value of the index itself (for example, on the physical stock market in New York).[47]

6.6.2 Index options

Options on stock market indices are the subject of much practical interest.[48] They raise some new theoretical problems.

First of all, there is the behaviour of the index itself, whose weighting depends on the value of the securities. As we have seen, it is very difficult to know exactly how the price of a share will behave over time; it is an even more delicate operation to determine the behaviour of a basket which may contain, according to case, several hundred different securities and whose weighting fluctuates. The fluctuations in the volatility of the index appear difficult to predict.

Also, since most stock market indices in the United States are the subject of futures contracts with regularly distributed maturity dates, it appears, strangely, that the volatility of the stock market index is noticeably greater in the vicinity of the expiry dates of these contracts. At least, this is what is revealed by the prices of options covering the corresponding indices.[49]

The value of the basket of securities is calculated by a weighted average of the various securities; according to case, the weighting may be constant or, on the other hand, reflect the relative market value of the various securities. In the latter case, the fluctuations of the index are the product of the variations in the prices considered individually and of the variations in the weightings. We could show that this produces a serial dependence in the behaviour of the index. No available pricing formula is capable of taking account of this serial dependence, which, in addition, complicates the statistical problem of volatility estimation.

Let us also mention two difficulties of a purely technical nature. The dates of dividend payments, for a basket containing numerous securities, are spread over the entire year. Besides the jump which they induce in the value of the index, they may also induce, in the case of an American option, an exercise of the option before maturity.[50]

Some options are in fact options on index *futures contracts*[51] and not direct options on the cash value of the index. Arbitrage and the hedging of positions in options will therefore be done most often using futures contracts; it is therefore the implicit rate of interest of futures transactions (forward transactions) which must be taken into account when evaluating the option. The price deviations already noted between stock market indices and the corresponding futures contracts make the negotiation of options on index futures hazardous.

6.6.3 Options on futures contracts written on financial securities

Options on futures contracts are level-three securities. From a primary underlying security, we may define a *futures* contract to buy this underlying asset (*see* Section 6.6.1); this is a level-two security. At level three, options on futures contracts are options which, in the event of exercise, grant to the bearer a futures contract to buy an underlying security.[52] Since the futures contract granted is marked to market, the bearer of the option who exercises receives in fact an *immediate cash payment* equal to the difference between the futures price quoted at the moment of exercise and the exercise price (and not equal to the discounted value of this difference). The maturity of the underlying futures contract obviously does not precede the maturity of the option.

There are two differences[53] between an option on a futures contract and an option on cash. Firstly, since the underlying asset is different, the Black-Scholes formula must be modified. [Black 1976] showed that the price of a European futures option is independent of the maturity of the futures contract and that, in order to price it, we need only replace the cash price S in the formula with the price F of the futures contract used as the underlying security, *multiplied by* e^{-rt} (or B_t), t being the remaining lifetime *of the option*. It is the remaining lifetime of the option which plays a role here – not the duration of the futures contract: this is due to the fact that on maturity *of the option* the bearer who exercises receives cash.

For the same reason, a second difference between a cash option and a futures option appears when the option is of the American type. Whilst it is never advisable to exercise prior to maturity a direct call option on a non-dividend-paying underlying security, it may be optimal to exercise a call option on a futures contract even when the primary security pays no dividend. The motive for this is the attraction of the cash, which is received on exercise, by the very nature of the option contract.

6.6.4 Currency options

We have already encountered, in Section 6.4, some of the difficulties attached to the evaluation of currency options – in particular, random fluctuations in the rate of interest on each of the two currencies and the opportunity which may arise of exercising such an option at any time, given that the interests on the currencies run continually. (The same difficulties are encountered when evaluating *commodities options*.)

Furthermore, the usual problems are present when identifying the process of the underlying asset, namely the exchange rate (cash exchange or futures contract depending on the definition of the option). Foreign exchange markets are characterized by periods of agitation, or high volatility, followed by periods of relative calm. In addition, some currencies are linked to others by exchange agreements and have a tendency to undergo sudden devaluations, that is, price jumps. For the reader interested in this type of option, [Chesney and Loubergé 1988] offers a useful summary of knowledge on the subject.

6.6.5 Exchange options

Under certain circumstances, it may be useful to know the value of an option which gives the right to exchange an underlying security for another security (the right of conversion), the bivariate random process followed by these two assets being assumed known. This is a problem which we have already solved without knowing it. The options we have considered up to now were options giving the right to exchange the underlying security for a specified amount of ECU, called the exercise price K, payable on the maturity date. In this case the ECU was a particularly useful unit of measurement, since it was in this unit that K was non-random.

Changing the unit of measurement, or numeraire, is a process which we have already used on occasion. In the present case, all we need to do is select as the numeraire one of the two securities in question. The *relative* price of these two securities is the ratio of their prices measured in ECU; its process is obtained from the bivariate process of the monetary prices: in particular, the volatility of the relative price results from the two individual volatilities and from the correlation between the two securities (*see* Chapter 7). In terms of this numeraire, the 'exercise price' of the option is equal to 1. In this case, the Black-Scholes formula – or the option pricing method adapted to the statement of the specific problem – gives the present value of the exchange option *relative to the price of the security chosen as a numeraire*. To arrive at the price of the option in ECU, all calculations having been made, we need only multiply the result obtained by the price in ECU of the numeraire security.[54]

6.6.6 'Primes'

Not so long ago, the Paris Stock Exchange dealt with derivative securities akin to options, which were called 'primes'. This type of contract, under which the buyer paid out nothing, may come back into fashion. Primes were similar to forward contracts, but conditional forward contracts, since the buyer reserved the right to retract at the moment of maturity (two days prior to settlement). If he retracted, he paid the seller a contractual penalty. The quotation was made on the 'price of the prime', which was in fact the conditional forward price (as opposed to the 'firm' forward price).

If we call the value of the prime K and the penalty D, it will be seen that on maturity the buyer who makes the purchase receives a profit $S - K$ and the one who pays the penalty pays out D. The payoff profile is therefore:

$$\text{Max}[S - K, -D] = \text{Max}[S - K + D, 0] - D \tag{6.4}$$

Apart from the transactions costs, the buyer prefers to retract if S is less than $K - D$.

The acquisition price of this prime may easily be obtained using the Black-Scholes formula, since the first term of the right-hand side of [6.4] represents an option with an exercise price equal to $K - D$, the second term being easily discounted since it is fixed.

However, the acquisition price of a prime is zero by construction, since an individual who takes a prime contract pays out no money, as opposed to what happens in the case of an option where this price is paid (the 'premium'). As a result, another variable must ensure the adjustment of supply and demand: this role is played by the quantity K. It is for this reason that we call it somewhat improperly the 'value of the prime': it is the (conditional) forward price of the underlying stock, on the understanding that the buyer may retract by paying the penalty.

To calculate the price of the prime, we need only set the acquisition price calculated by the Black-Scholes formula to zero, the unknown of this equation being K. The equation can then be solved by numerical iteration.[55]

6.6.7 Portfolio insurance

We saw in Section 6.2 that it is possible to reproduce a call option by combining a loan and a purchase of the underlying asset in proportions which vary over time (see propositions 1 and 3). In the same way, we may reproduce a put using a risk-free deposit and a short sale of the underlying asset.

It follows from this that individuals holding the underlying security may synthesize themselves a put on the underlying asset, by reducing their investment in the underlying asset and placing their money into a risk-free deposit as soon as the price of the underlying asset falls. This is the principle of portfolio insurance: to add a put is to procure a price safety net, that is, an insurance.

We have just shown that this may be done without necessarily having to resort to an actual existing put option, which is crucial since the maturity of most existing options is too close to offer the investor noteworthy protection. Long-term protection is obtained by transactions directly related to the underlying asset or, more commonly, by transactions on index futures contracts. The portfolio insurer manages a position on stock index futures contracts, buying futures when the market rises and selling them when it falls. This procedure increases exposure to upward fluctuations of the market and limits exposure to falls.[56][57]

The 'insurance contract' contains three elements: a management horizon (maturity), a floor, K, and a profit-sharing rate α. In total, on the maturity date, an insured investor will possess a capital equal to: $\max[\alpha S, K]$. Since the insurance premium is most often zero, these three elements adjust themselves accordingly. Given the maturity date and the floor, K, which is set, the determination of α, taking account of the starting capital, may be done using the Black-Scholes formula. In practice, given the problems posed by fluctuations in the volatility of the underlying asset, the insurer will have the good sense to promise a participation rate, α, which will depend on the volatility, σ, recorded.

6.7 Conclusion

The arbitrage pricing method has allowed us to bypass the extremely difficult modelling of general equilibrium and of the equilibrium of the financial market. It has allowed us to price secondary securities according to the price of primary securities with remarkable precision. However, it only operates from the moment that we posit the random processes governing the behaviour of primary securities over time. Since it is based on the hypothesis that the process given represents this behaviour correctly in general equilibrium, the bypass is obvious. The method is fruitful, but it depends on information which we do not in principle possess, short of possessing a theory of general equilibrium.

The fact remains that option pricing theory has undergone prodigious development in the space of a few years and has in many respects allowed the tools of financial theory to be sharpened (*see* Chapter 7). Furthermore, its empirical implementation will no doubt allow us, by an inverse argument, to deduce from the prices of options quoted on the market a good deal of information on the process of primary securities. In particular, options are an instrument for observing the behaviour of the volatility of primary securities, which leaves aside other aspects of their process. The options market therefore supplies a marvellous laboratory.

After going more deeply into some mathematical methods of financial theory in Chapter 7, we address in Chapter 8 some other applications of options theory, belonging to the field of corporate finance.

Appendix

The price limit obtained by the binomial method is the price given by the Black-Scholes formula [Cox *et al.* 1979]

Let us call u (up) and d (down) the two increase factors of the price of the underlying stock: at each time step, S is multiplied by u with a probability of p, or by d [with a probability of $(1 - p)$]. The price today being called S_n, at the end of n steps, the price arrived at, S_0, is:

$$S_0 = S_n \cdot u^j \cdot d^{n-j} \qquad\qquad\qquad\qquad [A.1]$$

or:

$$lnS_0 = lnS_n + j \cdot lnu + (n - j) \cdot lnd = lnS_n + j \cdot ln(u/d) + n \cdot lnd \quad [A.2]$$

if there have been j price jumps and $n - j$ falls, the probability of this event being $[n!/(j! \cdot (n - j)!)] \cdot p^j \cdot (1 - p)^{n-j}$.

Let us now establish the price C_n of the option as a fraction of S_n, when n periods remain to maturity. Let R be the rate of interest covering a period: we stipulate that $d < 1 + R < u$. By applying as many times as necessary the binomial method explained in the text of the chapter – involving reproducing the profile of the option using the underlying asset and a risk-free investment – and by calling the 'adjusted' probability of an upward jump:

$$\pi = (1 + R - d)/(u - d)$$

as in the text, we obtain the following formula for the price of the option:

$$C_n = (1 + R)^{-n} \cdot \{[n!/(j! \cdot (n - j)!)] \cdot \pi^j \cdot (1 - \pi)^{n-j} \cdot Max[0, S_n \cdot u^j \cdot d^{n-j} - K]\}$$

which we may also write as:

$$C_n = S_n \cdot \Phi_\pi(a; n) - (K/(1 + R)^{-n}) \cdot \Phi_\pi(a; n) \qquad\qquad [A.3]$$

if we adopt the following notations:

$\pi' = \pi \cdot u/(1 + R)$

$\Phi_z(a; n) = \Sigma_{j=a}^n [n!/j! \cdot (n-j)!] \cdot z^j \cdot (1 - z)^{n-j}$

a being the smallest integer such that: $S_n \cdot u^a \cdot d^{n-a} > K$

We can recognize in Φ the truncated binomial distribution law at level a (the probability of at least a price jumps in the course of n periods).

Now consider a length of time t left to maturity. We shall increase indefinitely the number n of periods which separate the present moment from the maturity date without changing the total length of time t left to run (another way of writing S_n would be S_t). Each period will therefore become extremely short. The size of the possible movements upwards and downwards during each period will need to be adjusted to the length of the period. We must specify how this adjustment is made. Let us choose to adjust the parameters of the jumps in the following manner:

$$u = e^{\sigma \cdot \sqrt{(t/n)}}, d = e^{-\sigma \cdot \sqrt{(t/n)}}, p = \tfrac{1}{2} + \tfrac{1}{2} \cdot (\mu/\sigma)\sqrt{(t/n)}, 1 + R = e^{rt/n} \qquad [A.4]$$

where μ and σ are constants.

We know that, when n is increased indefinitely, the binomial law converges towards a normal law whose expected value and variance are the limits of the expectation and the variance of the binomial law (*Moivre-Laplace theorem*).[58] This applies to the distribution of the numbers of jumps, or to any quantity which is linearly linked to it such as lnS_0 (see Equation A.2).

Let us therefore calculate the expectation and the variance of lnS_0, then substitute the values [A.4] of the parameters and take the limit when n→∞. We obtain:

$$E_p[lnS_0] = lnS_n + [p \cdot ln(u/d) + lnd] \rightarrow lnS_n + \mu \cdot t \qquad [A.5]$$

$$\text{var}_p[lnS_0] = p \cdot (1 - p) \cdot [ln(u/d)]^2 \cdot n \rightarrow \sigma^2 \cdot t \qquad [A.6]$$

Consequently, the variable $[ln(S_0/S_t) - \mu \cdot t]/(\sigma \cdot \sqrt{t})$ is standard normal.

Pursuing this argument, we wish to replace the binomial laws Φ_π and $\Phi_{\pi'}$ in [A.3] by their corresponding normal laws. We obtain the limits necessary to this calculation:

$$E_\pi[lnS_0] = lnS_n + n \cdot [\pi \cdot ln(u/d) + lnd] \rightarrow lnS_n + (r - \tfrac{1}{2}\sigma^2) \cdot t \qquad [A.7]$$

$$E_{\pi}[lnS_0] = lnSn + n \cdot [\pi' \cdot ln(u/d) + lnd] \rightarrow lnSn + (r + \tfrac{1}{2}\sigma^2) \cdot t \qquad [\text{A.8}]$$

$$\text{var}_{\pi}[lnS_0] = \pi \cdot (1 - \pi) \cdot [ln(u/d)]^2 \cdot n \rightarrow \sigma^2 \cdot t \qquad [\text{A.9}]$$

$$\text{var}_{\pi}[lnS_0] = \pi' \cdot (1 - \pi') \cdot [ln(u/d)]^2 \cdot n \rightarrow \sigma^2 \cdot t \qquad [\text{A.10}]$$

All substitutions having been made in [A.3], we obtain the Black-Scholes formula.

Notes to Chapter 6

1   It is not one of our objectives to explain investment strategies on the options market. This is the subject of specialized works, for example: [McMillan 1986].

2   For a classic empirical test of put–call parity, *see* [Stoll 1969].

3   If the rate is 6% per year, the unitary period in question is in the order of a month.

4   Readers with a background in economics will recognize here a form of 'Arrow-Debreu price': *see* [Debreu 1984] Chapter 7.

5   The generalization of this technique to two state variables enables us to extend its field of application; *see* [Boyle 1988].

6   *See* Section 7.5.2.

7   The passage to continuous time is not the only way of obtaining the Black-Scholes formula. Some hypotheses, covering not only the probability distribution of prices, *but also* the probability distribution of investors' future marginal utility, yield the same formula in discrete time; *see* [Brennan 1979] *or* [Rubinstein 1976].

8   A similar formula exists for European puts. It may be deduced from the formula below by noting, as we have already done, that buying a call attached to the sale of a put where both are of the European type and have the same exercise price, equates to a forward purchase of the underlying stock (a relationship known as parity). No analogous formula exists for American options.

9   If r is a continuously compounded interest rate.

10   Which means 'assuming the exercise takes place'.

11   This rate of return is, as it were, 'replaced' in the formula by the risk-free interest rate.

12   *See* [Cox and Rubinstein 1985], pages 287 to 317.

13   α represents the instantaneous expected return on the option, covering the infinitely small time interval between now and the immediate future. Rubinstein obtained a formula giving the expected rate of return of the option over a finite period of time; *see* [Cox and Rubinstein 1985], page 324.

14   The function $N(x)$ which appears in the formula may be approximated by a programmable polynomial expression which does away with the need to consult a table of the normal law:

$$N(x) = 1 - (1/\sqrt{2\pi})\ e^{-x^2/2}\ (b_1 k + b_2 h^2 + b_3 h^3 + b_4 h^4 + b_5 h^5)\ (x > 0)$$
where: $k = 1/(1 + ax)$; $b_1 = 0.319381530$; $b_2 = -0.356563782$; $b_3 = 1.781477937$; $b_4 = -1.821255978$; $b_5 = 1.330274429$; $a = 0.2316419$

See [Abramovitz and Stegun 1970], page 932.

15   [Black 1989].

16   Although they are not without importance in practice, we have given no space here to the somewhat unrealistic assumptions which pertain to the institutional framework of the market and which make possible complete and exact arbitrage (*see* the introduction to Part II).

17   *See* the price limit in the appendix, or Chapter 7, to understand the nature of the analogous process in continuous time.

18   Some very specific trinomial processes certainly do exist which, when the time interval tends towards zero, also lead to the Black-Scholes formula. However this 'generalization' is of little interest; the only trinomial processes to which this applies are those which differ less and less from binomial processes as the time divisions become smaller and smaller.

19   The price of a share also jumps on the day of a dividend payout. We shall return to the effect of dividends when discussing the exercise of options before maturity.

20   The prospect of a jump adds to the volatility of the underlying asset. The price comparison we are making extends to unchanged total volatility. Thus we compare the price of an option with a possible jump of the underlying asset to that of an option with no jump but with a higher σ.

21   Such a configuration appeared clearly over the days and weeks following the stock market crash of 19th October, 1987. Prices reflected the expectation of a second crash. *See* [Bates 1991].

22   This is a Poisson process.

23   To read further on this subject, *see* [Ball and Torous 1983, 1985], [Jones 1984], *and* [Bates 1988a,b].

24   This observation is equally applicable to stock options or options on currencies or bonds.

25   [Brenner and Subrahmanyam 1988] point out that for options at parity (more precisely, according to their definition, those whose exercise price is such that: $S = Ke^{-rt}$), we have: $C \approx 0.398\ S\ \sigma\ \sqrt{t}$, with the result that the price of the option rises linearly with the volatility.

26   In this case, two approaches may be considered. Either we assume that the fluctuations in volatility are a source of risk which is diversifiable and which, consequently, is not remunerated on the financial market by any risk premium: this is the approach taken by [Hull and White 1987], [Johnson and Shanno 1987] and [Scott 1987]. This clashes with the empirical findings of [Christie 1982] according to which the volatilities of different shares tend to vary together. Or we impose restrictions not only on the joint probability distribution of S and σ, but even on the joint distribution including S, σ *and* the marginal utility of the investors, which provides an explicit formulation of the risk premiums attached to the volatility of the volatility: this is the approach taken by [Wiggins 1987], [Nelson 1991] and [Melino and Turnbull 1991]. Whether we use one approach or the other, we must specify the behaviour of the volatility over time: we thus often use an ARCH (AutoRegressive Conditional Heteroskedasticity or autoregressive conditional variance) process as do [Scott 1987] and [Nelson 1991]. The empirical relevance of this type of process is tested by [Akgiray 1989] for shares of stock.

27   [Black 1976a] or [Black 1989].

28   *See* a corporate finance textbook such as [Brealey and Myers 1982], Chapter 12; *see also* Chapter 8 of the present work. An analogous empirical phenomenon also appears to exist on the currency market; the explanation is to date unknown. However, for currency the effect is much less discernible since its volatility also varies autonomously according to the economic context and the prospects of intervention by central banks on the foreign exchange market.

29   If the volatility of the underlying asset changes deterministically by being purely a function of time, the Black-Scholes formula remains applicable provided it is slightly amended. It is sufficient to replace the term $\sigma\sqrt{t}$ by the square root of $\int_0^t \sigma^2 (u)du$, where $\sigma^2(t)$ is the variance of the underlying asset t units of time before maturity.

30   We shall address later the problems of estimating volatility which occur when volatility is assumed constant. Regarding the more complex problem of estimating the two coefficients a and γ of the CEV model, let us mention here the work of [Tucker *et al.* 1988] and [Gibbons and Jacklin 1988]. [Bates 1988] measured the degree of asymmetry of the distribution of the underlying asset by comparing the prices of call options with those of put options.

31   Page 363.

32   Conversely, [Rubinstein 1983] considers the case of a firm possessing a portfolio of risky assets (whose variance is constant) and risk-free assets. When the value of the risky asset falls, its part in the total asset also falls so that the total volatility falls. The value of the firm follows a 'displaced diffusion process'. Such behaviour of the total risk of the firm does not apparently conform to reality, but it gives rise to an explicit option pricing formula.

33   Which may also be found in [Cox and Rubinstein 1985] page 414.

34   Economic theory gives only the relative prices, or prices of objects of choice *relative to one another*, the concept of the absolute price of a commodity item having no meaning since a transaction always consists of exchanging one commodity item for another. Rather than calculating all the relative prices of commodities taken two at a time, which would be superfluous, the economist will always choose a single reference commodity item, called the numeraire, which is used as a basis for pricing, relative to which we determine the prices of the other commodities and whose price is arbitrarily set at the value of 1. The

numeraire commonly chosen is a unit of consumption available on the current date or, in monetary models, a nominal currency unit. The change of measurement unit of which we are speaking here is the same thing as changing the numeraire. The numeraire used in the previous developments was the ECU (real or nominal) of today's date t. The new numeraire used by Merton is a bond with a face value of 1 ECU repayable at the maturity date of the option.

35   The value of the European call option $SN(d_1) - Ke^{-rt}N(d_2)$ has a lower bound imposed by $S - Ke^{-rt}$, and is therefore always greater than the value of an exercised option $S - K$.

36   For stock options, the case of a dividend paid continuously is neither relevant nor useful. However, it becomes very relevant when we consider options on currency or commodities. A call option on a foreign currency can be compared to the direct holding of the currency which would allow a continuous income to be received in the form of interest: this is the dividend in question. A perfect symmetry characterizes currency options: a call option on the dollar is identical to a put option on the ECU: continuous interest is received or constitutes an opportunity cost on both sides, depending on whether one has cash in hand or not.

37   See [Grabbe 1983] and [Carr 1988]. The procedure used is once again that used by [Merton 1973] for a random rate of interest and a nondividend-paying option (see Section 6.4.3). The random dividend and the random rate of interest play perfectly symmetrical roles and can be treated symmetrically. The volatility σ must therefore be that of the forward price of fixed maturity coinciding with that of the option.

38   If a call option on a foreign currency is exercised, the currency is received and may then be invested, allowing the foreign rate of interest to be earned continuously. As we have pointed out, this is an example of a dividend paid continuously by the underlying asset.

39   Exercise prior to maturity is not the only circumstance where the lifetime of an option is cut short. Some operations carried out by the firm issuing the underlying asset may have the same effect; mergers and acquisitions may be mentioned here. Incorporations of reserve may also change the nature of the option if by virtue of its definition contract the option is not 'protected'.

40   We will not be addressing the problems linked to transactions costs, margin calls and taxes. On these matters see respectively [Leland 1985], [Heath and Jarrow 1987] and [Dammon and Green 1987].

41   See [Dahlquist and Björck 1974]. Convergence is extremely rapid.

42   See [Chiras and Manaster 1978] or [Maloney and Rogalski 1989]. Further [Latané and Rendleman 1976] and [Chiras and Manaster 1978] show that the implicit volatility arising from the quoted option prices is a better predictor of future volatility than is past volatility. Preliminary tests carried out by Augros (see [Augros 1987], page 168) on volatilities observed on the Paris Stock Exchange do not appear to confirm the results obtained in the United States.

43   See [Patell and Wolfson 1979]. On the fluctuation of volatilities on the Paris Stock Exchange and their consistency across maturities, see [Augros 1987], page 162 onwards.

44   The Black-Scholes formula gives a value of $\partial C/\partial \sigma$ which is particularly high in the vicinity of the exercise price. The price of an option which is currently at parity therefore provides a better estimate of the volatility of the underlying asset: see [Beckers 1981].

45   For more detail, see [Cox and Rubinstein 1985], page 278, or [Black 1976].

46   See [Cox et al. 1981].

47   See [Stoll 1988] and [Stoll and Whaley 1990].

48   First appearing in 1982, several dozen types of index contract are quoted today in the United States, Britain, Australia and Canada, including index options specialized by industrial sector and options on stock exchange index futures contracts. In Paris, the opening in 1989 of an options contract on the CAC index marked an additional modernizing step. On maturity of the index options, settlement is purely in cash, on the basis of the level of the index noted: the contract does not provide for any delivery of securities.

49   See [Stoll and Whaley 1986] and [Day and Lewis 1988].

50   To make things worse, the time necessary to calculate the index makes it necessary to grant a delay in the exercise decision. *See* [Evnine and Rudd 1985].

51   *See* Section 6.6.6.2.

52   At the time of writing, no contract of this type exists where the primary underlying asset is a security price; the only existing contracts cover indices of security prices. They therefore simultaneously have properties linked to their character as index contracts (*see* above) and properties linked to their character as futures contracts. On the other hand, options do exist on currency futures (*see* [Ogden and Tucker 1988]) and on commodities futures (*see* [Jordan *et al.* 1987]).

53   The properties of options on futures contracts were addressed for the first time by [Black 1976]; the most complete treatment may be found in [Ramaswamy and Sundaresan 1985]; [Whaley 1986] is the best empirical study to date.

54   *See* [Margrabe 1978] *or* [Stulz 1982].

55   *See* [Dumas 1980], [Cox and Jacquillat 1984], [Moussi and Roger 1985].

56   Difficulties of implementation are numerous. Since the Black-Scholes formula is based on the same idea, we already know the limitations (*see* Section 6.4): random interest rate, variable volatility, price jumps. Nor must we forget transactions costs, which may rapidly become significant, anomalies of prices on the index futures market which we have already noted and the fact that the portfolio to be insured does not have the same composition as the market index relating to the available futures contracts.

57   Some commentators have accused portfolio insurers of precipitating the crash of 19th October, 1987. On this subject, an original thesis is expounded by [Grossman 1988]. *See also* the special edition of the *Journal of Economic Perspectives* (Summer 1988) on this issue.

58   The Moivre-Laplace theorem is usually stated (*see* [Métivier 1979], page 208) for the case where p = constant. We are applying here a generalization of this theorem. Another method which would allow the same limits to be obtained by using the theorem in its usual form would be to choose:

$$u = \exp[\mu t/n + \sigma\sqrt{(t/n)}], d = \exp[\mu t/n - \sigma\sqrt{(t/n)}], p = \tfrac{1}{2}.$$

References

[Abramovitz and Stegun 1970] M. Abramovitz and I. A. Stegun, *Handbook of Mathematical Functions*. Dover, 1970.

[Akgiray 1989] V. Akgiray, Conditional Heteroskedasticity in Time Series of Stock Returns: Evidence and Forecasts, *Journal of Business*, 62, 1989, 55–80.

[Augros 1987] J. C. Augros, *Finance; Options et Obligations Convertibles*. Economica, 1987.

[Ball and Torous 1983] C. A. Ball and W. N. Torous, A Simplified Jump Process for Common Stock Returns, *Journal of Financial and Quantitative Analysis*, 18, 1983, 53–65.

[Ball and Torous 1985] C. A. Ball and W. N. Torous, On Jumps in Common Stock Prices and Their Impact on Call Option Pricing, *Journal of Finance*, 40, 1985, 155–173.

[Bates 1988a] D. S. Bates, *The Crash Premium: Option Pricing Under Asymmetric Processes, With Applications to Options on Deutschmark futures*, Working Paper, Rodney White Center, University of Pennsylvania, 1988.

[Bates 1988b] D. S. Bates, *Pricing Options under Jump-Diffusion Processes*, Working Paper 37–38, Rodney White Center, University of Pennsylvania, 1988.

[Bates 1991] D. S. Bates, The Crash of '87: Was It Expected? The Evidence from the Options Market, *Journal of Finance*, 46, 1991, 1009–1044.

[Beckers 1981] S. Beckers, Standard Deviations Implied in Option Prices as Predictors of Future Stock Price Variability, *Journal of Banking and Finance*, 5, 1981, 363–382.

[Black 1976a] F. Black, Studies of Stock Price Volatility Changes, *Proceedings of the Meeting of the American Statistical Association*, Business and Economics statistics section, Chicago, 1976.

[Black 1976b] F. Black, *Fischer Black on Options*, 1, no 8, May 1976.

[Black 1989] F. Black, How to Use the Holes in Black-Scholes, *Journal of Applied Corporate Finance*, Winter 1989, 67–73.

[Black and Scholes 1973] F. Black and M. Scholes, The Pricing of Options and Corporate Liabilities, *Journal of Political Economy*, 81, 1973, 637–659.

[Boyle 1988] P. P. Boyle, A Lattice Framework for Option Pricing with Two State Variables, *Journal of Financial and Quantitative Analysis*, 23, 1988, 1–12.

[Boyle and Turnbull 1989] P. P. Boyle and S. M. Turnbull, Pricing and Hedging Capped Options, *The Journal of Futures Markets*, 9, 1989, 41–54.

[Brealey and Myers 1982] R. Brealey and S. Myers, *Principles of Corporate Finance*, 2nd ed., 1982.

[Brennan 1979] M. J. Brennan, The Pricing of Contingent Claims in Discrete-Time Models, *Journal of Finance*, 34, 1979, 53–68.

[Brenner and Subrahmanyam 1988] M. Brenner and M. Subrahmanyam, A Simple Formula to Compute the Implied Standard Deviation, *Financial Analysts Journal*, 1988, 80–82.

[Carr 1988] P. Carr, Option Pricing When Dividends and Interest Rates are Unknown, Working Paper, University of California, Los Angeles, August 1988.

[Chesney and Loubergé 1988] M. Chesney and H. Loubergé, Les options sur devises: une revue des modèles théoriques et des travaux empiriques, *Finance, Revue de l'AFFI*, 9, 1988, 7–34.

[Chiras and Manaster 1978] D. Chiras and S. Manaster, The Informational Content of Option Prices and a Test of Market Efficiency, *Journal of Financial Economics*, 6, 1978, 213–234.

[Christie 1982] A. A. Christie, The Stochastic Behavior of Common Stock Variances: Value, Leverage and Interest Rate Effects, *Journal of Financial Economics*, 10, 1982, 407–432.

[Cox and Jacquillat 1984]   J. C. Cox and B. Jacquillat, Une note sur
                               l'évaluation rationnelle des primes à la Bourse
                               de Paris, CESA Working Paper no. 241, 1984.

[Cox and Ross 1976]   J. C. Cox and S. Ross, 1976, The Valuation
                               of Options for Alternative Stochastic Pro-
                               cesses, *Journal of Financial Economics*, 3,
                               1976, 145–166.

[Cox and Rubinstein 1985]   J. C. Cox and M. Rubinstein, *Options
                               Markets*. Englewood Cliffs, NJ: Prentice Hall,
                               Inc., 1985.

[Cox *et al.* 1979]   J. C. Cox, S. Ross; and M. Rubinstein,
                               Option Pricing: A Simplified Approach,
                               Journal of Financial Economics, 7, 1979,
                               229–263.

[Cox *et al.* 1981]   J. C. Cox, J. Ingersoll and S. A. Ross, The
                               Relation Between Forward Prices and Futures
                               Prices, *Journal of Financial Economics*, 9,
                               4, 1981, 321–346.

[Dahlquist and Björck 1974]   G. Dahlquist and Å. Björck, *Numerical
                               Methods*, Englewood Cliffs, NJ: Prentice
                               Hall, Inc., 1974.

[Dammon and Green 1987]   R. Dammon and R. Green, Tax Arbitrage
                               and the Existence of Equilibrium Prices for
                               Financial Assets, *Journal of Finance*, 42,
                               1987, 1143–1166.

[Day and Lewis 1988]   T. E. Day and C. M. Lewis, The Behaviour of
                               the Volatility Implicit in the Prices of Stock
                               Index Options, *Journal of Financial Econo-
                               mics*, 22, 1988, 103–122.

[Debreu 1984]   G. Debreu, *Theory of Value. An Axiomatic
                               Analysis of Economic Equilibrium*, New
                               Haven, Conn. Cowles Foundation in Econo-
                               mics at Yale University, 1989.

[Dumas 1980]   B. Dumas, L'évaluation des titres condition-
                               nels non négociables à la Bourse de Paris,
                               document ESSEC no. 8014, February 1980.

[Evnine and Rudd 1985]   J. Evnine, and A. Rudd, 1985, Index Options:
                               The Early Evidence, *Journal of Finance*, 40,
                               1985, 743–756.

[Geske 1979]   R. Geske, The Valuation of Compound Options, *Journal of Financial Economics*. 7, 1979, 63–81.

[Gibbons and Jacklin 1988]   M. Gibbons and C. Jacklin, CEV Diffusion Estimation, Working Paper, Stanford University, November 1988.

[Grabbe 1983]   O. Grabbe, The Pricing of Call and Put Options on Foreign Exchange, *Journal of International Money and Finance*, 2, 1983, 239–253.

[Grossman 1988]   S. J. Grossman, An Analysis of the Implications for Stock and Futures Price Volatility of Program Trading and Dynamic Hedging Strategies, *Journal of Business*, 61, 1988, 275–298.

[Heath and Jarrow 1987]   D. Heath and R. Jarrow, Arbitrage, Continuous Trading and Margin Requirements, *Journal of Finance*, 42, 1987, 1129–1142.

[Hull and White 1987]   J. Hull and A. White, The Pricing of Options on Assets with Stochastic Volatility, *Journal of Finance*, 42, 1987, 281–300.

[Hull and White 1988]   J. Hull and A. White, The Use of the Control Variate Technique in Option Pricing, *Journal of Financial and Quantitative Analysis*, 23, 1988, 237–250.

[Johnson and Shanno 1987]   H. Johnson and D. Shanno, Option Pricing when the Variance is Changing, *Journal of Financial and Quantitative Analysis*, 22, 1987, 143–151.

[Jones 1984]   E. P. Jones, Option Arbitrage and Strategy with Large Price Changes, *Journal of Financial Economics*, 13, 1984, 91–113.

[Jordan *et al.* 1987]   J. V. Jordan, W. E. Seale, N. C. McCabe and D. E. Kenyon, Transactions Data Tests of the Black Model for Soybean Futures Options, *The Journal of Futures Markets*, 7, 1987, 535–554.

[Latané and Rendleman 1976]   H. Latané and R. Rendleman, Standard Deviations of Stock Price Ratios Implied in Option Prices, *Journal of Finance*, 31, 1976, 369–382.

[Leland 1985]   H. Leland, Option Pricing and Replication
                       with Transactions Costs, *Journal of Finance*,
                       40, 1985, 1283–1301.

[MacBeth and Merville 1979]   J. D. MacBeth and L. J. Merville, An Empi-
                       rical Examination of the Black-Scholes Call
                       Option Pricing Model, *Journal of Finance*,
                       34, 1979, 1173–1186.

[Maloney and Rogalski 1989]   K. Maloney and R. Rogalski, Call-Option
                       Pricing and the Turn of the Year, *Journal of
                       Business*, 62, 1989, 539–552.

[Margrabe 1978]   W. Margrabe, The Value of An Option to
                       Exchange One Asset for Another, *Journal of
                       Finance*, 33, 1978, 177–185.

[McMillan 1986]   L. G. McMillan, *Options as a Strategic
                       Investment*. New York Institute of Finance,
                       1986.

[Mclino and Turnbull 1991]   A. Molino and S. Turnbull, The Pricing of
                       Foreign Currency Options, *Canadian Jour-
                       nal of Economics*, 24, 1991, 251–281.

[Merton 1973]   R. C. Merton, Theory of Rational Option
                       Pricing, *Bell Journal of Economics and
                       Management Science*, 4, 1973, 141–183.

[Merton 1976]   R. C. Merton, Option Pricing When Under-
                       lying Stock Returns are Discontinuous,
                       Journal of Financial Economics, 3, 1976,
                       125–144.

[Métivier 1979]   M. Métivier, *Notions fondamentales de la
                       théorie des probabilités*, Paris, Dunod,
                       1979.

[Moussi and Roger 1985]   P. Moussi and P. Roger, L'évaluation d'un
                       contrat de prime à la Bourse de Paris,
                       CEREG Working Paper no. 8514, Université
                       Paris-Dauphine, 1985.

[Nelson 1991]   D. B. Nelson, Conditional Heteroskedasti-
                       city in Asset Returns: a New Approach,
                       Econometrica, 59, 1991, 347–370.

[Ogden and Tucker 1988]   J. P. Ogden and A. L. Tucker, The Relative Valuation of American Currency Spot and Futures Options: Theory and Empirical Tests, *Journal of Financial and Quantitative Analysis*, 23, 1988, 351–367.

[Parkinson 1980]   M. Parkinson, The Random Walk Problem: Extreme Value Method for Estimating the Variance of the Displacement, *Journal of Business*, 53, 1980, 61–65.

[Patell and Wolfson 1979]   J. Patell and M. Wolfson, Anticipated Information Releases Reflected in Call Option prices, *Journal of Accounting and Economics*, 1, 1979, 117–140.

[Ramaswamy and Sundaresan 1985]   K. Ramaswamy and S. M. Sundaresan, The valuation of Options on Futures Contracts, *Journal of Finance*, 40, 1985, 1319–1340.

[Rubinstein 1976]   M. Rubinstein, The Valuation of Uncertain Income Streams and the Pricing of Options, *Bell Journal of Economics and Management Science*, 7, 1976, 551–571.

[Rubinstein 1983]   M. Rubinstein, Displaced Diffusion Option Pricing, *Journal of Finance*, 38, 1983, 213–265.

[Rubinstein 1985]   M. Rubinstein, Non Parametric Tests of Alternative Option Pricing Models Using All Reported Trades and Quotes on the 30 Most Active CBOE Option Classes from August 23, 1976 through August 31, 1978, *Journal of Finance*, 40, 1985, 455–480.

[Rubinstein 1987]   M. Rubinstein, Derivative Assets Analysis, *Journal of Economic Perspectives*, 1, 1987, 73–73.

[Scott 1987]   L. O. Scott, Option Pricing When the Variance Changes Randomly: Theory, Estimation and an Application, *Journal of Financial and Quantitative Analysis*, 22, 1987, 4.

[Stoll 1969]   H. R. Stoll, The Relationship Between Put and Call Option Prices, *Journal of Finance*, 24, 1969, 801–824.

[Stoll 1988]   H. R. Stoll, Index Futures, Program Trading, and Stock Market Procedures, *Journal of Futures Markets*, 8, 1988, 391–412.

[Stoll and Whaley 1986]   H. R. Stoll and R. E. Whaley, Expiration Day Effects of Index Options and Futures, *Monograph Series in Finance and Economics*, New York University, Monograph 1986-3.

[Stoll and Whaley 1990]   H. R. Stoll and R. E. Whaley, The Dynamics of Stock Index and Stock Index Futures Returns, *Journal of Financial and Quantitative Analysis*, 25, 1990, 441–468.

[Stulz 1982]   R. Stulz, Options on the Minimum or the Maximum of Two Risky Assets: Analysis and Applications, *Journal of Financial Economics*, 10, 1982, 161–185.

[Tucker *et al.* 1988]   A. L. Tucker, D. R. Peterson and E. Scott, Tests of the Black Scholes and Constant Elasticity of Variance Currency Call Option Valuation Models, *The Journal of Financial Research*, 11, 1988, 201–213.

[van Hulle 1988]   C. van Hulle, Option Pricing Methods: An Overview, *Insurance: Mathematics and Economics*, 7, 1988, 139–152.

[Whaley 1986]   R. Whaley, Valuation of American Futures Options: Theory and Empirical Tests, *Journal of Finance*, 41, 1986, 127–150.

[Wiggins 1987]   J. B. Wiggins, Option Values Under Stochastic Volatility: Theory and Empirical Evidence, *Journal of Financial Economics*, 19, 1987, 351–372.

7

Option pricing in continuous time

The method of pricing financial securities in discrete time, studied in the previous chapter, makes use of an arbitrary concept: that of the unitary holding period of financial securities. In fact, we considered two successive instants t and $t + 1$, put into place an arbitrage portfolio at instant t, then examined the rebalancing of this operation at instant $t + 1$, the interval of time between t and $t + 1$ being fixed and given. A procedure of this type excludes the possibility of rebalancing at an intermediate instant. In practice, however, investors are free to operate on the financial market at any time.[1] A more natural procedure therefore involves using a continuous timescale. It is in this spirit that we showed in the previous chapter what the price limit of an option would be if we indefinitely reduced the interval of time between two successive instants. This procedure is, however, indirect. We shall now study, and apply to option pricing, a mathematical technique allowing us to reason directly in continuous time: the technique of stochastic differential calculus.

Section 7.1 is devoted to some mathematical concepts. Section 7.2 presents several ways to obtain the Black-Scholes partial differential equation; the result of this will be the Black-Scholes formula which is applicable, as we know (Chapter 6), to non-dividend-paying European options. The short Section 7.3 addresses options on securities paying a continuous dividend. Section 7.4 is devoted to exact or approximative methods of pricing American options. Given that, for most options, no formula may be obtained giving the price directly, we consider the available numerical methods in Section 7.5.

7.1   Basic concepts of stochastic differential calculus

When the timescale is continuous, it is possible to classify the random, or stochastic processes[2] followed by market prices into two categories, according to whether their sample paths are continuous or not. We are interested here only in those whose sample paths are continuous,[3] which means that the price in question is not liable to 'jump' suddenly from one level to another:[4] whatever its trajectory, it may be drawn without ever lifting pen from paper.

A *martingale X* is a stochastic process possessing the following property:[5]

$$X_t = E_t[X_{t+\tau}] \text{ for all } \tau > 0 \qquad\qquad [1.1]$$

In this equation, E_t denotes the expected value conditioned by the past trajectory $[X_\theta; \theta \le t]$ of the process X itself. The best forecast of the future values of a martingale, taking account of the realized path, is today's price. The accumulated wealth of a person who plays a game of tossing a coin, with a gain of +1 or −1 on each throw, follows a martingale.

7.1.1 Brownian motion[6]

Definition:
   A real process z is a *standard Brownian motion* if:

(a) The probability that a trajectory of z is a continuous function of t is equal to 1;

(b) Whatever the value of $0 \le s < t < \infty$, $z_t - z_s$ is a random variable of normal distribution with a zero expected value and a variance equal to $t - s$,

(c) Whatever the value of $0 \leq t_0 < t_1 < \ldots < t_k < \ldots < t_l < \infty$, the random variables $z(t_0)$ and $z(t_k) - z(t_{k-1})$, $1 \leq k \leq l$, are independent of one another, and

(d) $Pr(\{z_0 = 0\}) = 1$.

Condition (a) means that the Brownian is a continuous process. Condition (b) means that the variance of the increases in the process is equal to the time elapsed. Condition (c) means that successive increments are independent, and condition (d) specifies the initial condition.

On account of conditions (b) and (c), Brownian motion is a martingale. Also, since the variance of a sum of independent variables is equal to the sum of the variances, conditions (b), (c) and (d) mean that the expectation of the square of z_t is: $E_0(z_t^2) = t$. Since the expectation of the square exists, we say that the Brownian is a *square integrable martingale*.

Definition [Wiener 1923]:
   A real process w is a *Wiener process* if:

(a) The probability that a trajectory of w is a continuous function of t is equal to 1;

(b) w is a square integrable martingale and:

   $E_s[w_t - w_s]^2 = t - s; t \geq s;$

(c) $Pr[\{w_0 = 0\}] = 1$.

Theorem:
   (due to Paul Lévy):[7] Any Wiener process is a standard Brownian motion.

Brownian motion is, therefore, the only type of continuous martingale with an integrable square proportional to time.

7.1.2 Brownian motion as a limit of the random walk

Property (b) of Brownian motion will seem very natural if we picture the Brownian as the limit of a discrete time process known as the random walk. *The random walk z is defined as follows:*

$$z_{t+1} - z_t + e_{t+1} \tag{1.2}$$

where z_t is the value taken by the random walk at instant t, and e_{t+1} is a realization of a random variable of constant distribution (which we assume normal),[8] of zero expected value, independent of the preceding realizations.

In other words, a random walk results from the accumulation *of elementary increments independent of one another*, as illustrated by Figure 7.1. When var[e] = 1,[9] we say that it is a standard random walk.

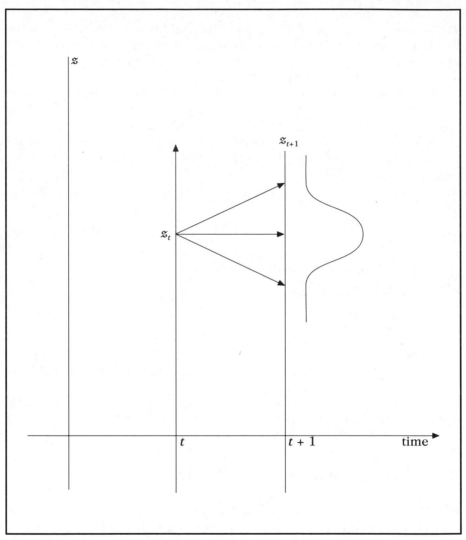

Figure 7.1   The random walk

It will be noted that a random walk is a *martingale*: the conditional expected value of the value which the variable will reach tomorrow is equal to the value reached today. Furthermore, the conditional expected value of the increase in z during any interval of time is zero.

Let us now consider the behaviour of the *variance* of a standard random walk:

$$\mathrm{var}[z_{t+\tau} \mid z_t] = \mathrm{var}[z_{t+\tau} - z_t \mid z_t] = \mathrm{var}[z_{t+\tau} - z_t]$$

$$= E[\sum_{i=1}^{\tau} (z_{t+i} - z_{t+i-1})^2] = \tau$$

[1.3]

the result once again stemming from the fact that the variance of the sum of several independent variables (here the τ successive realizations of e) is equal to the sum of their variances. This basic principle of probability theory therefore allows us to describe the behaviour of the variance of a random walk: the variance of the increase in z, during an interval of time equal to τ periods, is *proportional to τ*. When the random walk is standard, the variance of the increase is itself equal to τ, as we have just seen. The two properties mentioned so far indicate that the random walk, like the Brownian motion, is a *square integrable martingale*.

Let us reduce the interval of time which separates two successive values of z and do it in such a way that the *variance of the increment per unit of time remains constant*. If, for example, we divide by n the interval of time separating two successive values, the change from the value of z at instant τ to the value of z at the instant $t + \tau$, which previously was done in τ successive increments, is now done in $n\tau$ increments, each having a variance equal not to 1 but to $1/n$.

Under these conditions, it is clear that Equation 1.3 does not require correcting: however the time is divided up, the variance of the increase of z remains proportional (and even equal in the standard case) to the time elapsed:

$$\mathrm{var}[z_{t+\tau} - z_t] = E[\sum_{i=1}^{n\tau} (z_{t+i} - z_{t+i-1})^2] = n\tau \cdot (1/n) = \tau$$

[1.4]

By pursuing *ad infinitum* this process of subdivision,[10] it may be shown that, whatever t and t', the joint probability distribution of z_t and $z_{t'}$ converges towards the probability distribution of a Brownian. We converge towards the same Brownian however the time is divided up (*principle of invariance*). We have just stated *Donsker's theorem*.[11]

When the divisions of time become very small, the time interval $1/n$ between two successive values becomes a differential element which we write as dt and the random increase in z (which we write as dz) over the interval dt also becomes infinitely small. We must now indicate the sense in which dz is 'small'.

A first indication on this question is provided by Equation 1.4: the expected value of the square of each increase in z is equal to $1/n$. Using differential notation, we write:

$$E[(dz)^2] = dt$$

[1.5]

But this is not sufficient to specify the sense in which dz, a random quantity, is small. In Appendix 1, we give a meaning to the following equation which is more extraordinary:

$$(dz)^2 = dt \qquad\qquad\qquad [1.6]$$

This expression means that we are likening dt to the square of dz (and not just the expected value of this square). Whilst dz is random, $(dz)^2$, which is also random, will be likened to an infinitesimal real non-random element, namely dt. This is surprising. But beware! Whereas Equation 1.5 is an equality in the usual sense of the equality of real numbers, we give a different meaning to Equation 1.6: it is true *'in the sense of the mean square limit'*. This means that after summation along the trajectories of z, the expected square of the differences between the right and left-hand sides of [1.6] tends towards zero when the divisions of time become infinitely small:

$$\lim_{n \to \infty} \sum_{i=1}^{n\tau} E\left\{ \left[\left(z_{t+i} - z_{t+i-1} \right)^2 - \frac{1}{n} \right]^2 \right\} = 0$$

Since the square of dz is likened to dt, we may say, purely formally, that dz is 'of order of magnitude $\sqrt{(dt)}$'. This graphic statement has no strict mathematical meaning, beyond what we have just said, but it will guide our calculations. In particular, it will lead us to amend the rules of ordinary differential calculus (*see* Section 1.4).

7.1.3 Stochastic differential equations, Itō processes and diffusion processes

The drift of a process is the conditional expected value of its increase per unit of time. In the case of standard Brownian motion, the variance per unit of time was assumed to be equal to 1 and the drift per unit of time was assumed to be zero (martingale property). A *non-standard Brownian* has a variance per unit of time other than 1 and a non-zero drift. Both are assumed constant. When the drift is not zero, the expected future value of the variable is not equal to its present value: it differs from it by a quantity equal to the drift multiplied by the time separating this future value from today's date. At each instant, the drift imparts to the motion a certain direction, whilst a random impact of mean zero turns it away from this direction (*see* Figure 7.2).

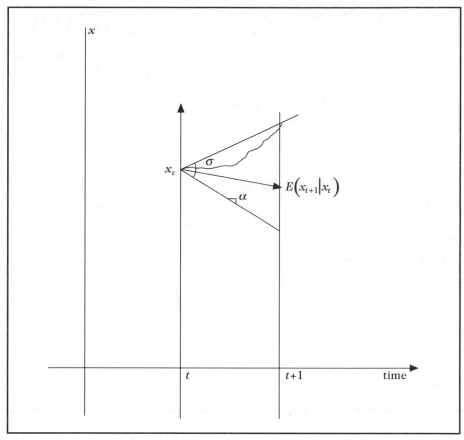

Figure 7.2   Drift and diffusion

A handy differential notation allows a non-standard Brownian motion x to be represented by the following equation:[12]

$$dx = \alpha dt + \sigma dz \qquad\qquad [1.7]$$

which is simultaneously equivalent to:

$$E[dx|x] = \alpha dt \qquad\qquad [1.7a]$$

and:

$$(dx)^2 = \sigma^2 dt \qquad\qquad [1.7b]$$

An equation of type [1.7], containing a random term, is called a *stochastic differential equation*. Its real meaning appears after integration:

$$x_{t+\tau} - x_t = \alpha \tau + \sigma (z_{t+\tau} - z_t) \qquad [1.8]$$

The integral form shows clearly that, in Equation 1.7, the drift term αdt must not be regarded as negligible in relation to the random term σdz, even though the first is of order of size dt, whereas the second is supposed to be of 'order of magnitude' $\sqrt{(dt)}$.[13] It is important to understand that the differential form [1.7] is based on unusual formulation, whereas the integrated form [1.8] has a direct meaning: the increase in x between t and $t + \tau$ is equal to the drift α times τ, plus a realization of the normal law of zero mean and of variance $\sigma^2 \tau$.

When α and σ are constants, Equation 1.7 is a particularly simple stochastic differential equation, since its solution [1.8] is obtained by simple stochastic integration of the two sides. More generally, a stochastic differential equation is an equation where the unknown is a process and which is written in the form:

$$dx = \alpha(x, t)dt + \sigma(x, t)dz \qquad [1.9]$$

It will be noted that the drift α and the standard deviation σ per unit of time are now functions of the unknown x and time t. These functions cannot be arbitrary, since the right-hand side must first of all be integrable.[14] Next, in order that the solution x to [1.9] exists and is unique for given initial conditions, we require that the functions α and σ satisfy two conditions called 'growth' and 'Lipschitz'.[15] The function σ is sometimes called the diffusion coefficient of x.

Any solution to a stochastic differential equation such as [1.9] is an *Itō process*. These processes are very similar to what are known as *diffusion*[16] processes whose definition property is that they possess a well-defined drift function $\alpha(.)$ and a diffusion function $\sigma(.)$.

Examples of Itō processes:

- the geometric Brownian process: this is a process whose increases are obtained by *multiplying* the present value by a random factor:

$$dx = x \cdot [\alpha dt + \alpha dz] \qquad [1.10]$$

where α and σ are constant. This process is frequently used to represent the behaviour of stock market prices; α and σ are in this case the expected value of the rate of return and the standard deviation of the rate of return on the security during the immediate time interval;

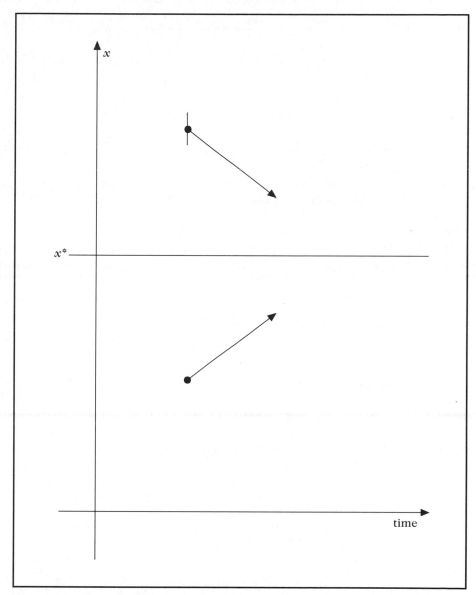

Figure 7.3   Ornstein-Uhlenbeck process

- the Ornstein-Uhlenbeck process is sometimes used to represent the behaviour of the short-term interest rate (*see* Chapter 10). The drift of this process represents an elastic force attracting the variable x towards a fixed value x^* (*see* Figure 7.3). The force is proportional to the distance between x and x^*, the coefficient of proportionality being denoted by β (>0). The instantaneous variance of the process is constant.[17] The corresponding differential equation is:

$$dx = \beta(x^* - x)dt + \sigma dz \qquad [1.11]$$

7.1.4 Itō's lemma or change of variable formula

We now turn to an Itō process y defined from process x of Equation 1.9 by means of a functional relationship $y = f(x, t)$, the function y being continuous and twice differentiable with respect to x, once differentiable with respect to t. We wish to obtain the stochastic differential equation $dy = ?$ which governs the behaviour of y.

Ordinary differential calculus would provide the following answer, which is incorrect. During the interval of time dt, t varies, obviously, as well as x. We would therefore have:

$$dy = f_x(x, t)\, dx + f_t(x, t)\, dt$$

where f_x and f_t represent the partial derivatives with respect to x and t respectively.

We are forced to question this rule of differential calculus by observing that, if terms of order greater than one are negligible and therefore legitimately absent from the right-hand side of this equation when x is a real variable, the same justification may no longer be valid when x is a random process. We have seen in fact that we would have to suppose that dz was of the order $\sqrt{(dt)}$. On account of this, a second-order term in $(dx)^2$ is no longer negligible before the term in dt. If we continue the differential development of dy, observing Taylor's rules of expansion, we obtain:

$$dy = f_x(x, t)dx + f_t(x, t)dt + \tfrac{1}{2}f_{xx}(x, t)\,(dx)^2 \qquad [1.12]$$

where f_{xx} represents the second derivative with respect to x. By using Equation 1.9,[18] we obtain:

$$dy = [f_x\alpha + f_t + \tfrac{1}{2}f_{xx}\sigma^2]dt + f_x\sigma dz \qquad [1.13]$$

which also means:

$$\cdot\, E[dy \mid x] = [f_x \alpha + f_t + \tfrac{1}{2} f_{xx} \sigma^2] dt \qquad\qquad [1.13a]$$

and:

$$(dy)^2 = [f_x \sigma]^2 dt \qquad\qquad [1.13b]$$

That is to say that the first term of Equation 1.13 supplies the drift of process y and the second term describes its random behaviour. Result [1.13] is known as 'Itō's Lemma' [Itō 1944].[19]

The presence of the term $\tfrac{1}{2} f_{xx} \sigma^2$ in formula 1.13a for the conditional expected value of dy may be understood intuitively as follows. We know that the second derivative f_{xx} of a function measures the curvature of its graph. Let us therefore examine in Figure 7.4 the special case of a function $f(x)$ passing through the origin, with a zero slope at the origin but with a non-zero curvature[20] at the same point. The variable x, on the x axis, is, in this particular case, a random variable of zero expected value. Let us now imagine how $E[y]$ would be calculated: when x takes a positive value such as a on the diagram, y is also positive; when x takes a negative value such as b on the diagram, y is still positive. It is therefore clear that $E[y]>0$, even though $E[x] = 0$ and $f(0) = 0$. The curvature therefore influences the value of $E[y]$ and it is this phenomenon which is faithfully taken into account by the term in question of formula 1.13a. The general rule of stochastic differential calculus is therefore that second-degree terms bringing in random elements are not negligible.

We shall now apply these concepts to the financial problem of option pricing in continuous time.

7.2   Option pricing in continuous time

Numerous, and quite different, approaches exist allowing the Black-Scholes formula to be obtained:

(1) the original argument of [Black and Scholes 1973] and [Merton 1973] is based on an instantaneous arbitrage between the option and the underlying security;

(2) the argument of [Merton 1977], as well as that of [Bergman 1981], is based on the construction of a portfolio which can be shown to reproduce exactly the payoff profile of the option. On a market without arbitrage, it must have the same value as the option itself. This is an identical procedure to that which we mainly followed in discrete time in Chapter 6;

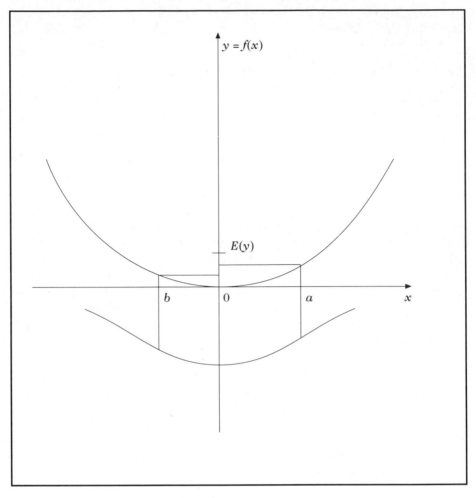

Figure 7.4   The intuitive meaning of Itō's lemma

(3) the approach of [Harrison and Kreps 1979] involves noting that a
    market where a random security and a risk-free security are exchanged
    is a 'complete market' in the sense that it is sufficiently rich in
    financial securities for us to be able to deduce, by a form of discount-
    ing, the value of any security whose payoff profile depends only on
    the value of the underlying random security. Harrison and Kreps
    explicitly calculated the relevant present value factors, applied them
    to the profile of the option and deduced from them the Black-Scholes
    formula. In Chapter 6, we alluded to an approach of this type, but
    applied in discrete time (*see* Section 2.2);

(4) in addition, we mentioned, also in the previous chapter (the proof in
    the appendix), that the formula could be obtained by taking the limit

of the binomial pricing method (this is the approach, it will be recalled, of [Cox *et al.* 1979].

(5) finally, it is also possible to derive the Black-Scholes formula by any one of the above arguments, but remaining in discrete time, and this on the condition of restricting the joint probability distribution of the investors' marginal utility and of the price of the underlying security on maturity (it must, for example, be log-normal, which would assume at the minimum that α is constant in Equation 2.1 in the text). We therefore lose out on generality in this way, but we avoid the hypothesis according to which the investors are in a position to carry out transactions in continuous time, that is, at any instant imaginable. On this subject, *see* [Rubinstein 1976] or [Brennan 1979].

The development below, which uses stochastic differential calculus, reproduces argument 2 above, that is, the one by [Merton 1977], and the presentation of it by [Bergman 1981].

7.2.1   The Black-Scholes partial differential equation

Suppose that the price S of a *non-dividend-paying* share follows, over time, the following process:

$$\frac{dS}{S} = \alpha(\cdot)\, dt + \sigma(S,t)\, dz \qquad [2.1]$$

This is a very general Itō process written in this form so that α may be interpreted as the conditional expected return on the security and σ is its volatility. α is permitted to follow any stochastic process (even autonomous from S and t) but σ depends only on S and t. We shall assume that S > 0 at $t = 0$ and that $\alpha(.)$ and $\sigma(S, t)$ take only finite values (so that $\alpha \cdot S$ and $\sigma \cdot S$ become zero when S becomes zero), so that the price of the security remains positive whatever happens.[21] Furthermore, we assume the existence of a risk-free investment at the instantaneous rate of interest r, where r depends at the most on S and t.

Let us give ourselves the task of pricing at each instant a European call contract (*see* previous chapter) whose underlying stock is the share with the price S above. The option contract is defined by the payoff profile on maturity T:

$$C(T) = \text{Max}[0, S(T) - K] \qquad [2.2]$$

where K is the exercise price. Furthermore, this contract does not produce any cash flow at the instants prior to maturity $t<T$.

Let us construct (at an initial instant $t = 0$) a portfolio (whose value in ECU is designated by V) by buying h units of the share in question S and buying b units[22] of a risk-free investment at the rate r whose unitary value evolves according to: $D(t) = D_0 e^{rt}$. We force h and b to vary over time as a function of S and t only: $h = h(S, t)$, $b = b(S, t)$. In addition, this portfolio must be subject to neither withdrawal nor investment of funds after its initial composition; this will be a *self-financed* portfolio. We have: $V(S, t) = h(S, t)S + b(S, t)D(t)$. We shall show that:

Theorem:
> The value V of the portfolio is the solution to the 'Black-Scholes partial differential equation' (p.d.e).

$$\frac{1}{2}\sigma^2 S^2 V_{SS} + rSV_S + V_t = rV \qquad [2.3]$$

The fraction held $h(S, t)$ is linked to the function V by:

$$h(S, t) = V_S(S, t) \qquad [2.4]$$

Proof: Since $V = hS + bD$, we have, by applying Itō's lemma:

$$dV = hdS + bdD + (dh)S + (db)D + (dh)(dS) \qquad [2.5]$$

In the absence of deposits or withdrawals of funds, the increases dV in the value of this portfolio can only result from the gains on the constituent elements (appreciations dS on the share and interest rdt on the risk-free investment):[23]

$$dV = hdS + bdD \qquad [2.6]$$

It must therefore be the case that:

$$(dh)S + (db)D + (dh)(dS) = 0 \qquad [2.7]$$

Stochastic differential equation 2.7 contains, as is usual, two equations, one concerning the terms in dz, the other the terms in dt. By equating the terms in dz to zero in [2.7], we obtain:

$$\frac{\partial h}{\partial S} S + \frac{\partial h}{\partial S} D = 0$$

but since $b = (V - hS)/D$, this gives $h = \partial V/\partial S$, that is to say [2.4], one of the desired results, and therefore also:

$$b = \frac{V - \dfrac{\partial V}{\partial S} S}{D} \qquad [2.8]$$

Now, grouping together the terms in dt of [2.7], we have:

$$\left[\frac{\partial h}{\partial S} \alpha S + \frac{1}{2}\frac{\partial^2 h}{\partial S^2} \sigma^2 S^2 + \frac{\partial h}{\partial t}\right] S + \left[\frac{\partial b}{\partial S} \alpha S + \frac{1}{2}\frac{\partial^2 b}{\partial S^2} \sigma^2 S^2 + \frac{\partial b}{\partial t}\right] D + \frac{\partial h}{\partial S} \sigma^2 S^2 = 0 \quad [2.9]$$

By substituting [2.4] and [2.8] into [2.9], we obtain [2.3], which was the other desired result.

Let us force the portfolio to satisfy, in addition to partial differential equation 2.3, the terminal condition:

$$V(S, T) = \text{Max}[0, S - K] \qquad [2.10]$$

and compare this portfolio to the European call option C whose price we wish to know. The portfolio and the option have the same terminal value: Max[0, S–K]. Moreover, the portfolio, like the option, gives rise to no cash flows between the initial instant 0 and the terminal instant T. They are therefore identical and their price must be the same: $C(S, t) = V(S, t)$, otherwise arbitrages could be implemented.

These arbitrages would involve buying (or selling) the option at the start and selling (or investing in) the self-financed portfolio, then managing this portfolio so that it contained at each instant $h = V_S$ units of the underlying security, the complement being invested in the risk-free security. This reasoning in no way assumes that the option itself may be traded at any instant or that its price on the market, at the dates after the initial instant, is an equilibrium price.[24] The formula $C = V(S, t)$ gives the price of the option at a given instant t, such that no arbitrage is possible, at this instant, between the option and the portfolio which reproduces it.

7.2.2 Solution of the Black-Scholes partial differential equation

By the use of economic reasoning, we have established that the function $V(S, t)$ giving the price of the option is the solution to [2.3] and verifies the terminal condition [2.2]. We must now solve the additional technical problem, which is to calculate the function $V(S, t)$, in one form or another.

Interpreting the terms of [2.3] may help us in this task. In the terms of the left-hand side, the formula of Itō's lemma will be recognized, giving the expected increase in the price, V, of the option over each interval of time, dt, except that the value of the expected increase in the price of the underlying asset taken into account is not $aSdt$, as might have been expected, but $rSdt$. The right hand side of [2.3] states that this expected price increase V must be equal to the repayment, at the risk-free rate of interest, r, of the capital V, which is $rVdt$. Therefore the price V must rise on average at the rate r. By accumulation over time, the resulting price V on any date is equal to the expected value, discounted at the risk-free rate, of the possible values of V on any later date. Furthermore, the terminal value of V in each state of nature is given by [2.2]. By this intuitive reasoning, we arrive at a formal solution to p.d.e. [2.3] which is provided by a mathematical result, known as the 'Feynman-Kac formula':[25]

$$V(S_t, t) = \hat{E}_t \left[\exp\left[-\int_t^T r(s)ds\right] \cdot Max[0, \tilde{S}_T - K] \right] \qquad [2.11]$$

This formula tells us that the price of the option is quite simply equal to the expected value of the discounted terminal payoff attached to the option. However, this expected value, designated by $\hat{E}$, must be calculated by assuming that the underlying variable S follows an artificial process, different from the 'true' process [2.1]. This 'adjusted' process $\hat{S}$ is defined by the following stochastic differential equation:

$$\frac{d\hat{S}}{\hat{S}} = rdt + \sigma dz \qquad [2.12]$$

In other words, we must calculate the adjusted expected value $\hat{E}$ by imagining that the underlying asset yields an expected return equal to the risk-free rate r. Once again, therefore, by an indirect route, we find proposition 6.2 of the previous chapter: options are priced as if investors were indifferent to risk and the underlying asset had an expected return equal to the risk-free rate of interest.[26]

In certain special cases, the solution $V(S, t)$ may be expressed in a more explicit form. If we are prepared to add two hypotheses, namely that the (risk-free) interest rate r and the volatility of the share σ are constant, we may verify that the solution sought is given by the Black-Scholes formula which we wrote in the previous chapter. This does indeed, therefore, give the price of the European option.

The check may be made by substitution, but the solution must then be known *a priori*. It is also possible to solve system [2.3–2.2] directly using Fourier's transformation (*see* [Farlow 1982]; other methods of solution are given by [Reinhard 1987]).

7.3 Options on securities paying a continuous dividend

The argument which we have just presented is not limited to European options, nor even to options in general. The terminal condition [2.2] was the only aspect of the argument which called on the characteristics of the option contract. Completely different boundary conditions, reflecting other contractual clauses and other payoff profiles, could have occurred without the conclusion changing one iota: from the moment that the payoff profile of a secondary security depends only on the price of a primary security and time, the value of a portfolio which reproduces the secondary security is given by the solution of p.d.e. 2.3; and, to avoid any arbitrage, the portfolio and the secondary security must have the same value at all times.

We must stress, however, that the Black-Scholes partial differential equation, as we have written it ([2.3]), applies to options on non dividend paying assets (and, conversely, those involving no holding or storage costs[27]). The argument is easily amended to take such flows into account. Recall that portfolio V is, by construction, a self-financed portfolio. If asset S which is part of this portfolio generated any cash flows, these would have to be reinvested.

Consider, for example, a continuous dividend with yield δ. In the presence of this, the gains arising from the portfolio are no longer given by Equation 2.6 but by:

$$dV = hdS + \underline{h\delta Sdt} + bdD \qquad [3.1]$$

so that Equation 2.7 becomes:

$$(dh)S + (db)D + (dh)(dS) = h\delta Sdt \qquad [3.2]$$

After all calculations have been completed, Black-Scholes' partial differential equation, thus generalized, is written as:

$$\frac{1}{2}\sigma^2 S^2 V_{SS} + (r - \delta)SV_S + V_t = rV \qquad\qquad [3.3]$$

Remember (*see* Section 6.4.4) that, for *European* options, valuation on the basis of the forward price allows us to deal without difficulty with any dividend – continuous or discrete, or even random, – on the condition, however, that the time series of forward prices, with a fixed maturity date coinciding with the maturity date of the option, has a volatility which depends, at most, on the forward price and the time: *cf.* [Grabbe 1983] or [Carr 1988].

7.4   American options

In this section, we study in particular American options, of which we know from the previous chapter that they can be priced by the binomial method. This gives an approximation of the price in continuous time. To price them directly in continuous time, we need to establish the boundary conditions which apply to this type of option.

All exercises before maturity are prompted by the prospect of receiving a 'dividend'. By this we mean any flow of cash which is received after exercise but which is not received if the option is not exercised and simply continues to be held. In Section 4.1, we consider the problem of exercise before maturity of options on securities which pay a dividend at isolated instants (example: options to buy shares with a maturity following later than a dividend payment date). The opposite case, that of the dividend received 'continuously', is the subject of Section 4.2. In conjunction with the boundary conditions which apply to this case, partial differential equation 2.3 has no explicit solution. We must therefore consider applying approximative methods of solution: we study two of these ([Geske and Johnson 1984] and [Barone-Adesi and Whaley 1987]) in Section 7.4.3.

7.4.1 Options with discrete and certain dividend

[Roll 1977] and [Geske 1979b] addressed the problem of pricing American call options written on shares on which a dividend payment occurs during the lifetime of the option. Let t be today's date, τ the anticipated dividend payment date and D the amount of the dividend respectively, and T the maturity date of the option. We assume that, when the dividend is paid, the price of the share suffers a fall equal to the amount of the dividend.[28] To ensure that the firm is in a position to pay the dividend D with certainty, we shall also assume that it has put into the bank, starting from today's date, an amount of liquid assets $D.\exp[-r(\tau - t)]$ sufficient to make D on the date τ. At dates prior to τ, we denote by S the price of the share reduced by this amount of liquid assets. It is S thus defined which follows a stochastic diffusion process. S may reach the value zero without this preventing the dividend payment.[29]

Just as, in the absence of a dividend, it is not advisable to exercise a call option before maturity (*see* Chapter 6), in the presence of a dividend it may be advisable to exercise the call option only at the instant preceding the date τ of the dividend payment. But exercising the option also means abandoning the advantages which, in the absence of a dividend, endow the option with its time-value. In particular, holding the option instead of the share means benefiting from a safety net in case of a later fall in price; furthermore, exercising the option means paying out the exercise price earlier. These costs and benefits depend on the price of the share. It is therefore necessary to determine the limit value S^* of the ex-dividend price above which it is advisable to exercise the option at the moment of payment. This value S^* fixes the limit-price of exercise at instant τ.

At the moment of payment and subsequently, $(t \geq \tau)$, the price of the option is given by the Black-Scholes formula: let us denote this by $V(S, t)$. At the instant τ of payment, the price of the unexercised option is therefore $V(S, \tau)$. We must compare this with the exercised value $S + D - K$. The exercise limit price S^* is the value of S for which the exercised price and the unexercised price are equal. It may therefore be determined from the beginning of the calculation, by solving the following equation, constructed on the Black-Scholes formula:

$$V(S^*, \tau) = S^* + D - K \tag{4.1}$$

The price of the option at date τ may therefore be expressed piecewise:

$$C(S, \tau) = \begin{vmatrix} S + D - K & \text{if } S > S^* & (\text{exercise}) \\ V(S, \tau) & \text{if } S \leq S^* & (\text{non-exercise}) \end{vmatrix} \tag{4.2}$$

Observe that at the dates prior to the payment date, the American call option is analysed as an option (with maturity τ) on an option (with maturity T), that is to say a '*compound option*', in the sense of [Geske 1979a]. The function $C(S, t)$ which gives the value at dates $t < \tau$ must be a solution of the Black-Scholes partial differential equation 2.3 attached to terminal conditions [4.2]. The solution is given by what is known as the 'compound option formula', attributed to [Geske 1979a].[30]

It is possible to generalize the result to options whose maturity is preceded by several dividend payments. But the formula rapidly becomes burdensome.[31]

7.4.2 Boundary conditions applicable to American options on securities paying a continuous dividend: 'smooth-pasting condition'

The problem of exercise before maturity is particularly difficult when exercising the option allows us to start receiving a flow of cash at *any time*. In this case, the decision to exercise or not to exercise is a decision which must be taken at every instant in the lifetime of the option. We shall refer to this case by speaking of a 'continuous dividend'.[32] In Chapter 6 we met three examples of this type of option, actually used in practice: put options, options on currency and commodities, and options on futures contracts.[33] In the case of exercise, these three types of option allow the value of the underlying asset minus the exercise price to be received in cash. This cash may then be reinvested; the interest constitutes the 'continuous dividend' to which we refer.[34] American puts, whose price we denote P, will serve as a canonical example.

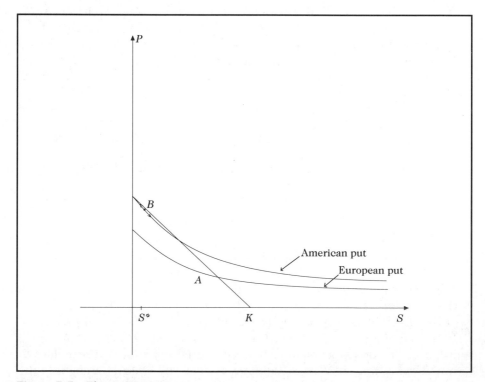

Figure 7.5   The American put

Consider an American put. Figure 7.5 represents the profile applicable on the maturity date T, which is also the exercise profile (the intrinsic value) at an earlier date $t \leq T$. The figure also contains, by way of a comparison, the profile of the European put at $t \leq T$. It can be seen that, for a sufficiently low value of the price of the underlying security (point A on the figure), the price of the European option passes below the exercised value. To the left of point A, an individual would prefer to exercise the option rather than hold it until maturity.

The choice which option contracts force their bearers to make is not one of exercising immediately or not exercising at all. If bearers do not exercise at the present instant, they retain the possibility of exercising one instant later. We may therefore guess that the optimal point of exercise is not point A and that it must in fact lie somewhere to the left of point A: we are in less of a hurry to exercise in the event of a fall in the underlying asset if we know that, if we do not do it immediately, we may still do it later. We set ourselves the task of writing the conditions which must be satisfied, jointly, by the location of the optimum points of exercise over time and the function giving the price of the optimally exercised American put.

Let us consider any 'exercise frontier' $S^*(t)$ and a policy of exercising the put option as soon as the price S_t of the underlying asset reaches the value $S^*(t)$.[35] The corresponding price of the option is given by a solution $P(S, t; S^*)$ to partial differential Equation 2.3, linked to this exercise frontier by the boundary condition:

$$P(S, t; S^*) = K - S, \text{ for all } S \leq S^*(t) \text{ and all } t \qquad [4.3]$$

This condition in particular entails:

$$P[S^*(t), t; S^*(t)] = K - S^*(t), \text{ for all } t \qquad [4.4]$$

Condition 4.4 is called a 'Value-Matching Condition'. The point on the x axis $S^*(t)$ is point B in Figure 7.5 and the solution we envisage is the curve passing through this point.[36]

Let us add the basic condition applicable to all puts:

$$\lim_{S \to \infty} P = 0 \qquad [4.5]$$

Amongst all the solutions to the partial differential equation satisfying [4.5] and amongst all the corresponding exercise frontiers, we wish to find those which, thanks to an optimum exercise policy, assure the buyer of a maximum price.

Let us fix instant t: since Equation 4.4 is true whatever S^*, we may differentiate it with respect to this variable:

$$\frac{\partial P}{\partial S}[S^*, t; S^*] + \frac{\partial P}{\partial S^*}[S^*, t; \ S^*] = -1 \qquad [4.6]$$

The decision variable being S^*, we wish to choose it so that $\partial P/\partial S^* = 0$.[37] This results in the following form of the first order condition:

$$P_S(S^*, t) = -1 \qquad [4.7]$$

If t is varied, we may deduce implicitly from this condition the function $S^*(t)$. This condition, added to [2.3] and [4.3], determines simultaneously the optimal curve $P(S, t)$, and the exercise frontier $S^*(t)$.

Condition 4.7 means that the maximum curve must be tangential to the segment $K - S$ giving the exercise price. In Figure 7.5, the maximum curve is that which passes through the exercise point B. At any instant t, the curve to the right of point B joins up with the right segment $K - S$, adopting at the joining point the tangent of the latter. There is therefore no kink but, on the contrary, a smooth join. The first order condition is known as the 'smooth-pasting condition'.

This condition has a general significance.[38] Since the marginalist or neoclassical tradition is very strong in economic theory, we are accustomed to thinking only in terms of gradual decision making. The decision involving exercising or not exercising an option is, by contrast, a binary or discrete decision.[39] When the frontier $S^*(t)$ is crossed, we switch from the situation where the option is not exercised to the situation where it is exercised. In this type of situation, the optimum frontier is determined by means of the smooth-pasting condition.

7.4.3 Approximate solution methods

Partial differential equation 2.3 – or Equation 3.3, according to case – with boundary conditions 4.4 and 4.7 has no known explicit solution. We must therefore leave this to approximate solutions or numerical solutions. Some generally applied numerical techniques are studied in Section 7.5 below: they require a sizeable amount of numeric calculation. Also, we saw in Chapter 6 that the binomial technique always provides as precise a numerical solution as we want (on the condition of multiplying the time stages). In this section, we describe some explicit approximative methods which are more effective and apply specifically to the problem of American options in the presence of a continuous dividend. The first is the compound option method of [Geske and Johnson 1984]; the second is the curiously named 'quadratic approximation' method, which we owe to [MacMillan 1986] and [Barone-Adesi and Whaley 1987].

7.4.3.1 The compound option method of [Geske and Johnson 1984]

This method involves artificially gathering the continuous dividend flows into a limited number of discrete payments. This brings us back to the case of the discrete dividend examined in Section 4.1 ([Geske 1979b]). In this type of approximation, we no longer use the smooth-pasting condition but conditions 4.1 and 4.2, since we do not envisage exercising the option at each instant, but only at the artificially chosen instants at which the dividend payments will take place.

7.4.3.2 The 'quadratic approximation' method of [Barone-Adesi and Whaley 1987]

As we have already pointed out, the Black-Scholes partial differential equation ([2.3], or [3.3] according to case) applies to the price-function of any secondary security, and therefore to the American put as well as to the European put. As this is a linear equation, it must therefore also apply to the exercise premium ε, defined as the difference between the price of the American put $P(S, t)$ and that of the European put, written here as $p(S, t)$:

$$\varepsilon(S, t) \equiv P(S, t) - p(S, t) \tag{4.8}$$

We wish to know the value of ε at today's date t, ε being the solution to [2.3] or [3.3], under the boundary conditions applicable to the exercise premium.

Let us consider, with Barone-Adesi and Whaley, a solution of the separable type:

$$\varepsilon(S, t) \equiv f(S) \cdot g(t) \tag{4.9}$$

the function $g(t)$ being chosen as follows:

$$g(t) \equiv 1 - \exp[-r(T - t)] \tag{4.10}$$

Bear in mind that t is the current date and T the maturity date. By substituting [4.9] into [2.3], we obtain a differential equation for the unknown function $f(S)$:

$$\frac{1}{2}\frac{f''(S)}{f(S)}\sigma^2 S^2 + \frac{f'(S)}{f(S)}rS = \frac{r}{g}$$ [4.11]

This differential equation is not properly separated, since the function g is a function of time.

Let us fix t and falsely treat g as a constant. This gives the solution:

$$f(S) = a \cdot S^q$$ [4.12]

where a is a constant coefficient and q is one of the roots of the characteristic equation:

$$\tfrac{1}{2}q(q - 1)\sigma^2 + qr = r/g$$ [4.13]

In the case of a put, we choose for q the negative root of [4.13] so that: $\lim_{S\to\infty} P = 0$. Remember that t played the role of a parameter in the determination of q; therefore: $q = q(t)$.

In the current state of our calculations, the American put is worth:

$$P(S, t) = p(S, t) + a \cdot S^{q(t)} \cdot g(t)$$

the price $p(S, t)$ of the European put being given explicitly by the Black-Scholes formula. We are left to determine, on date t, the factor a and the exercise point S^* for which the price of the American put satisfies boundary conditions 4.4 (value-matching) and 4.7 (smooth-pasting). These are, in the present case, written as:

$$P(S^*, t) + a \cdot (S^*)^{q(t)} \cdot g(t) = K - S^*$$ [4.14]

$$P_S(S^*, t) + a \cdot q(t) \cdot (S^*)^{q(t)-1} \cdot g(t) = -1$$ [4.15]

There is no difficulty in eliminating the a factor. This gives the following equation, which must be solved by successive iterations, in order to find S^* at instant t:

$$\frac{1}{q(t)} = \frac{K - S^* - p(S^*, t)}{-S^* - S^* p_S(S^*, t)}$$

[4.16]

Lastly, knowing S^*, the a factor may easily be deduced from Equation 4.15, which ends the calculation of the approximate price of the put at a given date t. The final result is not truly a separable function; this is the nature of the approximation.

The many numerical experiments by [Barone-Adesi and Whaley 1987] indicate that the price thus obtained is a good approximation of the true price of the put.

7.5 Introduction to numerical methods

It is often not possible to obtain the function $V(S, t)$, solution to [2.3] – [2.2], in an explicit form.[40] This is the case, for example, when the interest rate r or the volatility σ are not constant but are functions of S and t, or when the option in question is American and exercise before maturity becomes an event of non-zero probability (see Section 7.4), or when the boundary conditions describing the contract are more complex than those of the standard option (and are not pure linear combinations of it).

For want of an explicit expression for $V(S, t)$, we are forced to obtain numerical tables giving the function point by point, on a grid of values of S and t. Let us use h for the step of the grid in dimension S (the division of S is therefore: $S_i = ih$) and k for the step of the grid in dimension t (the division of t is: $T - t_j = jk$).[41] We therefore wish to obtain the values:

$$C_{ij} = V(ih, jk) \; ; \; i = 0, N; j = 0, M$$

which may be organized into a table as follows:

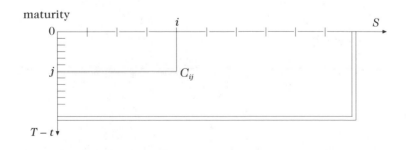

The most commonly used method of obtaining this numerical table is the 'finite difference method' which we study in Section 7.5.1. But we must also describe, at least briefly, another numerical method, Monte Carlo simulation (Section 7.5.2). Bear in mind, as well, that we may still resort to the binomial technique (*see* Chapter 6).

7.5.1 The finite difference method[42]

In this method, the calculation of C_{ij} is done line by line after replacing the differential equation by an approximately equivalent finite difference equation. We start with the first line ($j = 0$) which corresponds to the maturity date and where the conditions of the contract which, it will be recalled, are expressed by boundary conditions, supply the price of the security. For example, for the case of the call option, we know (by virtue of [2.2]) that: $C_{i0} = \text{Max}[0, ih - K]$.

We then go back in time from maturity to the date on which we wish to know the price of the secondary security.

Assuming the values of line j known, therefore, for all i:

$$C_{i,j} = V(ih, jk)$$

We wish to deduce from this, for all i, the unknown values of the following line $j + 1$:

$$C_{i,j+1} = V[ih, (j + 1)k]$$

by using partial differential equation 2.3.

Let us approximate as follows the partial derivatives which appear in [2.3]:

$$C_s \approx \frac{C_{i+1,j+1} - C_{i-1,j+1}}{2h}$$

$$C_{SS} \approx \frac{1}{h}\left[\frac{C_{i+1,j+1} - C_{i,j+1}}{h} - \frac{C_{i,j+1} - C_{i-1,j+1}}{h}\right] \qquad [5.1]$$

$$C_t \approx -\frac{C_{i,j+1} - C_{i,j}}{k}$$

Substituting these expressions into Equation 2.3, we obtain a finite difference equation:

$$\frac{1}{2}\frac{1}{h}\cdot\left[\frac{C_{i+1,j+1}-C_{i,j+1}}{h}-\frac{C_{i,j+1}-C_{i-1,j+1}}{h}\right]\cdot\sigma^2\cdot(ih)^2$$

$$+\frac{C_{i+1,j+1}-C_{i-1,j+1}}{2h}\cdot r\cdot(ih) \qquad\qquad [5.2]$$

$$-\frac{C_{i,j+1}-C_{i,j}}{k}=r\cdot C_{i,j+1} \qquad \text{for all } i$$

The original equation [2.3] must prevail at each point of the line (that is, for $i = 0,...N$). But it appears that we may only write [5.2] for $i = 1, ..., N - 1$, since this equation involves terms in C_{i-1} and C_{i+1}. We would thus have only $N - 1$ equations. The calculation of the values C_i for $i = 0$ and $i = N$, corresponding to the borders of the area, therefore requires special treatment. When the derivatives have been replaced by their finite approximation, we must add boundary conditions.

These are provided by two properties of the option. First, it is clear that the option has no more value than the security itself and that, consequently, if the security finds itself with a zero value, the option also has a zero value:

$$C(t) \leq S(t); C(t) = 0 \text{ if } S(t) = 0; C(0, t) = 0 \qquad\qquad [5.3]$$

Thus $C_{0,j+1}$, which must always be zero, is no longer really an unknown. On the other hand, $C_S \approx 1$ for large values of S, which is obvious from Figure 6.7 in the previous chapter.

This latter condition may be transcribed using an imaginary point $i = N + 1$ with the property: $C_{N+1} = C_N + h$. The imaginary point $N + 1$ allows us to write Equation 5.2 once more, which provides an Nth equation. It introduces one more unknown, namely C_{N+1}, but the relationship: $C_{N+1} = C_N + h$ constitutes an $N + 1$th equation which completes the system.

We therefore have, corresponding to a given line $j + 1$ of the table, a linear system of $N + 1$ equations where the $N + 1$ unknowns are the values $C_{i,j+1}$ for $i = 1,..., N + 1$. All that is required is to solve this system and then repeat the procedure for the next line, and so on. The linear system has the following particularly simple structure:[43]

$$
\begin{bmatrix}
\cdot & \cdot & & & \\
\cdot & \cdot & \cdot & & 0 \\
a_i & b_i & c_i & & \\
 & \cdot & \cdot & \cdot & \\
0 & & -1 & 0 & 1
\end{bmatrix}
\begin{bmatrix}
C_{1,j+1} \\
\cdot \\
C_{i,j+1} \\
\cdot \\
C_{N+1,j+1}
\end{bmatrix}
=
\begin{bmatrix}
\cdot \\
\cdot \\
d_i \\
\cdot \\
2h
\end{bmatrix}
$$

where a_i is the coefficient of $C_{i-1,j+1}$ in the ith equation, b_i is the coefficient of $C_{i,j+1}$ and c_i is the coefficient of $C_{i+1,j+1}$ in the same equation. By grouping the terms together, we have, more exactly:

$$
a_i = \tfrac{1}{2}\sigma^2 i^2 - \tfrac{1}{2}ri
$$
$$
c_i = \tfrac{1}{2}\sigma^2 i^2 + \tfrac{1}{2}ri
$$
$$
b_i = -\sigma^2 i^2 - \frac{1}{k} - r, \text{ for } i = 1, \ldots, N
$$

The right-hand sides d_i, for their part contain the values of the previous line j of the numeric table under construction:

$$
d_i = -\frac{C_{i,j}}{k}, \text{ for } i = 1, \ldots, N
$$

Thanks to the linear nature of the system, the solution presents no problems. The required reading on the solution of linear systems may be found in [Dahlquist and Björck 1974].[44]

A bias, of which we must be aware, has been introduced into the calculation. It concerns expressions 5.1 above, which we substituted into differential equation 2.3. Amongst these, the derivatives with respect to S (C_S and C_{SS}) were calculated approximately at point i on the basis of the unknown values[45] $C_{i-1,j+1}$, $C_{i,j+1}$, $C_{i+1,j+1}$ *all corresponding to instant $j +$ 1*, whilst the derivative with respect to time C_t was calculated approximately at point i on the basis of the difference between the values $C_{i,j}$ and $C_{i,j+1}$ of instants j and $j + 1$. The value obtained is not, in general, an approximation of the derivative at instant $j + 1$, nor of the derivative at instant j, but is equal (by virtue of the Mean Value Theorem) to the derivative taken at an intermediate instant between j and $j + 1$. Thus, we substituted into the same equation ([2.3]) the derivatives taken at instant $j + 1$ and the derivatives taken at an intermediate instant between j and $j + 1$.

The method of overcoming this problem involves calculating the derivatives C_S and C_{SS} not at instant $j + 1$, as in [5.1],[46] nor at instant j,[47] but taking an arithmetical mean of expressions 5.1 and the analogous expressions corresponding to instant j. For example, we would calculate C_S thus:

$$
C_S \approx \frac{1}{2} \frac{C_{i+1,j+1} - C_{i-1,j+1}}{2h} + \frac{1}{2} \frac{C_{i+1,j} - C_{i-1,j}}{2h}
$$

This method is called the 'Crank and Nicholson method' [Crank and Nicholson 1947]. It was applied to options by [Courtadon 1982].[48] The numerical results are more exact (for the same number of iterations) than those of the implicit method.

7.5.2 Another numerical method: Monte Carlo simulation

In contrast to those we have seen so far, the Monte Carlo method, which we describe below, does not allow American options to be dealt with easily. On the other hand, it is numerically more efficient when, for one reason or another, the number of variables, arguments in the evaluation function, is two or more. The reason is that its calculation time increases more or less linearly with the number of variables, whilst that of the other methods increases exponentially. The number of variables is greater than two when we wish, for example, to price an option on a security of random volatility in the presence of a risk-free interest rate which itself follows a random process. We thus have three variables (besides the time): the value of the underlying asset, the present value of the volatility and the value of the interest rate.

The Monte Carlo method allows the option to be priced on the basis of Equation 2.11 above. Since we are determining an expected value, we assume that we may obtain as good an approximation of it as we want by calculating the arithmetical mean of a sample of numbers drawn at random.

As, in the majority of cases, the joint probability distribution of all the required values is not known, we are forced to simulate the progression of the variables over time. For example, to simulate the behaviour of the underlying asset, we consider dividing the time into intervals Δt and replacing [2.12] by:[49]

$$
\Delta S_t = r_t S_t \Delta t + S_t \sigma_t \varepsilon_t \sqrt{(\Delta t)} \tag{5.3}
$$

In this equation, ε_t is a drawing of a normally distributed random variable. By sampling a series of values[50] of ε which are introduced successively into [5.3], we obtain an approximation of a possible path of S, which gives a possible price of the option on maturity. This terminal value is one realization out of all the possible terminal values. After simulating the trajectory of S a large number of times in this way, we may estimate the expected value $\hat{E}$ using the arithmetical mean of all the terminal values obtained.

Two very useful techniques allow us to reduce the quantity of numbers drawn at random to be used, whilst still keeping control of the accuracy of the final result.

The first is the technique of 'antithetical' variables by which two simulations are carried out in parallel, one using the samples ε and the other the numbers $-\varepsilon$. The estimate of the final value is then the mean of the two terminal values obtained from the two parallel simulations.

The second technique is that of the 'control variable'. It is often possible to find a case close to that being examined here, but in which the problem of valuation may be solved in the form of an explicit and exact formula; let us call this problem the 'control problem'. Option A is the option we wish to price. Option B has many characteristics in common with A, but its value V_B is known exactly in the form of an explicit expression. We now carry out two simulations (using the same random numbers and the same Δt) which give the approximate values V^*_A and V^*_B of the two options. We obtain an improved estimate of the value of A by calculating $V_A = V^*_A - V^*_B + V_B$.[51][52]

Conclusion

By way of a conclusion, here is a list of the methods for pricing options and other secondary securities which were introduced in this and the preceding chapter. They fall into three categories:

- Exact explicit formulae:[53]
    - The Black-Scholes formula, applicable to non-dividend-paying European options, options on securities of constant volatility, when the interest rate is constant;
    - Variations of the Black-Scholes formula, capable of taking into account a random interest rate or a continuous dividend (the Grabbe formula [Grabbe 1983]), on the condition that the option remains European and that the process of the forward price of the underlying asset has a constant volatility;
    - The Cox formula ([Cox and Rubinstein 1985]), applicable to options written on an underlying asset of variable volatility, but linked systematically to the price level, the relationship being isoelastic (Equation 6.4.1);

- The Geske formula ([Geske 1979a]), applicable to compound options and to American options on securities paying, at discrete instants, dividends whose amounts are known in advance (*see* Section 7.4).

- Approximate methods applicable mainly to American options on securities paying a 'continuous' dividend:
  - The compound option method of Geske and Johnson ([Geske and Johnson 1984]): *see* Section 7.4.3.1;
  - The Barone-Adesi and Whaley method ([Barone-Adesi and Whaley 1987]).

- Numerical methods:
  - The binomial method (Section 6.2 and appendix to Chapter 6);
  - The finite difference method: *see* Section 7.5.1;
  - The Monte Carlo method (Section 7.5.2);

the first two being practicable when the number of variables is relatively small (two, or three at the outside), and the third, on the other hand, not applicable to American options.

Appendix 1:

Variations of Brownian motion

Brownian motion is by definition a process whose sample paths are continuous with a probability equal to 1 ('almost surely' according to the time-honoured expression). We now wish to stress three other properties of the paths of Brownians: their variation is infinite[54], they are not differentiable, and their quadratic variation is finite. We shall begin with this last property.

Let us define the norm of a random variable A as being its quadratic mean:

$$\|A\| = E[A^2] \tag{A1.1}$$

and the corresponding distance (Euclidian) between two variables A and B by:

$$d(A, B) = \|A - B\| \tag{A1.2}$$

Let us introduce a discrete partition of the time interval $[t, t + \tau]$ into n sub-intervals.[55] Bear in mind that the increases $z_{t+i} - z_{t+i-1}$ have identical distributions (namely a centred normal distribution, of variance $1/n$) and are independent of one another. Let us calculate the quantity:

$$\left\| \sum_{i=1}^{n\tau} (z_{t+i} - z_{t+i-1})^2 - \tau \right\|$$
$$\equiv E\left\{ \left[\sum_{i=1}^{n\tau} (z_{t+i} - z_{t+i-1})^2 - \tau \right]^2 \right\} \tag{A1.3}$$

which may also be written as:

$$E\left\{ \sum_{i=1}^{n\tau} \left[(z_{t+i} - z_{t+i-1})^2 - \frac{1}{n} \right]^2 \right\}$$
$$= \sum_{i=1}^{n\tau} E\left\{ \left[(z_{t+i} - z_{t+i-1})^2 - \frac{1}{n} \right]^2 \right\} \tag{A1.4}$$

The first quantity [A1.3] is the expected square of the difference between the total length of time τ and the sum of the squares of the increases in z, whilst [A1.4] is the expected sum of the squares of the differences between the squares of the successive increases in z and their expected value, each equal to the increase in time $1/n$. These two quantities are equal by virtue of the independence of the successive increments.

Since the increases in z have a normal distribution of variance $1/n$, their fourth moment is equal to $3/n^2$, since the fourth moment of a normal variable is equal to three times the square of the second moment. The sum of the fourth moments of the successive increases minus $1/n^2$ may be recognized in the right hand side of expression A1.4. As they are $n\tau$ in number, the sum [A1.3] or [A1.4] is equal to:

$$2n\tau/n^2 = 2\tau/n \qquad\qquad [A1.5]$$

When the time division becomes smaller and smaller ($n \to +\infty$), this quantity tends towards zero. The expected squares of the differences which appear in the summation [A1.4] also tend towards zero.

Let us interpret this result in two different ways. It shows, first of all, that the quadratic variation of a Brownian is finite. This is true by definition of the quadratic variation: given that [A1.3] tends towards zero, the sum of the *squares* of the increases in z over a total interval of time τ may be likened to τ.

In a differential form (this is the second interpretation), we may also say that $(dz)^2$ may be likened to dt, as we stated in Equation 1.6.[56]

Let us return to the properties of the sample paths of a Brownian. Note that:

$$\sum_{i=1}^{n\tau} (z_{t+i} - z_{t+i-1})^2 \le \underset{i=1\ldots n\tau}{\text{Max}} \left| z_{t+i} - z_{t+i-1} \right| \cdot \sum_{i=1}^{n\tau} \left| z_{t+i} - z_{t+i-1} \right| \qquad [A1.6]$$

The left-hand side of this inequality converges towards τ, as we have just seen. The continuity of the paths of the Brownian implies that:

$$\underset{i=1\ldots n\tau}{\text{Max}} \left| z_{t+i} - z_{t+i-1} \right| \to 0$$

Consequently:

$$\sum_{i=1}^{n\tau} \left| z_{t+i} - z_{t+i-1} \right| \to \infty$$

,

In other words, the length of the trajectory (we say, the *variation*) of a Brownian, over a finite interval of time τ, is infinite, which gives a measure of the extreme agitation of the progression of Brownians. It will therefore be understood (although we shall not demonstrate this) that these progressions are not differentiable with respect to time; we cannot write dz/dt or $z'(t)$.

Appendix 2:

The stochastic integral with respect to Brownian motion

If stock market prices follow a Brownian motion, or a process derived from the Brownian, the infinite variation of these processes is liable to create problems when calculating the gains accumulated by an investor over an interval of time. Let z_t be the price of a security at instant t and f_t the number of shares held at the same instant (a real number; we ignore the indivisibility of the parts). The gains accumulated between instant 0 and instant τ are equal to

$$\int_0^\tau f_t \, dz$$

This integral with respect to time cannot be calculated traditionally as:

$$\int_0^\tau f(t)z'(t)dt$$

In fact, we have seen (Appendix 1), that $z'(t)$ has no meaning, taking into account the extreme agitation of the trajectories of z. We must therefore give a new meaning to the 'stochastic' integral

$$\int_0^\tau f_t \, dz_t$$

To do this, let us consider once again a division of the total interval of time $[0, \tau]$ into $n\tau$ subintervals and define the following random variable:

$$S_n = \sum_{i=1}^{n\tau} f_{i-1}\left(z_i - z_{i-1}\right) \tag{A2.1}$$

Under a condition of integrability to which we shall return later,[57] we may show, by a method of reasoning similar to that of Appendix 1 regarding the quadratic variation of z, that the series $\{S_n; n = 1...\}$ is a Cauchy series in the space of the random variables endowed with distance [A1.2]. As a result this series converges in quadratic mean towards a well-defined random variable which we shall call the stochastic integral of f with respect to z.

Without doing the mathematical proof,[58] let us illustrate the procedure used when calculating the following stochastic interval:

$$\int_0^\tau z_t \, dz_t$$

Here is the corresponding sum S_n:

$$S_n = \sum_{i=1}^{n\tau} z_{i-1}\left(z_i - z_{i-1}\right) = \frac{1}{2} z_\tau^2 - \frac{1}{2} \sum_{i=1}^{n\tau} \left(z_i - z_{i-1}\right)^2 \qquad [A2.2]$$

The first term of the right-hand side is explicit. As for the second, we know that it converges in quadratic mean towards τ. We therefore have the result:

$$\int_0^\tau z \, dz = \frac{1}{2} z_\tau^2 - \frac{1}{2} \tau \qquad [A2.3]$$

Let us make two very important observations regarding the definition of the stochastic integral, observations which are in fact linked. Firstly, the sum [A2.1] brings in the (random) value of f taken at instant $i-1$ and not at instant i or at an intermediate instant. In the context of ordinary integral calculus, the choice of the instant where f is evaluated in the interval $[i-1, i]$ would be of no importance, in the sense that the limit obtained would not depend on the point chosen. This is not true in the context of stochastic integral calculus. The reader may check, by way of an example, that $\Sigma z_i(z_i - z_{i-1})$ converges towards $(z_\tau^2 + \tau)/2$, which is different from [A2.3]. The value of f used in definition [A2.1] owes nothing to the realization of the future random factor $z_i - z_{i-1}$. We say that f is a process adapted to z.[59]

If, as we envisaged, the stochastic integral to which we refer represents the gains of an investor whose variable portfolio contains f_t shares of the security whose price would be z_t at instant t, this restriction means that only portfolios chosen on the basis of information available at the moment of purchase will be examined. This seems reasonable and leads us to the second observation regarding definition [A2.1].

The sum S_n gives the value of the integral taken from instant 0 to instant τ. This is clearly a process indexed by the upper limit τ, since we may envisage prolonging or shortening the interval of time over which the gains are calculated. We therefore write as S_τ the value of the integral, limit of the series S_n. *We need only perform the calculation to see that the process $\{S_\tau;\ \tau \in R^+\}$ verifies the definition [1.1] of a martingale*, the result depending on two things: (i) z is a martingale; (ii) f is adapted to z.

Therefore, *if the price of a financial security follows a martingale, any series of transactions on this security produces a cumulative gain which is itself a martingale*, which is to say that, on average, no tendency to make positive gains appears. It is satisfying to note that the definition chosen for the stochastic integral gives a result which, economically speaking, corresponds to intuition.

For the limit of the series S_n to exist, a technical condition of 'integrability' must still be satisfied. This condition is written as:

$$E\left[\int_0^\tau \left(f_t\right)^2 dt\right] < \infty \qquad\qquad \text{[A2.4]}$$

It will be understood that this condition is necessary for the calculation of the distance between two elements in the series $\{S_n\}$.

Economically speaking, f being interpreted as the number of shares held, the effect of condition (A2.4) is to limit the size of the positions taken by the investor.[60] We showed, in the introduction to the second (and current) part of this book, that an investor was in a position to make one ECU out of any game of chance, even though the expected gain on each occasion was zero, on the condition of being able to increase his stake indefinitely. This was the strategy of 'doubling stakes'. Condition A2.4 would have the effect of forbidding an investment strategy of this type. It is normal in the field of economics not to allow investors to increase their stakes indefinitely, since this would assume that they were given credit indefinitely once their personal funds were exhausted. Condition A2.4 is therefore a condition of solvency.

In this chapter, all the differential equations written acquired a meaning after stochastic integration of both sides. Since this integration is implicit, we must always assume that the condition of integrability [A2.4] is satisfied.

Notes to Chapter 7

1 Of course they are sometimes prevented from doing so by transactions costs and by difficulty in finding a counterpart. But arbitrarily fixing the interval of time between two successive transactions will obviously not take account of these two phenomena.

2 Intuitively, we denote by random 'process' a random variable whose probability distribution changes over time. In more rigorous terms, this is a family of random variables indexed by a parameter. This parameter, in all the applications we consider, will be time. It belongs to the set of non-negative real numbers. The set of processes indexed by a real number is constructed from the set of processes indexed by an integer in the same manner as we construct the set of real numbers from the set of integers. We arrive at a fundamental theorem whose existence is due to Kolmogorov.

3 Discontinuous price processes are dealt with by [Cox and Ross 1976].

4 In precise terms, a process is said to be continuous when the probability that a trajectory of this process is a continuous function of time is equal to 1.

5 Cf. [Feller 1966], page 210, or [Métivier 1979] page 214.

6 [Bachelier 1900], [Einstein 1905, 1906].

7 See [Karatzas and Shreve 1988], page 82.

8 Reminder: a sum of multivariate normal random variables is a normal random variable.

9 And when the time difference between instants t and $t + 1$ is equal to one unit of time.

10 Here, we assume a division into equal intervals to keep the explanation simple. In fact, this is not necessary. The more general condition commonly imposed on a partition t_i, $i = 1...n$ of the interval of time $[t, t + \tau](t_n = t + \tau)$ is that: $\mathrm{Max}_i \mid t_i - t_{i-1} \mid \to 0$ when $n \to \infty$.

11 See [Duffie 1988], p. 248 et seq., [Karatzas and Shreve 1988], p. 66 et seq. According to Donsker's theorem, there is convergence towards a Brownian even if the probability distribution of the increases $z_{t+1} - z_t$ is not normal. By virtue of the Central Limit theorem, it is sufficient that the increases are independent and of the same variance.

12 From now on, the symbol σ^2 indicates the variance per unit of time.

13 It is customary, in fact, to keep stochastic differential equations such as [1.7] in a form containing the differential elements dt and dz. It is not good practice to produce 'derivatives' by dividing both sides of Equation 1.7 by dt. The reason for this precaution is (see Appendix 1) that the trajectories of a Brownian are extremely erratic (non-smooth) and non-differentiable.

14 See Appendix 2 for the definition of the stochastic integral; in particular condition A2.4.

15 Cf [Arnold 1974], pages 105 ff.

16 There is, however, a significant difference between these two classes of process. Diffusion processes are, by definition, Markovian processes, whose movement depends only on the current value of the variable, whilst the class of Itô processes may be widened: $\alpha(\ )$ and $\sigma(\ )$ may depend on past values of x.

17 But, purely on account of the fact that the drift depends on x, the variance of an increase in x over a finite interval of time will also depend on x.

18 And by using the expression of $(dx)^2$ which results from this: $(dx)^2 = \sigma^2(x,t)dt$.

19 An Itô's Lemma also exists for functions of several random processes $y = f(x_1, x_2, t)$. It brings in the covariance between the random parts of x_1 and x_2.

20 It is positive in Figure 7.4.

21 We should also ensure that the functions α and σ are such that stochastic differential equation 2.1 possesses one and only one solution, that is to say that they satisfy the growth condition and the Lipschitz condition.

22 When reproducing a call option b is negative. In fact, this is then a borrowing position on the risk-free security.

23 The true mathematical meaning of Equation 2.6 is that of the corresponding integral equation giving the increase in value of the portfolio over an interval of time $[0, \tau]$:

$$V_\tau - V_0 = \int_0^\tau h_t dS_t + \int_0^\tau b_t D_t r dt = \int_0^\tau \left[h_t S_t \alpha_t + b_t D_t r \right] dt + \int_0^\tau h_t S_t \sigma_t dz_t$$

It is the first term on the right-hand side of the first line of this equation, or the last term of the second line, which requires the stochastic integral with respect to a Brownian to be defined (*see* Appendix 2). For this integral to exist, the integrability condition [A2.4] must be imposed on the portfolio:

$$E\left[\int_0^\tau \left(h_t S_t \sigma_t \right)^2 dt \right] < \infty$$

As we show in Appendix 2, it is this condition which prevents the portions invested in the risky security from growing indefinitely and which forbids strategies of the 'doubling strategy' type (*see* the introduction to Part II). From an economic point of view, this is a condition of solvency.

24   This is a notable advantage of this argument over Black and Scholes' original argument [Black and Scholes 1973]. Moreover, the present argument, as opposed to that of Black and Scholes, does not assume *a priori* that the price of the option is a twice differentiable function of the price of the underlying security. Here we constructed, without referring to the option, a twice differentiable function V. We then showed that the price of the option had to be identical to that of this function V.

25   See [Karatzas and Shreve 1988], page 267.

26   The change from drift α to drift r of the underlying asset induces a change in the probability distribution of the future values of S. If we know the 'true' probability distribution of these future values in the presence of drift α, we may obtain the 'adjusted' distribution resulting from a drift equal to r by means of the Girsanov theorem: *see* [Karatzas and Shreve 1988], page 190 *or* [Lipster and Shiryayev 1977], page 232.

27   Holding and storage costs may occur in relation to options on commodity or currency.

28   If we were in the presence of a tax system hitting dividends and capital gains differently, we could be less definite and assume that the drop in price is proportional to the dividend: we would then have to specify a coefficient of proportionality.

29   The opposite specification, in which the amount of dividend D actually paid on the date τ is limited by the total assets available, can only be solved by numerical methods (Section 7.4).

30   *See* Geske's article [Geske 1979a], *or* [Cox and Rubinstein 1985], page 414.

31   The 'ordinary' Geske formula, giving the price of an option on an option, calls in the *bivariate* normal distribution function, which must be calculated by numerical integration. The valuation of complex compound options 'on several levels' (an option on an option on an option...) requires numeric calculation of the multivariate normal law, which is extremely laborious.

32   An option gives the right to receive one security in exchange for another. Most often, one of the two securities is cash: a call is the right to receive a security in exchange for cash; a put is the right to receive cash in exchange for a security. We are speaking here of the dividend *attached to the security that is received*.

33   Recall that some options obey partial differential equation 3.3 rather than Equation 2.3.

34   Clearly, it is not the cash received itself which brings about the exercise before maturity. Without the plan to reinvest this cash, there would be no hurry to receive it.

35   Remember that the path of S is continuous. We assume here that: $S(0) > S^*(0)$, otherwise the option is exercised at instant 0.

36   The effective value of the put is then given by the curve to the right of point B and, to the left of this point, by the segment giving the exercise price $S - K$. This generally results in a kink in B.

37   We are reproducing here the reasoning of [Merton 1973], note 60.

38   *See* [Dumas 1991].

39   Note, however, that we obtained condition 4.4 from the condition: $\partial P/\partial S^* = 0$, which is of the marginal type. We assume here a small movement of the exercise frontier.

40   In the conclusion to this chapter, we review again the cases in which explicit, exact or approximate solutions are feasible and desirable.

41   That is, we count *the time backwards*, $j = 0$ corresponding to the date of (terminal) maturity of the option.

42   The reader will find a complete treatment of this method in [Smith 1978].

43   This is known as a tridiagonal structure.

44   It should be added that the finite difference method is applicable to American options. Exercise before maturity is taken into account by an additional stage of calculation: after calculating the prices of the non-exercised option on line $j + 1$, as shown, we need only compare them with the exercised price and keep the larger of the two before moving to the next time stage.

45   This method is known as an 'implicit method' as it calculates derivatives from values which are still unknown, which must be obtained by solving a system of simultaneous equations. The 'explicit' method would evaluate these derivatives at instant j, at which time all the values are already known. After substituting into the differential equation, the unknown value of C at point i at instant $j + 1$ would appear only once in the ith equation, in the term C_i. We could then solve each equation separately. This would be simpler, but the method is unfortunately often unstable (numerical errors will be magnified when moving from one line to the next). Furthermore, this method would introduce a similar bias, but with the opposite sign to that which we are about to describe in respect of the implicit method. We shall see that this bias may be eliminated by using an average of the implicit evaluation and the explicit evaluation of the derivatives with respect to S.

46   Expressions 5.1 represent, it will be recalled, (*see previous note*) the implicit method.

47   The derivatives estimated at instant j would be obtained by expressions analogous to [5.1] where $j + 1$ had been replaced by j.

48   *See also* [Smith 1978].

49   Here we give what is known as the Euler approximation. We may also simulate, with greater precision, the process solution to a stochastic differential equation using Runge-Kutta stochastic approximation. *See* [Rumelin 1982].

50   Most spreadsheets and statistical software are programmed with a function to generate numbers at random.

51   On the Monte Carlo technique applied to options, *see*, for example, [Boyle 1987].

52   The same method may be applied to the binomial technique of Chapter 6. The binomial technique is implemented twice: once for the main problem which we wish to solve and once for the control problem. Comparing the binomial solution of the control problem with its exact solution then provides an indication as to the error made in the binomial solution of the main problem and allows this to be rectified. *See* [Hull and White 1988].

53   We leave aside the formulae which apply to cases where the underlying asset may undergo jumps (mentioned in Chapter 6) or formulae linked to American options, the only known formulae being those which apply to American options with infinite maturity.

54   The 'variation' of a path is the length of the line which draws it.

55   We assume here a partition into equal intervals for ease of explanation. In fact, this is not necessary. *See note 10 above*.

56   Using slightly stronger hypotheses, it may even be shown that this equation is true almost certainly (that is with a probability equal to 1). *See* [Lipster and Shiryayev 1988], page 89.

57   *See* Equation A2.4.

58   This may be found, for example, in [Karatzas and Shreve 1988], page 137 or [Lipster and Shiryayev 1988], page 103.

59   *See* the much more precise definition of 'adapted' processes in the books already cited.

60   *See* [Dybvig and Huang 1988].

References

[Arnold 1974] L. Arnold, *Stochastic Differential Equations: Theory and Applications*. John Wiley & Sons, 1974.

[Bachelier 1900] L. Bachelier, 1900, Théorie de la spéculation, Annales des Sciences de l'Ecole Normale Supérieure, 3, 21–86, reproduced in P. H. Cootner, ed., *The Random Character of Stock Market Prices*. MIT Press, Cambridge, 1964.

[Barone-Adesi and Whaley 1987] G. Barone-Adesi and R. Whaley, Efficient Analytic Approximation of American Option Values, *The Journal of Finance*, 42, 1987, 301–320.

[Bergman 1981] Y. Z. Bergman, A Characterization of Self-financing Portfolio Strategies, Working Paper, Institute of Business and Economic Research, University of California, Berkeley, 1981.

[Black and Scholes 1973] F. Black and M. Scholes, The Pricing of Options and Corporate Liabilities, *Journal of Political Economy*, 81, 1973, 637–659.

[Brennan 1979] M. J. Brennan, The Pricing of Contingent Claims in Discrete-Time Models, *Journal of Finance*, 34, 1979, 53–68.

[Carr 1988] P. Carr, Option Pricing When Dividends and Interest Rates are Unknown, Working Paper, University of California, Los Angeles, August 1988.

[Courtadon 1982] G. Courtadon, A More Accurate Finite Difference Approximation for the Valuation of Options, *Journal of Financial and Quantitative Analysis*, XVIII, 1982, 697–704.

[Cox and Ross 1976] J. C. Cox and S. A. Ross, The Valuation of Options for Alternative Stochastic Processes, *Journal of Financial Economics*, 3, 1976, 145–166.

[Cox and Rubinstein 1985] J. C. Cox and M. Rubinstein, *Options Markets*. Prentice Hall, Inc., 1985.

[Cox *et al.* 1979]   J. C. Cox, S. Ross and M. Rubinstein, Option
                              Pricing: A Simplified Approach, *Journal of*
                              Financial Economics, 7, 1979, 229–263.

[Crank and Nicholson 1947]   P. Crank and P. Nicholson, A Practical
                              Method for Numerical Evaluation of Solu-
                              tions of Partial Differential Equations of the
                              Heat-conduction type, *Proc. Camb Phil. Soc.*,
                              43, 1947, 50–67.

[Dahlquist and Björck 1974]   G. Dahlquist and Å. Björck, *Numerical*
                              Methods, Englewood Cliffs, NJ: Prentice
                              Hall, Inc., 1974.

[Duffie 1988]   D. Duffie, *Security Markets, Stochastic*
                              Models. Academic Press, Inc., 1988.

[Dumas 1991]   B. Dumas, Super Contact and Related Opti-
                              mality Conditions, *Journal of Economic*
                              Dynamics and Control, 15, 1991, 675–685.

[Dybvig and Huang 1988]   P. H. Dybvig and C.-F. Huang, Nonnegative
                              Wealth, Absence of Arbitrage, and Feasible
                              Consumption Plans, *Review of Financial*
                              Studies, 1, 1988, 377–401.

[Einstein 1905]   A. Einstein, Annalen der Physik, 17, 1905,
                              549ff., reproduced as On the Movement of
                              Small Particles Suspended in a Stationary
                              Liquid Demanded by the Molecular Kinetic
                              Theory of Heat, in A. Einstein, *Investiga-*
                              tions on the Theory of the Brownian Move-
                              ment. R. Fürth, ed., Dover Publications,
                              1956.

[Einstein 1906]   A. Einstein, Zur Theorie der Brownschen
                              Bewegung, *Annalen der Physik*, 19, 1906,
                              371–381.

[Farlow 1982]   S. J. Farlow, *Partial Differential Equations*
                              for Scientists and Engineers. John Wiley &
                              Sons, 1982.

[Feller 1966]   W. Feller, *An Introduction to Probability*
                              Theory and its Applications, Volume II.
                              John Wiley & Sons, Inc., 1966.

[Geske 1979a]   R. Geske, The Valuation of Compound
                              Options, *Journal of Financial Economics*,
                              1979, 7, 63–82.

[Geske 1979b]   R. Geske, A Note on an Analytical Valuation
                                    Formula for Unprotected American Call
                                    Options on Stocks with Known Dividends,
                                    Journal of Financial Economics, 1979, 7,
                                    375–380.

[Geske and Johnson 1984]   R. Geske and H. E. Johnson, The American
                                    Put Valued Analytically, *Journal of Finance*,
                                    39, 1984, 1511–1524.

[Grabbe 1983]   O. Grabbe, The Pricing of Call and Put
                                    Options on Foreign Exchange, *Journal of
                                    International Money and Finance*, 2, 1983,
                                    239–253.

[Harrison and Kreps 1979]   M. Harrison and D. Kreps, Martingales and
                                    Multiperiod Securities Markets, *Journal of
                                    Economic Theory*, 20, 1979, 381–408.

[Lévy 1965]   P. Lévy, *Processus stochastiques et mouve-
                                    ment brownien*, 2nd edition. Gauthier-
                                    Villars, Paris, 1965.

[Hull and White 1988]   J. Hull and A. White, The Use of the Control
                                    Variate Technique in Option Pricing, *Jour-
                                    nal of Financial and Quantitative Analysis*,
                                    23, 1988, 237–251.

[Ingersoll 1987]   J. E. Ingersoll Jr., *Theory of Financial Deci-
                                    sion Making*. Rowman & Littlefield, 1987.

[Itō 1944]   K. Itō, Stochastic Integral, Proc. *Imperial
                                    Acad. Tokyo*, 20, 1944, 519–524.

[Itō 1946]   K. Itō, On a Stochastic Integral Equation,
                                    Proceedings of the Japanese Academy, 1,
                                    1946, 32–35.

[Itō 1951]   K. Itō, On Stochastic Differential Equations,
                                    *Memoir of the American Mathematical
                                    Society*, 4, 1951, 51.

[Karatzas and Shreve 1988]   I. Karatzas and S. E. Shreve, *Brownian
                                    Motion and Stochastic Calculus*. Springer
                                    Verlag, 1988.

[Lipster and Shiryayev 1977]   R. S. Lipster and A. N. Shiryayev, *Statistics
                                    of Random Processes I: General Theory*.
                                    Springer Verlag, 1977.

[MacMillan 1986]   L. W. MacMillan, Analytical Approximation
                          for the American Put Option, *Advances in
                          Futures and Options Research*, 1, 1986,
                          119–139.

[Merton 1973]   R. C. Merton, Theory of Rational Option
                          Pricing, *Bell Journal of Economics and
                          Management Science*, 4, Spring 1973,
                          141–183.

[Merton 1977]   R. C. Merton, On the Pricing of Contingent
                          Claims and the Modigliani-Miller Theorem,
                          Journal of Financial Economics, 5, 1977,
                          241-250.

[Métivier 1979]   M. Métivier, *Notions fondamentales de la
                          théorie des probabilités*. Dunod, 1979.

[Reinhard 1987]   H. Reinhard, *Equations aux dérivées par-
                          tielles*. Dunod, 1987.

[Roll 1977]   R. Roll, An Analytical Valuation Formula for
                          Unprotected American Call Options on
                          Stocks with Known Dividends, *Journal of
                          Financial Economics*, 5, 1977, 251–258.

[Rubinstein 1976]   M. Rubinstein, The Valuation of Uncertain
                          Income Stress and the Pricing of Options,
                          *Bell Journal of Economics and Manage-
                          ment Science*, 7, 1976, 551–571.

[Rumelin 1982]   W. Rumelin, Numerical Treatment of Sto-
                          chastic Differential Equations, *Siam
                          Journal*, 19, 1982, 604–613.

[Smith 1978]   G. D. Smith, *Numerical Solution of Partial
                          Differential Equations: Finite Difference
                          Methods*. Oxford University Press, 1978.

[Wiener 1923]   N. Wiener, Differential Space, *Journal of
                          Mathematical Physics*, 2, 1923, 131–174.

8

Evaluation of the liabilities and assets of a limited company; financial engineering

In the the last two chapters we discussed the pricing of call and put options in relation to the price of the underlying stock. In fact, the option pricing method has a much wider field of application: it allows us to evaluate the liabilities of a limited company (corporation) – that is, a company whose shareholders are protected by a limited liability clause – in relation to the price of the assets considered as underlying security. In some cases, it even allows us to determine the value of the assets in relation to certain variables affecting the profitability of the firm.

Any debenture security is generally subject to two types of risk:

- the default risk, which corresponds to the fact that the debt contract may not be totally honoured and that some payments have a non-zero probability of not being made,

- the interest rate risk, which is linked to the fact that a rise in market interest rates brings about a fall in the prices of debenture securities and vice versa.

In this book, the two types of risk are dealt with separately. In this chapter we address the default risk, by assuming that market interest rates are not only non-random but totally fixed. We shall study the interest rate risk to the exclusion of the default risk in Chapters 9 and 10. We therefore devote the most of this chapter to the valuation of the ordinary debt of a limited company (Section 8.1), then to studying the cost of the debt and the equity capital of a limited company (Section 8.2), and lastly to the valuation of convertible bonds and warrants (Section 8.3).

The circumstances in which assets may also be evaluated by the same techniques are addressed in Section 8.4.

8.1   Evaluation of ordinary debt

8.1.1   Single, zero-coupon debt with a one-off payment

Consider a company which has issued a single debt security giving rise to one terminal payment, with no other intermediate payment. This special case is only considered to simplify the explanation: it corresponds to a debenture security with a one-off payment in the absence of any other debt and in the absence of coupon payments to bondholders or dividend payments to shareholders. These other cases will be studied afterwards.

As usual, we address this problem of valuation by reasoning backwards in time. We shall therefore first ask ourselves the following question: what happens at the moment when the debt reaches maturity? In particular, what is the amount received by the debtholders? In answering these questions, it will be noted immediately that there are two possibilities:

- either the assets have a greater value than the redemption price of the debt (which we shall write as D) in which case the debtholders receive the redemption price,

- or the value of the assets is less than the redemption price, in which case the shareholders prefer to invoke the limited liability clause, abandon their title deeds and leave the company in the hands of the creditors, rather than compensate the creditors out of their own pockets.[1,2]

The payment eventually received by the debtholders therefore conforms to Figure 8.1 (the broken line). By considering the complement, it is equally easy for us to determine the amount of assets which remains in the hands of

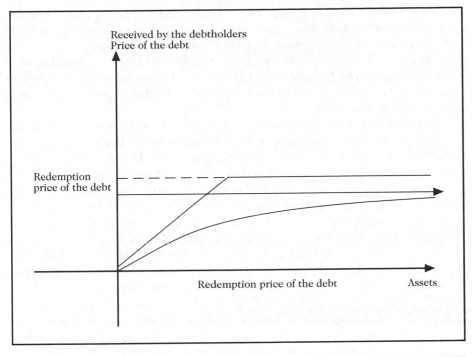

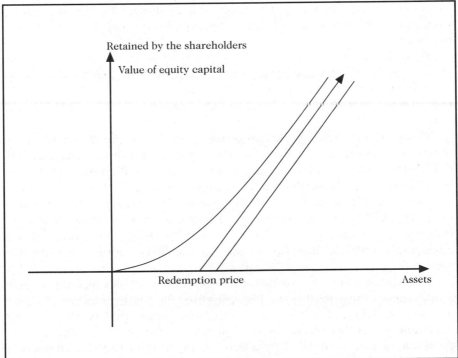

Figures 8.1 and 8.2

the shareholders after maturity: if the value of the assets is greater than the redemption price, they keep the difference, and if the value of the assets is less than the redemption price, they no longer have anything.

The curve in Figure 8.2 is clearly identical to that for a call option with an exercise price of D. This means that from a financial point of view, the shareholders, protected by limited liability, hold the equivalent of a 'call option' on the assets.[3]

At an instant preceding maturity, we need only apply the Black-Scholes formula to determine the share price;[4] this gives us the curve in Figure 8.2, where the asymptote is a half-line passing through the discounted value of the redemption price. Limited liability has the effect that the value of the share is never strictly zero, except for a value of the assets which itself was zero; even when the value of the assets is much less than the redemption price, the shareholders may nevertheless retain the hope of a rise in the value of the assets and have the safety-net of the limited liability clause.

By taking the complement again, we may return to Figure 8.1 to determine the value of the debt subject to a default risk, at instants preceding maturity (the curve in Figure 8.1). It will be noted that this value has a horizontal asymptote for very large values of the assets; this horizontal asymptote is located on the discounted value of the redemption price and is equal to the value which the debt would have on the market if it were risk-free. When the amount of assets is much smaller and close to, or less than, the redemption price, the value of the debt is itself much less than the value it would have in the absence of risk and is equal to or less than the value of the assets.

Thus, the Black-Scholes formula allows us to break down the total value of the assets into the value of the equity capital and the market value of the debt from the moment that the amount of debt issued, namely its redemption price, is given. There are two comments to be made on this result.

Firstly, it will obviously be noted that the value of the debt assumes an upper limit which is the value of the assets. Even if the firm increases the redemption amount (that is, the amount it owes) indefinitely, by issuing more debts, these cannot have a total market value greater than the value of the assets. Any increase in the amount owed is compensated by an increase in the probability that this promised payment will not be made. This is true even though bankruptcy, or rather non-payment, brings about no additional costs and simply modifies the division of the flows between shareholders and creditors.

Secondly, it will be remembered that the Black-Scholes formula involves a parameter: the volatility σ. The volatility for the evaluation of equity capital and debt will be the volatility of the assets, that is, the standard deviation of their instantaneous rates of return.[5] We know that the choice of assets is, in law, controlled by a general meeting of the shareholders or delegated to the board of directors. The shareholders therefore have every opportunity to harm the debtholders: if they replace less risky assets by more risky assets (larger σ) of equal value, the share price is immediately increased, as we saw when discussing options, and the value of the debt is immediately reduced, taking account of the higher probability of non-payment. The debtholders are exposed to a moral hazard, namely a risk linked to the behaviour of the shareholders, who have the power of decision so that the debtholders are effectively bound hand and foot.

The debtholders may however seek to protect themselves by certain clauses (covenants) in the debt contract which forbid the company from taking certain actions, in particular all those which would harm them.[6] This practice, common in Anglo-Saxon law, is appearing more and more frequently in France.[7]

8.1.2 Payments made to shareholders during the lifetime of the debt

By way of a generalization of the model suggested above, let us turn to the question of intermediate payments which may occur before the final repayment of the debt, dealing first of all with payments to shareholders in the form, for example, of dividends.

This question is clarified in Figure 8.3 where a time axis has been drawn with three instants marked instant 0, which is the instant of today, instant 1, which is an intermediate instant at which a dividend payment is to be made, and instant 2, which is that of the final repayment. At this final instant, the share price is given by the usual graph, which is shown at the top right of the figure. If we go back to instant 1, we need to mark off an instant which would immediately follow instant 1 and which we shall call instant $1 + \varepsilon$ and an instant which would immediately precede instant 1 and which we shall call $1 - \varepsilon$.

At instant $1 + \varepsilon$, the dividend having been paid, the share price is obtained by calculating the present value of the payment of instant 2; this calculation is very simply done using the Black-Scholes formula.

The transition from instant $1 + \varepsilon$ to instant $1 - \varepsilon$ introduces a discontinuity and calls for precise reasoning. Between these two instants, the dividend will have been paid (if the assets permit it), and this will have had two consequences: a corresponding amount of cash will have been deducted from the assets of the company, and then the payment of the dividend will have caused a fall of equal amount in the share price. The difference between the graph for instant $1 + \varepsilon$ and that for instant $1 - \varepsilon$ is therefore simply a movement of the origin along the first bisector representing the sudden variation in price, both of the assets and of the equity capital (the graph at the bottom left of Figure 8.3).

To continue the process of backward valuation, we must move from instant $1 - \varepsilon$ to instant 0 by solving the Black-Scholes partial differential equation (see Chapter 7, Equation 2.3), relying on the terminal condition

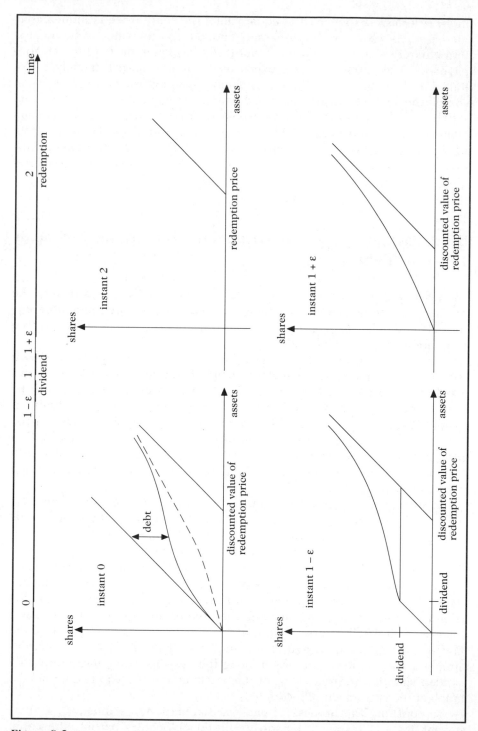

Figure 8.3

which gives the value, already obtained, of instant $1 - \varepsilon$. This can generally be done using the binomial method (*cf.* Chapter 6) or by numerical methods (*cf.* Section 7.5). In the case where the dividend payment at instant 1 is assured, the result is given by a slightly more complex formula than that of Black and Scholes, known as Geske's formula ([Geske 1979]), or the compound option formula (*see* Section 6.4.2 and Section 7.4.1), to which is added the discounted value of the dividend.

The result is, generally speaking, a curve slightly swollen up on the left which appears in the graph at the top left of Figure 8.3. The 'swell' is due to the prospect of a dividend payment which must occur before the compensation of the debtholders and which thus gives priority to the shareholders. If the result is compared with that which a simple Black-Scholes formula would have given us, ignoring the dividend (dotted curve in Figure 8.3, instant 0), we obviously find a higher share price. However, the difference becomes imperceptible for high values of the assets, since the probability of non-payment then becomes negligible and this makes the shareholders indifferent to the date of the dividend payment.

8.1.3   Payments made to debtholders

The problem of an intermediate payment to creditors in the form of an interest coupon or a partial repayment is dealt with in Figure 8.4. In this figure, the timescale is identical and the transition from instant 2 to instant $1 + \varepsilon$ is also the same as before. On the other hand, the transition from instant $1 + \varepsilon$ to instant $1 - \varepsilon$ is noticeably different.

When a payment is made to the debtholders, the assets are diminished by the amount of this payment, since it is taken from the company's earnings. The shares themselves, since they receive nothing, undergo no drop in price. The transition from the diagram for instant $1 + \varepsilon$ to the diagram for instant $1 - \varepsilon$ must therefore be effected by a simple movement to the right of the origin of the x axis. The diagram obtained for instant $1 - \varepsilon$ correctly reflects the fact that the shareholders will invoke the limited liability clause if and only if the value of available assets is less than the amount of the contractual coupon, in which case, they abandon their title deeds and have in hand a zero value.[8]

If we go back from instant $1 - \varepsilon$ to instant 0, we obtain the diagram at the top left of Figure 8.4, which is slightly flatter than one which would have been given by the Black-Scholes formula incorporating an exercise price equal to the sum of the redemption price and the dividend (dotted curve). The fact that the coupon occurs earlier provides some slight protection to the creditors and therefore reduces the share price. This explains why the majority of limited companies are obliged not only to pay dividends, but also to make certain repayments during the lifetime of the securities they have issued. These arrangements offer partial protection to the creditors.

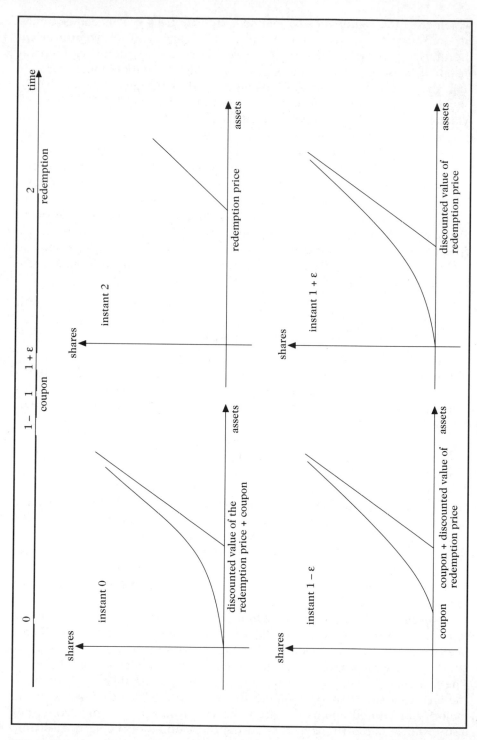

Figure 8.4

8.1.4   Subordinated debt

It is rare for a firm to issue only one class of bond during its existence. Let us therefore suppose in this section that the firm has issued three classes of financial security: (i) ordinary shares, (ii) priority bonds and (iii) subordinated bonds which will only be redeemed after a total paying-off of the priority creditors.

Let us consider the most simple case, where the shareholders receive no dividends and where the bonds are all of the zero-coupon type and have the same maturity.[9] Let us call the value of the assets of the firm V, the value of the equity capital V_a, and write $V_{d,p}$ for the value of the priority debt whose promised repayment at maturity amounts to D_p and $V_{d,np}$ for the value of the subordinated debt whose promised repayment amounts to D_{np}.

As with other financial securities, we shall address the problem of valuation by reasoning backwards. Let us first of all place ourselves at the maturity of the debts and examine the amounts received by the various backers of the firm. Three cases may arise:

- the assets have a value greater than the sum of the redemption prices of the priority debt and of the subordinated debt, that is to say, $V > D_p + D_{np}$. All the creditors receive the redemption price of their receivables. The shareholders retain the difference between the value of the assets and the total of the debts;

- the assets have a value between D_p and $D_p + D_{np}$. Only the priority creditors are entirely reimbursed, the non-priority creditors only receiving the difference between the value of the assets and the redemption price of the priority debt. The shareholders are left with nothing;

- the assets have a value less than the redemption price of the priority debt. The shareholders invoke the limited liability clause again and abandon the firm to the creditors. The non-priority creditors receive nothing and the priority creditors receive the value of the assets.

The value on maturity of the securities of the various backers may be summed up as follows: equity capital: $V_a = \max\,[0, V - D_p - D_{np}]$; priority debt: $V_{d,p} = \min[V, D_p]$; subordinated debt: $V_{d,np} = \max\{0, \min[V - D_p, D_{np}]\}$.

The curve for the equity capital corresponds to that of a call option with an exercise price of $D_p + D_{np}$; that of the priority debt is unchanged from that drawn in Figure 8.1: the priority creditors hold the assets but have sold in exchange a call option on these assets, with an exercise price equal to D_p, to the non-priority creditors. The non-priority creditors have simultaneously sold a call option with an exercise price of $D_p + D_{np}$ to the shareholders and bought a call option with an exercise price of D_p from the creditors.[10]

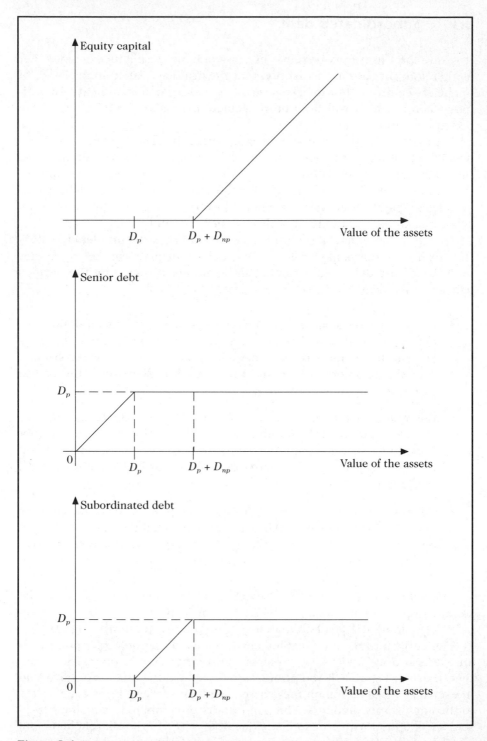

Figure 8.4

If we assume that the process governing the movements in the value of the assets of the firm is always of the type $dV = \alpha V dt + \sigma V dz$, the three classes of security must then satisfy the Black-Scholes partial differential equation (Equation 2.3 of Chapter 7) to which are added the appropriate boundary conditions corresponding to each of the securities in question.

It may therefore be shown[11] that, in contrast to priority debt, the value of subordinated debt may be an increasing function of the rate of interest, the time to maturity and the volatility of the value of the firm. Subordinated debt may even be more volatile than the actual assets of the company. In fact, when the value of the firm is low in relation to $D_p + D_{np}$, subordinated debt behaves more like equity capital than priority debt.

Before ending this section, let us stress that, in the above analysis, we have assumed that the two classes of debt issued by the firm had the same maturity. When this is not the case, and the maturities differ, some complications may appear, inducing strategic forms of behaviour on the part of the capital suppliers of the company, who will try to bypass the order of priority of reimbursement of debt.

By way of an illustration, suppose the maturity of the subordinated debt, t_1, precedes that of the priority debt, t_2, and that on this date, the assets of the firm are insufficient fully to reimburse the non-priority creditors: $V(t_1) < D_{np}$. Since the firm has defaulted on this payment, bankruptcy is declared. In such a case, it is generally expected that all the debts will be called in repayment. This situation is very disadvantageous to the non-priority creditors. In fact, since the assets are used first of all to compensate the priority creditors, the non-priority creditors are likely to find themselves with nothing (this will be the case in particular if $V(t_1) \le D_p$).

With this expectation, it is worth the non-priority creditors' while to re-negotiate their terms of engagement with the shareholders and renounce a fraction of their debt just large enough to avoid default by the firm. In this way, the non-priority creditors save part of their debt. It is clear that the consequences of this behaviour are entirely borne by the priority creditors, who will see themselves as being somewhat expropriated by the non-priority creditors: we are witnessing a transfer of wealth between liability holders within the firm. The strategy followed by the non-priority creditors allows them to overturn the theoretical order of priority of debt.

A detailed analysis of these strategic behaviour patterns and the resulting equilibria would mean resorting to game theory,[12] which lies outside the scope of this book. This type of analysis must not, however, be ignored as it plays a crucial role in corporate finance.

8.2   Costs of the various sources of funds

The reader may remember the value additivity principle and the celebrated Modigliani and Miller theorem (*see* Chapter 1). It says that in the absence of taxes on companies, the total value of the debt and of the equity capital of a company is independent of the relative proportion of these two components. The value of the firm is independent of the mix or of the financial leverage. A corollary to this theorem is often stated, which says that the weighted average cost of the capital is independent of the leverage, the weighted average cost being the average of the costs of financing (required expected return) attached to debt and equity capital.

To illustrate these results, we often draw the leftmost part of the curves in Figure 8.5. This figure has on the x axis the financial leverage, equal to the market value of the debt divided by the market value of the shares, and on the y axis the cost of the various sources of funds. The average cost is a constant, and the cost of the debt is equal to the risk free rate of interest, so long as the probability of non-payment is negligible. The result is that the cost of equity capital must grow linearly with the leverage. A higher leverage subjects the shareholders to a higher risk of return, which must be remunerated; this is known as the 'leverage effect'.

The usual treatment of the theory of corporate finance stops at this stage and rarely addresses the case where the probability of default becomes non-negligible. This case may well arise if we continue to increase the leverage. Since the value of the debt increases relative to the value of the assets, the creditors perceive that the probability of not being paid is not negligible and consequently demand a higher expected return from their debt. The cost of the debt must grow, as shown in Figure 8.5, without, of course, ever exceeding the average cost which reflects the business risk of the company. This is the risk of its industrial and commercial activity, which is the maximum risk that the creditors may ever have to take.[13] As for the cost of equity capital, it still increases with the leverage but less quickly than before, given that the shareholders are protected by the limited liability clause and assume a smaller increase in risk than before. The curved parts of the functions, which give the cost of the equity capital and the cost of the debt, are the product of this clause, which transfers risk from the shareholders to the creditors.

We wish to find an accurate measure of the costs of the various sources of funds, corresponding to the intuitive and approximate argument which we have just presented. This must be possible, since we know how to determine (Section 8.1) the value of the equity capital and the debt. As the cost of the equity capital is the expected return on the shares, and since a share may be likened to an option, we are led to make a digression on the expected return on an option.

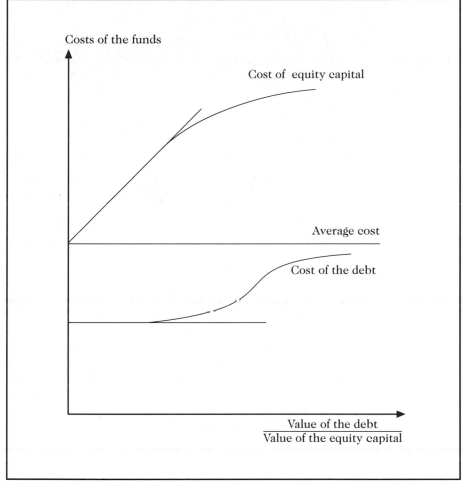

Figure 8.5

To do this, we refer to the previous chapter (Section 7.2), in which we established the Black-Scholes partial differential equation (Equation 2.3 of that chapter). We postulated there a random process for the underlying stock given by:

$$dS/S = \alpha\, dt + \sigma\, dz \qquad\qquad [2.1]$$

In this equation, α is the expected instantaneous rate of return on the underlying stock and σ the standard deviation of the instantaneous rate of return on this security (its volatility). We showed the existence of a continuous function twice continually differentiable with respect to S:

$$C(S, t) \hspace{10cm} [2.2]$$

linking the value of the option to the value of the underlying stock and time. We also showed that this function satisfies the Black-Scholes partial differential equation:

$$(1/2)\sigma^2 S^2 C_{SS} + rSC_S + C_t = rC \hspace{6cm} [2.3]$$

Let us apply Itō's lemma to the function C to calculate the expected variation of the price of the option, and thus the expected return on the option written α_C.

$$\alpha_C = \frac{(1/2)\sigma^2 S^2 C_{SS} + \alpha SC_S + C_t}{C} \hspace{5cm} [2.4]$$

We would be quite free to calculate the derivatives of the Black-Scholes formula and substitute them into Equation 2.4 to calculate this expected return. But a there is a simpler way. Let us denote Ω the elasticity of the price of the option in relation to the price of the underlying stock: $\Omega = (\partial C/\partial S)(S/C)$. This is the percentage of variation of the price of the option induced by a variation of 1% in the price of the underlying stock. Let us now substitute Equation 2.3 into Equation 2.4. This gives:[14]

$$\alpha_c - r = \Omega \times (\alpha - r) \hspace{6cm} [2.5]$$

or, in another form:

$$\frac{\alpha_c - r}{\Omega\sigma} = \frac{\alpha - r}{\sigma} \hspace{6cm} [2.6]$$

The interpretation of Equation 2.6 is simple if we think about what the volatility of an option is. Since the only random element influencing the price of an option is that of the underlying stock, the volatility of the option is equal to that of the underlying stock multiplied by the degree of sensitivity of the price of the option compared with that of the underlying stock, which is $\Omega \times \sigma$. Equation 2.6 therefore means that the risk premium[15] attached to an option per unit of volatility is the same as the risk premium per unit of volatility attached to the underlying stock. The underlying stock is therefore used as a reference in determining the premium. It will be noted, for practical calculations, that the elasticity Ω given by the Black-Scholes formula (Table 6.1) is as follows:

$$\Omega = \frac{S}{C} N(d_1) \tag{2.7}$$

Application of these developments to the calculation of the costs of the various sources of funds of a company is totally direct if we recall once again that a share equates to a call option on the assets. The share is now the option, and the underlying stock is made up of all the assets. We thus obtain the cost of equity capital:

$$k_a = r + \Omega_a(k-r) \tag{2.8}$$

where:

k_a = the cost of equity capital,

Ω_a = the elasticity of the price of the share in relation to the value of the assets (the elasticity supplied, as we have just seen (Equation 2.7), by the Black-Scholes formula),

k = the average cost of the capital, equal to the expected return on the assets.

We have, in completely similar fashion:

$$k_d = r + \Omega_d(k-r) \tag{2.9}$$

where:

k_d = the cost of the debt

Ω_d = the elasticity of the value of the debt in relation to the value of the assets.

This latter elasticity is easily obtained if we know that the average of the elasticities of the equity capital and the debt, weighted by their respective values V_a and V_d, is equal to the elasticity of the assets relative to one another, which is obviously 1:

$$\Omega_a \times (V_a/V) + \Omega_d \times (V_d/V) = 1 \qquad\qquad [2.10]$$

Application of formulae 2.7 to 2.10 would give exactly the curves of the graphs in Figure 8.5, which we have already interpreted.

We can see that the option pricing method has a considerable field of application which far surpasses its very limited name; in fact, it makes it possible to evaluate a good number of the legal clauses of risk allocation between one or another category of investor.[16]

8.3   Evaluation of convertible bonds

A convertible bond is a bond with an associated clause giving the bearer the right to exchange his or her bond for a number (fixed in advance) of shares in the same company. The number of shares received for each bond is called the conversion ratio.

It is important to note that the right of the bearer to convert his or her bond is exercised with the issuing company itself and not with a third party; when the bearer goes to the issuing company to make the exchange, the company issues new shares whose creation was authorized by an earlier general meeting. The fact that the bearer receives new shares implies that he or she shares the assets with the old shareholders; the assets are thus divided into a larger number of parts and there is consequently a dilution effect which must be taken into account. We shall study the problem of pricing convertible bonds by considering circumstances with increasing levels of difficulty, but also of realism.

8.3.1 A textbook case

We first address the problem of evaluating a convertible bond in the extremely simple case where this bond constitutes the only debt of the company, where it comprises only one payment (a one-off payment) and where no dividend is likely to be paid to the shareholders between today's date and the repayment date of the convertible bond. In addition, we assume that the final repayment may not be moved up by the issuing company (no call provision). These assumptions are never simultaneously satisfied in practice; nevertheless the exercise will allow us to address some concrete problems more conveniently later.

We shall reason as usual from the flows and values received by the bondholder at the moment of maturity, then go back to today's date to calculate the market value of the bond. At maturity, the bearer has the choice of receiving the redemption price of the bond or converting this bond into a share.

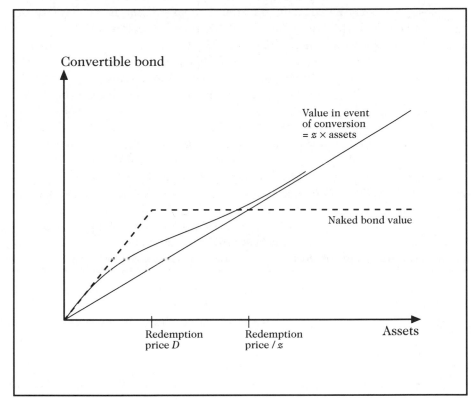

Figure 8.6

The payment of the redemption price is in no way guaranteed, since it is highly possible that the value of the assets is lower. Two cases therefore arise, as in the case of an ordinary bond, and this gives us the broken line known as the naked bond value at maturity which is shown in Figure 8.6.

On the other hand, if the bearer converts his bond into a share, he receives a certain fraction of the assets which we shall call z.[17] The fraction z incorporates the dilution effect occasioned by the issuing of new shares. The value of what he receives according to the value of the assets – the conversion value – is given by a proportionality relationship, that is, by a line passing through the origin, also drawn in Figure 8.6.

It is clear that the bearer, for each possible value of the assets at maturity, chooses whichever of the two possibilities has the greater value, which leads him to prefer repayment if the value of the assets is less than the redemption price divided by z, and conversion in the opposite case.

Our task now is to deduce from the value at maturity (the thick broken line in Figure 8.6) the value at earlier instants. Intuition suggests that we must obtain the curve which is drawn in Figure 8.6. But we wish to determine it precisely. This may be done by a combination of options.

The profile of what is received at maturity by the bearer, which we have just described, may be constructed from three elements. If the value of the assets is very low, the bondholders receive these assets; when the value of the assets exceeds the redemption price they receive only the redemption price and the shareholders keep the difference. This only reproduces the reasoning concerning ordinary debt; the naked bond value is equal to the value of the assets minus the value of a call option with an exercise price equal to the redemption price.

To this naked bond value we must add the value of the right of conversion. An examination of Figure 8.6 shows that this right of conversion is equivalent to a call option with an exercise price equal to the redemption price divided by z, except that the slope of the curve at maturity brought about by the right of conversion is not equal to 1 as was the case with an option. The slope is now z. This difference is easily taken into account if we consider not one call option with an exercise price equal to the redemption price divided by z, but z call options of this type ($z < 1$).

In total, therefore, we have:

naked bond value	$\begin{cases} \text{assets} \\ -\text{call option with exercise price } D \end{cases}$	
		[3.1]
right of conversion	$\begin{cases} +z \text{ call options} \\ \text{with exercise price } D/z \end{cases}$	

where D is the redemption price.

The Black-Scholes formula gives us very simply the two option values required, and consequently the value of the convertible bond. The total gives a curved-line graph as shown in Figure 8.6.

Let us now address two problems which always crop up in the real world where convertible bonds are concerned. These are, on the one hand, a payment of dividends to shareholders during the lifetime of the convertible bond and on the other, the possibility of anticipated redemption at the option of the issuing company.

8.3.2   Dividends paid during the lifetime of the bond

Dividend payments during the lifetime of the security give rise to a similar argument to that applied to ordinary debt in Section 8.1, using an identical time scale: the terminal instant is that of redemption, and an intermediate instant 1 is that of the dividend payment. We distinguish the minutes which follow the dividend payment from the minutes which precede it by writing them as $1 + \varepsilon$ and $1 - \varepsilon$.

At instant $1 + \varepsilon$ the value of the bond is supplied by the result we have just obtained, and it is the transition from instant $1 + \varepsilon$ to instant $1 - \varepsilon$ which requires a new argument. The situation facing the bearer at instant $1 - \varepsilon$ is shown in Figure 8.7. The bearer knows that a dividend must be paid and that, consequently, the assets will immediately be reduced accordingly. He can therefore obtain the price of his convertible bond in the absence of any conversion by shifting to the right the graph of instant $1 + \varepsilon$ (which is similar to that of Figure 8.6). However, he may convert and immediately receive a fraction z of the assets, dividend included. This adds to Figure 8.7 a line passing through the origin with a slope of z, which represents the immediate conversion price. Here again, the bearer chooses, for each possible value of the assets, the possibility which is most favourable to him, which gives the bold line.

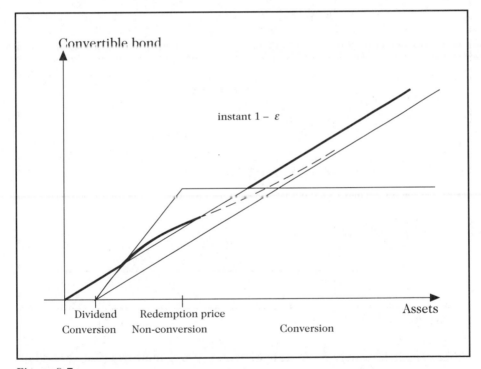

Figure 8.7

Note that we must distinguish three zones. In the central zone, that is, for a value of the assets which lies in the vicinity of the redemption price, the bearer chooses not to convert, whilst in the right-hand zone he chooses to convert. His reasoning is as follows: if the assets have a sufficiently high value, he prefers to receive the dividend as well as the shares, along with the risk which goes with it. For a lower value of the assets, he has the possibility of benefiting from the safety net offered to him by the non-converted bond on the condition of passing up the dividend, which is what he does. Lastly, for an even lower value of the assets (the left-hand zone) the safety net offered by the bond has no value since the firm is unlikely to repay; in this case, it is better to seize the dividend when it is offered. We can see that a dividend paid on the way may cause bonds to be converted, bearers wishing to hold the share in order to receive the dividend, whereas in the case which we examined previously (Section 8.3.1, Figure 8.6), no conversion could occur before final maturity.

8.3.3 Callable convertible debt

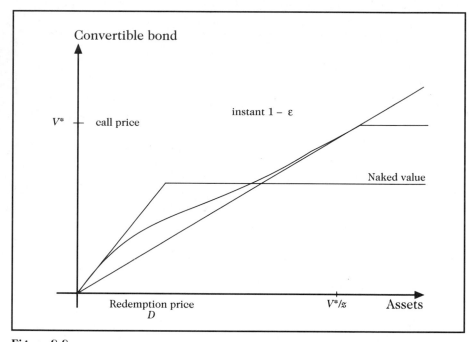

Figure 8.8

Other conversions may occur at instants preceding maturity if the bond has a call provision. This, when it is included in the debt contract, generally stipulates that, when the bond has reached a value on the stock exchange greater than or equal to a certain amount which we write as V^*, the issuing company has the right to offer the bearer the choice between conversion and an immediate payment equal to the redemption price. Since the value V^* is always greater than the redemption price, this is sufficient to prompt a conversion.

We thus obtain a graph for the price of the convertible bond which is shown in Figure 8.8, where it can be seen that this price may meet the conversion price before final maturity.

No simple method (except the numerical methods of Chapter 7 and the binomial technique which we apply below) allows us to calculate the value of the bond exactly in this case. We can nevertheless consider that the call provision has the approximate effect of subtracting from the price of the bond that of z call options at the exercise price of V^*/z, as shown in Figure 8.8.

$$
\begin{array}{lll}
\text{naked bond value} & \left\{ \begin{array}{l} \text{assets} - \\ \text{call option with exercise price } D \end{array} \right. & \\[2ex]
\text{right of conversion} & \left\{ \begin{array}{l} + z \text{ call options} \\ \text{with exercise price } D/z \end{array} \right. & [3.2] \\[2ex]
\text{call provision} & \left\{ \begin{array}{l} -z \text{ call options} \\ \text{with exercise price } V^*/z \end{array} \right. &
\end{array}
$$

This is how the value of the right to call possessed by the issuing company will be estimated. In fact, the price of the bond thus obtained is slightly underestimated as this method causes the graph of the price of the bond to cross the conversion line somewhere below V^*. The error is usually negligible, however.

8.3.5   Implementation of the binomial technique

Whilst, in the most simple of cases, the financial securities issued by firms may be interpreted directly in terms of call and put options on the firm, this is generally no longer the case as soon as securities include one or more complex clauses, such as the call provision written into most convertible bonds issued today. Whilst it is no longer possible to obtain an explicit formula for the value of the convertible bond, the pricing technique of options theory remains entirely valid. We shall illustrate this below with an example using the binomial technique.[18]

Consider a firm which has issued 750 ordinary shares and 500 convertible bonds which may at any time be exchanged for a new share. Each bond entitles its bearer to a coupon of 100 ECU at the end of the year as well as a repayment of 1000 ECU on maturity of the contract two years from now. The value of the firm today (just after a coupon payment of 50 000) is one million ECU and this value rises or falls by 50% each period.[19] The risk-free interest rate is 5%. The issuing firm reserves the right to call the bonds before maturity at the price of 1150 ECU.

First, let us calculate the global value of the convertible bonds on maturity, two periods from now. The movement of the value of the firm is as follows (in thousands of ECU):

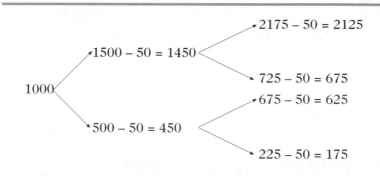

If the bondholders choose to convert their bonds on maturity, they will obtain a proportion $z = [500/(750 + 500)] = 40\%$ of the value of the assets. We may therefore immediately compare the value of the bonds at maturity with or without conversion.

Value of the firm	Value of convertible bonds (with conversion)	Value of convertible bonds (without conversion)
2125	850	500
675	270	500
625	250	500
175	70	175

The bondholders will only choose to convert if the value of the firm on maturity is 2125. Now let us proceed in reverse to calculate the value of the debt one period before maturity. To do this, we apply the binomial technique developed in Chapter 6. The value of the convertible bonds at the end of the first period in the state of nature where the value of the firm's assets has risen is equal to:

$$OC_u = \frac{0.55 \times 850 + 0.45 \times 500}{1.05} + \frac{50}{1.05} = 707.14$$

where 0.55 and 0.45 are the risk neutral probabilities.

If the creditors converted on this date, the overall value of their holding would only be $0.4 \times 1450 = 580$. The creditors would therefore prefer not to convert their securities and would keep them for one more period. However, the shareholders have reserved the right to call the debt at the price of 1.15 thousand ECU per bond and it is advantageous for them to do so in this case. In fact, they need only pay out on the entire issue 575 (= 500×1.15) to cancel a debt which on this date is worth 707.14. Thus forced, the creditors will prefer to convert their securities (receive 580) rather than accept the (global) repayment of 575, even though they would prefer not to convert their securities on this date. In this case we speak of a forced conversion. The value of the bonds on the other dates is easily calculated:

$$OC_d = \frac{0.55 \times 500 + 0.45 \times 175}{1.05} + \frac{50}{1.05} = 384.52$$

And finally,

$$OC = \frac{0.55 \times 580 + 0.45 \times 384.52}{1.05} + \frac{50}{1.05} = 516.22$$

which is 1032.45 ECU per convertible bond today.

In the same way, we may calculate the value of the convertible bond without a call provision, or the value of a non-convertible bond but with a call provision. The binomial approach is general and can deal with all situations.

8.3.6 Warrants and exercise strategy

Nowadays, firms rarely issue only ordinary shares or debt. Rather, we see issues of securities known as hybrids: that is, securities simultaneously including elements with characteristics of equity funds and elements with debt characteristics[20] such as shares with share warrants, bonds with share warrants, convertible bonds (which we have just studied in the section above), and so on.

Most of these securities may be broken down into a traditional security, such as a share or a bond, plus one or more warrants giving the right, against payment of an exercise price, to acquire a certain number of new shares in the company.

To end the section of this chapter devoted to evaluating the financial securities issued by limited companies, we shall analyse warrants and show that the optimal exercise strategy for these warrants may differ from that for traditional call and put options.[21]

Three characteristics of warrants[22] differentiate them from the traditional call options which were studied in Chapters 6 and 7. Firstly, the exercise prices paid by the holders of the warrants when they are exercised go to increase the assets of the issuing firm. Secondly, exercising the warrants gives rise to the creation of new shares, which has the effect of diluting the value of the old shares. Finally, as with all financial securities issued by limited companies, the underlying security to be taken into account for their evaluation is the total assets of the firm and not the ordinary shares covered by the warrant.[23]

Let us take the case of a firm which has only issued ordinary shares currently worth V_a and European warrants with a value of W. There are n shares and m warrants, each one allowing a new share to be acquired against payment of the exercise price K. In the case of exercise on maturity, each warrant will be worth:

$$W = \left[\frac{1}{n+m}\left(V + mK\right)\right] - K = \frac{1}{n+m}\left(V - nK\right)$$

where V represents the value of the assets of the firm on maturity just before the warrants are converted. Exercise is therefore only optimal if the value of the firm on maturity is greater than nK. In terms of a European call option,

$$W = [1/(n+m)]\, C(V, nK)$$

Each warrant corresponds to a fraction of a European call option on the total assets of the firm with an exercise price of nK.

We saw that exercising warrants or converting convertible bonds gives rise to the creation of new shares, which has the effect of diluting the value of the old shares. This dilution has the result that, in contrast to the case of ordinary calls and puts, it is no longer necessarily optimal to exercise all the securities in the same class simultaneously. In fact, it may be that when certain warrants are exercised, the value of the remaining warrants increases. We shall illustrate this case in the context of the binomial model.

Let us return to the above example of a firm which has issued n ordinary shares with a price of S, and m American warrants, each one allowing a new share to be acquired in return for a payment of K, the exercise price of the warrants. The value of the firm, V, changes each period according to the factors $u > 1$ and $0 < d < 1$ with risk neutral probabilities p and $1-p$.

Let us look at a situation one period before the maturity of the warrants. If none of these has been exercised previously, each is worth:

$$W(0) = \text{Max}\left\{ 0, \left(\frac{p}{1+r} \right) \left[\frac{uV + mK}{n+m} - K \right] + \left(\frac{1-p}{1+r} \right) \left[\frac{dV + mK}{n+m} - K \right] \right\}$$

On the other hand, if l warrants are already exercised, the $(m - l)$ remaining warrants are worth individually:

$$W(l) = \max\left\{ 0, \left(\frac{p}{1+r} \right) \left[\frac{u(V + lK) + (m-l)K}{n+m} - K \right] + \left(\frac{1-p}{1+r} \right) \left[\frac{d(V + lK) + (m-l)K}{n+m} - K \right] \right\}$$

If the value of the warrants is strictly positive,

$$dW(l) / dl = \left(\frac{1}{1+r} \right) \left[p(u - 1) + (1 - p)(d - 1) \right] \left(\frac{K}{n+m} \right) = \left(\frac{r}{1+r} \right) \left(\frac{K}{n+m} \right) \geq 0$$

In the context of this very simple model, each warrant exercised increases the value of the warrants remaining to be exercised. The optimal exercise strategy is therefore sequential and no longer simultaneous, as is the case for ordinary options. However, we know that if the underlying shares are non-dividend-paying, it is never optimal to exercise an option before its maturity date. No investor holding only a small fraction of the warrants will be prepared to exercise his warrants before maturity, as he personally would draw no benefit from this. This would, not however, be the case for an investor who held a significant fraction of the warrants. The loss made by exercising the first warrants may be recouped by the increase in value gained by the remaining warrants. It can be seen, therefore, that the exercise strategy followed will depend in particular on the way in which the various warrants are divided amongst the investors.[24]

8.4 Evaluation of assets

In the first three sections of this chapter, we saw how the field of application of options theory, developed during Chapters 6 and 7, went far beyond the restricted framework of options exchanged on financial markets, since it could also contribute to the evaluation of elements of the liabilities of a limited company, that is, the financial securities issued by such a company.

The object of this section is to show that there are also fruitful applications for options theory in evaluating the assets on the balance sheet, and notably, in evaluating investment projects.

8.4.1   Evaluation of investment projects

The most widely recommended method of selecting investment projects is that of *net present value* (*NPV*). The NPV of a project is the sum of the expected cash flows (negative for expenditures, positive for receipts) produced by the project, each flow being discounted by the corresponding opportunity cost. Mathematically:

$$\text{NPV} = \sum_{t=0}^{T} F_t / (1 + k_t)^t$$

where T is the life of the project, F_t is the expected cash flow (negative, positive or zero) raised by the project in period t and k_t is the discount rate retained for period t.

The selection criterion is to invest (not to invest) if the NPV of the project is positive (negative) and, in the case where several exclusive projects have a positive NPV, to retain the one with the highest NPV. The NPV represents the net increase in wealth created by the project.

This approach is, however, frequently criticized, notably by practitioners who accuse it of not taking account of the inherent flexibility of certain projects. In fact, the traditional method of calculating the NPV may greatly underestimate the economic value of projects in cases where they will require a whole series of sequential decisions on the part of the managers, with each decision representing an element of flexibility not valued by the traditional method of calculating the NPV.[25]

We must include under the heading of flexibility the options which are given to project managers to influence the progress of the project in one direction rather than another (size, timing, abandonment and so on). When the flexibility of investment projects may be expressed in terms of options,[26] options theory offers the relevant framework of analysis to quantify the value of this flexibility.

By way of example, here are some of the physical options which are most frequently encountered when evaluating investment projects:

The option of deferring the launch of the project

It is rare for an irreversible project to have to be launched immediately. When the launch date is not imperatively fixed, it is no longer sufficient for the present value of the project to be positive for it to be optimal to launch the project. In fact, it may well be that this net present value will be even

higher at a future date. The investment decision must rather be likened to
the decision to exercise an American call on a dividend-paying share. In
return for the cost of the project (the exercise price) we obtain the gross
present value of the project (the underlying asset). The cash flows produced
by the operation of the project correspond to the dividends paid by the
share. On a certain date, it becomes preferable to launch the project (exercise
the option) to benefit from the cash flows (the dividends) rather than wait
any longer.

Options theory allows us not only to calculate the value of the right of
ownership on this project, a value corresponding to the value of the call
option, but also to determine the optimal date on which investment should
be made.[27]

The option of abandonment

It is sometimes necessary to decide to abandon a project (either because it
has proved disappointing, or because the plant has aged, and so on) where
this is possible.[28]

The usual method involves calculating at each date t the NPV of the future
receipts and halting the project when this becomes negative. However, this
approach ignores the fact that not abandoning the project today allows it to
be abandoned at a later date, whilst the reverse is not true (there is an
irreversibility). The correct abandonment decision must take account of
this fact. This problem is formally identical to determining the optimal
exercise of an American put on a dividend-paying share. At any instant t,
we may abandon the project (exercise the option) and receive the resale
price of the assets (the exercise price) on delivery of these assets (the
underlying share). As in the previous example, the cash flows of the project
may be likened to the dividends received by the holder of the share.[29]

The option of expanding

Similarly, the question often arises whether it would be better to build a
factory A with a production capacity of X or a factory B with a production
capacity of Y, higher than X. The cost of the second factory is obviously
higher, but it offers the possibility of increasing production beyond X if
economic circumstances are favourable. Options theory once again allows
us to solve this problem. Project B may be seen as being equal to project A
plus the added option of increasing production by the amount $Y - X$. From
this, we may deduce that project B should only be chosen if its additional
cost does not exceed the option of expanding.

The option of a temporary halt to operations

We know from microeconomic theory that a firm wishing to maximize its
profits should only produce if its receipts cover at least its variable costs.
When receipts are insufficient, operation of the factory must be (temporarily)

stopped. When we wish to determine the value of a factory, we must not forget to include the value of the option to stop.[30]

We leave it to the reader to think up other examples.

8.4.2 Calculation of expanded net present value

It is of course rare that a project includes only one of the options mentioned above. Much more often a project will include a whole series of options, generally interdependent, some even being compound options.[31]

The value of such a project may therefore be likened to that of a portfolio of options.

This being the case, it would seem natural to widen the concept of NPV,[32] in order to take account of the options attached to (or implicit in) an investment project. [Trigeorgis and Mason 1987] suggest the new concept of 'expanded net present value' or ENPV. The ENPV of a project is equal to the net present value (NPV) of this project, calculated without taking account of any options (renamed 'static net present value'), expanded by a premium to take account of the flexibility of the project.

At first glance, we may therefore write: ENPV = NPV (static) + the value of the options attached to the project, on the condition that the options are precisely defined. In practice, however, it is easier to evaluate the ENPV directly rather than each of the two terms of the breakdown.

To illustrate how options theory allows us to calculate the value of a project, we present the model of [Brennan and Schwartz 1985] concerning the evaluation of a mine.[33] Running a mine is a complex operation requiring numerous decisions which may be modelled as option exercise decisions such as that of opening or not opening the mine (and on what date), closing it temporarily or, possibly, for good, choosing the rate of extraction of the ore contained in the mine, and so on.

Consider the evaluation of a goldmine. We assume that movements in the price of gold are described by the stochastic process:

$$dS/S = \mu dt + \sigma dz$$

The value of the mine at date t, $H = H(S, Q, t; j, \phi)$ is a function of the price S of the output, the stock Q of ore contained in the mine and the operating policy ϕ of the mine.[34]

To determine the value of the mine, we shall evaluate options as we did in Section 7.2.1. We construct (at an instant $t = 0$) a self-financed portfolio (whose value in ECU we shall denote H) by buying n units of ore (with a price of S) and buying b units of a risk-free investment at the rate r, whose unitary value changes according to:

$$B(t)=B_0e^{rt}$$

For the value of this portfolio to reproduce the value of the mine, the increases dH in the value of this portfolio must only result from the payoffs arising from the constituent elements of the portfolio (appreciations dS on the ore and interest rdt on the risk-free investment) increased by the value of the service flow, the 'convenience yield', $C(S, t)dt$, accruing to the holder of the ore[35] and reduced by the withdrawals corresponding to the instantaneous cash flows after tax, Kdt, produced by the running of the mine.[36]

An identical procedure to that of Chapter 7 leads to the partial differential equation which must be satisfied by the value of the mine, H:[37]

$$(1/2)\sigma^2S^2H_{SS} - qH_Q + H_t + K - rH - (r-c)SH_S = 0 \ (j = 0.1) \qquad [4.1]$$

Solving Equation 4.1 gives the value of the mine for any operation policy ϕ. It remains for us to determine the optimum operation policy, that which maximizes the value of the mine.[38] In general, there is no analytical solution to this problem. However, it is possible to solve this system numerically.

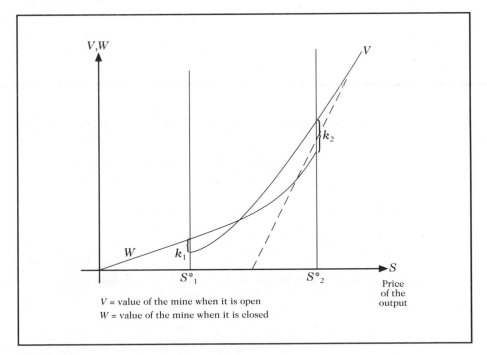

V = value of the mine when it is open
W = value of the mine when it is closed

Figure 8.9

Brennan and Schwartz manage to obtain an explicit solution at the expense of a few additional assumptions: (i) the stock of the goods item, Q, is infinite; (ii) the tax laws authorize total deduction of the losses; (iii) the rate of extraction is q^* when the mine is open and zero otherwise and (iv) the maintenance cost of the mine when it is shut is zero. The solution they obtain is illustrated in Figure 8.9 where V is the value of the mine when it is in operation and W is its value when it is closed:

$$V(S, Q, t) = \underset{\phi}{\text{Max}} \, H(S, Q, t; 1, \phi)$$

$$W(S, Q, t) = \underset{\phi}{\text{Max}} \, H(S, Q, t; 0, \phi)$$

The dashed line represents the present value of the cash flows produced by the mine when we assume it never closes. As we can see from the diagram, the value of the closure option falls steadily as the output price rises, eventually tending towards zero.[39] When the output price is very low, the mine is worth more closed (line W) than open (line V). The reverse is obviously true for high output prices. When the price of the output reaches S_2^*,[40] the value of the mine open exceeds the value of the mine closed by an amount just sufficient to cover the cost of reopening, k_2. When opening and closure costs tend to zero, S_1^* and S_2^* converge and the value of the mine is then represented by a single curve. On the other hand, when the cost of closure becomes very high, the value of the closure option tends to zero and the value of the mine when it is open tends towards the broken line.

8.4.3 Determining the optimum date at which to invest

It is important to realize that the approach developed above not only allows us to calculate the value of the mine, but also to determine the optimum time to invest.

To continue Brennan and Schwartz's example, the net present value corresponding to the construction of the mine is given by

$$NPV(S, Q, t) = V(S, Q, t) - I(S, Q, t)$$

where V represents the value of a mine in a state of operation whose stock of ore is Q, and $I(\ )$ represents the cost of the investment required to construct the mine and put it into operation.[41]

It is not sufficient, however, for this net present value to be positive for it to be optimal to invest immediately. Waiting may allow a higher net present value to be produced later. In fact, the project includes an option of deferring investment, an option which must be exercised optimally.[42]

The decision to invest is in fact similar to the decision to exercise an American call option on a dividend-paying share. We need only reinterpret the value of the call option as being the value of the right of ownership covering an unexploited mine with a stock Q of the goods item at the time t. In the case of investment (exercise of the option), the owner of the mine (the holder of the American option) receives, in return for payment of the investment cost (the exercise price), the present value of the future expected flows produced by the mine (the value of the underlying asset).

This example has illustrated how options theory allows complex investment projects to be evaluated. This approach seems particularly well adapted to the evaluation of projects whose value depends on a variable which is subject to quotation in the marketplace (natural resources, currency and so on) as well as research and development projects.[43]

One of the advantages of modelling investment choices on the basis of options theory lies in the fact that, as with financial options, only a very small number of parameters are required for the model. It will be noted in particular that knowledge of the expected future price of the output and the discount rate adjusted for the risk of the project is not part of the information necessary to solve the model, in contrast to the traditional approach to the calculation of net present value.

Conclusion

In conclusion, let us mention that the traditional approach finds new areas of application every day. We cite, for interest's sake, the evaluation of guarantees granted by governments and financial institutions ([Merton 1977a, b], [Sosin 1980], [Jones and Mason 1980]), covenants ([Mason and Bhattacharya 1981]), as well as applications to insurance ([Brennan and Schwartz 1976], [Merton 1977, 1978]), banking ([Sinkey and Miles 1982], [Crouhy and Galai 1986]), the management of assets and liabilities and so on.

The theory of options developed in Chapters 6 and 7 thus goes far beyond the context of calls and puts. However, remember that this approach is only operational from the moment we have a random process which governs the behaviour of the primary asset over time. For the applications which we have reviewed in the last three sections of this chapter, the process generally governs the movements in the market value of the total assets of the firm, an underlying security which is generally not directly observable and for which the estimation of volatility will be particularly difficult. These same limits will be encountered again when evaluating investment projects. Nevertheless, the applications of options theory to investment projects represent the most important step in this field since the 1960s.

Appendix

Optimization of the value of a mine

The maximum values of the mine when it is open, $V(S,Q,t)$, and closed, $W(S,Q,t)$, corresponding to the optimum exploitation policy $\phi^* = \{q^*, S_0^*, S_1^*, S_2^*\}$ are given by

$$V(S, Q, t) = \max_{\phi} H(S, Q, t; 1, \phi)$$

$$W(S, Q, t) = \max_{\phi} H(S, Q, t; 0, \phi)$$

The optimum values of the rate of extraction and of the mine must therefore satisfy the two equations [A.1] and [A.2].[44]

$$\max_{q} \left[(1/2)\sigma^2 S^2 V_{ss} + (rS - C)V_s - qV_Q + V_t + q(S - A) - T - (r + \lambda_1)V \right] = 0 \quad [\text{A.1}]$$

$$\left[(1/2)\sigma^2 S^2 W_{ss} + (rS - C)W_s + W_t - M - (r + \lambda_0)W \right] = 0 \quad [\text{A.2}]$$

Given the definition of S_0, S_1 and S_2, we know that

$$W(S_0^*, Q, t) = 0 \quad\quad\quad\quad\quad [\text{A.3}]$$

$$V(S_1^*, Q, t) = W(S_1^*, Q, t) - k_1 \quad\quad [\text{A.4}]$$

$$W(S_2^*, Q, t) = V(S_2^*, Q, t) - k_2 \quad\quad [\text{A.5}]$$

where k_1 and k_2 represent, respectively, the costs of closing and of opening the mine. Brennan and Schwartz also examine the hypothesis that the value of an exhausted mine is zero:

$$W(S, Q, t) = V(S, 0, t) = 0 \quad\quad\quad\quad [\text{A.6}]$$

Finally, as S_0^*, S_1^* and S_2^* are chosen so as to maximize the value of the mine, it follows from this that

$$W_S(S_0{}^*, Q, t) = 0 \tag{A.7}$$

$$V_S(S_1{}^*, Q, t) = W_S(S_1{}^*, Q, t) \tag{A.8}$$

$$W_S(S_2{}^*, Q, t) = V_S(S_2{}^*, Q, t) \tag{A.9}$$

Equations A.1 to A.9 constitute the global model of the mine. They define not only the value of the mine, whether it is open or closed, but also the optimum exploitation policy, that is, whether to open, close or abandon the mine, as well as the optimum rate of extraction of the ore. Unfortunately, there is generally no analytical solution to this problem. However, it is possible to solve this system numerically.

Notes to Chapter 8

1 In practice, when there is a default and therefore bankruptcy, the firm is placed under the control of the court. Two cases are therefore possible: either (i) the court sets up, in agreement with the creditors and shareholders, a plan of *reorganization*. There is a settlement of the liabilities, a reinjection of funds either by new, or by the old shareholders (there is therefore not necessarily a change of shareholdership) and the firm continues to operate. In this case, the old shareholders do not necessarily lose everything; or (ii) the court decides on a plan of transfer of assets by sale at auction. The firm ceases to exist and the creditors are compensated in order of priority. The balance, if it is positive, is recovered by the shareholders.

2 In the case of an administrative error by the shareholders, these may be called as fill-in liability even in a limited company.

3 We are considering here the financial point of view and not the legal point of view, according to which the shareholders are already the owners of the firm and consequently have no need of a call option. All that interests us here is evaluating the shares, and the formal analogy between the shares and a call option is particularly useful in this respect.

4 To apply the Black-Scholes formula, we must assume that the value of the assets of the firm follows the usual diffusion process, namely $dV = \alpha V dt + \sigma V dz$.

5 This is a period rate of return including not only the flows produced by the assets, but also the losses and gains in value. It is not, for example, the internal rate of return. The period return on an asset and its volatility are not easily determined, since the assets are most often not subject to quotation. But the volatility of the assets may be reconstructed from the volatility of the liabilities.

6 These 'covenants' may also be evaluated by options theory. *See* [Black and Cox 1976] *and* [Mason and Bhattacharya 1981].

7 Until recently, in France, debtholders, and in particular bondholders, constituting the 'bondholding class', could only call a general meeting to oppose a right of veto on the decisions of the firm. However, this possibility was very rarely used and the debtholders were badly protected against the shareholders' decisions.

8 There is no analogy here with the behaviour of a holder of call options on a share offering the prospect of a dividend (*see* Section 6.4.4 *and* Sections 7.4.1 and 7.4.2). The option holder may exercise his or her right prematurely. In the present case, the shareholder has no possibility of compensating the debtholders by prematurely paying them the redemption price. The only possible course of action available to the owners of the company is provided by the limited liability clause, in the case where the assets are less than the coupon amount.

9 This takes us back to the situation considered in Section 8.1.1, where there is no intermediate payment to the benefit of the shareholders or the creditors. However, we must now keep separate the risk of default attached to each category of debt. For the priority creditors, there is no change from the situation analysed in Section 8.1.1: their debt is still guaranteed by all the assets of the firm. On the other hand, the risk borne by the non-priority creditors is greater, since they will only be repaid after the priority creditors have been completely paid off (but nevertheless before the shareholders).

10 The sale of a call option made simultaneously with the purchase of another call option on the same underlying asset but with a higher exercise price is known to operators as a vertical spread.

11 *See* in particular [Black and Cox 1976].

12 Game theory deals with formalizing conflict situations between rational agents.

13 This is only accurate for priority debt or when the firm's debts are all of the same class. We mentioned in Section 8.1.4 that when the firm had issued more than one class of debt with different priorities, the subordinated debts could be more risky than the assets of the firm.

14 We have already encountered this result in Chapter 6 (Equation 3.4).

15 Expected return over and above the risk-free interest rate.

16 We speak here of the 'legal algebra' of financial engineering.

17 z is equal to the ratio of the number of shares issued at the time of complete conversion to the total number of shares after conversion (old shares + new shares): $z = (mq)/(n + mq)$, where n is the number of old shares, m the number of convertible bonds and q the number of shares issued per convertible bond in the case of conversion.

18 This example is adapted from [Cox and Rubinstein 1985], Chapter 7.

19 This level of volatility is excessive, of course, but it does simplify the calculations.

20 The reasons why firms choose to issue such securities rather than 'simply' debt or ordinary shares have given rise to a whole theoretical literature known as signalling theory and agency theory. It is mainly a question of minimizing the potential conflicts between the various partners of the firm as well as overcoming the problems caused by the asymmetry of information (the difference of information between firm managers and investors).

21 [Cox and Rubinstein 1985] includes a detailed biography (up-to-date in 1985) of the application of options theory to the evaluation of the various financial securities issued by firms. The reader may also consult [Smith 1979].

22 The discussion on the subject of warrants which follows applies also to convertible bonds.

23 [Crouhy and Galai 1991a, b, c] also show that the presence of warrants in the liabilities of the balance sheet will affect the volatility of the equity funds. As the volatility is no longer constant, the Black-Scholes formula can no longer be applied to evaluate call options on the shares of such a firm.

24 The reader interested in these questions is referred to the articles by [Emmanuel 1983], [Constantinides 1984] and [Constantinides and Rosenthal 1984], which showed, for example, (i) that a monopolist who held all the warrants could have an advantage in exercising the warrants one after another rather than simultaneously and (ii) that if the warrants were shared between many holders acting competitively, they may be led to undertake actions which would be unfavourable to them as a group, that is, which would bring them lower revenues than they could obtain if they co-operated.

25 It is important to realize that this critique does not so much concern the fundamental concept of the net present value of investments as the method of calculating this NPV.

26 We speak here of physical options to distinguish them from those exchanged on the financial markets.

27 For a numerical example, see [Brealey and Myers 1988], pages 496 to 498. For a more theoretical and complete treatment, refer to [McDonald and Siegel 1986]. They show that, in their case, it only becomes optimal to invest from the moment when the gross present value of the project is roughly double the cost. [Brennan and Schwartz 1985], [Trigeorgis and Mason 1987] and [Paddock et al. 1988] also deal with this issue.

28 A project which we may envisage being abandoned is more flexible than one for which this is impossible such as, for example, an investment undertaken for reasons of safety. This flexibility contributes to the value of the project.

29 For a detailed treatment, see [Myers and Majd 1983].

30 See [McDonald and Siegel 1985].

31 A compound option is an option whose underlying security is itself an option (cf. Chapter 7).

32 Remember that it is more a question of developing a method of calculation which allows us to take account of flexibility than of questioning the concept of net present value.

33 For other examples of the application of options theory to investment projects, read the surveys by [Mason and Merton 1985] and [Pindyck 1991].

34 This defines the rate of extraction of the output $q(S,Q,t)$ as well as three critical values of the price of the output: $S_1^*(Q,t)$, which is the price of the output at which the mine is closed, $S_2^*(Q,t)$, which is the price of the output at which the mine is reopened and $S_0^*(Q,t)$, which is the price of the output for which the mine is abandoned. Abandonment

is permanent, whereas closure may only be temporary. In this latter case, maintenance costs must be borne. As it is costly to close and then reopen the mine, the value of the mine will be different according to whether it is closed ($j = 0$) or open ($j = 1$).

35   By convenience yield we mean the service flow which is received by the holder of the ore but which would not be received by the holder of a forward contract on the ore. For example, the holder of the ore may choose the location where the goods are stored and the date on which the stock will be liquidated. Brennan and Schwartz introduce the assumption that the convenience yield is proportional to the price of the ore: $C(S,t) = cS$. This service flow thus corresponds to a continuous dividend at the rate c from which the holder of the ore benefits. It must therefore be included in the equation of dH. (How a dividend paid by the underlying stock is taken into account has already been dealt with in Section 7.3.)

36   In the Brennan and Schwartz model, this flow K is equal to $q(S - A) - M(1 - j) - \lambda_j H - T$, where $A(q,Q,t)$ is the average monetary cost of production of the output q at the time t and when the stock of ore in the mine is Q; $M(t)$ is the fixed cost after tax of maintaining the mine when it is closed; $\lambda_j(j = 0,1)$ is the proportional rate of tax when the mine is closed and opened and $T(q, Q, S, t)$ is the total tax on income levied on the mine when it is in operation. Brennan and Schwartz also introduce the hypothesis that $T(q, Q, S, t) = t_1 qS + \max\{t_2 q[S(1 - t_1) - A], 0\}$.

37   It will be noted that Equation 4.1 is very similar to Equation 3.2 of Chapter 7, which is not surprising since we followed the same reasoning as before. Two additional terms, qHQ and K, appear, however, reflecting the distinctive character of the problem here. Q being the stock of ore contained in the mine, the first term represents the impact of the variation of the stock on the value of the mine (observe that $dQ/dt = -q$), whilst the second represents the instantaneous cash flows produced by the operation of the mine (cf note 36 above).

38   The optimization of stochastic processes is outside the scope of this book. A brief presentation of the procedure to follow is given in the appendix to this chapter.

39   The value of the closure option is represented by the vertical distance separating the curve v from the segment of the broken line.

40   See note 34 above for the definition of S_1^* and S_2^*.

41   This formulation assumes that the construction of the mine is instantaneous. The above model may be modified to take account of delays in construction. See on this subject the example in [Siegel et al. 1988].

42   The reader will of course remember that it is also insufficient for the price of the underlying asset to be greater than the exercise price for it to be optimal to exercise the option.

43   Research and development may be modelled as a chain of interdependent options. The option of abandonment assumes a very special significance in this context.

44   The optimization of stochastic processes is beyond the scope of this book. The interested reader may consult [Merton 1971], Theorem 1, [Fleming and Rishel 1975], Chapter 6, and [Cox et al. 1978], Lemma 1. As far as we are directly concerned, we need only verify that the solution of this maximization problem gives us $V_Q = S - A$, of which the intuitive interpretation is immediate: at the optimum, the (marginal) value of one additional unit of the ore in the mine, V_Q, must be equal to the (marginal) value of one unit mined and sold, $S - A$.

References

[Black and Cox 1976]   F. Black and J. C. Cox, Valuating Corporate Securities: Some Effects of Bond Indenture Provisions, *Journal of Finance*, 31 (1976), 351–367.

[Brealey and Myers 1988]   R. A. Brealey, and S. C. Myers, *Principles of Corporate Finance*. Third Edition, McGraw-Hill, 1988.

[Brennan and Schwartz 1985] M. J. Brennan and Schwartz, E. S., Evaluating Natural Resource Investments, *Journal of Business*, vol. 58, no. 2 (1985).

[Constantinides 1984]   G. Constantinides, Warrant Exercise and Bond Conversion in Competitive Markets, *Journal of Financial Economics*, 13 (1984), 371–397.

[Constantinides and   G. Constantinides and R. Rosenthal, Strate-
Rosenthal 1984]   gic Analysis of the Competitive Exercise of Certain Financial Options, *Journal of Economic Theory*, 32, (1984), 128–138.

[Cox *et al.* 1978]   J. C. Cox, J. E. Ingersoll and S. A. Ross, *A Theory of the Term Structure of Interest Rates*, Research Paper No. 468, Stanford University, 1978.

[Cox and Rubinstein 1985]   J. C. Cox and M. Rubinstein, *Options Markets*, Prentice-Hall, 1985.

[Crouhy and Galai 1986]   M. Crouhy and D. Galai, An Economic Assessment of Capital Requirements in the Banking Industry, *Journal of Banking and Finance*, 10 (1986), 231–241.

[Crouhy and Galai 1991a]   M. Crouhy and D. Galai, Warrant valuation and equity volatility, *Advances in Futures and Options Research*, vol. 5, JAI Press, New York, 1991.

[Crouhy and Galai 1991b]   M. Crouhy and D. Galai, A Contingent-Claim Analysis of a Regulated Depository Institution, *Journal of Banking and Finance*, 15-1, (1991) 73–90.

[Crouhy and Galai 1991c]   M. Crouhy and D. Galai, Common Errors in the Valuation of Warrants and Options on Firms with Warrants, *Financial Analysts Journal*, September–October 1991, 89–90.

[Emmanuel 1983]   D. Emmanuel, Warrant Valuation and Exercise Strategy, *Journal of Financial Economics*, 12, (1983), 211–235.

[Fleming and Rishel 1975]   W. H. Fleming and R. W. Rishel, *Deterministic and Stochastic Optimal Control*. Springer Verlag, 1975.

[Geske 1979]   R. Geske, The Valuation of Compound Options, *Journal of Financial Economics*, 7 (1979), 63–81.

[Ingersoll 1987]   J. E. Ingersoll, *Theory of Financial Decision Making*. Rowman & Littlefield, 1987.

[Jones and Mason 1980]   E. P. Jones, and S. P. Mason, Valuation· of Loan Guarantees, *Journal of Banking and Finance*, vol. 4, 1980, 89–107.

[Mason and Bhattacharya 1981]   S. P. Mason, and S. Bhattacharya, Risky Debt, Jump Processes and Safety Covenants, *Journal of Financial Economics*, vol. 9, no. 3, 1981, 281–307.

[Mason and Merton 1985]   S. P. Mason and R. C. Merton, The Role of Contingent Claims Analysis in Corporate Finance, in Altman and Subrahmanyam, eds., *Recent Advances in Corporate Finance*. Irwin, 1985.

[Merton 1971]   R. C. Merton, Optimum Consumption and Portfolio Rules in a Continuous Time Model, *Journal of Economic Theory*, 3, (1971), 373–413.

[Merton 1974]   R. C. Merton, On the Pricing of Corporate Debt: The Risk Structure of Interest Rates, *Journal of Finance*, 19, no. 2 (1974).

[Merton 1977a]   R. C. Merton, On the Pricing of Contingent Claims and the Modigliani-Miller Theorem, *Journal of Financial Economics*, 15, no. 2 (1977).

[Merton 1977b]   R. C. Merton, An Analytic Derivation of the Cost of Deposit Insurance and Loan Guarantees: An Application of Modern Option Pricing Theory, *Journal of Business and Finance*, (1977).

[Merton 1978]   R. C. Merton, On the Cost of Deposit Insurance When There Are Surveillance Costs, *Journal of Business*, vol. 51, No. 3, 1978, 439–52.

[MacDonald and Siegel 1986] R. L. McDonald and D. R. Siegel, The Value of Waiting to Invest, *The Quarterly Journal of Economics*, November 1986.

[Myers and Majd 1983]   S. C. Myers and S. Majd, Calculating Abandonment Value Using Option Pricing Theory, Working Paper, Alfred P. Sloan School of Management, MIT (1983).

[Paddock *et al.* 1988] J. L. Paddock, D. R. Siegel and J. L. Smith, Option Valuation of Claims on Real Assets: The Case of Offshore Petroleum Leases, *The Quarterly Journal of Economics*, August 1988, 479–508.

[Pindyck 1991]   R. S. Pindyck, Irreversibility, Uncertainty, and Investment, *The Journal of Economic Literature*, vol. 29, No. 3, September 1991, 1110–1148.

[Sinkey and Miles 1982] J. F. Sinkey and J. A. Miles, The Use of Warrants in the Bail Out of First Pennsylvania Bank: *An Application of Option Pricing, Financial Management*, vol. 11, No. 3, 1982, 27–32.

[Smith 1979]   C. W. Smith, Applications of Option Pricing Analysis, in J. L. Bicksler, ed., *Handbook of Financial Economics*, North-Holland, 1979.

[Sosin 1980]   H. W. Sosin, On the Valuation of Federal Loan Guarantees to Corporation, *Journal of Finance*, vol. 35, No. 5, 1980, 1209–21.

[Trigeorgis and Mason 1987] L. Trigeorgis and S. P. Mason, Valuing Managerial Flexibility, *The Midland Corporate Finance Journal*, 1987.

Part III

Bonds and the term structure of interest rates

9

The term structure of interest rates

At a given moment, straight bonds[1] with different maturities exchanged on the same financial market have different prices.[2] In this chapter, we shall examine these differences in terms of yield, in order to make them comparable to each other. The relationship which is supposed to exist between the remaining lifetime of a security and its yield constitutes what is known as 'the term structure of interest rates'. The aim of this chapter is mainly descriptive and empirical. Of course, we shall see that these differences in price according to maturity are linked to the fluctuations in interest rates on the market and to the resulting risk to bonds. However, we leave it until the next chapter to model this aspect of things explicitly.

After a reminder of Chapter 1 on discounting under certainty, we define in Section 9.2 the concepts of yield to maturity and duration. In Section 9.3, we learn how to measure the term structure of interest rates using prices quoted on the Stock Exchange. Section 9.4 shows the influence of the taxation of debenture investments and Section 9.5 presents a management technique known as 'immunization', which allows the value of a portfolio of debenture securities to be protected against fluctuations in interest rates on the market. Finally, Section 9.6 is devoted to a brief discussion of the traditional theories which were developed to explain the term structure of rates.

9.1　Reminder on discounting

In applying the value additivity principle (*see* Chapter 1), we may break down any straight bond into a succession of payments. The value of this bond at any moment can still be calculated as the sum of these successive payments, each one being previously multiplied by a present value factor to be determined.

In Chapter 1, we referred to the special case – which will only hold our attention briefly – where the future and, more especially, the movement of interest rates, are fixed. In this case present value factors are particularly simple to determine: they result from the composition of the successive interests which apply to the future periods. Let us once again consider[3] the example of a security which, at the successive instants $t = 1$, $t = 2$ and $t = 3$, will give rise to a payment of 500 ECU, 500 ECU and 10,500 ECU respectively. This succession of payments defines the security and it remains for us to define the financial market on which the security is to be evaluated. Suppose that during the three successive periods in question, the rates of interest are 6%, 7% and 8% respectively. The value of the security at each instant is therefore obtained by starting from the terminal value of the security – which is 10,500 ECU – and, by discounting period by period, taking care each time a coupon is paid to add back its value:

$$9722.22 = 10500/1.08$$
$$9553.48 = (500 + 9722.22)/1.07 \qquad [1.1]$$
$$9484.41 = (500 + 9553.48)/1.06$$

This is how we calculated the movement of the price of a security over time (Figure 1.1).

Remember that the rate of return on a security is defined period by period and is equal to the period earnings divided by the price at the start of the period. It therefore amounts to the earnings per ECU invested which are received by an individual who bought the security at the start of the period, held it for the whole period and resold it at the end of the period.[4] The earnings include the cash received by the bearer, as well as any capital gains or losses. If we apply this definition to the security described above, in relation to the first period, for example, we find:

$$(500 + 9553.48 - 9484.41)/9484.41 = 0.06 \qquad [1.2]$$

We can check that calculation 1.1 allowed us to establish the prices such that the security (of whatever type) would have, during each period, a rate of return equal to the interest rate for the period. The equality of the rate of return on all the securities under certainty – and the equality of the rate of return on all securities with the same level of risk[5] in the random future – result from the freedom which the investors have, at the start of each period, to sell one security and buy another: if the expected returns were not aligned, everyone would want to buy and sell the same securities, which is obviously not a situation of equilibrium.[6]

9.2   Yield to maturity, duration and convexity

9.2.1 Yield to maturity

As we have just reminded ourselves, the only rates of return which are essential to all securities are period rates of return. Nevertheless, actuaries like to define an average rate of return which covers the entire lifetime of a security, that is, the period of time separating today's date from final maturity. To do this, they define the 'yield to maturity'. This is defined as follows:

Yield to maturity is the constant discount rate such that the present value of future payments calculated at this rate is equal to today's market value.

If we apply this definition to the security we used as an example, the yield to maturity is a number, with an unknown value x, such that:

$$9484.41 = \frac{500}{1+x} + \frac{500}{\left(1+x\right)^2} + \frac{10500}{\left(1+x\right)^3} \qquad [2.1]$$

The solution to this equation is calculated by successive approximations (see Figure 9.1, which shows what is known as the secant method[7]) and we find: $x = 6.9633\%$.

The idea which led to defining yield to maturity according to Equation 2.1 is as follows. It is a quite natural generalization of calculation 1.1 above, the difference being that in [2.1] all the periods are incorporated into one calculation, whereas [1.1] incorporates each period separately. It will be noted in particular that the yield to maturity calculated for a security with no more than one period remaining is reduced to its period rate of return.[8] Also, the yield to maturity (6.9633%) is a mixture of the three period rates: 6%, 7% and 8%. But this is a complex mixture which is neither an arithmetic mean, nor a geometric mean, nor a harmonic mean.

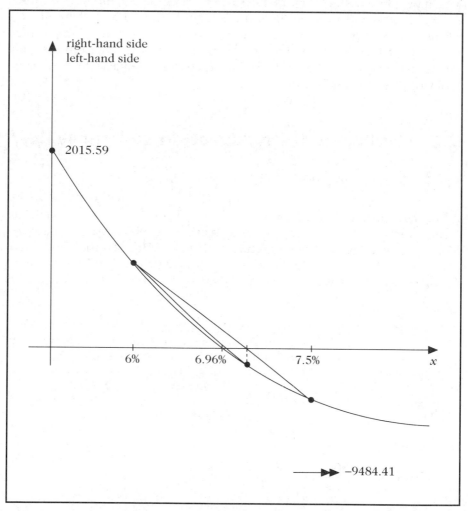

Figure 9.1

The important point is that this mixture involves in its calculation the payment schedule of the security. Consequently, the yield to maturity is specific to each security and is, in principle, neither comparable nor transposable from one security to another, in contrast to period rates of return, which are imposed on all securities. The yield to maturity of one security having been determined, it is not correct to calculate the price of another security[9] by applying this same constant discount rate, whereas it would be correct to apply to both the same period discount rates. We shall return to this important warning presently, by means of an illustration.

Before continuing our study, let us pause for a moment to calculate the term structure of rates for the example developed above. Remember that the term structure of rates shows the relationship which exists between the rates of yield to maturity of pure-discount bonds, also called spot rates, and the maturities of these bonds. A pure-discount bond is a bond which pays no coupon. In compensation for the absence of coupons, the bond is issued and quoted at a price lower than its redemption price on maturity. The remuneration is thus received entirely in the form of an increase in value.

The yield to maturity of a bond of this type is very easily calculated, since the only cash flow received by the holder of the bond is the redemption of his or her bond on maturity. If $P(t,T)$ is the price at t of a pure-discount bond paying one ECU with certainty at T, the yield to maturity of the bond is the rate, $R(t,T)$ verifying

$$P(t, T) = [1 + R(t, T)]^{-(T-t)}$$

If we return to our example, the prices of pure-discount bonds with the respective maturities of one, two and three years, are, respectively, $P(t, t + 1) = 0.9434$, $P(t, t + 2) = 0.88168$ and $P(t, t + 3) = 0.81637$, which gives us the following rates of yield to maturity (spot rates):

$$R(t, t + 1) = 6\%$$

$$R(t, t + 2) = 6.498\% = [(1.06 \times 1.07)^{1/2} - 1] \times 100$$

$$R(t, t + 3) = 6.996\% = [(1.06 \times 1.07 \times 1.08)^{1/3} - 1] \times 100$$

and, therefore, a term structure of rates which is increasing.

Since the future is not certain, randomness is in fact attached to the interest rates of the future periods, which in our example were conveniently assumed to be known and equal to 6, 7 and 8%. Of course, by a calculation which is the reverse of what we did in [1.1], the quoted prices of straight bonds may be used to deduce an estimate of the interest rates of the future periods,[10] as they are anticipated by the market: these are known as 'forward rates'. But the rates which prevail in the future may well differ from the forward rates calculated today.

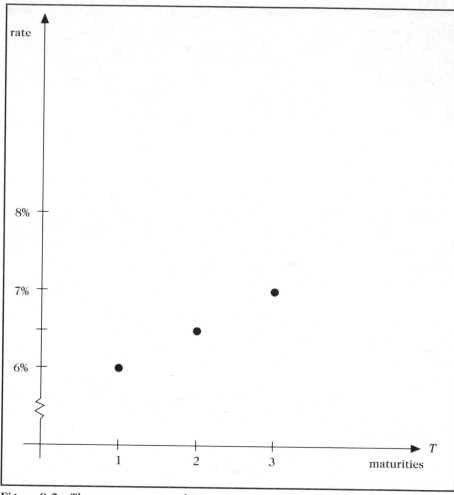

Figure 9.2 The term structure of interest rates

Period forward rates, $f(t, T)$, are defined on the basis of the prices (or the rates of yield to maturity) of pure-discount bonds:

$$f(t,T) = \frac{P(t,T)}{P(t,T+1)} - 1 = \frac{[1 + R(t,T+1)]^{T+1-t}}{[1 + R(t,T)]^{T-t}} - 1$$

This is therefore the rate for the period $(T, T + 1)$ defined implicitly by the term structure of rates.[11, 12] Continuing our example, we obtain[13]

$$f(t, t) = 6\% \qquad f(t, t + 1) = 7\% \qquad f(t, t + 2) = 8\%$$

Finally, the immediate period spot rate $r(t)$, which applies to the period $(t, t + 1)$, is defined by

$$r(t) = f(t, t) = R(t, t + 1)$$

Note that under certainty, period rates are equal to the forward rates defined by the present term structure. This will not generally be the case when the future is uncertain.

If, during a period of time, the interest rates required by the market rise, the prices of bonds must fall (and vice-versa) in order that the bonds may produce over the coming periods a higher return than before. By the mechanical effect of discounting, it is clear that their rise can only lead to a fall in the price obtained, since the period rates appear in the denominator of calculation [1.1]. So the randomness attached to the market rates causes randomness in the price of the bonds. Although they assure fixed payments during their entire lifetime, bonds are a risky security in the eyes of any investor who envisages buying and selling them when he or she wishes and not holding them until their maturity. Randomness in rates makes the period rates of return on bonds random.

9.2.2 Duration

Duration is a useful, if heuristic, method of measuring the degree of risk of a bond. This quantity is the mathematical transcription of what we said in the preceding paragraph. It answers the following question: if interest rates had just risen today (date 0), by how much would the price of the bond fall? When all present value factors rise proportionally, that is to say, when the present value factor $(1 + R_t)^{-t}$ which applies to the flow of period t, F_t, is multiplied by $(1 + u)^{-t}$, we may proceed as follows. We begin by rewriting the price of the bond according to the parameter u:

$$P(u) = \Sigma_t F_t [(1 + R_t)(1 + u)]^{-t} \qquad [2.2]$$

In formula 2.2 we wrote R_t instead of $R(0, t)$ in order to simplify notation. Note that for $u = 0$ we find the price of the security. We then apply the following calculation:

$$\frac{dP(u)}{du} = \frac{d}{du} \left(\Sigma_t F_t [(1 + R_t)(1 + u)]^{-t} \right)$$

$$= -\frac{1}{1 + u} \Sigma_t F_t t [(1 + R_t)(1 + u)]^{-t}$$

an expression which we must evaluate at the point $u = 0$, corresponding to the price of the security just before the change of rates. We may also write:

$$-\frac{1+u}{P}\frac{dP}{du}\bigg|_{u=0} = \frac{\Sigma_t tF_t(1+R_t)^{-t}}{\Sigma_t F_t(1+R_t)^{-t}}$$

[2.3]

The right-hand side of expression 2.3 may be analysed as an average of the payment dates of the various flows, weighted by the discounted values of these flows. This quantity is known as 'duration'. The duration therefore gives the logarithmic derivative[14] of the price in the vicinity of the point $u = 0$. This logarithmic derivative measures the elasticity of the price in relation to a proportional variation of the discount rates. If the 'length' of a security is measured by its duration, the longest securities are most affected by variations in interest rates. This is not surprising if we consider the formula which gives the price of the security. In this formula, the more distant a payment is, the higher is the power of $1 + R_t$ produced by the accompanying present value factor.

Care must be taken not to confuse the definition of duration given above with a more traditional definition known as Macaulay's duration. In Macaulay's definition ([Macaulay 1938]), the discount rate of all flows is the rate of yield to maturity of the security itself:

$$D' = -\frac{1+x}{P}\frac{dP}{dx} = \frac{\Sigma_t tF_t(1+x)^{-t}}{\Sigma_t F_t(1+x)^{-t}}$$

[2.4]

As shown by [Ingersoll *et al.* 1978], this last definition is only a correct measurement of the impact of an infinitesimal variation in interest rates on the price of the security when all spot rates are equal and vary by the same amount in the event of a shock, which corresponds to the case of a flat term structure of rates subject to parallel movements.[15]

These results have a definite meaning only under certainty, since they are based on the discounting method. Strictly speaking, they address the following question: since the future rates of interest are known whatever happens, to what extent do the prices of bonds differ according to whether rates are higher or lower? There is obviously a link, but not a strict link, between this question of comparative statics under certainty and another fundamentally different question, which is: if interest rates were random, their volatility having been determined, which would be the bonds whose prices were the most volatile? It is natural to reply that the longest bonds are the most risky and that duration constitutes a measurement of the risk attached to a bond. This is a leap of logic which is hazardous but which has given rise to some widely used empirical methods. We will therefore pursue this investigation further.

9.2.3 The link between yield to maturity and duration

If duration measures the risk of a bond, it is reasonable to think that the bonds whose durations are the highest must have the highest rates of return, since risk must be remunerated. And, at the very least, bonds with the same duration would have to be comparable in their rates of return. From this idea there has resulted a method of arbitrage on the debenture market guided by the following principle:

Two bonds with the same duration[16] quoted on the same market must have the same yield to maturity.[17]

To illustrate this method and, simultaneously, to demonstrate that it is inaccurate (even under certainty), we shall examine several financial securities quoted on the same market. The market which we are considering is defined by the 'present value factors' of Table 9.1 applicable to the various future maturities:

Date	0	1	2	3
Present value factor	1	0.893	0.783	0.675

Table 9.1

These present value factors represent the present value (at date 0) of one ECU payable at a future date. In the example considered, the future rates of interest which are implicit in the present value factors used are equal to 12%, 14% and 16% for the three successive periods ($0.893 = 1/1.12$; $0.893/0.783 = 1.14$ and so on).

The first security we examine is defined by the series of cash flows shown in Table 9.2. By applying the present value factors in Table 9.1 to these future flows, a price results from them:

Security 1

Date	0	1	2	3
Flow		900 ECU	900 ECU	10900 ECU
Price	8865.90 ECU			

Table 9.2

Taking account of these flows and of this price quoted today, the yield to maturity defined by the equation:

$$8865.90 = \frac{900}{(1+x)^1} + \frac{900}{(1+x)^2} \frac{10900}{(1+x)^3}$$

is equal to:

$$x = 13.875\%$$

For this value of x, $900/(1 + x)$ constitutes 8.9% of the total price of 8865.90 ECU, whilst $900/(1 + x)2$ represents 7.83% and $10900/(1 + x)3$ represents 83.26%. The duration of the security is therefore:

$$1 \times 0.089 + 2 \times 0.0783 + 3 \times 0.8326 = 2.743 \text{ years}$$

Let us now compare the first security to other securities and, first of all, to a security 2 which includes a coupon of 1000 ECU, rather than 900 ECU as in Table 9.3:

Security 2

Date	0	1	2	3
Flow		1000 ECU	1000 ECU	11000 ECU
Price	9101.00 ECU			

Table 9.3

This security, quoted on the same market, has a price of 9101 ECU, taking into account the present value factors we specified earlier. There results from this price a yield to maturity equal to 13.863% and a duration equal to 2.722 years. By proceeding in similar fashion for a series of securities with different coupons, we obtain the upper curve of Figure 9.3, linking yield to maturity (on the y axis) to duration.

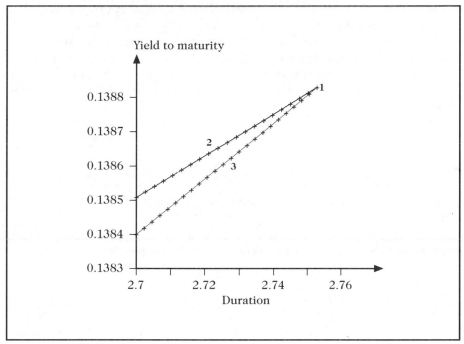

Figure 9.3

Let us now vary, not the coupon rate, but the payment schedule of the principal. If, for example, the coupon rate remains at 9% whilst a partial repayment of 200 ECU occurs at instant 2, we have the following sequence of flows:

Security 3				
Date	0	1	2	3
Flow		900 ECU	1100 ECU	10682 ECU
Price	8875.35 ECU			

Table 9.4

This security has a yield to maturity equal to 13.8612% for a duration of 2.726 years. If we compare it with securities 1 and 2, it will be noticed that it cannot lie on the same curve as they do. Moreover, by proceeding in similar fashion for a series of securities paying different intermediate amounts, we obtain the lower curve of Figure 9.2, which is obviously not superimposed on the previous one.

The principle under which securities with the same duration must have the same yield to maturity is therefore incorrect. If, to evaluate security 3, we had used a discount rate deduced from the yields to maturity of securities 1 and 2, the resultant error would have been approximately 1 ECU. This is not much, but it may be much greater when we try to evaluate securities with a longer duration.[18] In concrete terms, the yield-to-maturity technique may only be applied accurately to the comparison of securities with a one-off payment and with the same maturity.

9.2.4 Convexity

Duration is only a first-order approximation of the impact of a variation in rates on the price of bonds.

By way of an example, let us return to our bond with successive payments of 500 ECU, 500 ECU and 10500 ECU and the spot rates $r_1 = 0.06$, $r_2 = 0.0649883$ and $r_3 = 0.0699688$.[19] Its price is 9484.41 ECU and its duration 2.854.[20]

Now let us suppose that all present value factors, $(1 + r_t)$ suddenly rise by 1% ($u = 0.01$). The price of the bond is now worth only 9218.92 ECU,[21] which represents a fall of 2.80% (($9218.92 - 9484.41)/9484.41$). If, on the other hand, the present value factors had fallen by 1% ($u = -0.01$), the bond would be worth 9760.52, producing an immediate increase in value of 2.91%. In both these cases, it will be noted that the variation in the value of the bond (expressed as a percentage) is very close to the duration calculated above, but is not identical. This difference is easily explained: duration is a local measurement resulting from the calculation of a derivative. As the function $P(u)$ is convex, the approximation is only good for (very) small rate variations.

To correct (the greatest part of) the error made, we need only add the second order term in the Taylor expansion of $P(u) = S_t F_t [(1 + R_t)(1 + u)]^{-t}$:

$$dP = \left(\Sigma(-t)F_t(1 + R_t)^{-t}(1 + u)^{-t-1}\right)du +$$

$$+ \frac{1}{2}\left(\Sigma_t t(t + 1)F_t(1 + R_t)^{-t}(1 + u)^{-t-2}\right)(du)^2 +$$

$$+ \text{ higher order terms}$$

which must be evaluated in $u = 0$. We may rewrite this as:

$$\frac{dP}{P}\bigg|_{u=0} = -Ddu + \frac{1}{2}\left(D + \frac{\Sigma t^2 F_t(1+R_t)^{-t}}{P}\right)(du)^2 + \dots \qquad [2.6]$$

where D represents the duration (Equation 2.3).

When we take account of convexity, we obtain:

$$dP/P = -2.854 \times 0.01 + 0.5 \times (2.584 + 8.3697) \times 0.0001 = 0.02798 \text{ or } 2.798\%$$

which is now very close to the real variation of 2.799%.

As we may observe in Figure 9.4, the convexity of the function dP/P means that duration overestimates the negative impact of a rise in the discount rate and underestimates the impact of a fall in the rate, which corroborates the numerical results obtained above.

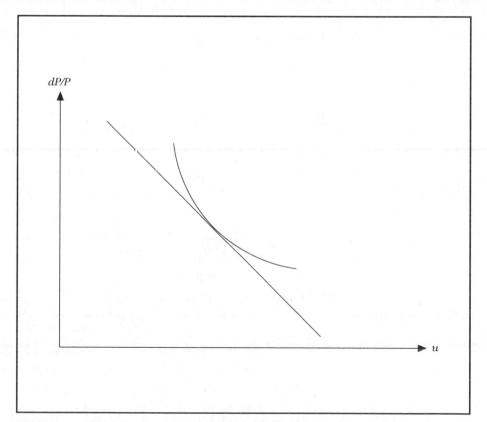

Figure 9.4   The convexity of function $dP(u)/P(u)$

Two securities or portfolios of securities with the same duration may thus react differently to variations in rates if their convexities are not equal. The higher the variation in rates, the greater will be the difference. This is why it is a good idea to calculate not only the duration but also the convexity of a portfolio in order to obtain a good perspective on the rate risk attached to it.

9.3 Measuring the term structure of interest rates

Since it is the period rates of return and the present value factors – that is, the yields-to-maturity of pure-discount bonds – which are common to all securities quoted on the same market and apply to the payments of the various maturities, it seems more judicious to estimate these factors from existing coupon bonds rather than use for them the contrivance of yield to maturity.[22] The problem is apparently simple, but its solution runs into some serious practical difficulties.

To calculate the present value factors corresponding to three future dates, let us treat these as three unknowns z_1, z_2 and z_3:

Date	0	1	2	3
Present value factor	1	z_1	z_2	z_3

We need then only observe the quoted prices of these three securities, for example those of securities 1, 2 and 3 in the tables above, to deduce from them the three present value factors: the prices quoted must satisfy the following equations[23]:

Security 1	$8865.9 = z_1\, 900 + z_2\, 900 + z_3\, 10900$
Security 2	$9101 = z_1\, 1000 + z_2\, 1000 + z_3\, 11000$
Security 3	$8872.6 = z_1\, 900 + z_2\, 1100 + z_2\, 10682$

and, consequently:

$$z_1 = 0.893$$
$$z_2 = 0.783$$
$$z_3 = 0.675$$

In practice, unfortunately, a seemingly insignificant difficulty[24] complicates matters: in contrast to what was assumed in the above example, the payment dates of the various existing securities do not coincide. When worse comes to worst, if each of the n securities quoted makes payments at m different dates, it is not m but $m \times n$ factors which we have to determine. This is obviously not possible with n equations, in which case we must resort to an interpolation function, called a discounting function, dependent on a small number of parameters which will be substituted for the collection of present value factors corresponding to the various maturities. The unknown parameters are adjusted to minimize the sum of the squares of the differences between the prices quoted on a given day and the values obtained by the discounting formula. Restrictions are imposed on this discounting function: it must be strictly and uniformly positive and strictly monotonically decreasing according to the distance of maturity. An example of a discounting function is given in Section 9.5.

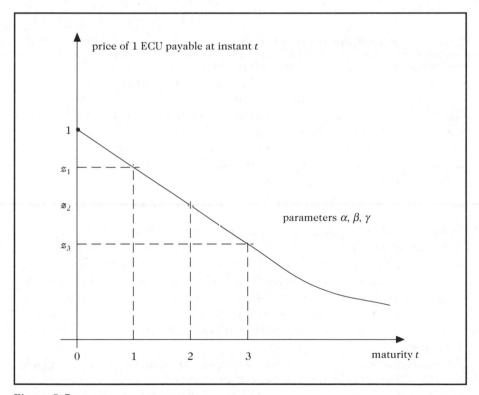

Figure 9.5

Since we lack a more precise theory (*see next chapter*), it is not possible to restrict further the choice of this discounting function. This choice therefore remains largely arbitrary. Here are some examples of commonly used discounting functions:

- cubic splines[25] are pieces of third-degree polynomials linked in such a way that the resulting curve is continuous and smooth.[26] The parameters to determine are therefore the coefficients of the polynomials and the locations of the points of linkage;[27]

- Bernstein polynomials[28] constitute a family each of whose members is a monotonically decreasing function and of which a linear combination is taken. The parameters to determine, by minimization of least squares, are the (positive) coefficients of the combination;

- exponential functions of third degree polynomials have been implemented by some analysts who fitted a linear combination of three functions of this type, so that twelve parameters had to be estimated, namely the three coefficients of the linear combination and the three parameters of each of the three polynomials.[29] Problems with stability of the parameters over time were encountered.

9.4   The influence of taxes

The principle under which the same collection of present value factors applies to all securities is in truth only correct in a world devoid of taxes. The world we know is subject to taxes. A financial security is most often defined on the basis of the flows which it produces before personal income tax.[30] The net flows of taxes differ from one investor to the next. Consequently, no series of common present value factors applies to the observed pre-tax cash flows of all the securities.

We may attempt to group investors together into categories according to their fiscal status and assume that common present value factors apply to the securities held by the same category of investor. It is clear that different categories of security are most often held by different fiscal populations,[31] so that each of these populations applies its own present value factors separately. In extreme cases, everything happens as if the securities destined for the various categories of bearer were quoted on separate markets. In order to determine the discounting functions, we would therefore have to apply the methods described above to the securities held by the same population.

Unfortunately, data on the effective holdings of securities are not available. [Schaefer 1981] therefore decided to shift the emphasis of the problem and to go by the collection of securities which each fiscal population ought to hold, the calculation of the optimal portfolio of each population being done using linear programming. The method therefore involves simultaneously determining the optimum portfolio and the discounting function for each fiscal population. It does not, however, permit the adjustment of the portfolio during the lifetime of a security; that is to say, each security held is supposed to be held until its maturity. This is a great pity, in view of the large volume of operations on the debenture market with the aim of avoiding tax.

This question is studied by [Constantinides and Ingersoll 1984], who determine the management strategy of a debenture portfolio which is optimal from a fiscal point of view. They show in particular that since short-term appreciations (less than one year) are generally taxed more heavily than long-term appreciations (more than one year),[32] it is often advantageous to take one's losses in the short term, that is, during the current tax year, and on the other hand to defer making one's gains in order that they be treated as long-term gains. The tax system therefore creates a 'timing' option which generally makes holding the portfolio until maturity less than optimal.

Constantinides and Ingersoll show that measurements of the term structure of rates obtained by assuming that the portfolios are held until maturity (Schaefer's hypothesis), rather than managed dynamically from a fiscal point of view, lead to estimates of interest rates which are biased upwards. However, their results are obtained under the hypothesis of a single fiscal clientele of investors. It therefore remains to combine the approaches of Schaefer and of Constantinides and Ingersoll to obtain a complete model of the effect of taxation on the prices of bonds.

9.5 Immunization

We saw in Section 9.2.2 above that duration was a useful, if heuristic, method of measuring the degree of risk of a bond.[33] The intention of this section is to illustrate a method of managing the interest rate risk based on duration: immunization. A bond or a portfolio of bonds is immunized against a variation in the rate of interest for a given period if the return made on this period after a variation in the rate is at least equal to that which would have been made in the absence of the variation in rates.

Let us put ourselves in the position of an investor who has bought a bond which he or she wishes to hold until a future date T. A variation in the rate of interest occurs. What impact will this have on the rate of return on the debenture investment?

A variation in interest rates has two consequences for the holder of a portfolio of bonds. The first effect is a variation in the value of the portfolio, a variation which has the opposite sign to that of the variation in the rates. This effect, illustrated in detail in Sections 9.2.2 and 9.2.4 above, is known as the *price effect*. It is generally measured at t, that is, at the moment of the variation in rates. In the context of immunization, we are interested in the impact of the variation in rates on the price of the security not at t but on the date $t' = t + D$ corresponding to the duration of the security.

The other effect of a variation in rates is linked to the reinvestment of the coupons paid by the bond. A rise (fall) in rates means that future coupons may be reinvested at a higher (lower) rate than the initial rate. We refer to this as the *reinvestment risk*.

The impact of a variation in rates corresponds to the sum of these two effects. It will be noted that the risks of price and reinvestment act in opposite directions. In fact, although a rise in rates leads to a fall in the value of the security, this rise, on the other hand, allows successive coupons to be reinvested at more advantageous conditions, and vice versa in the case of a fall in rates.

If the investor retains the security until the date coinciding with the duration of the security, these two effects cancel each other out so that the impact of the variation in rates on the return made on the investment over the period $[t, t + D]$ is zero: the holder of the security is immunized against rate variations.[34][35]

By way of an example, let us take our bond whose successive payments are 500 ECU, 500 ECU and 10,500 ECU. Suppose, to simplify the explanation, that the spot rates are 5% for all maturities. In order to offer a rate of return of 5%, the bond must be valued at 10,000 ECU. Its duration is equal to 2.589.

Now suppose the spot rates rise suddenly to 6%. This leads to a depreciation (price effect), measured at $t' = t + 2.859$, of 13.88 ECU, which is compensated by a gain of 14 ECU made on the same date on reinvestment of the first two coupons.

This situation is illustrated in Figure 9.6.[36] Suppose we have a bond or a portfolio of bonds with a value of $V(x)$ when the yield to maturity is x, and with a duration of $D(x)$. Suppose that one instant later, the range of rates moves upwards in parallel to the level $x^* > x$. The immediate consequence is a fall in the value of the bond from $V(x)$ to $V(x^*)$. However, this lower value $V(x^*)$ will now increase over time at the new rate $x^* > x$. After an interval of time equal to the duration (calculated at the initial rate x) the capitalized value (at the rate x^*) of $V(x^*)$[37] makes up for the capitalized value (at the rate x) of $V(x)$ so that the return made on the bond over the period $[t, t + D]$ is equal to the initial rate x.[38]

We may sum up the analysis as follows:

- When the period during which an investor holds a security is equal to the duration of the security, a change in the discount rate occurring immediately after the acquisition of the security will have no impact on the return made by the investor. Price effect[39] and reinvestment effect cancel each other out, so that the investment is immunized against rate variations.

- When the holding period is less than the duration of the security, the price effect prevails over the reinvestment effect. The return made on the investment will be less (greater) than the initial yield-to-maturity[40] if rates rise (fall) just after acquisition of the security.

- When the holding period is greater than the duration of the security, the reinvestment effect prevails over the price effect. The return made on the investment will be greater (less) than the initial yield-to-maturity if rates rise (fall) just after acquisition of the security.

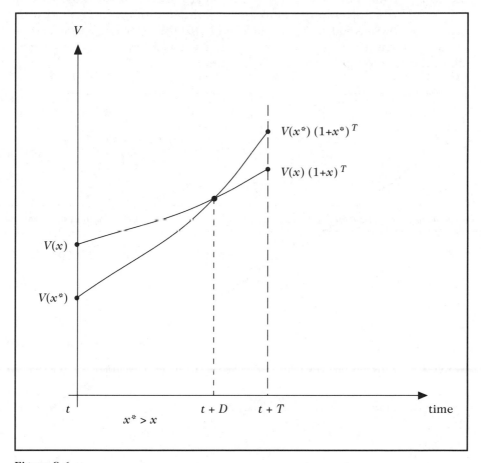

Figure 9.6

We can easily show that the duration of a portfolio of bonds is equal to the weighted average of the durations of the bonds which make up the portfolio, the duration of each security being weighted by the ratio of the value of the security to the total value of the portfolio. Portfolio managers may thus increase (reduce) the sensitivity of their portfolio to variations in rates by increasing (reducing) the duration of their portfolio. They need only buy (sell) securities with a long duration and sell (buy) securities with a short duration.

The results stated above emphasize the relevance of the concept of duration to bond management. Before concluding, however, two remarks must be made.

Firstly, the duration of a security varies with the time to maturity of the security, the size of coupons (face value) and the yield to maturity. It can be verified that duration increases with time to maturity but at a decreasing rate and that it decreases with the coupon rate and the yield to maturity. The simple passage of time modifies the duration of the portfolio and therefore the horizon for which it is immunized. This effect is illustrated in Figure 9.7, which shows the movement of the duration of the bond with respective flows of 500 ECU, 500 ECU and 10500 ECU as we approach the maturity of the security. It can be observed that after each coupon payment, the duration undergoes a positive jump.

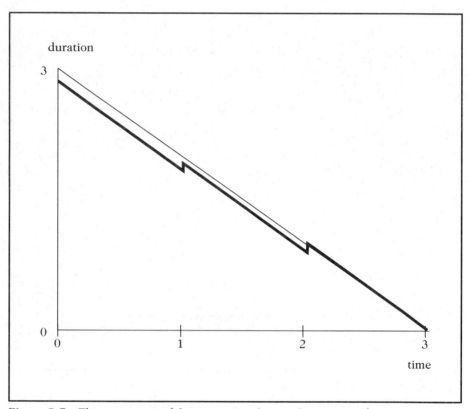

Figure 9.7   The movement of duration according to the passage of time

Managers will therefore need to recalculate duration regularly and reallocate the elements of their portfolio in order to preserve the desired duration. Management of the rate risk implies dynamic management which must be a compromise between the precision of the hedge and the transactions costs linked to the reallocations of the portfolio.

Secondly, in the example developed above, the term structure is flat and undergoes a parallel movement. When this is not the case, the analysis of immunization given above remains valid as long as the shocks affecting the interest rates are infinitesimal and uniform (that is, proportional) and for a duration calculated according to Equation 2.3.[41] More sophisticated immunization techniques will be based on a more complete description of the range of rates and a model which we develop in Chapter 10. But before that, let us take a few moments to review the traditional theories developed to explain the form of the term structure of rates.

9.6 Traditional theories of the term structure of interest rates[42]

Several theories have been proposed to explain the relationships between the rates corresponding to different maturities. We generally recognize the expectations hypothesis ([Fisher 1896], [Hicks 1939], [Lutz 1940]), the liquidity preference theory ([Hicks 1939]) and the theory of preferred habitats ([Culbertson 1957], [Modigliani and Sutch 1966]).

9.6.1 The expectations hypothesis

Strictly speaking, no explicit version of the expectations hypothesis exists. Rather, this hypothesis embodies the points of view of several authors who have expressed an opinion on this subject. In its most restrictive version, the expectations hypothesis requires that at equilibrium there is both equality between the expected rates of return on all securities and equality of them for all possible holding periods. Unfortunately, these two requirements are incompatible. The example which follows shows this clearly.

If we assume that the first condition above is satisfied, the expected return on the period (t_0, t_1) of a bond reaching maturity at t_2 $(t_2 > t_1)$, must be equal to the certain return received on a bond reaching maturity at t_1:

$$1 / P(t_0, t_1) = E[P(t_1, t_2)] / P(t_0, t_2) \qquad [6.1]$$

where $P(t,T)$ is the price at t of a pure-discount bond with no risk of non-payment reaching maturity at T.

Furthermore, by virtue of the second condition, the return received on the period (t_0, t_2) by investing in a security with a maturity at t_1 and reinvesting the product made at t_1 in a second security, with a maturity at t_2, must be equal to the certain return made on a security with a maturity at t_2:

$$1 / P(t_0, t_2) = \{ 1 / P(t_0, t_1) \} E\{1 / P(t_1, t_2)\} \qquad [6.2]$$

These two equations taken together imply

$$E\{1 / P(t_1, t_2)\} = P(t_0, t_1) / P(t_0, t_2) = 1 / E[P(t_1, t_2)]$$ [6.3]

which, by virtue of Jensen's inequality,[43] can only be true in the absence of any uncertainty. We have thus shown that it is impossible for the expected returns to be equal for all securities and all holding periods.

In order to escape from this incompatibility, different authors have relied on more restrictive statements and have used them to deduce the relationship between the rates which was to result from them. Four different (and incompatible!) versions of the expectations hypothesis are currently known. It may seem surprising to see four incompatible hypotheses appearing under the same heading of 'expectations hypothesis'. The problem results from the attempt which has been made to transpose into uncertainty, future results obtained initially under certainty. To understand how we managed to get where we are, let us pause to consider a world where the future is certain.

As we saw in Section 9.2.1 above, the forward rate, f, is defined by the equation:

$$f(t,T) = \frac{P(t,T)}{P(t,T+1)} - 1 = \frac{[1 + R(t,T+1)]^{T+1-t}}{[1 + R(t,T)]^{T-t}}$$

Let us apply this definition recurrently. We obtain the non-arbitrage condition

$$P(t,T) = \frac{1}{[1 + r(t)][1 + f(t,t+1)]\ldots\ldots[1 + f(t,T-1)]}$$ [6.4]

But, since under certainty all future flows are known for certain,

$$f(t,T) = r(T) \qquad \forall\, t \le T$$ [6.5]

and Equation 6.4 may be rewritten as

$$[P(t,T)]^{-1} = [1 + r_t][1 + r_{t+1}]\ldots\ldots[1 + r_{T-1}]$$ [6.6]

The fixed return made on a bond with a maturity of T received when the security is held until its maturity is equal to the return obtained on a succession of one-period securities with the same total length. In terms of the rate of yield to maturity,

$$1 + R(t,T) = \{[1 + r(t)][1 + r(t + 1)]\ldots\ldots[1 + r(T{-}1)]\}^{(t-T)} \qquad [6.7]$$

Finally, [6.6] also allows us to write

$$\frac{P(t+1,T)}{P(t,T)} = 1 + r(t) \qquad [6.8]$$

Under certainty, the return made on any given period must be the same for all securities and equal to the spot rate of the period.

We now possess the elements which allow us to understand the origin of the different versions of the expectations hypothesis which we shall expand upon below. The expectations hypothesis, as we mentioned above, results from the attempt to transpose to risky situations, the results obtained under certainty. Each of the incompatible versions of the expectations hypothesis takes as its starting point one of equations 6.5–6.7. Unfortunately, whilst these equations are compatible under certainty, they no longer are under uncertainty.

Local expectations hypothesis

In this version of the hypothesis, we assume that the expected returns on all securities must be equal over a period of time one unit long and no longer arbitrary as was the case in the initial statement. Formally,

$$E_t\{P(t + 1,T)\} / P(t,T) = 1 + r_t \qquad [6.9]$$

where r_t represents the spot rate for the period $(t, t + 1)$. This version therefore has as its starting point the formulation corresponding under certainty to Equation 6.8 above.

By expanding expression 6.9 recursively, we obtain the equilibrium condition

$$P(t,T) = E_t\{[(1 + r_t)(1 + r_{t + 1})\ldots\ldots(1 + r_{T-1})]^{-1}\} \qquad [6.10]$$

Expectations hypothesis of the rate of return until maturity

Other authors specify instead that, at equilibrium, equality must be established between the rate of return on two investment strategies: the fixed one made on any (long term) security held until maturity and the expected return over the same period by investing successively in securities with a maturity of one period (short term). Formally,

$$1/P(t,T) = E_t\{(1 + r_t)(1 + r_{t+1})\ldots\ldots(1 + r_{T-1})\} \qquad [6.11]$$

The origin of this version may be found in Equation 6.6 of the formulation in certain time.

Expectations hypothesis of the yield to maturity

This third version postulates that, at equilibrium, equality must be established, this time between the rates of yield to maturity of the same two strategies.[44] Formally,

$$[P(t,T)]^{-1/(T-t)} = E_t\{(1 + r_t)(1 + r_{t+1})\ldots\ldots(1 + r_{T-1})]^{1/(T-t)}\} \qquad [6.12]$$

We now have three different versions of the expectations hypothesis. Unfortunately, these three versions are incompatible. In fact, by denoting $Y = [(1 + r_t)(1 + r_{t+1})\ldots\ldots(1 + r_{T-1})] - 1$, Equations 6.10, 6.11 and 6.12 above may be rewritten as:

$$P = E\{Y\}$$
$$P^{-1} = E\{Y^{-1}\}$$
$$P^{-1/(T-t)} = E\{Y^{-1/(T-t)}\}$$

Jensen's inequality assures us that at most one of these equations is true.

Unbiased expectations hypothesis

Finally, there is a fourth version of the expectations hypothesis, perhaps the best known, which postulates equality at equilibrium between the implicit rates (also called forward rates) and the expected future spot rates:

$$P(t,T)/P(t,T+1) = E_t\{1 + r_T\} \qquad [6.13]$$

or,

$$1 / P(t,T) = (1 + r_t) \, E_t\{1 + r_{t+1}\}.........E\{1 + r_{T-1}\} \qquad [6.14]$$

This last version is not compatible with the three preceding ones either.[45]

In the above analysis, we used the concept of a holding period without explicitly defining its length. It would be useful to know whether the incompatibility emphasized above could be avoided by judiciously choosing the length of the reference period. We could, for example, retain the shortest period imaginable, that of infinitely short length. The choice of continuous time is the one which we make in Chapter 10, as it is the most natural and because it has received the favour of modern theoretical analyses.

When the expectations hypothesis is modelled in continuous time, we can show that the unbiased expectations hypothesis is equivalent to the expectations hypothesis of the yield to maturity, which was not the case in discrete time. The choice of the length of the period also plays a crucial role in the statement of these theories. Unfortunately, the change to continuous time does not allow the existing incompatibilities between the three other versions to be removed.[46]

In an important article, [Cox *et al.* 1981] showed that only the local expectations version was compatible with an equilibrium of rational expectations. This is therefore the version which we must bear in mind when speaking of the expectations hypothesis. Cox *et al.* also stress that, despite appearances, the local expectations hypothesis can be justified not by the hypothesis of neutrality to risk of economic agents but rather, in some cases, by the logarithmic utility function hypothesis.

9.6.2   Liquidity preference and preferred habitat

In the expectations hypothesis, expected returns do not explicitly include risk premiums. This characteristic has been the subject of numerous criticisms. Some authors have therefore developed new theories explicitly aiming to take account of risk premiums. Amongst them, [Hicks 1939] developed the liquidity preference theory. According to Hicks, firms wish to issue securities with long maturities in order to guarantee their sources of financing whilst lenders, that is, investors, prefer to invest in the short term. To encourage the latter to hold long-term securities, they must therefore be offered a risk premium. Moreover, as fluctuations in the prices of bonds increase with the time to maturity, risk premiums must be increasing functions of maturity.

[Culbertson 1957], in his market segmentation hypothesis, assumes that economic agents have very marked preferences for certain maturities and that quite distinct markets exist in parallel for each of these maturities. From a more moderate point of view, [Modigliani and Sutch 1966], in the theory of preferred habitats, assume that investors have preferences for certain maturities, but that they are also prepared to consider other maturities if they are correctly compensated by an appropriate risk premium.[47 48]

In the theory of preferred habitats, the investment horizon, corresponding to the investor's consumption date, therefore plays a crucial role, a role which is absent in the expectations hypothesis where we are only concerned with a one-unit period length. The determination of risk premiums becomes an integral part of the more general problem of the intertemporal choice of consumption.

Conclusion

Having reviewed the main concepts linked to bonds and bond management – yield to maturity, duration, convexity, immunization – we have now mentioned the difficulties encountered when attempting to estimate the term structure of interest rates in practice. This quite naturally leads us to wish to fill in the gaps in empirical observation by developing models of the term structure of rates. This is the subject of Chapter 10, to which we now turn our attention.

Appendix 1

Bond repurchases (sinking funds)[49]

Most straight bonds are not bonds with a one-off payment. The contract for most of them obliges the issuer to amortize the bond at fixed dates during the lifetime of the security. To this end, the issue of bonds is divided into 'series', each series grouping together a certain number of shares. At each contractual repayment date a drawing of lots designates the series which will be repaid by the issuer. The holders of the securities thus designated, or their agents, must remit their securities to the issuer, who compensates them in cash on the basis of the contractual redemption price, which is often parity (or face value). The drawing of lots may be a favourable or unfavourable event for the bearer. Everything depends on the market price of the bond and therefore eventually on the interest rates prevailing at the moment of the draw. If rates are low, the draw is unfavourable since the unlucky holder will be repaid at parity for a security which is worth more than parity.[50]

In the basic case, the lucky or unlucky event is the result of pure chance, that is, of the drawing of lots. Very often, however, the drawing clause is in fact a draw-repurchase clause which entitles the firm to repurchase securities on the stock exchange at the market price, instead of repaying them by lot. We shall see that this clause adds to the security a delivery option which is favourable to the firm. When this clause exists, the bond ceases to be a straight bond even if the market appears to take little account of this 'hidden option'.

At first sight, the right of the firm to repurchase bonds on the market appears totally insignificant. Superficial reasoning could lead us to think that a repurchase at the market price, and not at a price fixed in advance, is a neutral operation, not liable to affect the previous value of the security. It would only be a question of replacing a certain number of flows by their discounted value.

In fact, the option which the firm possesses has a real value even though the repurchase is made at the market price. The reason is subtle. Before drawing, the shares of all series receive an identical price on the market, since they all have the same characteristics. The issuer repurchases on the market, at this undifferentiated price, the shares of any series. Nevertheless, the contractual clause gives him the right to credit every repurchase against the *next* repayment. If on the next repayment date, the issuer is supposed to amortize 10000 securities (at a redemption price fixed in advance) and if he can show that, since the last repayment maturity, he has repurchased 7689 new securities on the market, only 2311 shares will be drawn out and repaid.[51]

Repurchasing on the stock exchange thus allows the issuer to reduce the next repayment. He will therefore make repurchases on the stock exchange if the quoted price (undifferentiated) is less than the discounted value of the next repayment (discounted at the short-term interest rate). An option exercised when the market price of the underlying asset is less than a threshold has a profile which is similar to that of a put option, even though we are speaking of repurchasing. As soon as the term structure is ascending, which is frequent, the long rates higher than the short rates give the quoted price a value less than the discounted value of the next repayment and it is in the issuer's interest to repurchase.

Naturally, the prospect of future repurchases will normally have a (downward) influence on the quoted price. In the extreme case where the market had the certainty that all repayments would be repurchased at 100% (assuming that the contract authorizes this), the quoted price of the bond would have to be equal to that of a bond with a one-off payment. Repurchases increase the implicit duration of the security.

A term structure calculated from the prices of such bonds, treated as straight bonds with repayment on the way, would be marred by a measurement error.

By way of an example, let us consider a three-year bond, with a face value of 1500, amortized yearly, with a coupon rate of 12%, the repurchase option applying only to the next repayment. We reason under an assumption of certainty. The period rates of the successive years are 10%, 16.7% and 18%.

This bond, treated as a straight bond without repurchase, would give rise to the following cash flows:

---

end of the first year: repayment of one series = 500
+ interest on three series = 3×60
total = 680 ECU

end of the second year: repayment of one series = 500
+ interest on two series = 2×60
total = 620 ECU

end of the third year: repayment of one series = 500
+ interest on one series = 60
total = 560 ECU

Repurchasing during the last year is pointless and repurchasing during any year is equivalent, from the point of view of value, to repurchasing at the end of the year a few seconds before repayment. Consider therefore the decision to repurchase at instant $2 - \varepsilon$ whilst two repayments remain. At this instant, the value of the bond in the absence of any repurchase is:

$$500 + 120 + (500 + 60)/1.18 = 1094.58 \text{ ECU}$$

At the same instant, the value with complete repurchase of a series (a purchase which will be credited on repayment 2) is an unknown, V, which satisfies the following equation:

$$V = V/2 + 60 + (500 + 60)/1.18$$

In fact, the issuer pays out the value, $V/2$, of one of the two remaining series, plus the interest on series 3, and will still remain liable for this last series. We find: $V = 1069.15$ ECU, which is less than 1094.58 ECU. It is therefore in the issuer's interest to repurchase.[52] Knowing this, the market will set the effective price of the bond at $2 - \varepsilon$ at the level of 1069.15 ECU and will fix the price at earlier instants by discounting this figure.

Consider the decision to repurchase at instant $1 - \varepsilon$ whilst three blocks remain. The value of the bond at this instant, in the absence of repurchase, is:

$$500 + 180 + (1069.15)/1.167 = 1596.15 \text{ ECU}$$

as the market knows that the issuer will repurchase repayment 2 during the following year. At the same instant, the value with full repurchase of a block (a purchase which will be credited on repayment 1) is an unknown, V, which satisfies the following equation:

$$V = V/3 + 120 + (1069.15)/1.167$$

In fact, the issuer pays out the value, $V/3$, of one of the three remaining series, plus the interest on series 2 and 3, and will be still liable for these last two series. We find: $V = 1554.23$ ECU, which is less than 1596.15 ECU. It is therefore in the issuer's interest to repurchase. Knowing this, the market will set the effective price of the bond at $1 - \varepsilon$ at the level of 1554.23 ECU.

At the initial instant 0, the price of the bond is thus equal to: $1554.23/1.10 = 1412.94$ ECU. We can verify that this price is equal to that of the bond with a one-off payment:

$$\{180 + [180 + (1680/1.18)]/1.167\}/1.10 = 1412.94$$

In the presence of uncertainty about future rates, the valuation of a bond with a draw-repurchase clause requires a method of the optional type. We address problems of the same type, but slightly more simple, in Chapter 10. It would be necessary to solve a pair of partial differential equations where the variables were the factors of the term structure and where the unknown functions were the two values, with and without repurchase, of the bond at each instant, the effective price being established at the minimum of these two values.

Appendix 2

The expectations hypothesis in continuous time

When time moves continuously, the definitions of the various rates which we introduced during Chapter 9 must be slightly modified.

If $P(t,T)$ still represents the value at t of a pure-discount bond paying 1 ECU with certainty in T, the yield to maturity of this bond is the rate $R(t,T)$ such that:

$$P(t,T) = \exp\{-R(t,T)[T-t]\}$$

The implicit rate $f(t,T)$ which applies to the period $(T,T+dt)$ is itself equal to:

$$f(t,T) = \frac{-\partial P(t,T) / \partial T}{P(t,T)}$$

and the period rate is simply:

$$r(t) = f(t,t) = R(t,t)$$

In continuous time, the four versions of the expectations hypothesis are therefore stated mathematically as follows:

(a) Local expectations hypothesis:

$$E\{dP(t,T)\}/P(t,T) = r(t)dt$$

or,

$$P(t,T) = E\left\{\exp\left(-\int_t^T r(s)ds\right)\right\}$$

(b) Expectations hypothesis of the return until maturity:

$$1/P(t,T) = E\left\{\exp\left(\int_t^T r(s)ds\right)\right\}$$

(c) Expectations hypothesis of the yield to maturity:

$$\left[\frac{-1}{(T-1)}\right]ln[P(t,T)] = E\left\{\left[\frac{1}{(T-1)}\right]\int_t^T r(s)ds\right\}$$

(d) Unbiased expectations hypothesis:

$$\frac{-\partial P(t,T)/\partial T}{P(t,T)} = E[r(T)]$$

which may also be rewritten as:

$$-ln[P(t,T)] = \int_t^T E\{r(s)ds\}$$

It therefore appears that in continuous time the unbiased expectations hypothesis is equivalent to the expectations hypothesis of the yield to maturity. However, the change to continuous time does not get round the incompatibility between the three other versions.[53]

Notes to Chapter 9

1   By a straight bond we mean a security whose contract unconditionally specifies the future payments which the issuer must make.

2   Refer to what was said in the introduction to Chapter 8. In exact contrast to what we did in that chapter, we now examine bonds whose signature risk is assumed to be zero. This means that the probability of regular payment of dividends and repayments is equal to 1. For all that, the security is not risk-free over a given period of time, since interest rates on the market fluctuate and produce fluctuations in the prices of bonds. It is this aspect which now requires attention.

3   As in Section 1.2.

4   This concept obviously supposes that it is possible to define a unitary holding period for securities to which every investor would conform. This means that all operators intend re-equilibrating their portfolio on the same dates by choosing to resell some securities and buy others. The choice of securities is guided by their respective rates of return, as we saw in Chapter 3, which dealt with portfolio choices. The most natural hypothesis, and the one which gives the greatest freedom to investors, involves reducing this holding period until it is infinitely small. Investors are then free to adjust their portfolio at each instant of the real line. We shall do this in Chapter 10.

5   The appropriate method of determining the level of risk for the various securities was shown in Chapter 4.

6   Furthermore, if the period rates of return were different from one security to the next, the present value factors resulting from the composition of the rates of return would also be different and the market values would not be additive: that is to say, a security whose sequence of flows was exactly equal to the sum of the sequences of two other securities would not have a price equal to the sum of the prices of these securities.

7   Any iterative algorithm must be initialized. A first approximation of yield to maturity which may be used as a starting point for the calculation is given by the coupon plus the average appreciation divided by an average price:

$$\frac{500 + (10500 - 9484.41)/3}{(10500 + 9484.41)/2} = 8.39\%$$

On the properties of this approximation, see [Hawawini and Vora 1979].

8   The reader will recall that a yield is a ratio of cash flows to an initial price, whereas a rate of return incorporates the appreciation produced on a security during a given holding period. It is therefore correct to speak of yield, and not rate of return, to maturity. In fact, definition 2.1 establishes a relationship between the cash flows paid by the security on the one hand, and the initial price on the other.

9   For this calculation to mean anything, the two securities must be comparable. In the paragraphs which follow, we examine the possibilities of transposition to securities of the same 'duration' (see below). We shall see that even then, the procedure is incorrect.

10   A calculation of this type is described in detail in Section 9.3.

11   More generally, the forward rate $f(t,T,T^*)$ for a period starting at T and ending at T^* is calculated as follows:

$$f(t,T,T^*) = \left(\frac{P(t,T)}{P(t,T^*)}\right)^{1/(T^*-T)} - 1 = \left(\frac{[1 + R(t,T^*)]^{(T^*-t)}}{[1 + R(t,T)]^{(T-t)}}\right)^{1/(T^*-T)} - 1$$

12   By 'forward rates' we mean the implicit future rates deduced from prices quoted today for bonds with different maturities. 'Spot rates', on the other hand, are the rates covering a period of time of any length but whose starting date of lending or borrowing is today's

date. These 'spot' rates therefore correspond to the yield to maturity of zero-coupon bonds. In the eyes of investors, the spot rates of interest which will prevail at the various future dates are random variables. They constitute a stochastic process in the sense of Chapter 7. However, the calculation of forward rates, as defined above, yields real numbers and not random variables. Forward rates are, in a sense to be defined, 'certainty equivalents' of future rates. Nothing indicates that these are unbiased estimators of these future rates. (An estimator is unbiased if its expected value is equal to the quantity to be estimated.) We return to this question in Chapter 10.

13   By applying the above definition, we calculate

$$f(t,t) = \frac{P(t,t)}{P(t,t+1)} - 1 = \frac{1}{0.9434} - 1 = 0.6$$

and so on for $f(t,t+1)$ and $f(t,t+2)$.

14   A logarithmic derivative is a derivative in terms of relative variations. It indicates by what percentage the price falls when the discount rate increases by 1% from what it was previously.

15   For our bond (with successive flows of 500, 500 and 10500) and spot rates of 6%, 6.49883% and 6.99688%, the duration calculated by discounting all the flows at the yield-to-maturity (6.9633%) is equal to 2.8554, whereas it is 2.8541 when each flow is discounted at the spot rate corresponding to the date of the flow. The difference may, however, be starker for bonds with more distant maturities.

16   In this case, duration in the sense of Macaulay.

17   Another break with logic will be noted here: we have just stated in the previous paragraph that securities having the same level of risk ought to have the same rate of return. The principle stated is curiously based on a comparison of the yields to maturity. We have already said that yields to maturity were not transposable from one security to another. But it is so much more convenient to assume that they are!

18   This weakness in the principle is of course known to actuaries, who specify that yield to maturity only 'means anything' if the hypothesis of a constant rate of reinvestment is adopted. In the example considered, we have seen that the envisaged future rates are 12, 14 and 16% successively.

19   Cf. Section 9.2.1.

20   The duration formula is given in Section 9.2.2, Equation 2.3.

21   This amount is the result of discounting the successive flows 500, 500 and 10500 at the respective spot rates of 7.06%, 7.564% and 8.067%.

22   Let us repeat: if the yields to maturity were common to all the securities, the rates of return on the various securities during successive periods would differ from one another, which would offer arbitrage opportunities to any investor in a position to buy and sell when the time seemed right.

23   Although the prices of three securities are sufficient, it would be inefficient not to use the prices of the n securities quoted; as these in practice do not all exactly satisfy a system of n equations with three unknowns, we choose the values of z_1, z_2 and z_3, which minimize the sum of the squares of the differences between the right and left-hand sides of the system.

24   Another much less insignificant difficulty lies in the fact that the majority of bonds give rise to interim repayment. Furthermore, many issuing firms have in their contracts the option of substituting for repayment by repurchase of their bonds on the Stock Exchange. See Appendix 1 of this chapter.

25   Cf. [McCulloch 1971, 1975].

26   That is, in such a way that its derivative is continuous.

27   Given the hypotheses of continuity, these parameters are not independent of one another.

28   Used by [Schaefer 1981] and [Bonneville 1983].

29   The constant terms of the polynomials must be zero since the present value factor corresponding to immediate maturity is equal to 1.

30   Securities exempt from tax are an exception to this general rule. The valuation of these securities requires, therefore, that they are compared with other securities whose revenues are taxable.

31   In the presence of taxes, it may be that at equilibrium, even the net flows of taxes of different securities are discounted differently, the gains and losses of an investor not always being treated the same in the calculation of tax. As well as this, fiscal arbitrage often leads the investor to wish to sell bonds short (or to take forward contracts of sale). The tax on short sales (negative holdings of securities) is not symmetrical to the tax which hits pure and simple holdings of securities. This is added to the usual obstacles which are encountered when attempting to sell securities short. These various phenomena may lead certain fiscal categories not to hold any bonds, either positively or negatively, whereas other categories only hold some specific types of security (the 'corner' solution).

32   This is the case at least in the United States.

33   Remember that we are dealing here exclusively with the risk linked to movements in interest rates. Default risk was dealt with in Chapter 8.

34   It is important to realize that until now the implicit holding period which we have considered was that of one unit of time, whether in discrete time $[t, t + 1]$ or in continuous time $[t, t + dt]$. The holding period we are dealing with here $[t, t + D]$ may (and probably will), on the other hand, cover several units of time.

35   More precisely, the return made on the date of the duration may not be less than the return which would have been made in the absence of a variation in rates, but may be greater.

36   As in the numerical example, we assume that all the spot rates are equal. The reasoning remains valid in situations other than this, however, on condition that the duration is correctly defined. *Cf* Note 41 below.

37   Including reinvested coupons.

38   For mathematical proofs of the results of this section, *see*, for example, [Bierwag 1987], Chapter 4.

39   Remember that this is the price effect measured on the date corresponding to duration, and not at t!

40   That is, the yield to maturity of the security when it is acquired.

41   For other configurations of the range of rates or other types of shock, the analysis of immunization given in this chapter remains equally valid as long as new definitions of duration are used. *See*, amongst others, [Ingersoll *et al.* 1978], [Bierwag *et al.* 1988], [Hawawini 1987], [Schaefer 1984]. [Schaefer 1984] shows, however, that from an operational point of view, conventional immunization strategies (using Macaulay's duration) generate results practically as good as those based on more sophisticated models.

42   This section is largely similar to [Cox *et al.* 1981] and [Ingersoll 1987].

43   Jensen's inequality: if X is a random variable with an expected value of $E(X)$ and $g(.)$ a convex function, then

$$E(g(X)) \geq g(E(X))$$

Except in special cases, therefore,

$$E(g(X)) \neq g(E(X))$$

44   Either investing in a long security with maturity T, or investing successively in securities with one-period maturities.

45   It would be equivalent to the expectations hypothesis of the rate of return until maturity, Equation 6.11, if the levels of the future rates were not correlated between themselves, which is not verified empirically.

46   *See* Appendix 2 to this chapter.

47   Here, risk premiums which are no longer necessarily an increasing function of the time to maturity, as was the case with Hicks.

48   Hicks' liquidity preference theory therefore becomes a special case of the preferred habitat theory, one in which the investors' preferred habitat is the very short term.

49   This appendix was written with the help of Bertrand Jacquillat, to whom we extend our thanks. Sinking-fund provisions vary greatly from country to country and from bond to bond. A good theoretical treatment is [Ho 1985].

50   It is in order to diversify this randomness that buyers of bonds, who buy a sufficient portion of the same issue, prefer to buy shares which are spread over several series. Bond valuation theories are therefore allowed to neglect the risk of the draw.

51   The draw is then made on the shares and no longer on the series. It may often be done on half-series, as the repurchase clause often sets a ceiling on repurchases and permits the issuer to repurchase at maximum a half a repayment block.

52   We disregard the costs involved in this type of operation.

53   To check this, define

$$Y = \exp\left(-\int_t^T r(s)ds\right)$$

rewrite the three different versions of the hypothesis and use Jensen's inequality.

References

[Bierwag 1987]   G. O. Bierwag, Duration Analysis: *Managing Interest Rate Risk*. Ballinger, Cambridge, MA, 1987.

[Bierwag *et al.* 1988]   G. O. Bierwag, G. G. Kaufman and C. M. Latta, Duration models: A taxonomy, *Journal of Portfolio Management*, Autumn 1988.

[Bonneville 1983]   M. Bonneville, *Le prix des obligations sur le marché de Paris*. Thèse de Doctorat d'Etat soutenue à l'Université de Lille, 1983.

[Cox *et al.* 1979]   J. C. Cox, J. E. Ingersoll and S. A. Ross, Duration and the Measurement of Basis Risk, Journal of Business, 52/1, 1979, 51–61.

[Cox *et al.* 1981]   J. C. Cox, J. E. Ingersoll and S. A. Ross, A Re-examination of Traditional Hypotheses about the Term Structure of Interest Rates *The Journal of Finance*, 36, No. 4, 1981.

[Culbertson 1957]   J. Culbertson, The Term Structure of Interest Rates *Quarterly Journal of Economics*, 1957.

[Fisher 1896]   I. Fisher, Appreciation and Interest, *American Economic Association Publications*, 1896.

[Hawawini 1987]   G. Hawawini, Controlling the Interest Rate Risk of Bonds: An Introduction to Duration Analysis and Immunization Strategies, *Finanzmarkt und Portfolio Management*, No. 4, 1986/87.

[Hawawini and Vora 1979]   G. A. Hawawini and A. Vora, *On The Theoretic and Numeric Problem of Approximating The Bond Yield to Maturity*, Working Paper No. 160, Salomon Brothers Center for the Study of Financial Institutions, New York University, 1979.

[Hicks 1939]   J. Hicks, *Value and Capital*. Oxford University Press, 1939.

[Ho 1985]   T. S .Y. Ho, The Value of a Sinking Fund
                                   Provision under Interest-Rate Risk, in E. I.
                                   Altman and M. G. Subrahmanyam, *Recent
                                   Advances in Corporate Finance*. Dow Jones
                                   Irwin, 1985.

[Hodges and Schaefer 1977]   S. D. Hodges and S. Schaefer, A Model for
                                   Bond Portfolio Improvement, *Journal of
                                   Financial and Quantitative Analysis*, 1977,
                                   243–259.

[Ingersoll 1987]   J. E. Ingersoll, *Theory of Financial Decision
                                   Making*. Rowman & Littlefield, 1987.

[Ingersoll 1989]   J. E. Ingersoll, Interest Rates, in *The New
                                   Palgrave – Finance*. Norton, 1989.

[Ingersoll *et al.* 1978]   J. E. Ingersoll, J. Skelton and R. L. Weil,
                                   Duration Forty Years Later, *Journal of
                                   Financial and Quantitative Analysis*,
                                   November 1978, 627–650.

[Litzenberger and Rolfo 1984]   R. H. Litzenberger and J. Rolfo, Arbitrage
                                   Pricing, Transaction Costs and Taxation of
                                   Capital Gains. A Study of Government
                                   Bonds with the Same Maturity Date,
                                   Journal of Financial Economics, 13, 1984,
                                   337–351.

[Lutz 1940]   F. Lutz, The Structure of Interest Rates,
                                   Quarterly Journal of Economics, 1940.

[Macaulay 1938]   F. R. Macaulay, *Some Theoretical Problems
                                   Suggested by the Movements of Interest
                                   Rates, Bond Yields, and Stock Prices in the
                                   U.S. since 1856*, National Bureau of Eco-
                                   nomic Research, New York: Columbia
                                   University Press, 1938.

[McCulloch 1971]   J. H. McCulloch, Measuring the Term Struc-
                                   ture of Interest Rates, *Journal of Business*,
                                   44, 1971, 19–31.

[McCulloch 1975]   J. H. McCulloch, The Tax-adjusted Yield
                                   Curve, *Journal of Finance*, 30, 1975,
                                   811–830.

[Modigliani and Sutch 1966]   F. Modigliani and R. Sutch, Innovations in
                                   Interest Rate Policy, *American Economic
                                   Review*, 1966.

[Nougier 1983]   J.-P. Nougier, *Méthodes de calcul numérique*. Masson, 1983.

[Schaefer 1981]   S. Schaefer, Measuring a Tax-Specific Term Structure of Interest Rates in the Market for British Government Securities, *Economic Journal*, 1981, 415–438.

[Schaefer 1984]   S. Schaefer, Immunisation and Duration: A Review of Theory, Performance and Applications, *Midland Corporate Finance Journal*, 2, Autumn 1984, 41–58.

10

The movement of interest rates and the price of bonds

A basic principle of financial theory is that today's prices result from investors' expectations with regard to tomorrow's prices. Consequently, the prices of bonds with differing maturities reflect the expected (random) movement of interest rates. This does not mean that the term structure of interest rates is simply the expected value of what it will be tomorrow, as risk premiums are involved in determining this: bonds whose maturities are longest are the most risky, and they must therefore have a higher expected return. The aim here is to develop a single formula for determining the price of a bond incorporating both the movement of future rates and the variation in the risk premium relating to the same bond as it approaches its maturity.

In the first four sections we develop a model of the range of rates based on a hypothesis describing the movement of the underlying rates. In the cases developed by [Vasicek 1977] and, more recently, by [Cox *et al.* 1985b], the term structure depends only on one random factor, the spot rate (Sections 10.1, 10.2 and 10.4) whilst for [Brennan and Schwartz 1982]

331

it is determined by the movement of the short rate (spot rate) and the long rate. Section 10.5 is devoted to the valuation of new forms of bond: indexed bonds and bonds which are puttable or callable. The final section of the chapter is devoted to a generalization to two factors of Cox, Ingersoll and Ross' model, *viz.* the model of [Longstaff and Schwartz 1992].

10.1   The price of a bond on a market subject to one random factor

We shall consider here a collection of pure-discount bonds exempt from default risk but evaluated on a market where interest rates fluctuate and induce random variations in prices and therefore in rates of return. As a first approximation, we can work on the assumption that the prices of all the bonds have a tendency to fluctuate together: they rise when the short-term interest rate falls and they fall when it rises.

We therefore postulate that the price at instant t of a pure-discount bond reaching maturity at instant s ($s \geq t$) is a function of the short-term interest rate r:[1]

$$P = P(t,s,r) \qquad [1.1]$$

This relationship, which we assume exists, is an unknown function on which we wish to impose conditions. To establish these conditions, we postulate the Itō process followed by the rate of interest r:

$$dr = \mu(r,t)\, dt + \sigma(r,t)\, dz \qquad [1.2]$$

where $\mu(r,t)$ and $\sigma(r,t)$ are specific functions: μ is the 'drift' or trend of the interest rate and σ is its volatility. The first step in the task of valuing the bonds will therefore involve identifying this process by statistical means or, at minimum, postulating the form of the functions μ and σ in order then to estimate the value of the parameters which provides the best approximation to the prices quoted on the stock market. For example, we could postulate for r an Ornstein-Uhlenbeck process (*see* Section 7.1.3 *and* Section 10.2 below).

Given the behaviour [1.2] of the interest rate, that of the price of the fixed maturity bond can be deduced by the following reasoning. Let us apply Itō's lemma to the functional relationship postulated in [1.1]:

$$dP = \left[\frac{\partial P}{\partial t} + \frac{\partial P}{\partial r}\mu + \frac{1}{2}\frac{\partial^2 P}{\partial r^2}(\sigma)^2 \right]dt + \frac{\partial P}{\partial r}\sigma dz \qquad [1.3]$$

The second-order term, representing the curvature of the function, enters into the calculation of the anticipated trend of P, due to the random nature of the variable r.[2]

To obtain the partial differential equation determining the price of all the bonds and thus the range of rates, we now implement an arbitrage operation between two bonds with different maturities s^1 and s^2, with prices which we shall denote as follows in order to simplify matters:

$$P^1 = P(t,s^1,r)$$
$$P^2 = P(t,s^2,r)$$

This arbitrage involves buying one bond with a maturity of s^1 (at the price P^1) and selling h bonds with a maturity of s^2 (at the price P^2), the number h being chosen such that:

$$\frac{\partial P^1}{\partial r} - h\frac{\partial P^2}{\partial r} = 0 \qquad\qquad [1.4]$$

that is to say:

$$h = \frac{\partial P^1 / \partial r}{\partial P^2 / \partial r} \qquad\qquad [1.5]$$

The aim of condition 1.4 is to cancel out the instantaneous risk of the arbitrage position; we can confirm this by noting that, in formula 1.3, the random component of the price of the bond is quite simply equal to the randomness in the rate, $\sigma\, dz$, multiplied by the reaction of the price to a one-unit variation in the rate. This reactivity or sensitivity of the price is the determining factor of the volatility which is specific to the security in question; the other determining factor, namely the volatility of the interest rate, is common to all the securities. Condition 1.4 therefore stipulates that an appropriate choice of h allows the volatility of the arbitrage position to be reduced to zero.

In a correctly functioning market, the rate of return on a risk-free position must be equal to the risk-free short-term interest rate. This condition will be sufficient for us to determine the price of the bond.[3]

Since we are speaking here of pure-discount bonds, their remuneration is derived entirely from the increases in value calculated in [1.3]. Thus, the income from our arbitrage position when h satisfies [1.5] is equal to:

$$\frac{\partial P^1}{\partial t} + \frac{\partial P^1}{\partial r}\mu + \frac{1}{2}\frac{\partial^2 P^1}{\partial r^2}(\sigma)^2 - h\left[\frac{\partial P^2}{\partial t} + \frac{\partial P^2}{\partial r}\mu + \frac{1}{2}\frac{\partial^2 P^2}{\partial r^2}(\sigma)^2\right]$$

and the rate of return, equal to the income per ECU invested, is calculated by dividing this amount by the starting value of the position, which is:

$$P^1 - h\,P^2$$

The equality of the rate of return and the risk-free rate of interest supplies us with the equation:

$$\frac{\frac{\partial P^1}{\partial t} + \frac{\partial P^1}{\partial r}\mu + \frac{1}{2}\frac{\partial^2 P^1}{\partial r^2}(\sigma)^2 - h\left[\frac{\partial P^2}{\partial t} + \frac{\partial P^2}{\partial r}\mu + \frac{1}{2}\frac{\partial^2 P^2}{\partial r^2}(\sigma)^2\right]}{P^1 - hP^2} = r$$

where h is given by [1.5]. By substituting the value of h and grouping together on each side the terms relating to each of the two bonds, we obtain:

$$\frac{\frac{\partial P^1}{\partial t} + \frac{\partial P^1}{\partial r}\mu + \frac{1}{2}\frac{\partial^2 P^1}{\partial r^2}(\sigma)^2 - rP^1}{\frac{\partial P^1}{\partial r}} = \frac{\frac{\partial P2}{\partial t} + \frac{\partial P^2}{\partial r}\mu + \frac{1}{2}\frac{\partial^2 P^2}{\partial r^2}(\sigma)^2 - rP^2}{\frac{\partial P^2}{\partial r}}$$

In other words, this amount is the same for all the bonds. The same is obviously also true for the amount:

$$\lambda = \frac{\frac{\partial P}{\partial t} + \frac{\partial P}{\partial r}\mu + \frac{1}{2}\frac{\partial^2 P}{\partial r^2}(\sigma)^2 - rP}{-\frac{\partial P}{\partial r}\sigma} \qquad [1.6]$$

that is to say, $\lambda = \lambda(r,t)$ is constant when comparing the various bonds at a given moment.[4]

This law is relatively simple to interpret. If we divide the numerator and the denominator of [1.6] by P, we find in the numerator the instantaneous return on a bond over and above the risk-free rate. The numerator is therefore a risk premium which enters into the determination of the rate of return on the security. The denominator, after dividing by P, is:

$$-\frac{1}{P}\frac{\partial P}{\partial r}\sigma$$

which is equal to the standard deviation of the interest rate (in interest rate points; *cf.* Equation 1.3), multiplied by the reactivity of the price of the bond to the rate of interest. The denominator is the risk (standard deviation) of the rate of return on the bond.

Relation 1.6 applied to the various bonds therefore means that the risk premium for each of them is proportional to its standard deviation, or that a linear relationship exists between rate of return and instantaneous volatility. We shall call the coefficient of proportionality, λ, the 'market price of the interest rate risk'.[5]

Equation 1.6 gives the result that the price function $P(t,s,r)$ of any bond (and generally of any security whose price depends only on the rate of interest r), must satisfy the partial differential equation

$$\frac{\partial P}{\partial r}(\mu + \lambda\sigma) + \frac{1}{2}\frac{\partial^2 P}{\partial r^2}(\sigma)^2 + \frac{\partial P}{\partial t} = rP \qquad [1.7]$$

to which is added, for a straight bond, the terminal condition according to which the price on maturity is equal to the redemption price:

for all r: $P(s,s,r) = 1$ ECU   [1.8]

Although the market price of the interest rate risk λ is, at a given moment, equal to a constant when comparing bonds with one another, there is nothing to show that it is constant over time. Generally:

$$\lambda = \lambda(t, r)$$

This function, like the functions μ and σ which specify the process of the rate, must be supplied if we wish to solve Equation 1.7. In practice, and for want of a better hypothesis, we shall assume that λ is constant in time: the risk of a bond varies (with $-[\partial P/\partial r]\ (t,s,r)$) as maturity is approached and the rate r changes, but the premium per unit of risk is assumed constant. This constant will be determined empirically on the basis of the observed prices of the bonds.

The only general formula which gives the solution to Equations 1.7 and 1.8, that is, the price of the bond at any instant t for any value of the rate of interest r, involves an expected value which remains to be calculated:

$$P(t,s,r) = \hat{E}_t \exp\left(-\int_t^s r(\tau)\, d\tau \right) \qquad [1.9]$$

This expression simply shows that the price of the bond results from future interest rates. The risk premium is taken into account, since the expected value $\hat{E}_t$ in this formula must be calculated (by integration) on the basis of the probability distribution of a rate process modified as follows:

$$dr = (\mu + \lambda\sigma)\, dt + \sigma\, dz \qquad [1.10]$$

In other words, we artificially alter the drift of the interest rate to take the risk premium into account: it is not the 'true' anticipated rates but the rates thus modified which are incorporated into formula 1.9. When $\lambda = 0$, no risk premium is required and it is the 'true' anticipated rates which are reflected in the prices of the bonds: this special case is called the 'unbiased expectations hypothesis'.[6]

Although useful to comprehension, formulae 1.9 and 1.10 can only be used for calculation when the probability distribution of the future rates resulting from movement 1.10 is known. In other cases, prior determination of the probability distribution requires the solution of a partial differential equation as complex as [1.7] and it is therefore simpler to deal with this latter equation, which gives the price directly.

10.2   Example: the Vasicek formula

Most often, the price function, the solution to Equations 1.7 and 1.8, can only be obtained point by point, in the form of tables, by means of numerical methods which involve approximating derivatives by finite differences, taken between two points of the graph of the function.

Nevertheless, in order to illustrate the properties of the solutions, we shall now consider a special case for which a solution exists in the form of an explicit formula. This is the special case where λ is constant and where the interest rate r follows the Ornstein-Uhlenbeck process:

$$dr = \alpha\,(\gamma - r)\,dt + \sigma\,dz$$

Vasicek showed that in this case the solution to [1.7] is:

$$P(t,s,r) = \exp\left\{\frac{1}{\alpha}\left(1 - e^{-\alpha(s-t)}\right)\left(R(\infty) - r\right) - (s-t)R(\infty) - \frac{\sigma^2}{4\alpha^3}\left(1 - e^{-\alpha(s-t)}\right)^2\right\}$$

where

$$R(\infty) = \gamma + \frac{\sigma\lambda}{\alpha} - \frac{1}{2}\frac{\sigma^2}{\alpha^2} \qquad\qquad [2.1]$$

Another way of writing this solution involves giving the yield to maturity of this bond until its maturity, that is to say the rate R, such that:

$$P = 1\ \text{ECU} \times e^{-(s-t)R}$$

that is:

$$R = \frac{1}{s-t}\ln P$$

and therefore:

$$R(t,s,r) = -\left\{\frac{1}{\alpha}\left(1 - e^{-\alpha(s-t)}\right)\left(R(\infty) - r\right) - \frac{\sigma^2}{4\alpha^3}\left(1 - e^{-\alpha(s-t)}\right)^2\right\} / (s-t) + R(\infty)\, [2.2]$$

We can verify that:

$$R(t,t,r) = r$$

that is to say that the yield of a bond reaching maturity instantaneously is equal to the instantaneous interest rate. Furthermore,

$$R(t,\infty,r) = R(\infty)$$

which explains the notation and shows that the rate of return on a very long bond is a constant whose value is given in [2.1].

The 'term structure of interest rates', according to the accepted expression, that is, the yield to maturity R at a given instant t according to the maturity s as supplied by Equation 2.2, is shown in Figure 10.1 (solid lines). Three cases arise:

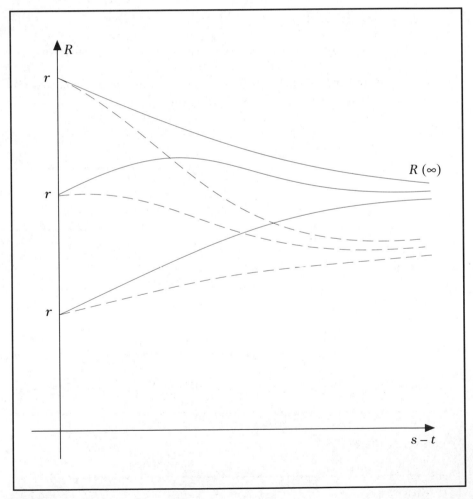

Figure 10.1

- if the present interest rate is high (to be precise, if $r > R(\infty) + (1/4)\sigma^2/\alpha^2$) the structure is monotonically decreasing and obviously reflects the anticipated fall in rates;

- if the rate is low, (to be precise, if $r < R(\infty) - (1/4)\sigma^2/\alpha^2$) the reverse is true;

- for intermediate values of r, the graph is first increasing and then decreasing.

The Vasicek formula not only takes account of the anticipated movement in interest rates, but also of the variation in the risk of the bond (and of the risk premium attached to it), until its maturity. For proof, it is useful to compare the structure obtained to that which would have prevailed in the absence of a risk premium ($\lambda = 0$), in which case the unbiased expectations hypothesis would have applied; this structure is shown by the dashed lines in Figure 10.2. Whereas we take 'risk premium' to mean the additional instantaneous return (over a short holding period) created by the market price of the interest-rate risk, 'liquidity premium' means the corresponding additional yield to maturity.[7] The two types of premium exist simultaneously and are simply two representations of the same phenomenon. The liquidity premiums are therefore read in Figure 10.1 as the differences between the solid lines and the dashed lines: they are obviously higher for the longest bonds.

The parameter α, which determines the average force of reversion of the interest rate towards its long term value γ, plays a dual role in the final result:

- α determines the anticipated trajectory of the rate;

- α has an influence on the uncertainty which hits the rate in the course of a finite period: if α were infinitely large, the rate, whatever the shock received, would be brought back infinitely quickly towards γ and would therefore hardly ever differ from it. On account of this, the rate would become non-random.

Thus, when the present interest rate is low, an increase in parameter α will have an influence on the price of the bond which will result from two antagonistic effects:

- a more rapid rise in rates will be anticipated, and this will reduce the price of the bonds,

- a lower risk will be taken into account, and this will increase the price of the bonds.

However, when the current rate is high, the effect of an increase in α is unambiguous: the prices of the bonds rise.

Whatever the validity of the Vasicek formula, it has one unsatisfactory property from an empirical point of view: the extremity $R(\infty)$ of the structure of the rates is completely immutable, even though the rest of the structure fluctuates with the short-term rate. We shall now see whether we can remedy this state of affairs.

10.3   The price of a bond on a market subject to two random factors

In order to make the structure of the rates more flexible and to allow it to adapt better to the prices of the bonds we are observing, the most simple method involves 'freeing' its extremity, until now immutable, by considering it as a new exogenous random factor.

This means that, from now on, the financial market in question will be subject to two random factors represented by the two extremities of the structure, chosen as 'primary rates':

- r: the interest rate of immediate maturity,
- l: the yield to maturity of a bond of infinitely long maturity.

The precise definition of l is a matter of taste. Here, we follow Brennan and Schwartz by defining l as the yield to maturity of a perpetual bond continuously paying a coupon of 1 ECU per unit of time.[8] For this reason alone, we will be led to take account of a coupon in calculating the rate of return on a bond.

On the basis of the two extremities of the structure and their behaviour in time, we mean to determine all the prices of the bonds.

Returning to the reasoning of Section 10.1, we postulate the existence of a function which links the price at instant t of a bond with a maturity of s ($s \geq t$) to the two primary rates r and l:

$$P = P(t,s,r,l) \tag{3.1}$$

Then, we postulate the joint process of the two rates:

$$dr = \mu_1(r,l,t)\, dt + \sigma_1(r,l,t)\, dz_1 \tag{3.2a}$$

$$dl = \mu_2(r,l,t)\, dt + \sigma_2(r,l,t)\, dz_2 \tag{3.2b}$$

completed by the correlation $\rho(r, l, t)$ which links the two white noise terms dz_1 and dz_2.

A particularly interesting example of a process of this type would be provided by the following generalization of the Ornstein-Uhlenbeck process:

$$dr = \alpha(l-r)\, dt + \sigma_1\, dz_1 \qquad\qquad\text{[3.3a]}$$

$$dl = \sigma_2\, dz_2 \qquad\qquad\text{[3.3b]}$$

This process would represent the behaviour of a short-term rate whose 'long-term value' was equal to the long-term rate, the speed of return being proportional to the difference between the two rates.

Having postulated [3.1] and [3.2], an arbitrage reasoning analogous to that of Section 10.1 would allow us to conclude that two numbers λ_1 and λ_2 must exist, which are two 'market prices of risk' corresponding to the two sources of risk, and which are applicable to all bonds so that for each one, the following partial differential equation must be verified:

$$\frac{\partial P}{\partial t} + \frac{\partial P}{\partial r}\mu_1 + \frac{\partial P}{\partial l}\mu_2 + \frac{1}{2}\frac{\partial^2 P}{\partial r^2}(\sigma_1)^2$$

$$+\frac{1}{2}\frac{\partial^2 P}{\partial r}(\sigma_2)^2 + \frac{\partial^2 P}{\partial r\partial l}\sigma_1\sigma_2\rho + c - rP \qquad\qquad\text{[3.4]}$$

$$= -\lambda_1\frac{\partial P}{\partial r}\sigma_1 - \lambda_2\frac{\partial P}{\partial l}\sigma_2$$

The left-hand side of this equation contains the expected income of the bond (capital gain plus any coupon[9]) over and above the risk-free income. It is therefore a risk premium (in ECU). The right-hand side is a record of the total risk: short-term interest rate risk 'charged' at the price λ_1 and long-term interest rate risk 'charged' at the price λ_2.[10]

In fact, as in the case of options, a perfect arbitrage exists between all pairs of bonds on the one hand, and the perpetual bond of infinite maturity on the other, where the price of the latter, taking account of the definition of l, is equal to:

$$1/l \qquad\qquad\text{[3.5]}$$

The best proof of this is that we can eliminate the market price λ_2 (as well as the drift μ_2) from Equation 3.4 by noting that the price [3.5] of the perpetual bond must, like all prices, satisfy [3.4]. By substituting [3.5] into [3.4] we obtain:

$$-\frac{1}{(l)^2}\mu_2 + \frac{1}{2}\times 2\frac{1}{(l)^3}(\sigma_2)^2 + 1 - r\frac{1}{l} = \lambda_2\frac{1}{(l)^2}\sigma_2$$

By next substituting the value of λ_2 thus obtained into [3.4], we can conclude that the price of any (pure-discount) bond must satisfy the following partial differential equation:

$$
\frac{\partial P}{\partial r}(\mu_1 + \lambda_1 \sigma_1) + \frac{\partial P}{\partial l}\left(\frac{1}{l}(\sigma_2)^2 + l^2 - rl\right)
$$

$$
+\frac{1}{2}\frac{\partial^2 P}{\partial r^2}(\sigma_1)^2 + \frac{1}{2}\frac{\partial^2 P}{\partial l^2}(\sigma_2)^2 + \frac{\partial^2 P}{\partial r \partial l}\sigma_1 \sigma_2 \rho \qquad [3.6]
$$

$$
+\frac{\partial P}{\partial t} = rP
$$

to which the following limit condition is attached:

$$
P(s,s,r,l) = 1 \text{ ECU} \qquad [3.7]
$$

System 3.6 and 3.7 may be solved when we postulate the (possibly constant) functions: μ_1, λ_1, σ_1, σ_2, r. This theory was implemented on the Canadian and American markets by Brennan and Schwartz, who proceeded in three steps:

Step 1:   Estimate process 3.2 of the primary rates

Using monthly data gathered from the US markets covering the period December 1958 to December 1979, Brennan and Schwartz estimated [3.2] by interpreting r as the yield to maturity of 30-day Treasury Bills, and l as the yield to maturity of US Government Bonds of more than 20 years. The functional form of the process was postulated *a priori* and not identified from the data. Estimation of the parameters by statistical methods[11] gave the following results:

$$
\frac{r_t - r_{t-1}}{r_{t-1}} = -\frac{0.0887}{r_{t-1}} + 0.1102\left(\frac{l_{t-1}}{r_{t-1}} - 1\right) + \xi_{1,t} \qquad [3.8]
$$
$$
(0.0526) \quad (0.0301)
$$

$$
\frac{l_t - l_{t-1}}{l_{t-1}} = 0.00891 + 0.00358\ r_{t-1} - 0.0037\ l_{t-1} + \xi_{2,t}
$$
$$
(0.0069) \quad (0.0017) \qquad (0.0020)
$$

$$
\sigma(\xi_1) = 0.1133;\ \sigma(\xi_2) = 0.0298;\ \rho(\xi_1, \xi_2) = 0.2063
$$

The numbers in parentheses under the estimators show their standard deviations. The links in both directions between the short and long rates are significant. The autocorrelations of the errors are equal to -0.195 for the first equation and -0.064 for the second. Improvements in the process postulated can therefore be envisaged; they would have the aim of explicitly representing these delayed effects.

Step 2:   Solve partial differential equation 3.6, 3.7 and compare the prices obtained with the prices quoted

Since the functions μ_1, μ_2, σ_1, σ_2 are supplied by Equation 3.8, which has just been estimated, Brennan and Schwartz solved Equation 3.6 by numerical methods, by assuming λ_1 to be constant. The estimate of the value of λ_1 which optimized the approximation between the data and the theory was made by grouping together all the US Government Bonds into ten portfolios containing bonds with similar maturities. The value found was:

$$\lambda_1 = 0.45$$
$$(0.028)$$

A comparison was then made between the prices quoted every month for 20 years on all the US Government Bonds taken individually (some 11669 observations), and their theoretical prices obtained once again by solving [3.6]. Brennan and Schwartz found a mean absolute error,[12] on a bond with a normalized nominal value of $100, of only $1.58. For these same bonds, the mean absolute error made on the yield to maturity was 0.55% per year.

Step 3:   Analyse the behaviour of price errors

Although the difference between theoretical prices and quoted prices may seem small, the above model does not completely take account of the behaviour of the debenture market. Brennan and Schwartz stated in fact that price errors tend to occur together (and in the same direction), for bonds with different maturities; that is to say, a third factor common to all securities, over and above the two prime rates r and l treated explicitly, apparently influences the debenture market.

The autocorrelation of this factor is nevertheless very strong (in the order of 0.8 for a difference of one month between two successive values); that is to say, it moves only slowly. On account of this, although the omission of this factor may cause non-negligible differences in absolute prices, it has little consequence in the explanation of price variations from one month to the next. The model may be very useful as a guide to investment: the difference between theoretical price and quoted price indicates the trend: on average 15% of this difference translates into a price adjustment in the month which follows, and 30% in the quarter which follows.

Although the models by Vasicek and Brennan and Schwartz may still be used in practice, they in fact suffer from several weaknesses. One of the main ones is that the market price of the risk and the parameters of the process(es) of the rate(s) are specified independently of one another, which may lead to internal inconsistencies and therefore to arbitrage opportunities.

We present below the model by [Cox *et al.* 1985b], which was developed, amongst other things, with the aim of ruling out this kind of inconsistency.

10.4   The Cox, Ingersoll and Ross model

In the models by Vasicek and Brennan and Schwartz, the stochastic process of the rate(s) of interest and the functional form of the risk market price are given exogenously. By taking this course, we run the risk of obtaining results which are not consistent with a general equilibrium of the capital assets market.[13] To offset this weakness, [Cox *et al.* 1985b] consider the problem of the term structure of interest rates in the more general context of an intertemporal capital asset pricing model. From very strong hypotheses on intertemporal consumption preferences and the attitude towards risk of the representative economic agent and by assuming that the output of the production process is governed by a single (technological) random factor, Y, whose dynamics are:

$$dY = [\xi Y + \zeta]\, dt + v \sqrt{Y}\, dz$$

they obtain *endogenously* the stochastic process followed at equilibrium by the risk-free instantaneous interest rate:

$$dr = k\,(\theta - r)\, dt + \sigma \sqrt{r}\, dz$$

For k, $\theta > 0$, the interest rate follows a first-order autoregressive process with reversion towards θ. The parameter k determines the speed of adjustment of the rate. The properties of this process are as follows:

- if $\sigma^2 \leq \zeta k \theta$ the interest rate never takes a negative value. This is due to the presence of the term $\sqrt{r}$ in the expression of the volatility of the short rate.[14] When the rate approaches zero, its instantaneous volatility diminishes proportionally, which prevents the origin from being crossed;
- the absolute variance of the interest rate increases with the rate;
- there exists a long term equilibrium distribution of the rate.[15]

A similar reasoning to that of Vasicek then allows us to obtain the partial differential equation which must be verified by the price P of all pure-discount bonds, λ being a constant:

$$(1/2)\sigma^2 r P_{rr} + k(\theta - r)P_r + P_t - \lambda r P_r - rP = 0 \qquad [4.1]$$

to which we must add the usual boundary condition

$$P(r, T, T) = 1$$

The solution to Equation 4.1 is:[16]

$$P(r, t, T) = A(t, T)e^{-B(t, T)r}$$

where

$$A(t, T) = \left[\frac{2\gamma e^{[(k+\lambda+\gamma)(T-t)/2]}}{(\gamma + k + \lambda)(e^{\gamma(T-t)} - 1) + 2\gamma} \right]^{2k\theta/\sigma^2}$$

$$B(t, T) = \frac{2(e^{\gamma(T-t)} - 1}{(\gamma + k + \lambda)(e^{\gamma(T-t)} - 1) + 2\gamma}$$

$$\gamma = ((k + \lambda)^2 + 2\sigma^2)^{1/2}$$

As regards yield to maturity and therefore the range of rates, the Cox, Ingersoll and Ross model leads to the following result[17]:

$$R(r, t, T) = [rB(t, T) - \log A(t, T)]/(T-t)$$

When the maturity of the bond draws near, the yield to maturity approaches the instantaneous rate, as expected. Conversely, when the maturity approaches infinity, $R(r,t,T)$ goes to $2k\theta/(\gamma + k + \lambda)$, its long-term value.

When the instantaneous rate is less than this long-term value, the term structure of the rates is uniformly increasing. When the rate is greater than $k\theta/(k + \lambda)$, the term structure is decreasing. When the rate takes intermediate values, the term structure has a hump.

It must be noted that if, as in the Vasicek model, the price of the bonds only depends on a *single random factor*, in this case the spot rate, the Cox, Ingersoll and Ross model has the dual advantage (1) of avoiding negative rates of interest and (2) of ensuring that the process of the instantaneous interest rate, $r(t)$, and the functional form of the market price of the risk, $\lambda(r,t)$, both being determined endogenously, are consistent. An examination of the respective partial differential equations of Vasicek and Cox, Ingersoll and Ross shows us that the market price of the risk for Cox, Ingersoll and Ross, λ^{CIR}, is linked to the market price of the risk for Vasicek, λ^V, in the following manner

$$\lambda^{CIR} = \lambda^V\sqrt{r}/\sigma$$

where λ^V had wrongly been assumed to be a constant. Cox, Ingersoll and Ross thus demonstrate that, in contrast to the hypothesis made by Vasicek, the market price of the risk will not generally be independent from the process followed by the spot rate at equilibrium.[18]

10.5 New forms of bond

Our task until now has involved pricing classic pure-discount or fixed-coupon bonds, repayable according to a predetermined schedule. Although it shows satisfactory empirical results, the proposed method is probably less accurate for these bonds than the traditional actuarial techniques of Chapter 9. The advantage of this method lies in its generality: Equation 3.6 applies to bonds of all types, evaluated on a market subject to two random factors. Only boundary conditions (Equation 3.7 for classic bonds) differentiate the bonds and express the terms of the debenture contract.

However, large fluctuations in interest rates have led firms and financial institutions to issue new debenture securities, which we shall divide into two categories:

- Some securities have a floating or indexed half-yearly coupon. At the beginning of each half-year, the coupon to come is determined according to a contractual formula which takes into account an indexing base: the present rate of the money market or of the debenture market.

- The contract of some others contains an early exit clause, that is, a possibility of early redemption, either at the option of the bearer (puttable bond), or at the option of the issuer (callable bond). Often, there are even two early exercise clauses together, one at the option of the bearer, the other at the option of the issuer. The contractual clause specifies in each case on what dates and at what price fixed in advance the redemption may be made. The beneficiary of the clause chooses, when he or she has the opportunity to do so, either redemption at the price fixed, or continuation of the normal life of the security at the price quoted on the stock exchange.

The object of both types of clause is to stabilize the price of the bond in question. Its capital value fluctuates less than that of a straight bond; but the cash flows which it generates are more random since they adjust to market conditions.

When the solution to the partial differential equation ([1.7] if there is one factor, [3.6] if there are two) is obtained by numerical methods, there is no difficulty in taking these new clauses into account. Following a basic principle of finance, the solution is always obtained by going backward in time: starting from the given final repayment, we fill in line by line the table of values of the bond corresponding to closer and closer instants (see Figure 10.2). If a coupon is paid at a precise instant, its amount must be added back to the price of the bond to determine its previous values.

This technique is adapted to the clauses mentioned above in the following manner:

Indexation clauses:

Since the move from line j to line $j + 1$ of the table is made by solving the partial differential equation, a coupon must be added to the result $j + 1$ if this date (or a date between j and $j + 1$) is a coupon payment date. In the case of a straight bond, a coupon is a fixed number of ECU which is added to all the cells of the line, whatever the corresponding value of the random factor. In the case of an indexed coupon bond, it is sufficient to introduce the indexing base as a random factor entering into the evaluation, and to vary the amount of the coupon added to each cell of the line, by applying the contractual formula. The most simple case is that where the indexing base is the short-term rate r; the coupon is then a given function $c(r)$ and we therefore add to the boxes in line $j + 1$ the coupon amounts corresponding to the various values of r: $c(r_1)$, $c(r_2)$, and so on. A floating or indexed coupon is no more difficult to deal with than a fixed coupon. At worst, it involves the introduction of an additional factor which must appear in the partial differential equation. For example, the indexing base may be, not the present short-term rate, but an average of recent short-term rates; this average, itself random, must therefore appear as a separate factor.

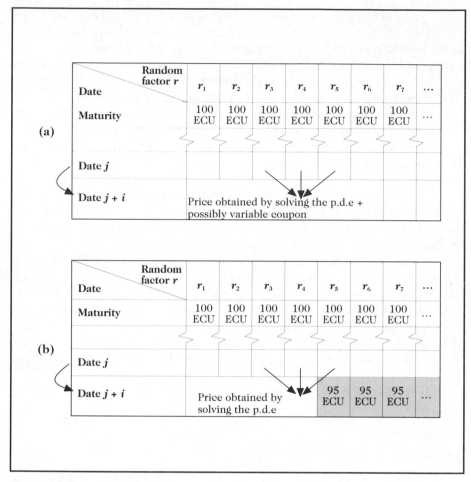

Figure 10.2

Put and call features:

Let us first of all consider a redemption clause at the option of the bearer (puttable bond). Bearers always choose the option which is the most favourable, that is, the one which leads to the highest value of their wealth. If, therefore, $j + 1$ is an exercise date of the redemption option, the bearer compares the value of the bond, where the option at instant $j + 1$ has not been exercised,[19] to the fixed redemption price. This comparison determines whether or not the bearer requests repayment: the true value of the bond at $j + 1$ is therefore the larger of these two amounts. After solving the partial differential equation and moving to line $j + 1$, we need only examine this line cell by cell and use the redemption price (for example: 95 ECU if the bond has a nominal value of 100 ECU) to replace the cells of the line which are less than this price (see the grey cells of Figure 10.2b).

The treatment of a call feature is symmetrical: issuers prefer to repay at the best possible conditions. Thus, if $j + 1$ is an exercise date of the repayment option held by the issuer, he compares the price of the bond, where the option is unexercised, to the redemption price. This comparison leads him to repay or not to repay the security, and the true value of the bond in $j + 1$ is therefore the smaller of these two amounts. The numerical procedure may be deduced from this.

The flexibility of this method is therefore total. Its limits are only those of the numerical technique used: a limitation in practice to three random factors, rounding-off errors and errors resulting from the replacement of derivatives by finite differences.

In the final section of this chapter, we present briefly an extension to two factors of the Cox, Ingersoll and Ross model.

10.6 Recent developments

In Section 10.4 above, we presented Cox, Ingersoll and Ross's general equilibrium approach to the term structure of interest rates. [Longstaff and Schwartz 1992] extend this approach by including a second state variable in the model, the instantaneous variance of changes in, or volatility of, the short-term rate.[20] By following the same general equilibrium approach as Cox, Ingersoll and Ross, they guarantee that the dynamics and factor risk premiums of both factors, which are endogenously determined in the model, are consistent with the absence of arbitrage.[21] The inclusion of a second factor, however, greatly increases the flexibility of the model and enables it to generate a wider range of term structures.

Longstaff and Schwartz assume that the return on physical investment generated by a constant return-to scale technology is described by.

$$\frac{dQ}{Q} = \left(\mu X + \theta Y\right)dt + \sqrt{Y}\,dz_1$$

where μ, θ and σ are positive constants, X and Y are state variables and z is a scalar Wiener process. Note that when setting $\mu = 0$ we again find Cox, Ingersoll and Ross's one-factor model. The dynamics of the two state variables are:

$$dX = \left(a - bX\right)dt + c\sqrt{X}\,dz_2$$
$$dY = \left(a - eY\right)dt + f\sqrt{Y}\,dz_3$$

where $a, b, c, d, e, f > 0$ and where it is assumed that z_2 is uncorrelated with z_1 and z_3.[22]

Longstaff and Schwartz make the same strong assumptions on the representative consumer's intertemporal preferences as did Cox, Ingersoll and Ross, and show that a simple change of variables makes it possible to rewrite all expressions in terms of the short-term rate, r, and its instantaneous volatility, V, two variables which have a strong economic intuition. Like Cox, Ingersoll and Ross, they obtain closed-form expressions for pure-discount bond prices and for yields to maturity, but these are now functions not only of the short-term rate and the time to maturity of the bond but also of the volatility of the short-term rate.

Longstaff and Schwartz show that in this more general model, the partial derivative of the bond prices with respect to time to maturity can be either negative or positive, whereas it is always negative in one-factor models. This is because an increase in time to maturity can, in some circumstances, lead to a reduction in production uncertainty and in the bond term premium, yielding a smaller expected rate of return for the bond and, correspondingly, a higher bond price. The partial derivative of the bond price with respect to the volatility of the short rate is also ambiguous, again because of the impact on the term premium.

Notes to Chapter 10

1   The rate r will be interpreted as the instantaneous yield of a risk-free investment of immediate maturity. In a non-random market, this rate would be used as a continuous discount rate: for example, if r is constant, the present value at instant t of one ECU paid at instant s $(s > t)$ is: $\exp[-r(s - t)]$.

2   It will be remembered that the second derivative of a function measures its curvature.

3   This is not entirely accurate: we shall add the assumption, crucial and not justified, that the market price of the risk is constant.

4   In other words, λ does not depend on the *maturity* of the bonds.

5   The dimension of λ is, according to Equation 1.6:

$$\{ECU \text{ tomorrow/time}\}/\{ECU \text{ tomorrow}/\sqrt{time}\} = 1/\sqrt{time}.$$

6   *See* Chapter 9.

7   In other presentations, the liquidity premium is taken as the difference between the forward rate and the expected value of the corresponding spot rate.

8   This type of bond is known as a 'consol bond'.

9   This is the rate of continuous payment per unit of time. c is equal to 1 ECU per unit of time for the consol bond.

10   $-(\partial P/\partial r)\,\sigma_1$ is the volatility of the bond linked to the short-term rate and $-(\partial P/\partial l)\,\sigma_2$ is that linked to the long-term rate.

11   Generalized least squares, which take account of the correlation between the residuals of the two equations and their serial correlations.

12   The 'root mean square error'.

13   An example of this type of inconsistency leading to arbitrage opportunities is given by [Cox *et al.* 1985b], page 398.

14   In view of this characteristic of the Cox, Ingersoll and Ross model, it is also known as the square root process.

15   The reader may check that when k tends towards ∞, the expected value tends towards θ and the variance tends towards zero, and that when k tends towards 0, the conditional expected value of r tends towards $r(t)$ and the conditional variance tends towards $\sigma^2 r(t)(s - t)$.

16   The dynamic of the price of the bonds is:

$$dP = r[1 - \lambda B(t,T)]P\,dt - B(t,T)P\sigma\sqrt{r}\,dz$$

17   The definitions of the yield to maturity, spot rate and forward rate concerning continuous time are given in Appendix 2 of Chapter 9.

18   Remember that this formulation depends crucially on the hypotheses made by the authors, which greatly limits the generality of their result.

19   Because of the calculations made earlier, this value nevertheless takes into account possible *later* exercises of the option.

20   Longstaff and Schwartz rationalize the choice of the volatility of the short rate for the second factor by quoting an empirical study by [Dybvig 1989] according to which the short rate and its volatility are the two most important factors in explaining movements in the term structure.

21   The reader is referred to Section 10.4 for a brief discussion on this point.

22   Therefore, given that z_2 is uncorrelated with z_1 and z_3, changes in X cannot be hedged and its risk is unpriced. We are thus left with only one market price of risk, as was the case in [Cox *et al.* 1985a].

References

[Brennan and Schwartz 1979]   M. J. Brennan and E. S. Schwartz, A Continuous-Time Approach to the Pricing of Bonds, *Journal of Banking and Finance*, 3, 1979, 135–155.

[Brennan and Schwartz 1982]   M. J. Brennan and E. S. Schwartz, An Equilibrium Model of Bond Pricing and a Test of Market Efficiency, *Journal of Financial and Quantitative Analysis*, vol. 17, no. 3, September 1982.

[Cox *et al.* 1985a]   J. C. Cox, J. E. Ingersoll and S. A. Ross, An Intertemporal General Equilibrium Model for Asset Prices, *Econometrica*, vol. 53, No. 2, 1985, 363–384.

[Cox *et al.* 1985b]   J. C. Cox, J. E. Ingersoll and S. A. Ross, A Theory of the Term Structure of Interest Rates, *Econometrica*, 53, 1985b, 385–407.

[Dybvig 1989]   P. H. Dybvig, Bond and bond option pricing based on the current term structure, Working paper, Washington University, St. Louis, Missouri, 1989.

[Longstaff and Schwartz 1992]   F. A. Longstaff and E.S. Schwartz, Interest rate volatility and the term structure: A Two-Factor General Equilibrium Model, *The Journal of Finance*, vol. 47, 1259–128, 1992.

[Vasicek 1977]   O. Vasicek, An Equilibrium Characterization of the Term Structure, *Journal of Financial Economics*, 5, 177–188, 1977.

11

Options on interest rates and on interest-sensitive instruments

The wide fluctuations in interest rates that have occurred in recent years have led to the creation of numerous instruments that serve as hedges against interest rate risk. Among them are 'caps', 'floors' and other 'swaptions', which are all options on the term structure of interest rates.[1] When an interest rate option is exercised, it is settled in cash, which means that there is no delivery of the underlying asset; instead, a sum of money is paid by the seller (issuer) to the holder of the option. Interest rate options differ from options on government bonds (Treasury Bonds and Bills in the United States, Obligations Assimilables du Trésor (OATs) in France, and so on) for which, in the event of exercise, the seller of the option delivers the underlying asset (the bond) against the payment of the exercise price. They also differ from the option clauses tagged on to some modern forms of bond, such as callability (early repayment at the option of the issuer of the bond), or puttability (repayment at the option of the holder of the bond). These were discussed in Chapter 10. However, all these securities are contingent on the term structure of interest rates.

The first models to value interest-rate-sensitive options[2] were based on the models of the term structure of interest rates by [Vasicek 1977] and

353

[Brennan and Schwartz 1982], which were discussed in Chapter 10. This was a two-stage procedure. The first stage aimed to obtain a theoretical representation of the term structure on the basis of a one-factor (such as Vasicek) or two-factor (such as Brennan and Schwartz) model. The second stage valued options on the term structure.

The two-stage approach to bond options differs markedly from the approach of Black and Scholes to stock options. In the Black-Scholes stock option pricing theory, the behaviour of the underlying asset price is postulated and the theory proceeds directly to value options on the basis of absence of arbitrage.[3] This is a one-stage procedure.

The two-stage approach applied to bond options increases the chance of a poor fit of the theory with the data, because the errors made in the first-stage model of the term structure have repercussions on the valuation of options.[4] In other words, the first-stage bond prices do not generally fit exactly the actual term structure that prevails at the time the option is being valued. Hence, the second stage values the option on the basis of theoretical prices, as opposed to observed prices, for the underlying asset.

Why not instead dissociate the two undertakings as much as possible: the pricing of bonds on the one hand (for which we have done our best in Chapter 10), the pricing of options on bonds on the other? In the second undertaking, we can simply take as given the current prices of all the bonds traded in the exchange and use all that information to price options on one of them, without questioning the process by which the market has established those prices. This would be analogous to what has been done for stock options: we have priced stock options given the current price of the under-lying stock security. We have only established a relationship between them (for instance, the Black and Scholes formula). The formula gives the 'right' price for the option if in the first place the price observed for the stock is the 'right' one. That, however, is a separate issue. The same approach may be envisaged for bonds.[5,6]

Such an approach has been developed in the literature of finance, notably by [Ho and Lee 1986], [Heath *et al.* 1992], [El Karoui and Rochet 1989] and [Hull and White 1990, 1993a, 1993b]. These models are based on the concept of a 'risk-neutral', or risk-adjusted probability. We first need to remind the reader of this important concept (Section 11.1). We then present a simple binomial representation of the term structure (Section 11.2). In Section 11.3, we show how, in continuous time, we can equally well postulate the behaviour of bond prices, of forward rates, or of yields to maturity. Finally, in Sections 11.4 (binomial approach) and 11.5 (continuous-time approach), we indicate how the postulated behaviour of bond prices leads to a model of bond option prices.

11.1 Reminder on 'risk-neutral' probabilities

[Harrison and Kreps 1979] show that in the absence of arbitrage, there exists a probability measure, called adjusted probability or risk-neutral probability, such that the price of every security today is equal to the expected value (under this probability) of its price tomorrow discounted at the riskless rate: that is, the discounted prices of all securities are 'martingales'.[7] In other words, under this probability the expected rate of return on all assets is equal to the riskless rate.[8]

We have already met the adjusted probability measure on several occasions. In Section 6.2, we evaluated stock options within the binomial framework. In formula 6.2.8, the effective probability, p, of an 'up' move was replaced by an adjusted probability, π, and discounting was then accomplished by means of the riskless rate. The change of probability is what allowed us to discount the expected value of the terminal option payoff at the riskless rate, even though the option is, of course, a risky asset.

That same idea was carried further in Section 7.2.2, where we showed that the price of an option, the solution to the Black-Scholes partial differential equation, could be written as the expected value of the terminal payoff discounted back at the riskless rate. In mathematical literature, this is known as the Feynman-Kac formula.[9] Once again, however, that expected value was understood as being calculated under the adjusted probability measure, which is different from the effective probability.

Under the effective probability, the price of the underlying stock security followed the diffusion process:[10]

$$dS/S = \alpha dt + \sigma dz \tag{1.1}$$

Under the risk neutral probability, the price follows the process:[11]

$$dS/S = r dt + \sigma dz \tag{1.2}$$

Note a very important property of this change of probability: the volatility, σ, of the rate of return is the same under both probabilities.

As for the price at time t, $V(S(t),t)$, of any derivative security (European option, pure discount bond, and so on) with a single, fixed maturity T, written on an underlying asset with price $S(t)$, this is given by the following expected value formula:

$$V(S(t),t) = \hat{E}\left\{ \exp\left[-\int_t^T r(s)ds \right] V(S(T),T) \Big| \Phi(t) \right\} \tag{1.3}$$

where Φ represents the information available and $\hat{E}$ indicates that the expected value must be calculated under the adjusted probability. In Chapter 10, we used that same line of reasoning a third time to obtain the price of a bond in a one-factor model (Equation 1.9).

We are now ready to consider stochastic representations of the term structure of interest rates and options written on it.

11.2 The Black, Derman and Toy example

[Black *et al.*1990] employ a binomial probability tree, as did [Cox *et al.* 1979] for stock options.[12] The information, which is available from the start and which Black, Derman and Toy use to build their tree, is in two parts: first, the yields to maturity of all the pure-discount bonds of different maturity dates, second, the volatility of these yields. The yields are observable but the volatilities are postulated.[13]

Black, Derman and Toy make an assumption of risk neutrality which is not restrictive if the purpose is only the pricing of derivative assets. It is not restrictive because risk aversion would only affect the required expected returns on securities, that is, their drifts, not their volatilities.[14]

Black, Derman and Toy show that the information on yields and yield volatilities is sufficient, under the assumption of risk neutrality, to deduce uniquely the future possible behaviour of yields along the tree or, equivalently, the future behaviour of bond prices or, again equivalently, the future behaviour of spot interest rates. Here, we shall content ourselves with verifying that the future behaviour of yields, prices and interest rates produced by Black, Derman and Toy is consistent with the original information.

In their example (reduced to three periods), the assumed term structures of yields and yield volatilities at time 0 are given as follows:

Maturity (years)	Yield %/year	Yield volatility (%/year) (standard deviation of yield)
1	10	
2	11	19
3	12	18

We now verify that the probability tree for one-period short rates which is consistent with the above information is the following one (assuming equal probabilities of up and down moves):

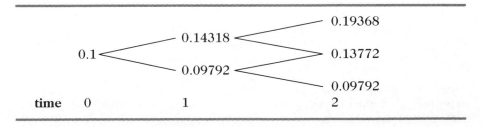

| time | 0 | 1 | 2 |

First, note that the one-period interest rate at time 0 for maturity 1 is indeed equal to 10% as stipulated. Second, note the volatility of the two-period yield over the time interval 0 to 1. Over that time interval the two-period yield becomes a one-period yield. Volatility of yields is defined by Black, Derman and Toy as the standard deviation of time increments in logarithms of yields. We verify that:[15]

$$ln(0.14318/.09791)/2 = 0.19$$

as stipulated by the original information on yield volatility. At this point, we could easily calculate the volatility of the price of the two-year pure-discount bond as well.

Working backwards, as we have been used to doing ever since the first chapter of this book, that tree can now serve to compute the price at time 0, under risk neutrality, of a pure-discount bond maturing at time 2:

$$\frac{0.5\dfrac{100}{1.4318} + 0.5\dfrac{100}{1.09791}}{1.1} = 81.16247$$

This price implies a yield to maturity for a two-year bond at time 0 equal to:

$$\sqrt{(100/81.16247)} - 1 = 11\%$$

as was required.

Working in a similar fashion, we can obtain by backward induction the tree of prices taken at time 0, 1 and 2 by a pure-discount bond maturing at time 3:

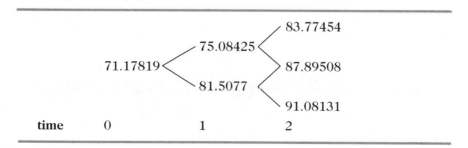

The corresponding yields for that bond in the future are:

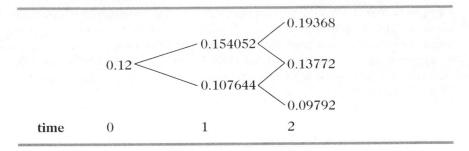

Note first that the yield at time 0 on the three-year bond is 12%, as was required by the original data. Secondly, note the volatility of the three-year yield (becoming a two-year yield) over the interval of time 0 to 1:[16]

$$ln(0.154052/0.107644)/2 = 0.18$$

which was the last piece of information from the original data that was to be checked. We have completed the task of checking that the postulated tree conforms with the original requirements. At this point, we could easily calculate the volatility of the price of the three-year zero coupon bond.

Note also that we could have calculated the forward interest rates and their volatilities at every point in time.

This small example from Black, Derman and Toy goes a long way towards making one threefold point: it makes no difference whether we take as a starting point the term structure of yields and yield volatilities or the risk-neutral tree of one-period rates, or the risk-neutral tree of pure-discount bond prices, or the risk-neutral tree of yields to maturity. Similarly, we could have started the whole exercise with the data on the term structure of prices and price volatilities (as was done for stock securities in the Black-Scholes theory), or, for that matter, with the term structure of forward interest rates and forward rate volatilities.

In the next section, we make the same points in the context of continuous-time theory. In Section 11.4, we return to the Black, Derman and Toy tree to show how it can be used in the manner of Cox, Ross and Rubinstein to price an option on a bond.

11.3 Specifying the behaviour of the term structure in continuous time[17]

In this section, we mimic the Black-Scholes approach to stock options and adapt it to bond options. The stochastic process (the future evolution) of the stock price is postulated and the current value of the stock price (the initial condition for the process) is given.

We first specify the behaviour of bond prices, as did [Hull and White 1993a, b] and [El Karoui and Rochet 1989]. But we then show that we could equally well specify the behaviour of forward interest rates, as did [Heath *et al.* 1992], or that of the instantaneous spot rate as in [Black *et al.* 1990] or [Hull and White 1990]. These three routes are equivalent.

11.3.1   Specifying the behaviour of bond prices

As we specify the initial conditions and the later behaviour over time of the entire vector of bond prices – as opposed to the behaviour of only one stock price in the theory of Black and Scholes – we need to be mindful of the fact that an arbitrary specification could lead to a situation in which arbitrage opportunities would open up between the various bond prices. Some restriction must be imposed on the assumed future behaviour of bond prices so that arbitrage possibilities have a zero probability of occurring.[18]

The easiest way to accomplish this task is to specify directly the behaviour of prices under the risk-neutral probability measure, which exists in the absence of arbitrage opportunities.

Under that probability, we write:

$$\frac{dP(t,T)}{P(t,T)} = r(t)dt + \sum_{j=1}^{n} \sigma_j(t,T)dt_j(t) \qquad [3.1]$$

where $P(t,T)$ is the price at t of a pure discount bond maturing at T, $r(t)$ is the instantaneous spot rate at t,[19] t_j ($j = 1...n$) are independent standard Brownians,[20] and σ_j ($j = 1...n$) represent the instantaneous volatilities of the rates of return on bonds.

We impose the conditions that n is finite, that each σ_j is only a *deterministic function*[21] of time, t, and maturity date, T, and that: $\sigma_j(T,T) = 0$ for all j, since the terminal price of a bond is certain.

In order to simplify notation, we assume in what follows that $n = 1$. This is a one-factor formulation which implies that the term structure is subject to only one source of risk and that the rates of return on all bonds are perfectly correlated with each other. Readers interested in the general case may go to the references which are supplied at the end of the chapter.

Formula 3.1 is slightly awkward. First of all, it is incomplete without some knowledge of the behaviour, $r(t)$, of the instantaneous spot rate over time. We show below that that behaviour is implied. Secondly, despite the assumed existence of the risk neutral measure and the fact that all bonds return r, absence of arbitrage is still not guaranteed because we have an apparent conflict between terminal conditions, $P(T,T) = 1$ for pure-discount bonds, and the initial conditions provided by the time-t observed term structure of bond prices.

In order to clarify these points, we now draw the implications of [3.1] for forward and spot rates.

11.3.2 Specifying the behaviour of forward interest rates in continuous time [22]

We now derive from [3.1] the behaviour of forward rates over time. The forward rate, implied in the time-t term structure, for the future loan period $[T_1, T_2]$ is defined as:

$$f(t,T_1,T_2) = \frac{lnP(t,T_1) - lnP(t,T_2)}{T_2 - T_1} \tag{3.2}$$

Applying Itō's lemma to the logarithm of bond prices (as per [3.1] above), we get:

$$df(t,T_1,T_2) = \frac{\sigma(t,T_2)^2 - \sigma(t,T_1)^2}{2(T_2 - T_1)} dt + \frac{\sigma(t,T_1) - \sigma(t,T_2)}{T_2 - T_1} dt(t)$$

The process for the instantaneous forward rates is obtained by taking the limit of the above expression as $T_2 \rightarrow T_1$ (let us then call both numbers T):[23]

$$df(t,T) = \sigma(t,T)\sigma_T(t,T)\, dt + \sigma_T(t,T)\, dt(t) \tag{3.3}$$

where $\sigma_T(t,T)$ stands for the partial derivative of volatility, $\sigma(t,T)$, with respect to T.

Therefore, the drift and diffusion terms of the stochastic process for forward rates, under the risk-neutral probability, depend only on the *volatilities* of rates of return on bonds, not on the prices of bonds or on the riskless interest rate, except perhaps indirectly via their impact on the volatility of bond returns. Once the volatilities of bond returns are specified for all maturities, the process for forward rates under the risk-neutral measure follows uniquely. The drift of the process for the forward rate can also be written as:

$$\sigma^f(t,T)\int_t^T \sigma^f(t,\tau)d\tau$$

where σ^f denotes the volatilities of forward rates. This relationship between the drift and the volatility of forward rates comes from the arbitrage condition.

The comparison between [3.1] and [3.3] highlights a simple relationship between the volatilities of bond returns, σ^P, and those of forward rates, σ^f:

$$\sigma^f = \partial\sigma^P/\partial T$$

It has become clear that modelling the process for forward rates, as did [Heath *et al.* 1992], is equivalent to modelling the process for bond prices. It is easy to shift from one formulation to the other. The choice of formulation is a matter of convenience.

11.3.3 Specifying the behaviour of spot rates in continuous time [24]

The instantaneous spot interest rate is one of the instantaneous forward rates:

$$r(t) \equiv f(t,t)$$

Since:

$$f(t,t) = f(0,t) + \int_0^t df(s,t)$$

we can obtain from Equation 3.3 above:

$$r(t) = f(0,t) + \int_0^t \sigma(s,t)\sigma_t(s,t)ds + \int_0^t \sigma_t(s,t)dt(s) \qquad [3.4]$$

We obtain the corresponding process for the riskless rate (still under the risk-neutral probability) by taking increments over time in [3.4] and by making use of the requirement that at maturity, the volatility of the return on a bond is zero, $\sigma(t,t) = 0$:[25]

$$dr(t) = f_t(0,t)dt + \left\{ \int_0^t \left[\sigma(s,t)\sigma_{tt}(s,t) + \sigma_t(s,t)^2 \right] ds \right\} dt$$

$$+ \sigma_t(t,t)dt(t) + \left\{ \int_0^t \sigma_{tt}(s,t)dt(s) \right\} dt$$

[3.5]

Note that, generally speaking, the process for the instantaneous rate, which is implied by a Gaussian, Markovian specification for bond prices such as [3.1], is Gaussian[26] but is not Markovian; that is, stochastic differential equation 3.5 indicates that the evolution of the rate of interest from time t onwards depends on the past since time 0. Furthermore, the last term in [3.5] depends on the trajectory of the Brownian motion, $t(t)$.[27]

We can show that, within the family of volatilities that are functions of the bond's time to maturity, $\tau = T - t$, only two functional forms are compatible with spot interest rates that follow a Markovian process. These are:[28]

a) the exponential form: $\sigma_j(r) = n_j \, [1 - \exp(-ar)]/\alpha$ [3.6]

which is the form reached by the Vasicek (1977) one-factor model (*see* Chapter 10)[29] and:

b) the linear form: $\sigma_j(r) = \eta_j \, r$

where α and the η_js are constants.

Here again, the volatilities to which we are referring are those of bond rates of return, not those of forward rates as in [Heath *et al.* 1992]. However, we saw that there is a close correspondence between the two, so that the two separate approaches lead to the same process [3.4] for the short rate.

11.4 Pricing options in the Black, Derman and Toy example

Having specified the behaviour of the underlying bonds in three equivalent ways, we now show how an option on one of those bonds can be priced.

Assume that the risk-neutral bond price behaviour of the Black, Derman and Toy tree (*see* Section 11.1) is correct and consider a European call option maturing at date 2 written on a pure-discount bond maturing at date 3 and struck at 85. The tree of bond prices and terminal option values is the following:

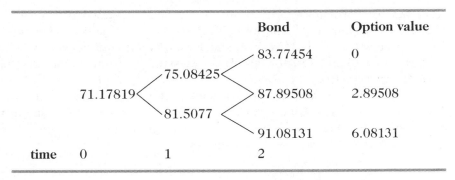

		Bond	Option value
		83.77454	0
	75.08425		
71.17819		87.89508	2.89508
	81.5077		
		91.08131	6.08131
time 0	1	2	

Seen from the upper node at time 1, the option is equivalent to holding, during the time period 1 to 2, the following fraction of the bond:

$$h = \frac{2.89508 - 0}{87.89508 - 83.77454} = 0.70298$$

along with the following amount of one-period riskless asset:

$$B = 0 - h \times 83.77454 = -58.8598 \text{ ECU}$$

Hence, the option at the upper node of time 1 is worth:[30]

$$h \times 75.08425 + B/1.14318 = 1.266243 \text{ ECU}$$

Working backwards in a similar fashion, we find that the option is worth 4.087951 ECU at the lower node of time 1 and 2.433725 ECU at time 0.

It would have been equivalent to work not with the tree of risk-neutral prices for the three-year pure-discount bonds but with the tree of 'undiscounted risk-neutral bond prices' or forward bond prices to time 2:

83.77454

$0.5 \times 83.77454 + 0.5 \times 87.89508 = 85.8348$
(in lieu of 75.08425 which is 85.8348/1.14318)

$0.4899 \times 85.8348 + 0.5101 \times 89.48820$
(in lieu of 71.17819)

87.89508

$0.5 \times 87.89508 + 0.5 \times 91.08131 = 89.48820$
(in lieu of 81.5077)

91.08131

Note that the probabilities at time 0 have been modified to reflect the absence of discounting.[31] The probability 0.4899, for instance, is equal to $0.5 \times (1.11)^2/(1.1 \times 1.14318)$. Remember that 11% is the two-year yield at time 0, and 10% and 14.318% are the successive short rates along the 'up' branch stemming from the original node.

We can now use the same tree as support for the calculation of undiscounted values of the option (forward values of the option to its maturity date, which is time 2). For instance, at the upper node of time 1, the forward value of the option we can calculate as:

$$h \times 85.83481 + B = 1.447544 \text{ ECU}$$

After the calculation has reached time 0, we would switch back to the discounted (that is, spot, as opposed to forward) value of the option in one fell swoop using the price of the two-period bond as a discount factor.

We will now price options in the same manner but directly using continuous-time mathematics.

11.5 Pricing options in continuous time

On the basis of the spot rate process, Equation 3.4, one may evaluate any interest-sensitive derivative security by means of the risk neutral probability.[32]

Under the assumption that the volatility of pure discount bond returns depends only on the time, t, and maturity date, T, of the bond, [Hull and White 1993] show that the price of an option written on a pure discount bond paying 1 ECU at T, with an exercise price equal to K and a maturity date of T_K, is equal to:

$$C(P_T, P_{T_K}, t; T_K, T, K) = P_T N(h + \sigma_P) - K P_{T_K} N(h) \qquad [5.1]$$

where: $N()$ is the cumulative normal function,
P_T and P_{T_K} are the given prices at time t of pure-discount bonds maturing at date T and at date T_K respectively,

$$h = ln\left[(P_T / KP_{T_K})\right] / \sigma_P - \sigma_P / 2,$$

and $$\sigma_P^2 = \int_t^{T_K} [\sigma(s,T) - \sigma(s,T_K)]^2 \, ds$$

Under the stronger condition that:[33]

$$\sigma(t,T) = \eta^2 \{1 - \exp[-a(T-t)]\}/a \qquad [5.2]$$

we can verify that:

$$\sigma_P^2 = (\eta^2/2a^3) \{1 - \exp[-a(T-T_K)]\}^2 \{1 - \exp[-a(T_K-t)]\}$$

and Equation 5.1 becomes identical to a formula derived by [Jamshidian 1989] and applying to European options on pure-discount bonds.

Under the assumption of exponential volatility [5.2], [El Karoui and Rochet 1989] established a formula for European options on coupon paying bonds:

$$C(P_{T_i}, i = 1\ldots N, P_{T_K}, t; T_K, T, K) = \sum_{i=1}^{N} P_{T_i} N(h + \sigma_{P_i}) - KP_{T_K} N(h) \qquad [5.3]$$

where: T_i, $i = 1\ldots N$ are the payment dates of the N coupons,
T_K, the maturity date of the option, satisfies: $T_K < T_1$,
F_i are the ECU amounts of the coupons on the bond,
P_{T_i} and P_{T_K} are the given prices at time t of pure-discount bonds maturing at date T_i and at date T_K respectively,

$$\sigma_{P_i}^2 = \int_t^{T_K} [\sigma(s,T_i) - \sigma(s,T_K)]^2 \, ds$$

and h is defined implicitly by:

$$\sum_{i=1}^{N} F_i P_{T_i} \exp\left[-\frac{1}{2}\sigma_{P_i}^2 + h\sigma_{P_i}\right] = KP_{T_K}$$

To reach this result, El Karoui and Rochet first price the option relative to the bond which matures on date T_K, which is the maturity date of the option. That is, they obtain the undiscounted (or T_K forward) value of the option. Readers have already encountered this idea on several occasions.[34]

They know that, in such a case, the volatility which is relevant for option pricing purposes is not the volatility of the spot price of the underlying asset but that of its forward price, which is its spot price divided by the price of a T_K pure-discount bond. That is precisely why the σ_ps are defined the way they are. The quantity:

$$- [\sigma_{P_i} - \sigma_{P_K}]^2$$

is the instantaneous variance of returns on:

$$P_{T_i} / P_{T_K}$$

since the prices of all bonds (under the assumption of only one Brownian factor) are perfectly correlated. Then, the σ_p^2s are time integrals of the instantaneous variances. The use of the T_K bond as numeraire is especially convenient.

Conclusion

The material we have covered in this chapter has appeared very recently in the specialist literature. The challenge faced was to model the evolution of the term structure in such a way that the postulated process would not contradict the initial term structure, which was taken as given. It was found that the specification of the initial term structure and the assumption of a prespecified, deterministic volatility were enough to obtain the entire future time path of interest rates, yields, forward rates and bond prices under the risk-neutral probabilities.

The knowledge of these variables under the risk-neutral probability is all that was needed to price any option on rate-sensitive instruments.

Notes to Chapter 11

1   A 'cap' protects its holder against a rise in interest rates. If the rates rise above a ceiling prescribed in the contract, the seller of the cap pays the holder an amount of money equal to the difference in interest rates multiplied by a notional contract amount. A 'floor' offers the same kind of protection against a fall in interest rates. A 'swaption' is an option on a 'swap'. A 'swap' is an agreement between two parties to exchange the cash flows associated with two debt instruments on the basis of a pre-established formula.

2   *See* [Rendlemann and Bartter 1980], [Courtadon 1982] *and* [Schaefer and Schwartz 1987].

3   *See* Chapter 7.

4   Errors occur potentially when specifying and estimating the market price of interest-rate risk, and when estimating the drifts of the long and short rates. Besides, as indicated in Section 6.4, the intertemporal behaviour of the rates and the market price of risk should not be set independently of each other; this was the substance of the Cox, Ingersoll and Ross critique [Cox *et al.* 1985].

5   Along with the current, initial values of bond prices, we also need to have information on the future evolution of those prices. We remember from stock option theory that the crucial piece of information when pricing options is the specification of the volatility of the price of the underlying security. The specification of the drift of that price is less crucial.

6   It is possible to dissociate bond pricing from option pricing by simply generalizing or 'extending' the models of Chapter 10 in such a way that they tautologically fit the current term structure. For instance, the Vasicek model, which was originally developed on the basis of an Ornstein-Uhlenbeck process for the short rate, can be extended to the following process:

$$dr = (\theta(t) - \alpha r)\, dt + \sigma dz$$

where $\theta(t)$ is a function of time designed to fit current bond prices once formula 10.2.1 for $P(t,s,r)$ has been extended to that case. The only relevant information in the process for the short rate is the fact that its volatility is constant. As with the basic model, the extended Vasicek model leads to a volatility for bond rates of return which is deterministic and exponential: $\sigma[1 - \exp(-\alpha(s - t)]/\alpha$, where s is the maturity date of the bond. We shall encounter this form of volatility again.

7   For a definition of 'martingales', *see* Chapter 7.

8   Not only does the change of probability imply a change of expected return from its effective value to one equal to the riskless rate, it is also true that this change of rate of return (or drift) fully characterizes the change in measure. This is the message of the Girsanov theorem (*see* [Karatzas and Shreve 1988]).

9   *See* Equation 2.11 in Chapter 7.

10   In Equation 1.1, z is a standard Brownian under the effective probability. This means that its drift and standard deviation under that measure are equal to zero and one respectively, and that their increments are independent.

11   In Equation 1.2, z is a standard Brownian *under* the *adjusted probability*. Its drift and standard deviation computed with this probability measure are equal to zero and one respectively. The Brownian in [1.2] is not identical to the Brownian in [1.1].

12   *See* Section 6.2.

13   These might have been derived from the quoted prices of some bond options. See the material of Section 11.5. In that case, of course, the material of Section 11.5 would become circular. But it could serve to price options other than those which were used to derive the volatility information.

14   If the Black, Derman and Toy tree were to be used as a representation of the effective process of future bond prices, the assumption of risk neutrality would have to be taken literally.

15   Computing the standard deviation in conventional manner, we write:

> mean = $0.5 \times ln(0.14318) + 0.5 \times ln(0.09791)$;
> standard deviation = $0.5 \times [ln(0.14318)]^2 + 0.5 \times [ln(0.09791)]^2 - \text{mean}^2 = 0.19$.

16   Note the volatility of the two-period yield over the time interval 1 to 2 (remember that over this time interval the two-period yield becomes a one-period yield):

> $ln(0.19368/0.13772)/2 = ln(0.13772/0.09792)/2 = 0.1705 = 0.18^2/0.19$.

17   This section is based on [Hull and White 1993a,b].

18   Fortunately, a change of drift leaves the set of zero-probability events unchanged, provided that the drift (loosely speaking) is never infinite. In the language of mathematics, a change of drift is identical to a change of probability measure on future events, by virtue of the Girsanov theorem. In this change of measure, the old and new measures are 'equivalent', which means that the set of events which receive a zero probability of occurring is the same under both measures. The Girsanov theorem applies under the 'Novikov condition' (see [Karatzas and Shreve 1988] page 198), which limits the choice of drifts.

19   As indicated, under the adjusted probability measure, the instantaneous expected rate of return on any security is equal to the instantaneous spot interest rate.

20   Under the adjusted probability, the drift of t is equal to zero and the standard deviation is equal to one.

21   [Hull and White 1993a,b] also allow σ_j to be a function of bond prices.

22   Similarly, we could have derived from [3.1] an expression for the yields to maturity of the various bonds.

23   Equation 3.3 is written for a fixed T, as t varies.

24   The result that the dynamics of bond prices (or yields) and the term structure of volatilities were sufficient information to determine the behaviour of spot rates was first established by [Ho and Lee 1986] in a discrete-time context.

25   Note that stochastic differential equation 3.5 is not a special case of Equation 3.3 for forward rates, even though $r(t)$ is a special forward rate: $r(t) = f(t,t)$. This is because [3.3] was written for a fixed maturity date T ($df(t,T) = ...$), whereas $dr(t) = df(t,t)$; that is, the increment [3.5] in the instantaneous spot rate is calculated with a 'sliding', immediate maturity date t.

26   The Gaussian feature implies that the interest rate can become negative. This is a consequence of the assumption that bond volatilities are deterministic (that is, $\sigma_j(t,T)$ is a function of t and T only).

27   One advantage of Markovian processes for the interest rate is that their discrete-time representation can be accomplished by means of a *recombining* binomial tree. This is important for options whose price must be calculated numerically. The Markovian character is necessary for it to be possible to use a recombining tree.

28   They make up the family of 'linear Gaussian processes'. Where there are several factors ($j = 1...n$), the same α parameter must be common to all the factor-specific volatilities σ_j.

29   We have also noted (see Note 6) that the 'extended' Vasicek model implies the same exponential form for bond return volatility.

30   See the tree of one-period rates in Section 11.1.

31   In the parlance of applied mathematicians, we are making use not of the risk-neutral tree and probabilities, but of the 'forward neutral' tree and probabilities (see [El Karoui and Rochet 1989] or [El Karoui and Geman 1991]). Changing the tree and probabilities is equivalent to changing the numeraire: instead of calculating the value of the option in current monetary units at each point in time, we have computed the value of the option in terminal (maturity-date) monetary units, that is, its forward value. For an application of

this concept in continuous time, *see* Section 11.5. This change of numeraire was proposed by [Merton 1973] to accommodate time-varying interest rates (*see* Section 7.4.3).

32   Note in this connection that the market price of risk, whose estimation posed a problem in Chapter 10, is not present in the process for the spot rate under the risk-neutral probability. The only parameters which appear in such a case are observable or can be easily estimated. In particular, the estimation of volatilities can be done in the usual manner from observed rates of return, since the volatilities are not affected by the change of measure; they are identical under the two probabilities provided that returns are observed over short enough intervals.

33   Remember that this condition implies that the interest rate follows a Markov process (*see* Section 11.3.3).

34   *See*, for instance, Section 7.4.3, where we examined the case of stock option prices under time-varying interest rates. El Karoui and Rochet use a special vocabulary. They introduce the concept of a 'T_K forward neutral' probability measure. That is, they consider a probability measure equivalent (that is, with the same-zero probability events) to the effective one or to the risk-neutral one, which has the property that the prices of all assets, divided by the price of the bond maturing at T_K – that is, the T_K forward prices – are martingales under that probability measure.

References

[Black et al. 1990] F. Black, E. Derman and W. Toy, A One-factor Model of Interest Rates and its Applications to Treasury Bond Options, *Financial Analysts Journal*, 46, 1990, 33–39.

[Brennan and Schwartz 1982] M. J. Brennan and E. S. Schwartz, An Equilibrium Model of Bond Pricing and a Test of Market Efficiency, *Journal of Financial and Quantitative Analysis*, 17, 1982.

[Courtadon 1982] G. Courtadon, 1982, The Pricing of Options on Default-free Bonds, *Journal of Financial and Quantitative Analysis*, 17, 1982, 75–100.

[Cox et al. 1979] J. C. Cox, S. A. Ross and M. Rubinstein, 1979, Option Pricing: A Simplified Approach, *Journal of Financial Economics*, 7, 1979, 229–263.

[Cox et al. 1985] J. C. Cox, J. E. Ingersoll and S. A. Ross, A Theory of the Term Structure of Interest Rates, *Econometrica*, 53, 1985, 385–407.

[El Karoui and Geman 1991] N. El Karoui and H. Geman, The Valuation of General Floating-Rate Notes and Swaps: a Probabilistic Approach, mimeo. 1991.

[El Karoui and Rochet 1989] N. El Karoui and J.-C. Rochet, A Pricing Formula for Options on Coupon Bonds, working paper #8925, University of Paris VI, 1989.

[Heath et al. 1992] D. R. Heath, R. Jarrow and A. Morton, Bond Pricing and the Term Structure of Interest Rates: a New Methodology for Contingent Claims Valuation, *Econometrica*, 60, 1992, 77–105.

[Ho and Lee 1986] T. S. Ho and S. Lee, Term Structure Movements and Pricing Interest Rate Contingent Claims, *Journal of Finance*, 41, 1986, 1011–1029.

[Hull and White 1990]   J. Hull and A. White, Pricing Interest-Rate-Derivative Securities, *The Review of Financial Studies*, 3, 1990, 573–592.

[Hull and White 1993a]   J. Hull and A. White, One-Factor Interest-Rate Models and the Valuation of Interest-rate Derivative Securities, *Journal of Financial and Quantitative Analysis*, 28, 1993, 235–254.

[Hull and White 1993b]   J. Hull and A. White, Bond Option Pricing Based on a Model for the Evolution of Bond Prices, in *Advances in Futures and Options Research*, 6, 1993, 1–13.

[Jamshidian 1989]   F. Jamshidian, An Exact Bond Option Formula, *The Journal of Finance*, 44, 1989, 205–209.

[Karatzas and Shreve 1988]   I. Karatzas and S. E. Shreve, *Brownian Motion and Stochastic Calculus*. Springer Verlag, 1988.

[Rendlemann and Bartter 1980]   R. J. Rendlemann Jr. and B. J. Bartter, The Pricing of Options on Debt Securities, *Journal of Financial and Quantitative Analysis*, 1980.

[Schaefer and Schwartz 1987]   S. Schaefer and E. Schwartz, Time-Dependent Variance and the Pricing of Bond Options, *Journal of Finance*, 42, 1987, 1113–1128.

[Vasicek 1977]   O. Vasicek, An Equilibrium Characterization of the Term Structure, *Journal of Financial Economics*, 5, 1977, 177–188.

Index